CAMBRIDGE TEXTS IN THE
HISTORY OF POLITICAL THOUGHT

PLATO
The Republic

CAMBRIDGE TEXTS IN THE HISTORY OF POLITICAL THOUGHT

Series editors

RAYMOND GEUSS

Reader in Philosophy, University of Cambridge

QUENTIN SKINNER

Regius Professor of Modern History in the University of Cambridge

Cambridge Texts in the History of Political Thought is now firmly established as the major student textbook series in political theory. It aims to make available to students all the most important texts in the history of Western political thought, from ancient Greece to the early twentieth century. All the familiar classic texts will be included, but the series seeks at the same time to enlarge the conventional canon by incorporating an extensive range of less well-known works, many of them never before available in a modern English edition. Wherever possible, texts are published in complete and unabridged form, and translations are specially commissioned for the series. Each volume contains a critical introduction together with chronologies, biographical sketches, a guide to further reading and any necessary glossaries and textual apparatus. When completed the series will aim to offer an outline of the entire evolution of Western political thought.

For a list of titles published in the series, please see end of book

PLATO

The Republic

EDITED BY

G. R. F. FERRARI

University of California, Berkeley

TRANSLATED BY

TOM GRIFFITH

CAMBRIDGE
UNIVERSITY PRESS

PUBLISHED BY THE PRESS SYNDICATE OF THE UNIVERSITY OF CAMBRIDGE
The Pitt Building, Trumpington Street, Cambridge, United Kingdom

CAMBRIDGE UNIVERSITY PRESS
The Edinburgh Building, Cambridge CB2 2RU, UK
40 West 20th Street, New York, NY 10011-4211, USA
477 Williamstown Road, Melbourne, VIC 3207, Australia
Ruiz de Alarcón 13, 28014 Madrid, Spain
Dock House, The Waterfront, Cape Town, 8001, South Africa

http://www.cambridge.org

© In the translation and editorial matter Cambridge University Press 2000

This book is in copyright. Subject to statutory exception
and to the provisions of relevant collective licensing agreements,
no reproduction of any part may take place without
the written permission of Cambridge University Press.

First published 2000
Sixth printing with corrections, 2003
Eighth printing 2005

Printed in the United Kingdom at the University Press, Cambridge

Typeface Monotype Ehrhardt 9.5/12 pt.   *System* QuarkXPress™   [SE]

A catalogue record for this book is available from the British Library

Library of Congress Cataloguing in Publication data
Plato.
[Republic. English]
The republic / Plato ; edited by G. R. F. Ferrari ; translated by Tom Griffith.
p.   cm. – (Cambridge texts in the history of political thought)
Includes index.
ISBN 0-521-48443-X (pbk) – ISBN 0-521-48173-2 (hardback)
1. Political science–Early works to 1800. 2. Utopias–Early works to 1800. I. Ferrari,
G. R. F. (Giovanni R. F.) II. Griffith, Tom. III. Title. IV. Series
JC71.P35 2000
321'.07–dc21   00-024471

ISBN 0 521 48173 2 hardback
ISBN 0 521 48443 X paperback

Contents

Translator's preface

If you tell people you are translating Plato's *Republic*, the question they almost invariably ask is 'Why? Surely there are plenty of translations already.' The answer is fairly simple. For whatever reason, Plato chose to put his philosophical thoughts in dialogue form, and I believe that when he did so, he intended these dialogues to sound like conversations. Maybe not straightforward, everyday conversations, but conversations nonetheless. And it is still true, though things have improved in recent years, that there are many translations of Plato where you cannot read a complete page without coming across something which no English-speaking person would ever say, or ever have said. So in balancing the conflicting demands of the translator, I have tried to give the highest priority, with only a few exceptions, to the requirement that what I wrote should sound like a conversation. The danger in this, since I am not a professional Plato scholar, was that in trying to make it sound conversational I might commit myself to an interpretation which ran counter to the agreed and accepted views of those who were scholars. That being so, I have been exceptionally fortunate to have had John Ferrari as my academic minder. I would never have undertaken the project without his encouragement and guarantee of help and support. And once embarked on it, I found him ready and willing to give up huge amounts of his time to the task of vetting my early drafts – a laborious task which involved reading the whole text against the Greek, flagging the hundreds (literally) of passages where he did not agree with what I had written, explaining in precise detail why he disagreed, and (bless him) suggesting an alternative in each and every instance. His influence is strongest in those passages where the translation of key terms has been the subject of much critical discussion, but there is no part of the translation which has not benefited immeasurably from his comments, advice and suggestions, and it should be seen, to a very considerable extent, as a joint effort rather than mine alone. It has been an enormous labour for him, and I am greatly in his debt for performing it.

TOM GRIFFITH

Editor's preface

The thought of translating Plato's *Republic* is not unlikely to cross the mind of any Platonist. Whenever it crossed mine, I dismissed it firmly. Too many scholarly ghosts hovered about its text, too many pitfalls lurked on every page, and the impossibility of satisfying all of the readers all of the time was only too easy to anticipate. Then I discovered Tom Griffith's remarkable translation of Plato's *Symposium*, and saw that there could after all be a role for me in producing a new translation of the *Republic*, a technical, advisory role, and that the effort would be repaid many times over. I have had the privilege of exceptionally close editorial collaboration with Tom as his translation took shape, and he co-operated with unfailing intelligence, patience and tact. For all my relentless editing of details, the translation remains essentially his. I have contributed the introduction, notes, and other ancillary material – all of which have benefited from Tom's scrutiny.

JOHN FERRARI

Introduction

Plato's Republic *is the first great work of Western political philosophy, and has retained its grip on the imagination of political thinkers for over two thousand years. It was also very much the product of particular historical circumstances. In this introduction we will consider the political instability of the Greek world in the late fifth and early fourth centuries BC and investigate the cultural factors most likely to have influenced Plato when he came to write the* Republic, *bearing in mind that he was not only a pre-eminent philosopher but also a literary writer, an educator, and, not least, an Athenian aristocrat (pp. xi xxii). We will then assess the* Republic's *position within political philosophy (pp. xxii–xxv), and present the essentials of its argument (pp. xxv–xxxi). We begin with a harrowing episode from Athenian history – an episode in which Plato's family played a major role.*

The Thirty

Plato's mother's cousin was a tyrant. In the course of a single convulsive year, from summer to summer, 404–403 BC, Critias son of Callaeschrus made himself leader of a thirty-man junta imposed on Athens by a foreign power, disarmed the populace, ordered the murder of hundreds of prominent persons – some for their money, some to settle old scores, others because they were rivals – and died fighting the band of exiles that soon after restored the city to democracy. The discussion narrated in Plato's *Republic* takes place in the home of a family that was to come to grief at the hands of the Thirty. Polemarchus, according to the tale his brother Lysias survived to tell, was one of those murdered for their money. Lysias

xi

himself went on to fund the democratic resistance and supply it from the family's arms business. The resistance was based in the Piraeus, the port-district of Athens, a magnet not only for successful immigrant families such as that of Lysias and Polemarchus, whose home was there, but also for the lower ranks of society, who manned and serviced the Athenian navy. The label 'men of the Piraeus' came to identify those who fought for the democracy. The decisive battle – the conflict in which Critias lost his life – took place by the temple of Bendis, the goddess whose inaugural festival gave Socrates, the leader of the discussion at Polemarchus' house, a reason to come to the Piraeus in the first place. Another who lost his life there was Charmides, an associate of the Thirty with special responsibility for the Piraeus. He was Plato's uncle. Not Plato's only, but uncle too of Glaucon and Adeimantus, for Plato gives a major role in the discussion to his own two brothers, and puts them on the best of terms with a family whom their kinsmen will ruin. Socrates was for his part to incur the hostility of the returning democrats because he counted the likes of Critias and Charmides among his philosophic companions.

It is difficult to know what to make of Plato's *mise-en-scène*, and tempting to turn to an autobiographical passage of his *Seventh Letter* (324c–326b), which purports to describe his own dealings with the Thirty. Letters from celebrities were a favourite production of fiction writers and outright forgers in antiquity, and none of the Platonic letters is above suspicion – although scholars these days are inclined to regard the seventh as authentic. But let it stand to Plato only as Plato's *Apology of Socrates* stands to the actual speech of defence that Socrates delivered when on trial for his life; still it would remain the most important interpretation of Plato's political motives to survive from antiquity. Plato speaks of being invited by his relatives and by others he knew in the junta to throw himself in with their enterprise, and of how this excited an idealistic youth – he was in his early twenties – with hopes of a better society and zeal for the power to bring it about. Disenchantment came swiftly. An incident involving Socrates is chosen to serve as an emblem for the regime's immorality: its attempt to co-opt him into the vindictive arrest of a citizen that it had designated a public enemy, and his courageous refusal to do so.

The revived democracy, however, turned out to have as little regard for Socrates' independent character as had its despotic predecessor, and prosecuted him for subverting traditional religious belief – a very serious charge, tantamount to treachery, and a favourite to employ against intellectuals. The resulting execution of his philosophic mentor came as Plato was once again considering, although more cautiously than before, an entry into politics; and once again he was brought up short. As age sharpened his awareness of the barriers to good government, he tells us in this open letter, he came eventually to understand that no form of government in any existing state was satisfactory, and was driven to declare that there would be no end to the general wretchedness until philosophers, who see justice in all its complexity, were given political power, or until existing rulers learned true philosophy.

Faction

It is a good story, and a poignant preface to the life of a politically engaged philosopher who came to adulthood in the Greek world of the early fourth century BC – a world of small civic communities, independent of each other and jealous of the status conferred by citizenship, yet willing to strike alliances with other cities for self-protection and the discomfiture of their enemies, willing even to accept the hegemony of those cities that sought to extend their power by offering protection, but with all sides aware how readily allegiance grounded only in self-interest can shift. Attempts made during the fourth century to unite the Greek world in 'panhellenic' resistance against Persia went hand in hand with the nostalgic claim that that world had once possessed a sense of its common good, a century earlier, when it had repelled the Persian invader. But if it had ever possessed such a sense, its behaviour belied this now. The common good was rather an ideal for each civic community to espouse within its own boundaries. Indeed, it was by looking to this ideal that the Greeks maintained resistance to the Persian king on a conceptual level even as some of them struck deals with his agents. Throughout the Persian empire, they told themselves, there lived only one free man, its king, whose subjects were his slaves; but Greek cities – those that were not themselves in the hands of tyrants – were self-governing republics, no matter whether oligarchic or democratic, however closely held the privileges of their ruling classes, however restricted their roster of full citizens. For whether political freedom belonged to few or to many, it belonged also to the republic itself.

That such was the ideal is only confirmed by the tendency of Greek political theorists to take a jaundiced view of political reality, and see it as driven by the resentment, avarice and ambition of interest groups. Not only was the common good forgotten in the hurly-burly of factionalism within individual cities – that is, in the arena where that good was thought to find its natural home – but the factionalism fed off the absence of a common good outside that arena, in the network of relations between Greek cities. Thucydides' *History* (3.82) explains how war between Athens and Sparta at fifth century's end afforded factions in lesser cities a pretext to summon external powers to their aid – Athens if the faction sought democracy, Sparta if it sought oligarchy. In such times, powerful allies were to be had for the asking. The general pattern did not cease with the war of which Thucydides wrote, but persisted and ramified well into the fourth century even as the power blocs became less well defined – Sparta declining, Athens reviving, and Thebes becoming prominent. It was characteristic of the political discourse of the time to polarise the troubles into an antagonism between oligarchy and democracy, and this in turn into an antagonism between rich and poor.

Such an analysis was not wholly accurate, as Plato knew. Some oligarchies and democracies were more oligarchic or democratic than others; the dichotomy did not in any case exhaust the range of political systems; in many places there existed what the Greeks too called a middle class. However frequent the calls for cancelling debts and redistributing land, the prize contested was political at least as much as economic. Democratic Athens had its disparities of wealth – indeed, the rich were relied upon to fund public services – but political power and legal entitlement extended to all adult male Athenians. Everywhere struggle would typically begin as a division within the elite: between those who would and those who would not strike political bargains with the populace. Despite these caveats, it is understandable that a concerned observer in the fourth century would think the world trapped on a factional see-saw. A reader of the *Seventh Letter* can well believe that Plato, who saw the man he declared the most virtuous of his time suffer first under Critias and his oligarchy and again under democracy, would finally cry: a plague o' both your houses.

So it is at first sight surprising when Callipolis, the ideal city conceived in the *Republic*, turns out not only to conform to the constitution that Critias sought to impose on Athens, but to push it further than perhaps even Critias could have imagined.

A Spartan utopia?

The foreign power that supported Critias' coup was Sparta. For a well-born Athenian such as Critias to be a lover of Spartan ways was nothing unusual. His varied writings, of which we have only fragments, included laudatory descriptions of the Spartan system, and he was followed in this practice by another of the gentlemen among Socrates' companions, Xenophon, whose *Spartan Constitution* survives entire. Athenians with oligarchic sympathies or elitist attitudes were often accused of acting like Spartans, and some went so far as to dress and wear their hair in the Spartan fashion. But none went so far as Critias, who seems to have wanted to remake all Athens in the image of Sparta.

The contrasts between the Athenian and Spartan systems were stark in a number of ways. In social geography: while Athens was at pains to distribute the privileges of citizenhood uniformly through the district under its direct control, the Spartan region had a core of citizens surrounded by non-citizen subordinates in the villages and countryside. In their economy: whereas Athenians of all social ranks could engage in a full range of commercial, agricultural and other activities likely to produce wealth, the small and tight-knit group of full Spartan citizens lived off the agricultural surplus produced by a large body of public serfs, and were expected to hold themselves aloof from money-making pursuits. In their military organisation: Spartiates (Spartan citizens) were full-time warriors, who messed together even when not on campaign, and identified themselves by the privilege of bearing arms that non-citizens were issued only at need; most soldiers and sailors who fought for Athens, by contrast, were called up at times of campaign from the body of regular citizens. In their degree of openness: Athens encouraged foreigners to settle (as the statesman Pericles encouraged Polemarchus' father Cephalus to emigrate from Sicily), naturalised religious cults (as with the cult of Thracian Bendis), and welcomed artistic variety and experiment; Sparta was far more cautious on all these fronts.

Seen against this background, the actions of the Thirty reflect the values of their sponsors. They drew up a list of some 3,000 supporters – about the number of Spartiates at the time – disarmed the rest, and banned them from living within the city limits. They made particular targets of immigrants. The relation they began to establish with the 3,000 was analogous to that between the conservative *gerousia* or senate of Sparta and the collective body of Spartiates. They did all this, we are told, in the cause of purging the city of unjust men and inclining it to virtue and justice. For the fame of Sparta depended not on its actions abroad or its glamour at home but on a distinctive way of life. Sparta was nothing without the lengthy, rigorous and uniform education towards virtue that it imposed on the Spartiate youth, with the aim of producing well-disciplined men and indeed women of honour, bearers of an austere and martial culture that smothered internal faction and gave the place its reputation for *eunomia*, law and order.

If the rule of Critias was too brief and too harried for us to be sure of its ultimate direction, there can be no doubt that a contemporary reader would have detected more than a whiff of Sparta in his cousin's Callipolis. It too is a city distinguished by the way of life of its military elite, the guardians, who devote themselves entirely to the tasks of defence and policing, and have their material needs provided by a subordinate class of farmers and artisans. The city stands or falls by the upbringing and education of its guardians, a notably austere and conservative process of inculcating discipline and shaping good character. Women among the guardians share the men's way of life to an unusual degree. And in a remarkable passage at the end of Book 7, it is suggested that the quick and easy way to bring all this about would be for those in power to ban everyone over the age of ten from living within the city limits, so as to educate the children in isolation from their parents.

But what would the contemporary reader have made of this quasi-Sparta, this post-Critian coup, when he discovered that the rulers of Callipolis were to be no mere senate of worthies, but philosophers, intellectuals risen from the guardian ranks and educated in mathematics and disputation? Such subjects formed no part of Spartan education; Sparta was a notoriously unbookish place, whose fighters prided themselves on avoiding fancy talk. And would the counts laid against 'timocracy', the first of the unjust societies considered in Book 8, have reinforced this reader's puzzlement, or dispelled it? The timocratic society values militarism and puts the man of honour above all others; its failings are those of a contemporary Sparta, untempered by the intellectual virtues.

For all that the institutions of Callipolis draw inspiration from historical revolutions and familiar societies, in the end they transcend anything known to the Greek world. The discussion sets itself the task of discovering a just city, but finds that it cannot stop short of utopia. How seriously Plato took this utopian vision has long been a controversial issue. The main line of debate divides those who see Callipolis as an ideal whose function is to motivate efforts at personal, not civic, perfection, from those who see it as a guide for future progress on the political, not just the individual level. A different school of thought has denied that Plato intended Callipolis even to seem desirable, let alone practicable. The question whether the *Republic* is a work primarily of moral or of political philosophy will be addressed in later sections (pp. xxii–xxix). While we are still tracing the work's historical context, let us consider instead the utopian ideas current in Plato's day. Here the fantastic and serious elements are more readily distinguishable than in the *Republic*.

The fantastic we find most clearly in the comedies of Aristophanes – in the Cloud-cuckoo-land of *Birds*, the city in the sky where dreams of absolute power come true; in the means to panhellenic peace and salvation proposed in *Lysistrata*, when the women bring their warring husbands to terms by going on a sex-strike; in the women's rule that comes about in *Women at the Assembly* (or *Ecclesiazusae*), in which the women of Athens, disguised as men, first vote themselves into power, then achieve social concord by equalising distribution of the two great objects of social desire: women and wealth. Equal distribution of property was first proposed, we are told, by a serious utopian theorist, a certain Phaleas of Chalcedon. Less shadowy is Hippodamus of Miletus – a likely model for the Aristophanic geometer and town-planner Meton who offers to lay out the 'streets' of Cloud-cuckoo-land on a radiating pattern. Hippodamus' theories were those of the social engineer and the architect, and sometimes of both together, as in his proposal to divide land according to the occupations and needs of the various classes in the city. He argued for a strict division of the citizenry into three functional groups, although his were farmers, artisans and warriors rather than the producers, warriors and philosopher-kings of the *Republic*. In town-planning his name was associated with the strictly regular geometric line, and some of his layouts were actually built – among them that for the Piraeus, where he lived and worked. In general, the modern reader should bear in mind the ease with which cities in the Greek world could be rebuilt, relocated, or started from scratch. Although Socrates in the *Republic* makes it clear that he is using a metaphor when he calls himself and his discussion partners the founders of Callipolis, starting a new township would not have been regarded as pie-in-the-sky. There is a story that Plato himself was asked to write the laws for one such city, Megalopolis in Arcadia, but refused on the grounds that the new citizens were unwilling to accept equality of possessions.

Yet the town-planner's vision of utopia, the detailed topographic fantasy that became a fixture of utopian writing in Plato's immediate aftermath and marks out the canon from Thomas More's *Utopia* to William Morris' *News from Nowhere*, is notably absent from the *Republic*.

Plato reserves this motif for the twin dialogues *Timaeus* and *Critias*, in which a character Critias who is either the familiar tyrant or an ancestor meant to remind us of him takes a social system purporting to be that of Callipolis and projects it backwards in time onto a primeval Athens. He then tells the tale of its struggle with the now vanished island city of Atlantis, whose glittering palaces and concentric network of canals he lovingly describes. The kinds of writing with which the *Republic* invites comparison have less of Shangri-La about them and are more overtly political.

The philosopher and the king

One of these genres we have encountered already, exemplified by Critias' and Xenophon's writings on the constitution of Sparta. Their manner of contributing to the lively contemporary debate on the relative merits of different constitutions was to offer a partisan, idealised description of just one. Alternatively, a single constitution might be selected for criticism, not praise – as with the *Athenian Constitution* that survives from the late fifth century by an unknown author often called 'The Old Oligarch'. The traditional title of the *Republic* conceals an allusion to such works as these. For if *Politeia* can in Greek name a kind of community that governs itself and has no truck with tyranny – '*Republic*' is not an outright misnomer – it is also the normal Greek word for 'constitution'. It was not, then, a *Spartan Constitution* or an *Athenian Constitution* that Plato wrote, but simply a *Constitution*.

When judging constitutions against each other, fourth-century theorists often grouped them into three broad types, complicating the earlier antithesis of oligarchy and democracy by the addition of monarchy. The figure of the king became an important focus for reflection on the powers of men – not only the power of the ruler over those he rules, but the power of a human being to live successfully. The concentration of authority in a single individual fused the moral with the political, made the king's actions on the political plane an expression of his personal virtue and an exercise in self-development. This at least was the theme of a second kind of writing that bears comparison with the *Republic*. It is represented for us by works such as Xenophon's *Education of Cyrus*, a romanticised biography of the Persian king, in which the difficult relation between republican and imperial politics is filtered through the virtues of that princely paragon. Here too belong the Cyprian orations of Isocrates (*To Nicocles*; *Nicocles, or the Cyprians*; and *Evagoras*), which contain his opinions on the duties that bind kings to their subjects and subjects to their kings. Cyrus was long dead by Xenophon's time, King Nicocles of Cyprus not only alive but an active patron of Isocrates; yet both writers fictionalise their enlightened monarchs.

And if the king was no enlightened monarch but an arbitrary despot whose will was law? Then a Xenophon could imagine him confessing his unhappiness, as in *Hiero*, in which the Sicilian tyrant of that name laments his loveless life in conversation with the wise Simonides, who consoles him with some careful advice on gaining popularity. The early model for such a scene – the confrontation of philosopher and tyrant – can be found in Herodotus' *History* (1.30–33), where Solon, Athenian sage and statesman, and ancestor of Plato, denies King Croesus the satisfaction of being judged the most fortunate of men.

Xenophon and Isocrates had both been associates of Socrates; other 'Socratics' too, to judge by the titles of their lost or fragmentary works, wrote on the topic of kingship and government, and Plato was not the first among them to write Socratic dialogues. The *Education of Cyrus* was already matched with the *Republic* in antiquity. Isocrates never wrote a Socratic dialogue, but did establish a school of 'philosophy' – his name for what he taught, although he rejected speculative and cosmological inquiry as too abstruse and offered himself rather as a master of the art of words and a model for emulation by the civic-minded and politically thoughtful. The school seems to have maintained an uneasy rivalry with the group of students and companions that Plato attracted to his home near a public park just outside Athens, named after an obscure local divinity, Academus. In this Platonic 'Academy' astronomers and mathematicians were welcome, and the training given to philosopher-kings in the *Republic* is usually taken to reflect this fact. *Philosophia* was still an elastic word, and embraced intellectual activities of many sorts.

Plato wrote the *Republic*, then, not only as a concerned member of the political elite and a keen observer of contemporary troubles, but as a writer who looked back at literary models and askance at literary competitors. The *Republic* fits a mould when it indicts the wretched condition of the tyrant from the perspective of the sage, and when it brings its political and moral reflections to a focus in the figure of the enlightened king. But Socrates, although he is a wise man summoned by the social elite to say his piece on virtue and happiness, is not in dialogue with either kings or tyrants; rather, in this case the advice of the philosopher is that the philosopher should remain no mere adviser but should himself become king, or kings become philosophers. We are to imagine a sage who could counsel himself on kingly happiness, for he would himself be king. Here Plato breaks the literary mould.

Indeed, we may suspect that the considerable fanfare that attends Socrates' proposal is Plato's way of claiming originality more as a literary writer and educational theorist than as a political reformer. Socrates treads very carefully and makes a great show of hesitation before coming out with his advice; his audience reacts to it as if it were quite outrageous (473c–474a). Yet, historically, the coincidence of philosophic ability and political power in notable individuals was by no means unprecedented. One intellectual who drafted a code of law has already been mentioned: Solon, Plato's sixth-century ancestor, who not only brought social reform to Athens but composed poetry on the political issues he was responsible for resolving. Another example is furnished by the 'sophist' (itinerant professor) Protagoras, who wrote the laws for Thurii, and is mentioned in the *Republic* (600c). We have seen that Critias too could have thought himself, at first, something of a philosopher-king.

More generally, philosophers of the sixth to fifth centuries tended to belong to the upper echelon of their communities and for that reason alone would have been called upon for political office – a duty not a few of them are reported to have fulfilled. Or consider the Pythagoreans, who followed a strict regimen of life designed to prepare their souls for the next world, a regimen that ranged dietary taboos together with the practice of philosophy. Beginning in the fifth century, they rose to political power in southern Italy. Many aspects of Pythagorean philosophy, including its mathematical emphasis, are thought to have left their mark on Plato – although the issue of intellectual indebtedness is complicated by the scarcity of good evidence for Pythagoreanism in its early days. But one Pythagorean philosopher, we are told, was not only an intellectual influence on Plato but his political ally and his host: Archytas of Tarentum, seven times elected to the leadership of his city. He was an expert in military ballistics as well as mathematical theory, and his city was later praised by Aristotle for its innovative and socially cohesive politics. Archytas plays a considerable role in the *Seventh Letter*; and some have detected him behind the mask of Timaeus, the otherwise unknown and doubtless fictional philosopher from southern Italy whom Plato makes the principal speaker in his dialogue of that name, and who is introduced as one who has scaled the twin heights of political office and philosophic achievement.

So Plato is exaggerating when he allows the prospect of philosophers in power to seem as preposterous and laughable as ever Aristophanes did the spectacle of the rule of women. Why does he do it? One likely reason is that the reaction to this proposal justifies Socrates in giving a lengthy defence of his conception of the genuine philosopher, in the course of which he explains the position of philosophers in Athenian society, both those who are worthy of the title and those who are not, and lays out a curriculum of philosophic education. From that curriculum the art of words taught by the likes of Isocrates is strikingly absent. A common word for politician at Athens was simply 'speaker', *rhētōr*, for it was by speaking in public assembly that a citizen typically made his way to prominence. Glaucon, whose impetuousness is both displayed and remarked upon in the *Republic*, apparently attempted to speak in the assembly before he was twenty years old – a mark of extreme political ambition. Certainly he and his brother are given the longest and most eloquent political speeches in the work. In the preface to his *Nicocles*, Isocrates writes of the hostility aroused by the eloquence of those who study philosophy – in his sense of the term – and how they are suspected of aiming at selfish advantage rather than virtue. The philosopher-kings whose viability Socrates eventually gets Glaucon and Adeimantus to accept are truer to the Spartan model, and avoid eloquence. Their political rhetoric is a matter of knowing how to keep things hidden from citizens whom the truth would only harm; their art of disputation, the coping-stone of their education, aims to tell things as they are. All this, of course, from the pen of a consummate master of the art of words. Plato is taking his stand, not against eloquence as such, but against its contemporary place in politics and in the education of those who took part in politics.

Both Plato and Isocrates educated politicians. But whereas Isocrates began from his communicative art, and argued that the task of discovering the most decorous considerations with which to frame discourse directed at others on the worthiest of topics cannot but leave its mark on the practitioner's conduct, whether public or private, Plato seems rather to have begun from a conception of virtue as self-possession and self-understanding – attributes that are in a way the precondition of the philosophic life, yet also expressed by it, and in another way its goal – and to have wanted the character of the man to stamp his political discourse, not the discourse to stamp the man.

Nevertheless, it would be easy to exaggerate the contrast between Plato and Isocrates. Both men seem in practice to have been more interested in promoting competent government of whatever form than in seeing a particular constitution come into being. Plato's associates and students in the Academy were a diverse company: some were connected to the school for many years, and lived primarily intellectual lives, interrupted in a few cases by stints as lawgivers or ambassadors; others were young men from prominent families who came to complete their education. There were foreigners in both categories. While some among the prominent visitors returned home to rule as autocrats, others went back to tumble autocrats from power. In general, almost all varieties of political sympathy can be found among Plato's associates, whether in foreign affairs (pro-Spartan, pro-Athenian, pro-Macedonian) or in constitutional preference.

Plato's own most notable political adventure fits the grand tradition of Solon and Croesus. He became involved with the politics of Syracuse and the dynasty of Dionysius I, the outstanding tyrant of his age, who won himself an empire in Sicily and made Syracuse the glittering embodiment of his personal wealth and magnificence. Dionysius became stereotyped as an enemy of liberty, and his rise to power is thought to have helped shape Plato's account of the onset of tyranny in Book 8. A notable aspect of his court's magnificence was its hospitality towards poets, artists, intellectuals; and Plato was one of the visitors. Stories of his debunking the tyrant's self-image to his face seem too good to be true, too closely modelled on Herodotus. More credit is given to the narrative of Plato's later visits to serve as philosophic mentor for the tyrant's successor, Dionysius II, and of his failure to influence the unworthy and recalcitrant young autocrat. For the details we must rely once more on the *Seventh Letter*. Yet even trusting its portrait of a Plato bent on practising what he has hitherto preached, what we find here are political proposals at once bland and constrained by the Sicilian context. Dionysius was to have some moral fibre infused in him, then to be sent out to unite the Sicilian cities against Carthage, the foreign invader. There is no talk of a guardian class, no call to give women a role in government or to redistribute wealth – no Callipolis in view.

Plato was a thinker, a teacher, a writer fully enmeshed in the controversies of his time, both political and intellectual. Had he been less of his time he would not, perhaps, live so fully on our page.

A political work?

For all the historical particularity of the *Republic*, it has also achieved enduring recognition as a classic of political philosophy. Its position within the range of political philosophy, however, has proved more difficult to pinpoint than the work's canonical status might lead one to expect. Some, indeed, have wondered whether it ought to be considered a political work at all. Does it not set out to answer a problem of individual rather than collective action, and demonstrate the claim of morality on individual choice and its effect on individual well-being, regardless of social consequences (367b–e)? Does Socrates not explicitly subordinate politics to psychology, describing social structures only as an analogue for corresponding structures of character within the individual (369a)? In which case, it would be better to think of the *Republic* as a work of moral philosophy. Others have chosen to emphasise the fact that its proposals for social reform – its utopian refashionings of education, of property-rights, of the very structure of the family – go well beyond what correspondence with the individual would require, and seem to be developed for their own sake. Even where that correspondence is more strictly observed, in the parallel analyses of unjust societies and individuals that fill Book 8, the critique of actual social conditions that emerges from the correspondence has a relevance and bite of its own.

Yet if the *Republic* would on this account merit its classification as a political work, disagreement returns with the attempt to classify its political stance. Concentrate on its desire to secure collective happiness (420b), its warnings against disparities of wealth and against the mercantile ethos (421d–c, 556c), its efforts to avoid oppression of the weak by the powerful in society, and you may find in it the first stirrings of socialism. Look rather towards its restriction of political power to a tiny elite (429a, 491a), consider their status as moral paragons and saviours (487a, 463b), their centralised control of the moral and cultural as well as economic life of the society, their eugenic techniques (458c–461e), their resort to censorship and to outright deception in order to preserve order and promote good behaviour (389b–c, 414b, 459c–d), and you may think you are reading a prescient charter for fascism – as did some scholars, approvingly, before the Second World War, and many, disgustedly, in its aftermath.

One modern stance whose ancestry it would occur to no one to trace back to the *Republic* is liberalism. What could be further from an ideal of collective self-rule through elected government and uncensored discussion than the political life of Callipolis? In a liberal society, there are for political purposes no morally superior human types, but Callipolis – to describe it now in its own terms rather than with modern categories – is an aristocracy of the virtuous. Philosophers qualify to form its ruling class by their moral and intellectual excellence – their natural superiority, reinforced and perfected by careful education. Should the *Republic*'s theoretical descendants therefore be sought rather in the varieties of republicanism, which, broadly understood, elevates ideals of citizenship and community over individualism, and assigns to politics the goal of promoting virtue? Certainly, Socrates does not hesitate to attribute wisdom and courage to Callipolis as a whole even though the virtues in question are restricted to small classes within the populace (428b–430c) – much as each Greek republic called itself a free and self-governing community no matter how restricted its citizen-roll or governing class. He sets himself the goal of making the entire society flourish, preventing any particular class or individual from flourishing at the expense of the whole (420b–421c). And he sums up the task of his philosopher-kings as that of modelling the community as closely as possible on permanent ideals of virtue (501b).

Yet for all that, it is rather Aristotle's *Politics*, with its famous declaration that man is a political animal, and that the purpose of society is not mere life but a good life, that is the more whole-hearted inaugurator of this tradition. A reader of the *Republic* is unlikely to come away with so celebratory a sense of the possibilities of the self-governing community. Reservations come to a focus at one of the work's central and most disconcerting ideas: that a society should be governed by those who show least eagerness for the task. The idea appears in other writers, including Isocrates and Aristotle, but in connection with conventional political complaints. They frown upon excessive ambition, or sigh for an earlier age when the socially eminent engaged in public life from a sense of their station and its duties. Such thoughts make their appearance in the *Republic* also (347b, 520b–d), but are developed in the direction of outright disenchantment with the political life – famously allegorised in the philosophic soul's escape from the dim and constricted cave of its cultural environment to the sunlit, open spaces of true understanding (514a–517c).

The philosopher, even the philosopher who becomes king, does not look to society as the realm in which to exercise his freedom and realise his virtue, but looks rather to the life of the mind for his liberation; nor does he define himself by his social station or the values of citizenship, but by his individual search for wisdom. For a work that is, in truth, no ancestor of liberalism, the *Republic* lays an unusual emphasis on the individual; however, it regards individuality not as a possession that confers rights on all and gives society its defining basis, but as an achievement of the few – an achievement in which society can play, at best, only a supporting role. Small wonder, then, that some have doubted whether the *Republic* is truly a political work. One might say, rather, that it is counter-political.

City and soul

Consider how the discussion develops in its early stages. Glaucon offers an account of the origins of justice and law. Human beings were driven to accept legal limits on their urge to take advantage of each other because they judged the unfettered satisfaction of that urge not worth the distress of finding themselves at the receiving end of the conduct to which it prompted others also – a result that only the strongest could entirely avoid (358e–359b). To establish settled laws as the criterion of right and wrong is therefore to impose restrictions on nature, for it is human nature to thrust oneself forward at the expense of others. There is loss as well as gain: the pre-eminence of natural superiority vanishes. A 'real man', one who could always prevail, would never agree to restrict his power (359b). The story of society's origins that Socrates hypothesises in reply presents communal life rather as an organic development that brings us happiness at no cost to our nature. Since none of us is self-sufficient, each will seek to co-ordinate his efforts with others so as to provide for the needs common to all. Individuals will gravitate towards the tasks for which they are naturally suited, and specialise in those, because their needs will be more efficiently addressed in this manner (370c). The process gives rise to a simple, rustic community of farmers, artisans and tradesmen, who live a contented and god-fearing life with no apparent need for rulers or laws (372a–b). They co-ordinate their labour as two men will co-ordinate their rhythm when rowing a boat. Identical needs and a common rationality suffice to produce co-operation even in the absence of hierarchy.

This happy scene is firmly dismissed by Glaucon, who finds it quite devoid of the civilised graces – a 'city of pigs' (372d). Socrates permits himself to be drawn into discussion of a community equipped with urban luxuries, including a sophisticated cultural life. This place, unlike the rudimentary society first considered, would have room for intellectuals; yet Socrates' parting description of the city of pigs is that it is 'the true city – the healthy version, as it were' (372e). The healthy city sets its goals no higher than economic stability and co-operative order among its citizens; the sophisticated city is by contrast bloated and inflamed, and will be driven to make war on its neighbours to feed its excessive appetites (373d–e). However, when the education and discipline necessary for its military class has required a purge of decadent influences in the general culture, and so re-imposed austerity on the city as a whole (399e), is there not a return to health and indeed an achievement of beauty in Callipolis – the word means 'city of beauty' – far superior to the simple happiness of the city of pigs? The matter is not as clear-cut as it may seem. That Plato thought the world a better place for having philosophers in it, we cannot doubt; but we may legitimately doubt whether the goals of Callipolis as a society are any higher than those of the healthy city, the true city that it replaces in the discussion.

One way in which such doubts might arise is from consideration of the similes used to describe the task of the good ruler. The philosopher-king is like a ship's captain or helmsman, who recognises that to steer the ship of state one must have knowledge of the stars, the seasons, the winds. It is not enough, as politicians in a democracy believe, merely to persuade the shipowner – the populace – to let one take the tiller in hand (488a–e). A port of destination has no importance in this analogy and is not mentioned. When the demagogic sailors take control, their aim is not to set a new course but to feast on the ship's stores and turn the voyage into a carousal. Society is simply a ship at sea, not a ship headed for a particular port. What the true helmsman will do that these sailors will not is use his knowledge of navigation to avoid storms and shoals – to keep the ship afloat. His political goals are limited to security, stability, social harmony. Certainly, he aims to instil virtue into his city, as is clear from another of the similes for the philosopher-king's task, in which he is compared to a painter working on the canvas of his citizens' characters (501a–c); but what he paints there are merely the social virtues needed in the city at large, discipline and justice above all (500d). He himself has become, through his philosophic activity and the perfectly rational order of things to which it has given him access, as godlike as it possible for a human being to be. The city that he paints on the model of this rational order, however, is described not as a divine but only as a human likeness, and its general citizenry are not themselves godlike but only 'as pleasing to god as human characters can be' (500d vs. 501b–c).

The virtuous society and the virtuous individual are indeed alike in point of virtue, and so the philosopher – that paragon of virtue – is akin to the finest of cities, Callipolis, the city ruled by philosophers (435b, 498e). But consider what this correspondence amounts to. Wisdom guides the life of the philosophically inclined individual and ensures that his material desires do not grow distractingly materialistic — enforcing that prevention, if necessary, with the aid of an ambitious self-respect. The analysis derives from the *Republic*'s theory of the tripartite soul, according to which each person is characterised by a rational or wisdom-loving element, a desiring, material, or profit-loving element, and an ambitious or honour-loving element. Only in the truly virtuous person, however, are these elements properly balanced. Similarly in Callipolis political life is under the guidance of wise philosophers, who ensure that the farmers and artisans supplying the city's material needs keep to their tasks and neither unbalance the economy nor are permitted disruptive inequalities of income, but instead only a decent sufficiency. Should enforcement be required, the military class, which defends the honour of the entire city, can do the policing.

Because of the manner in which the correspondence between society and individual is established – because it is a correspondence of elements and of the relations between those elements – the virtues of the best society and of the best individual can be declared the same even though they come to something quite different. Justice – that multivalent word, in Greek as in English – was first discussed in connection with the keeping of agreements: repaying what one owes, and avoiding fraud (331b). By fastening on the broadest construal of what one owes and is owed, namely as what is deserved, the discussion reviews a traditional conception of justice unemancipated from vengeance, according to which 'an eye for an eye' is the counterpart of 'one good turn deserves another' – this is Polemarchus' contribution (331d–336a). Under Thrasymachus' provocation it considers the idea that what you deserve is whatever your strengths and skills enable you to acquire for yourself. This is the idea that Glaucon reconfigures as the state of nature, and against its background justice appears once more as a matter of keeping agreements, but in the much wider sense of abiding by the convention of law.

Eventually the discussion settles on a definition of justice as 'doing one's own' (433b), where what is one's own is not whatever one is able to get, but what is best for one (586e). Callipolis is a just city because each of its three elements – philosopher-kings, warriors and producers – is performing the task to which it is best suited, and each stands in the appropriate relation to the others. The civic life that this permits is one of economic stability and harmonious order – values not essentially different from those of the city of pigs, the healthy city. The just individual, by contrast – he of the healthy soul, with its three elements in harmony (444e) – turns out to be no contented pig but a full-blown philosopher, for to take wisdom as one's guide in life is not merely to be rational and prudent in the ordinary sense but to make the disinterested pursuit of understanding one's ultimate value. Only so is the rational element liberated, open to the full range of tasks for which it is best suited: not just controlling the other elements but pursuing wisdom for its own sake (441e, 581b, 586e).

The life that such a person leads is, accordingly, not merely stable and harmonious but godlike and glorious. 'Doing one's own', when it comes to the individual, is more than doing one's part for the community; it is to conduct the business of oneself. Individuality is an achievement, and only the philosopher has the talent to achieve it, for only he provides each element in his make-up with what is best for it. All others may be a part of the just community, but cannot themselves, as individuals, be just. As individuals, Socrates is even prepared to call them the 'slaves' of the just man, the philosopher; as citizens of Callipolis, however, they are called by their rulers not slaves but paymasters and providers, and regard those rulers not as masters but as saviours and defenders (590d, 463b). Each citizen is to find his level; none is to keep his place by virtue of birth alone, but, in theory at least, is to be promoted or demoted as appropriate (415b–c, 423c–d). In this way, Socrates attempts to preserve the pre-eminence of natural superiority that Glaucon thought political life must renounce. Yet he manages also to maintain the benefits of harmonious coexistence that Glaucon claimed as justifying the rule of law in the first place.

The disparity between the philosopher's ambition as an individual and the goals of the city ruled by philosophers becomes only more marked when we consider how the correspondence between individual and society falls out in its unjust forms (Books 8 and 9). It is a spectrum of increasing moral decay that runs from timocracy and the timocratic man, through oligarchy and democracy, and ends with tyranny and the demonstration that the tyrannically inclined man who succeeds in becoming an actual tyrant is the unhappiest wretch of all, and can fulfil no part of his inner being. (Although this decay is presented as a sequence in time, the succession of regimes does not match the history known to Plato – see pp. xiii–xiv – or does so only in certain details, not in its general pattern. But the pattern is not purely symbolic. For one thing, it surrenders even Callipolis to the prospect of eventual downfall.) Unlike the philosopher, each of the lesser types of person can see only as far as a horizon set by society. The timocrat seeks honour, the oligarch money, the democrat freedom and equality, the tyrannical man an exploitative self-indulgence. It is not simply that these ambitions require a relatively sophisticated civic environment – that much was true also of philosophy – but that they express themselves entirely in social terms, as a matter of one's relations with others.

Mathematics and metaphysics

It may be thought, however, that if Callipolis is ruled by wise philosophers, its civic life is better than stable and harmonious, it can itself be considered wise. And surely the careful filtering of decadent or socially disruptive images and thoughts from the education of the guardians could only be successful if the cultural environment of the entire community were characterised by the austere gracefulness with which the military class must in particular be imbued (401b–d)? Certainly, the *Republic* contains one of the earliest extended analyses (in Books 2, 3 and 10) of the power of cultural artefacts of all sorts to mould the ethos of large groups – a type of analysis familiar in our day from controversies over the influence of advertisements and the censorship of pornographic or violent images. Yet even the inhabitants of so primitive a place as the city of pigs sang praises to the gods – one part of the poetry permitted in Callipolis, with its verses in praise of the gods and of good men (372b, 607a). Similarly, the gracefulness instilled in the guardians by their musical and poetic education aims at and reflects nothing more elevated than social harmony and cohesiveness, together with a piety and a patriotism that fall short of true understanding (386a, 389d–e, 522a).

The education of the most talented among them does not stop, however, at the musical and poetic, but continues with mathematics and philosophy. (Indeed, in retrospect it is suggested that even the youngsters should be made familiar with basic mathematics, 536d.) It is the public policy of the society as a whole that supports this higher education, and provides the conditions in which those with a gift for philosophy can fulfil themselves both intellectually and morally. These are conditions that neither a healthy but rudimentary community nor in its different way a sophisticated but decadent city can provide. Here, in a political system worthy of him, the philosopher's 'own growth will be greater, and he will be the salvation of his country as well as of himself' (497a; compare 492a). On the other hand, when in Book 4 the whole city ruled by guardians is declared wise by virtue of the knowledge possessed by its ruling class alone, that knowledge has the city for its object – it is expertise in domestic and foreign policy (428d). Only later in the discussion does Socrates make it clear that the knowledge which truly qualifies a guardian to rule is philosophic wisdom, having for its object the whole cosmos (484d, 486a). The question is, how intimate is the connection between this knowledge and the philosopher's political activity?

It is a question surprisingly difficult to answer. As part of the process of qualifying for political power, the guardians are given ten years' education devoted to advanced mathematics, crowned by five years of 'dialectic'. About dialectic Plato is deliberately cagey. It is or involves philosophic disputation, as befits its etymological connection with the Greek word for 'conversation' (534d, 539b–d); it takes a global, unifying view of its topic (537c); it aims to discover the definitions of things, and thereby the unchanging principles of all that exists – the 'forms' – arriving finally at an understanding of the ultimate principle, the form of the good (511b–c, 532a–b, 533b). But we are not told how it achieves this feat, and scholars dispute whether dialectical activity is some kind of meta-mathematics, or whether it quite transcends the ground that mathematics has prepared.

On the one hand, ten years of mathematics seems too long a stretch for a study that would merely be meant to sharpen the intellect in a general way. Yet we need not regard the education of the philosopher-king, at the other extreme, as an internalisation of mathematical structures that function as blueprints for applying his knowledge of the good to the social world. This would have the consequence that, when we read of philosophers looking to the forms in order to paint virtues on the canvas of the citizens' character, we should take them to be embodying in society a mathematical proportion whose structure they have first discovered in abstraction.

A middle ground between these two positions would be the following. A full ten years' preparation in mathematics is required because only long exposure to the rational order of its objects, in combination with dialectic, can succeed in transmitting to the soul of the sympathetic learner a similarly rational order and proportion (500c). This is consonant with the ennobling effects attributed to the study of astronomy and cosmic harmony in the *Timaeus* (47b, 90d). Once educated, however, the political use to which the philosopher-king puts his mathematical and analytic training consists in resolving particular problems that arise while he is taking his turn at running the city. He does not apply his mathematical expertise to the overall structure of the community and its institutions. He has inherited that structure – ultimately, from Socrates as 'founder' of the imaginary city (519c) – and is charged simply to preserve it. The frequent glances back and forth at the painter's model, the erasures and corrections – these would represent the work of day-to-day judgment, minor legislation, and management of established institutions, whose details Socrates claims there is no need to supply (501b; compare 423e, 425d). Book 5 of Aristotle's *Nicomachean Ethics* perhaps gives us some idea how mathematics was thought relevant to such work. Its topic is justice, but its talk is mostly of 'proportionate equality', 'diagonal exchange' and the like – concepts involved, on the one hand, in the economics of just distribution and commerce, and, on the other, in the ratios of gain and loss, reward and penalty, that make for rectificatory justice.

The work of running Callipolis and assuring the continuance of its system is regarded by philosophers not as a privilege, not as something grand, but as a necessity (540b; compare 520e, 347d). Each takes his tour of duty, but finds his greatest pleasure in philosophic activity, conducted in the company of his peers. His attitude towards political life is intriguingly reminiscent of that which Glaucon attributed to the conventionally just person, for whom justice is a compromise to be practised not willingly, as one would practise something thought to be beneficial, but rather as something unavoidable (358c). There is this difference, however, between the two attitudes: the philosopher does not rule unwillingly – at least if that is taken to mean that he would avoid ruling if he could – but rather in recognition of what is necessary if things are to turn out for the best, both for himself and for his fellow-citizens (592a, 520c–d). The grand and godlike thing is only philosophy, but the philosopher is not only a philosopher. He is a human being, beset by a variety of needs and desires, adrift amid a variety of fellow human beings. Because he is a philosopher, he makes the best of things – for only in a paradise where souls are simply wise could the best alternative be to engage in continuous and perfect contemplation (519c–d, 611c–612a). The politics of the *Republic* draws its strength from a sense of loss.

A guide to further reading

Bibliographical note to the introduction

For those who wish to explore issues arising directly from the editor's introduction, the following works are recommended.

For the **general historical and cultural background**, fundamental and remarkably lively are the volumes of *The Cambridge Ancient History*, 2nd edition, that deal respectively with the fifth and the fourth centuries BC: vol. v, ed. D. M. Lewis *et al.* (Cambridge: Cambridge University Press, 1992) and vol. vi [abbr. *CAH* 6], ed. D. M. Lewis *et al.* (Cambridge: Cambridge University Press, 1994). An important work of reference is K. J. Dover, *Greek Popular Morality in the Time of Plato and Aristotle* (Oxford: Blackwell, 1974, repr. Indianapolis: Hackett, 1994).

A detailed account of the rule of **the Thirty** can be found in Peter Krentz, *The Thirty at Athens* (Ithaca: Cornell University Press, 1982). Plato's *Letters* can be studied in the translation, with critical essays, of Glen R. Morrow, *Plato's Epistles* (Indianapolis: Bobbs Merrill, 1962).

M. M. Austin gives a succinct account of **faction** in *CAH* 6 pp. 528–535 ('Social and political conflicts'). There is a full survey in A. W. Lintott, *Violence, Civil Strife and Revolution in the Classical City, 750–330 BC* (Baltimore: Johns Hopkins University Press, 1981). Martin Ostwald, *From Popular Sovereignty to the Sovereignty of Law: Law, Society and Politics in Fifth-Century Athens* (Berkeley: University of California Press, 1986), is a detailed conceptual history. G. E. M. de Ste Croix, *The Class Struggle in the Ancient Greek World: From the Archaic Age to the Arab Conquests* (Ithaca: Cornell University Press, 1981), views the issues from a Marxist perspective. An important study of political groupings at

Athens is W. Robert Connor, *The New Politicians of Fifth-Century Athens* (Princeton: Princeton University Press, 1971, repr. Indianapolis: Hackett, 1992).

A very readable social history of **Sparta** and of its polarity with Athens is Anton Powell, *Athens and Sparta: Constructing Greek Political and Social History from 478 BC* (London: Routledge, 1988). The account of the *Republic* given by W. K. C. Guthrie, *A History of Greek Philosophy*, vol. IV [*Plato: The Man and His Dialogues, Earlier Period*] (Cambridge: Cambridge University Press, 1975), is representative of the approach to the *Republic*'s **utopianism** that understands Callipolis as a personal ideal (see esp. pp. 483–486). M. F. Burnyeat, 'Utopia and fantasy: the practicability of Plato's ideally just city'. 175–187 in Jim Hopkins and Anthony Savile, eds., *Psychoanalysis, Mind and Art: Perspectives on Richard Wollheim* (Oxford: Blackwell, 1992), argues that Plato was serious about the political reforms projected in Callipolis. The approach that puts in question whether Plato intended Callipolis even to seem desirable is identified with Leo Strauss: see the second chapter ('On Plato's *Republic*') of *The City and Man* (Chicago: University of Chicago Press, 1964). The interpretive essay in Alan Bloom's translation of the *Republic* (New York: Basic Books, 1968) is a more accessible version of this approach. A survey of utopian theory is included in W. Robert Connor's chapter 'Historical writing in the fourth century BC and in the Hellenistic period': 458–471 in P. E. Easterling and B. M. W. Knox, eds., *The Cambridge History of Classical Literature*, vol. 1 [*Greek Literature*] (Cambridge: Cambridge University Press, 1985). The chapter is also relevant to the issues mentioned next.

A wide selection of **political theory before Plato**, including important but relatively obscure texts such as the 'Old Oligarch' and the fragments of Critias, is translated in Michael Gagarin and Paul Woodruff, eds., *Early Greek Political Thought from Homer to the Sophists* [Cambridge Texts in the History of Political Thought] (Cambridge: Cambridge University Press, 1995). On **Xenophon** as a political writer and Socratic see the chapter by Christopher Bruell in Leo Strauss and Joseph Cropsey, eds., *History of Political Philosophy* (3rd edn, Chicago: University of Chicago Press, 1987). Martin Ostwald and John Lynch give an account of **Isocrates** and of the relation between his and Plato's schools in chapter 12a of *CAH* 6 ('The growth of schools and the advance of knowledge'). The opening chapter of Charles Kahn's *Plato and the Socratic Dialogue: The Philosophic Use of a Literary Form* (Cambridge: Cambridge

University Press, 1996) is a survey of the literature written by the **Socratics** as a group. Diskin Clay, 'The origins of the Socratic dialogue': 23–47 in Paul A. Vander Waerdt, ed., *The Socratic Movement* (Ithaca: Cornell University Press, 1994), analyses the models and the background for **Socratic dialogue** as a literary form. The classic modern work on the **Pythagoreans** is Walter Burkert, *Lore and Science in Ancient Pythagoreanism* (trans. E. Minar, Jr., Cambridge, Mass.: Harvard University Press, 1972). For the political involvement of **members of Plato's Academy**, in addition to chapter 12a of *CAH* 6 mentioned in this paragraph, see chapter 10 ('Plato's academy and politics') of P. A. Brunt, *Studies in Greek History and Thought* (Oxford: Clarendon Press, 1993), which includes an account of Plato's connections with the elder and younger **Dionysius**, as do chapters 5 and 13 of *CAH* 6 (David Lewis' 'Sicily, 413–368 BC' and H. D. Westlake's 'Dion and Timoleon').

On pp. xxii–xxv of the introduction: the controversy over whether the *Republic* should be considered a proto-fascist work came to a head with the publication of vol. I of Karl Popper, *The Open Society and its Enemies* (London: Routledge 1945; last revised edn 1966). The question can be profitably studied in the collection of articles *Plato, Popper and Politics*, ed. R. Bambrough (Cambridge: Heffer, 1967).

On pp. xxv–xxxi of the introduction: see the works on psychology, on metaphysics, and on mathematics listed under the heading 'Specific aspects of Plato's thought and of the *Republic*'.

General studies of Plato and of *The Republic*

Two good introductory books on Plato are Bernard Williams, *Plato* (New York: Routledge, 1999), and C. J. Rowe, *Plato* [Philosophers in Context] (New York: St Martin's Press, 1984). G. M. A. Grube, *Plato's Thought* (2nd edn, Indianapolis: Hackett, 1980) remains useful. The discussion of the *Republic* in vol. IV of Guthrie's *History of Greek Philosophy* (full reference at p. xxiii above) is useful in its own right and as a gateway to more particular topics; and the same can be said of Guthrie's entire account of Plato and of particular dialogues in vols. IV and V. Ernest Barker's classic *Greek Political Theory* (London: Methuen, 1918), despite its title, is devoted entirely to Plato and the pre-Platonic context of political thought. George Klosko, *The Development of Plato's Political Theory* (New York: Methuen, 1986), is a useful modern discussion of political themes in the dialogues.

R. L. Nettleship, *Lectures on the Republic of Plato* (2nd edn, London: Macmillan, 1901) is still well worth reading. Bernard Bosanquet, *A Companion to Plato's Republic for English Readers* (2nd edn, London: Rivingtons, 1925), which is a philosophic commentary keyed to a translation, remains interesting, especially for its Hegelian perspective. Two books of value from mid-century are N. R. Murphy, *The Interpretation of Plato's Republic* (Oxford: Clarendon Press, 1951), and, at a more introductory level, R. C. Cross and A. D. Woozley, *Plato's Republic: A Philosophic Commentary* (London: Macmillan, 1963). The subsequent generation of works written by philosophers and intended as introductions includes Nicholas P. White, *A Companion to Plato's Republic* (Oxford: Blackwell, 1979) and Julia Annas, *An Introduction to Plato's Republic* (Oxford: Clarendon Press, 1981). More ambitious are C. D. C. Reeve, *Philosopher-Kings: The Argument of Plato's Republic* (Princeton: Princeton University Press, 1988), and T. H. Irwin, *Plato's Ethics* (Oxford: Oxford University Press, 1995) – a work which, while not exclusively about the *Republic*, gives an influential account of its theory of justice. Studies that show the influence of Strauss (see p. xxiii above) and are important in their own right include Seth Benardete, *Socrates' Second Sailing: On Plato's Republic* (Chicago: University of Chicago Press, 1989), and Leon Craig, *The War Lover: A Study of Plato's Republic* (Toronto: University of Toronto Press, 1994).

Specific aspects of Plato's thought and of *The Republic*

There is an extensive bibliography arranged by topic in Richard Kraut, ed., *The Cambridge Companion to Plato* (Cambridge: Cambridge University Press, 1992).

Those who wish to investigate the **metaphysical** themes sounded in the *Republic* could begin with chapter 9 of the *Companion* just mentioned, Nicholas P. White's 'Plato's metaphysical epistemology', and move on to the more adventurous territory of Richard Patterson's *Image and Reality in Plato's Metaphysics* (Indianapolis: Hackett, 1985) and the difficult but brilliant work of Terry Penner, *The Ascent from Nominalism: Some Existence Arguments in Plato's Middle Dialogues* (Dordrecht: Reidel, 1987). Quite different is the approach of the 'Tübingen school', which understands the metaphysical arguments contained in the dialogues as allusions to a Platonic metaphysics never described in them. Little of this work is available in English, but note the succinct and accessible account by Thomas A. Szlezák, *Reading Plato* (New York: Routledge, 1999).

For **Plato's psychology** in general, consult the accounts given by Sabina Lovibond, 'Plato's theory of mind': 35–55 in Stephen Everson, ed., *Psychology* [Companions to Ancient Thought] (Cambridge: Cambridge University Press, 1991), and Charles Kahn, 'Plato's theory of desire', *Review of Metaphysics* 41 (1987) 77–103. Probing modern studies of the tripartite soul in the *Republic* include Bernard Williams, 'The analogy of city and soul in Plato's *Republic*': 196–206 in E. N. Lee *et al.*, eds., *Exegesis and Argument* (*Phronesis* supplementary vol. 1, 1973), and John M. Cooper, 'Plato's theory of human motivation', *History of Philosophy Quarterly* 1.1 (1984) 3–21. They should be read alongside the quite different J. L. Stocks, 'Plato and the tripartite soul', *Mind* 24 (1915) 207–221.

For discussion of **Plato on literature and culture** see G. R. F. Ferrari, 'Plato and poetry': 92–148 in George Kennedy, ed., *The Cambridge History of Literary Criticism*, vol. 1 [Classical Criticism] (Cambridge: Cambridge University Press, 1989), Christopher Janaway, *Images of Excellence: Plato's Critique of the Arts* (Oxford: Clarendon Press, 1995), and M. F. Burnyeat, 'Culture and society in Plato's *Republic*', *Tanner Lectures on Human Values* 20 (1999) 215–324. For a different perspective, see chapter 3 ('Plato and the poets') of H.-G. Gadamer, *Dialogue and Dialectic: Eight Hermeneutical Studies on Plato* (trans. P. Christopher Smith, New Haven: Yale University Press, 1980). Andrew Barker, *Greek Musical Writings* (2 vols. Cambridge: Cambridge University Press, 1984, 1989) includes an annotated translation of all passages in Plato having to do with music. For the wider context, see H. I. Marrou, *The History of Education in Antiquity* (trans. G. Lamb, New York: Sheed and Ward, 1956).

Ian Mueller provides a useful survey of the place of **mathematics** in Plato's thought in his 'Mathematical method and philosophic truth', chapter 5 of *The Cambridge Companion to Plato* (full reference at p. xxxv above). Important studies that take opposing views of mathematics are F. M. Cornford, 'Mathematics and dialectic in the *Republic* VI–VII', *Mind* 41 (1932) 37–52; repr.: 61–95 in R. E. Allen, ed., *Studies in Plato's Metaphysics* (London: Routledge, 1965), and M. F. Burnyeat, 'Plato on why mathematics is good for the soul', in T. Smiley, ed., *Mathematics and Necessity in the History of Philosophy* [Dawes Hicks Lectures on Philosophy, British Academy] (Oxford: Oxford University Press, 2000).

Cornford emphasises distinctions between the mathematical and the moral in the *Republic*, Burnyeat emphasises their kinship. The standard history of Greek mathematics as a whole is that of T. L. Heath, *A History of Greek Mathematics* (2 vols., Oxford: Clarendon Press, 1921, repr. New York: Dover, 1981). A classic study of the curriculum in Plato's Academy and of the place of mathematics within it is Harold Cherniss' *The Riddle of the Early Academy* (Berkeley: University of California Press, 1945, repr. New York: Garland, 1980).

Principal dates

The chronology includes no guesses as to when Plato wrote the various dialogues. For the issues and difficulties involved in such attempts, see the quick overview in pp. xii–xviii of the introduction to John M. Cooper, ed., *Plato: Complete Works* (Indianapolis: Hackett, 1997), or the full treatments of Holger Thesleff, *Studies in Platonic Chronology* (*Commentationes Humanarum Litterarum* 70, 1982), and Leonard Brandwood, *The Chronology of Plato's Dialogues* (Cambridge: Cambridge University Press, 1990).

Plato			*Political events*
		431	War declared between Athens and Sparta ('Peloponnesian War')
427	Birth of Plato		
		411	Oligarchic revolution of 'The Four Hundred' at Athens
		410	Democracy restored at Athens
		405	Dionysius I of Syracuse rises to power
		404	Spartan victory over Athens, oligarchic regime of 'The Thirty' imposed
		403	Democracy restored at Athens

Plato		Political events	
		399	Execution of Socrates
		395	Athens, Thebes, Corinth in alliance against Sparta ('Corinthian War')
388	Visits south Italy and Sicily, meets Archytas the Pythagorean and Dionysius I of Syracuse		
c. 387	Founds Academy after return to Athens		
		386	'The King's Peace' imposed by Persia on the parties to the Corinthian War
		386–378	Sparta in the ascendant in the aftermath of the King's Peace
		378	Athens and Thebes in alliance against Sparta; foundation of Second Athenian League
		371	Thebes defeats Sparta at Leuctra; Spartan military supremacy comes to an end
		370 362	Thebes in the ascendant after Leuctra; Athens in alliance with Sparta against Thebes
		367	Death of Dionysius I of Syracuse; Dionysius II succeeds him
367–366	Plato visits Dionysius II in Sicily		
361–360	Plato revisits Dionysius II		

Plato			*Political events*
		360	Philip II (father of Alexander the Great) accedes to throne of Macedon and begins to build empire in Greece; Athens at first in alliance, but from 357 onwards at war with Macedon
		357	Dionysius II is ousted by Dion, member of the Syracusan royal family and Plato's confidant and student
		354	Dion is assassinated
347	Death of Plato		
		338	Final victory of Philip of Macedon at Chaeronea

Abbreviations and conventions

CAH 6   D. M. Lewis *et al.*, eds., *The Cambridge Ancient History*, 2nd
        edition, vol. VI [*The Fourth Century BC*] (Cambridge:
        Cambridge University Press, 1994)
DK   H. Diels, *Die Fragmente der Vorsokratiker* (6th edn, rev. W.
        Kranz, Berlin: Weidmann, 1951–1952)
EGPT   Michael Gagarin and Paul Woodruff, eds., *Early Greek Political
        Thought from Homer to the Sophists* [Cambridge Texts in the
        History of Political Thought] (Cambridge: Cambridge
        University Press, 1995)
GPM   K. J. Dover, *Greek Popular Morality in the Time of Plato and
        Aristotle* (Oxford: Blackwell, 1974, repr. Indianapolis: Hackett,
        1994)

Line references to works by ancient Greek prose writers are keyed to the
Oxford Classical Text.

Editor's synopsis of *The Republic*

Book 1

327a: Socrates and Glaucon are detained at the Piraeus. The scene is set at Polemarchus' house (328b). – 328c: Socrates converses with Cephalus about old age (328e) and the benefits of wealth (329e), and introduces the topic of justice (331c): it is not simply a matter of being truthful and returning what one owes. – 331d: Discussion between Socrates and Polemarchus. Justice, it is proposed, is a matter of giving what is appropriate: to friends, giving good, to enemies, bad (332c). But in what context (332d)? And won't the just person also be best at injustice (333e)? Besides, who *are* our friends and enemies (334c)? And is it just to treat even an enemy badly (335b)? – 336b: Thrasymachus speaks up. His definition: justice is what is good for the stronger (338c). But does this mean: whatever the stronger *thinks* is good (339b)? Clarification is volunteered by Polemarchus and Cleitophon (340a). Thrasymachus insists that the stronger, to the extent that he *is* stronger, does not make mistakes (340d). Socrates counters with an analysis of art or skill: it aims at what is good for its object, not its practitioner (341c). Thrasymachus objects: shepherds do not aim at what is good for their sheep (343b). Socrates distinguishes the shepherd's concern for his sheep from his concern to earn a living (345c). He suggests that the best rulers are reluctant to rule (347a). He offers three arguments in favour of the just life over the unjust life: (i) the just man is wise and good, the unjust man ignorant and bad (349b); (ii) injustice produces internal disharmony and prevents effective action (351b); (iii) the just person lives a happier life than the unjust person (352d). But it remains to be discovered what justice is (354b).

Book 2

357a: Glaucon, as devil's advocate, renews Thrasymachus' challenge. – 359a: His speech against justice: (i) justice has its origin in a compromise; (ii) is practised only because unavoidable (the Gyges story) (359c); (iii) is desirable only for its rewards, which can be gained by the mere appearance of justice (360e). – 362d: Adeimantus' speech reinforcing Glaucon's critique. Two ways of describing justice are widespread: as something praiseworthy not for itself but for its rewards (363a), or as something dissociated from pleasure and happiness (364a); both these views tend to corrupt the young (365b). Socrates is requested to praise justice for itself, not for the reputation it brings (367b). 368a: Socrates comes to the defence of justice. He proposes to look for justice in the city first, then for its equivalent in the individual; and begins by imagining the origins of civic life (369a). – 372c: In response to Glaucon's objection that this hypothetical city is uncivilised, Socrates describes instead a luxurious city. He proposes that a professional army will be needed to guard the city (373e), made up of guardians who must be fierce to enemies but gentle to their own people (375c), and educated with special care (376d). Traditional stories about the gods are to be censored (377b); god should be presented to them as good, and as a cause only of good (379a); also as unchanging (380d), and as refraining from deception (381e).

Book 3

386a: Discussion of the guardians' education continues. The qualities that stories should promote in them, in addition to the respect for authority and the social harmony already considered, are (i) courage (386b), (ii) resistance to grief (387d), (iii) resistance to laughter (388c), (iv) respect for truth, but including a willingness to tell lies when necessary (389b), (v) self-discipline (389d). – 392d: Discussion turns from the contents of stories to the manner in which they are told, and Socrates makes a distinction between simple narrative and narrative through imitation. He imposes limitations on the guardians' familiarity with and performance of imitative poetry (394e). They should confine themselves to the austere style and not use either the elaborate or the mixed styles (396c). – 398c: Equivalent restrictions are imposed on the types of music to be included in the guardians' education. – 400e: Finally, Socrates makes a generalisation about the importance of good art in forming good character, and connects the beauty of art with the beauty that inspires erotic attachment (402d). – 403c: Turning to the guardians' physical education, Socrates recommends a straightforward diet and avoidance of recourse to doctors, which he associates with the avoidance of litigation (404e). Physical education should aim to benefit the soul rather than the body (410b); a balance between intellect and spiritedness is the ideal (410d). – 412b: Socrates describes how rulers should be selected from among the guardians. He designs a patriotic myth to be believed by subsequent generations in the newly founded city (414c), and briefly sketches the guardians' social organisation, forbidding them private property (415d).

Book 4

419a: Adeimantus objects: Will the guardians be happy (419a)? Socrates explains that the task is to make the whole city happy, not any particular group within it (420b). He mentions further requirements if the city as a whole is to be happy: both its wealth (421d) and its size (423b) must be limited. He emphasises once more the importance of education (423e), and urges conservatism when it comes to amending laws (425e). For its religious rituals the city can defer to the traditional authorities (427b). – 427d: Now that the city has been theoretically established, discussion turns to its justice. Socrates proposes that its justice will be what remains after its wisdom, courage and self-discipline have been identified (427e). The city's wisdom is located in its ruling class (428b); its courage is located in the army (429a); and its self-discipline consists in the fact that its subjects are willing to be ruled by those best suited to rule (430d). Its justice, finally, is a matter of each class performing its proper function (432b). – 434d: The corresponding virtues in the individual are now to be identified. First, the general correspondence between city and individual is defended (435a), prompting the question whether the three elements in the soul, corresponding to the three classes in the city, have distinct functions (436b). Socrates distinguishes the function of the rational from that of the desiring element (439a), and that of the spirited element from each of the others in turn (439e, 440e). He explains how the virtues of the individual correspond in their elements and their structure to those of the city (441c). An individual is just when each of the elements internal to his soul performs its proper function (442d). This account is compatible with conventional beliefs (442e). Justice, then, is a healthy balance of the soul's components, and injustice an unhealthy imbalance (444e). – 445a: Socrates now comes to the question which Glaucon and Adeimantus originally asked him to answer: which is more profitable, justice or injustice? A proper response will require examination of the various unjust societies and of the unjust individuals that correspond to each.

Book 5

449a: Socrates is about to describe the varieties of unjust society when he is distracted by a whispered transaction between Polemarchus and Adeimantus. Invited to speak up, they demand a more detailed account from him of the proposal that women and children should be held in common among the guardians. – 451c: Socrates begins with an argument that female members of the guardian class should perform the same tasks as male guardians. Against the objection that women should be assigned different tasks from men because they differ from men by nature (453b), he responds that this natural difference is not relevant when it comes to running a city (453e). Having shown that this proposal is feasible, he also argues that it is optimal (456c). – 457d: Socrates' second proposal is that there should be no separate families among the guardians. He postpones consideration of its feasibility in order to consider its optimality (458a), and begins by explaining the sexual and eugenic regulations that will be required of the guardians (458c), before describing how these arrangements will achieve a unity among the guardians that can then extend to all the citizens (462a). He points out that, living this way, the guardians are likely to be extremely happy (465d) Once again the feasibility of these arrangements is mooted (466d). Socrates launches into an account of how the guardians will make war (466e), but is presently interrupted by Glaucon, who demands to know precisely how it is possible for a society such as this to come into being (471c). – 472a: After a preamble explaining that the theoretical model of the ideal city remains valid even if its feasibility cannot be demonstrated, Socrates responds that the model cannot become reality unless philosophers become kings, or kings philosophers (473c). To justify this claim, an analysis of philosophy is required (474b). Only philosophers recognise and take pleasure in the single form behind the multiplicity of appearances (476a). Socrates offers an argument to distinguish the philosopher's knowledge from mere opinion (476e).

Book 6

484a: Given the superior discernment of philosophers, Socrates continues, it is to them that the city should look for guidance, provided they can also be shown to be capable of gaining practical experience and of achieving the full range of human virtue. The character traits of the philosopher do in fact cover this range, being love of learning, truthfulness, self-discipline, greatness of spirit, courage, justice, quickness of mind, good memory, refinement and charm (485a). – 487a: Adeimantus objects that actual philosophers are either useless or bad. Socrates responds with an analogy (the ship of state) to show that it is not philosophers who are to blame for their uselessness, but those who refuse to make use of them (488a). He describes how the philosophic nature tends, because of its very excellence, to become distorted by society, which would ignore a less outstanding character (489e). He warns against various impostors who claim the mantle of philosophy (495c), and who far outnumber the few philosophers who manage to escape corruption by society (496b). He explains how it is possible for a city to cope with the challenge of philosophy (497d), and to become free of the prejudice against it (500a). He concludes that Callipolis is both optimal and not unfeasible (502c). – 502d: Turning to the question of how philosopher-kings should be educated, Socrates argues that their most important branch of study will be the study of the good (505a), and offers three analogies to explain it: (i) the sun (507a); (ii) the line (509d).

Book 7

514a: The final analogy to explain the study of the good is that of (iii) the cave. Education ought to turn the eye of the soul away from the shadows with which it is surrounded in the cave of society and lead it to true understanding in the sunlit world above (518c). But philosophers who attain this understanding must be made to return to the cave and rule there (519d). – 521d: Socrates explains how it is the study of mathematics that will do the job of drawing the soul out of the cave. He analyses each branch of mathematics in turn: (i) arithmetic and number (522c); (ii) plane geometry (526c); (iii) solid geometry (528b); (iv) astronomy (528e); (v) harmonics (530d). – 531d: The culmination of the philosopher-king's education is the study of dialectic, which brings him to understand the good. But Socrates cannot give Glaucon a clear idea of what dialectic is, or how it achieves its end. – 535a: Instead, they discuss what qualifications are necessary for such a course of study, and at what age the various studies should be undertaken (536d). Socrates concludes with a suggestion about the easiest way to bring Callipolis into being (541a).

Book 8

543a: Socrates and Glaucon take stock of the argument so far, and resume the topic that was interrupted at the beginning of Book 5. The four main types of unjust regime will be systematically described, together with the corresponding types of unjust individual, beginning with the least degenerate and proceeding to the most. Socrates once again offers a general justification of the correspondence between city and individual (544e) – 545b: He explains how timocracy arises from aristocracy, the characteristics of timocracy (547d), the character of the correspondingly timocratic individual (548d), and how an individual becomes timocratic (549c). – 550c: Oligarchy. How it arises from timocracy, its characteristics (551c), how the correspondingly oligarchic individual becomes oligarchic (553a), and what his character is (554a). – 555b: Democracy. How it arises from oligarchy, its characteristics (557b), how the correspondingly democratic individual becomes democratic (558c), and what his character is (561a). – 562a: Tyranny. How it arises from democracy, and what its characteristics are (566d).

Book 9

571a: The tyrannical individual. How he becomes tyrannical, and what his character is (573c). Socrates demonstrates this individual's unhappiness by applying the correspondence between city and individual (576c). Unhappiest of all is the tyrannical individual who becomes tyrant of a city (578b). Socrates concludes this first proof that the just are happier than the unjust with a final ranking of the individual characters in respect of happiness (580b). – 580d: Second proof that the just are happier than the unjust. Socrates distinguishes three fundamental human types, the lovers of wisdom, of honour, and of profit, and argues that we should trust the wisdom-lover's judgment that his way of life is the most pleasant. – 583b: Third proof that the just are happier than the unjust. Socrates analyses the nature of pleasure. Relief from pain can seem pleasurable (583c), and most, even if not all, bodily pleasures are no more than a relief from pain (584b). The only truly fulfilling pleasure, by contrast, is that which comes from understanding (585b). – 586d: Socrates concludes with the claim that each element in the soul can find its proper pleasure if the part that loves wisdom is in control. He calculates the multiple by which the best life is more pleasant than the worst (587a). He offers a final vindication of justice with the help of a comparison between the soul and an imaginary creature of multiple form (588b).

Book 10

595a: Socrates returns to the topic of poetry, last discussed in Books 2 and 3. What is imitation? Socrates answers his question by considering the example of a couch, and distinguishing between the form of the couch, the manufactured couch, and a painting of a couch (596a). He concludes that the products of imitation are far removed from truth (597e). – 598e: Poets, like painters, are imitators. Socrates argues that if they really had the expertise conventionally attributed to them, they would not have been content to remain mere poets (599b). Their knowledge is in fact inferior to a maker's knowledge, which is in turn inferior to a user's knowledge (601c). – 602c: Socrates turns from the topic of what imitators know to that of how they affect their audiences. Using a comparison with optical illusions (602c), he argues that imitative poetry aims to stir the irrational element in the soul (603c). Worst of all, it can corrupt even decent people (606c). He concludes that there is no place for such poetry in Callipolis, but only for verses in praise of the gods and of good men (606e). – 608a: Via the claim that imitative poetry prevents the immortal soul from attaining its true reward, Socrates makes the transition to a proof of the soul's immortality (608d). He insists that the soul cannot be understood in its true nature if we consider only its association with the body, as we have been doing in this discussion (611b). – 612b: Finally, Socrates describes the rewards of justice, as permitted by the rules of their discussion now that justice has first been vindicated without appeal to its reputation or rewards. He briefly reviews the rewards of justice and the penalties for injustice in this life (612d), then narrates an elaborate myth, the myth of Er, describing the rewards and penalties that await us after death (614a). The souls of the dead meet on a meadow to discuss their experiences of reward and punishment (614c); they travel to a place from which they can view the whole cosmos (616b); they choose their next lives (617d); they are reincarnated (620e). Socrates ends the discussion with a farewell (621c).

Book 1[1]

327 I went down to the Piraeus yesterday with Glaucon the son of Ariston, to offer a prayer to the goddess.[2] Also I wanted to watch the festival, to see how they would conduct it, since this was the first time it was being celebrated.[3] The parade of Athenians struck me as excellent, and the show put on by the Thracians was every bit as impressive, I thought. We offered our prayers, watched the festival, and then started off on our journey back

b to town. We were already on our way home when we were spotted by Polemarchus the son of Cephalus. He got his slave to run after us and tell us to wait for him. The slave tugged at my cloak from behind, and said, 'Polemarchus says you are to wait.' I turned round, and asked him where his master was.

'There he is,' he said, 'coming along behind you. Wait for him.'

'We will,' said Glaucon.

c In a few moments Polemarchus reached us, with Glaucon's brother Adeimantus, Niceratus the son of Nicias, and a few others. They had been watching the procession, apparently. And Polemarchus said, 'It looks as if you're all on your way back to the city, Socrates. You're not staying, then?'

---

[1] It has been traditional since antiquity to divide the *Republic* into ten 'books'. Each book corresponds to a single roll of papyrus, the format in which Plato's writings were archived, distributed, and read in the ancient world. We do not know whether the division into ten books was made by Plato himself or by a later editor. The numbers and letters in the margin follow the pagination of the sixteenth-century edition of Plato by Stephanus. It is the pagination normally used to circumvent differences of format among subsequent editions and translations.

[2] Bendis, as we are eventually told at the end of Book 1 (354a).

[3] We can date this occasion only to a window of time between 431 and 411 BC.

'That's a pretty good guess,' I replied.

'Do you see how many of us there are?' he asked.

'Yes.'

'Well, then,' he said, 'you must either get the better of all these people, or else stay here.'

'There is another possibility,' I said. 'We might persuade you that you should let us go.'

'And do you really think you could persuade us,' he said, 'if we refused to listen?'

'Of course not,' said Glaucon.

'In that case, make your decision on the assumption that we are *not* going to listen.'

328   'Haven't you heard about the torch race?' Adeimantus added. 'This evening, on horseback, in honour of the goddess?'

'On horseback?' I said. 'That's something new. Do you mean a relay race on horseback, passing torches from one to another?'

'Yes,' said Polemarchus. 'And they're going to have an all-night ceremony as well, which should be worth watching. We can go out and watch

b   it after dinner. There'll be lots of young people there. We can spend some time with them, and talk to them. Do stay. Please say "yes."'

'It looks as if we shall have to,' said Glaucon.

'If that's your decision,' I said, 'we shall.'

So we went back to Polemarchus' house, where we found Polemarchus' brothers Lysias and Euthydemus – as well as Thrasymachus of Chalcedon, Charmantides from the deme[4] of Paeania, and Cleitophon the son of Aristonymus. Also there, in the house, was Polemarchus' father

c   Cephalus. It was a long time since I had seen him, and I found him much aged. He was wearing a garland, and sitting on a sort of cushioned stool. He had just been conducting a sacrifice in the courtyard.[5] There was a circle of stools round him, so we sat down with him.

As soon as he saw me, Cephalus started to make me welcome. 'You don't often come down to visit us in the Piraeus, Socrates,' he said. 'You should, though. If I were still strong enough to make the journey up to

d   town without difficulty, there would be no need for you to come here. We would go to you. But as things are, you should come more often. I can assure you, speaking for myself, that the more the pleasures of the body

---

[4] The territory of Athens and its surrounding countryside was subdivided into districts called 'demes', each with some degree of self-government.

[5] Cephalus' garland is an item of sacrificial uniform.

fade, the greater become one's desire and taste for conversation. So do please spend some time with these young men. Do come here and visit us. Regard us as your friends – as your family, even.'

e   'With pleasure, Cephalus,' I replied. 'I love talking to the very old. It's as if they're a long way ahead of us on a road which we too are probably going to have to travel. I feel we should learn from them what the road is like – whether it's steep and rough going, or gentle and easy. In particular, I'd very much like to hear how it strikes you, now that you've actually reached the time of life which the poets call "old age, the threshold."[6] What is your report on it? Would you call it a difficult time of life?'

329   'I'll tell you exactly how it strikes me, Socrates. There's a group of us who meet fairly often. We're all about the same age, so we're following the words of the old proverb.[7] When we meet, most of them start complaining; they say they miss the things they used to enjoy when they were young, and they recall their sexual exploits, their drinking, their feasting, and everything connected with those pleasures. They get upset, as if they'd suffered some great loss – as if then they had led a wonderful life, b whereas now they're not alive at all. Some of them also complain about the lack of respect shown by their families towards old age, and under this heading they recite a litany of grievances against old age. I think they're putting the blame in the wrong place, Socrates. If old age were to blame, then not only would I have felt the same way about old age, but so would everyone else who has ever reached this age. And yet I've met several people who are not like this – most notably Sophocles the poet. I was there c once when someone asked him, "How is your sex life, Sophocles? Are you still capable of making love to a woman?" "Don't talk about it, my good sir," was Sophocles' reply. "It is with the greatest relief that I have escaped it. Like escaping from a fierce and frenzied master." I thought that a good reply at the time, and I still think it a good one now. Old age is altogether a time of great peace and freedom from that sort of thing.

d   'When our appetites fade, and loosen their grip on us, then what happens is exactly what Sophocles was talking about. It is a final release from a bunch of insane masters. Both in this, and in your relations with your family, there is only one thing responsible, and that is not old age, but your character. For those who are civilised and contented, then even

---

[6] That is, the threshold of death. The phrase is common in Homer and other epic poets.

[7] The proverb runs, literally, 'People of the same age please each other' and has no exact proverbial match in English – but compare 'birds of a feather flock together'.

old age is only a slight burden. Otherwise – for those who are not like this – both old age and youth prove hard to cope with.'

e I was very impressed by what he said, and I wanted him to go on talking. So I prompted him further: 'I suspect most people don't believe you, Cephalus, when you say that. They think it is not your character which makes old age easy for you, but the fact that you have plenty of money. The rich, they say, have many consolations.'

'You're right,' he said. 'They don't believe me. And there's some truth in what they say. But not as much truth as they think. Themistocles' 330 famous saying is very much to the point here. A man from Seriphus started making disparaging remarks about him, and telling him that his fame was due not to his own merits, but to those of his city. Themistocles' reply was that though he himself would never have been famous if he had been born in Seriphus, neither would the other man have been if he had been born in Athens. The same applies to those who are not rich, and who find old age hard to bear. In poverty, even the right temperament will not find old age altogether easy, whereas the wrong temperament, even with the aid of wealth, will never be at peace with itself.'

'Did you inherit most of the money you possess, Cephalus?' I asked. 'Or is most of it money you made yourself, on top of your inheritance?'

b 'Did I add to it, Socrates? When it comes to making money, I'm somewhere between my grandfather and my father. My grandfather – my namesake – inherited about as much wealth as I now possess, and increased it many times. My father Lysanias reduced it to even less than it is now. I shall be happy if I can leave these boys not less, but a little bit more, than I inherited.'

c 'The reason I asked,' I said, 'is that you've never struck me as being particularly fond of money. And that's generally the attitude of those who haven't made it themselves. Compared with most people, self-made men are doubly fond of their money. Those who have made a fortune are devoted to their money in the first place because it is their own creation – just as poets love their poems, or fathers love their children – and in the second place for what they can do with it, just like anyone else. This makes them very poor company, since they can see no value in anything except money.'

'You're right,' he said.

d 'Yes,' I said. 'But I have another question for you. What would you say is the greatest benefit you have derived from your possession of great wealth?'

'One which many people might not be inclined to believe, if I told them. But you can take my word for it, Socrates, that when you are confronted by the thought of your own death, you are visited by fear and anxiety about things which never troubled you before. The stories told about what happens in Hades, that anyone who is unjust here will have to
e   pay for it there – stories you once laughed at – begin to trouble your mind. You wonder if they may be true. You start seeing that world for yourself, either through the infirmity of old age, or because you are already in some way closer to it. Suddenly you are full of suspicion and fear; you start calculating and considering whether you've done anyone any sort of injustice. And if you find many acts of injustice in your own life, you keep
331 waking in a panic in the middle of the night, the way children do. You live in a state of apprehension. The person with nothing on his conscience, by contrast, has fine and pleasant hopes – a nurse to his old age, as Pindar puts it. He found just the right words for it, Socrates, when he said that anyone who lives his life in righteousness and purity will find that

> Sweet hope, old age's nurse, which chiefly guides
> Men's wayward minds, accompanies his heart
> And so protects him.[8]

He's right – couldn't be more right. And that's why I attach the greatest
b   importance to the possession of money. Not for everyone, but for those of good character. If you want to avoid defrauding people, or lying to them, however reluctantly, or going to the world below in a state of terror after failing to pay what you owe – whether sacrifices to a god, or money to a man – then the possession of money contributes in no small measure to this end. Of course it has many other uses as well, but weighing one thing against another I would rate this as one of the most important uses of money, in the eyes of anyone with any sense.'
c   'That's admirably put, Cephalus,' I said. 'But since you've brought up the subject of justice, can we say, quite simply, that it is truthfulness, and returning anything you may have received from anyone else? Or is it sometimes right to behave in these ways, and sometimes wrong? Let me give you an example. Suppose you borrowed some weapons from a friend when he was in his right mind. Suppose he later went mad, and then asked for them back again. Everyone would agree, I imagine, that you shouldn't give them back to him, and that anyone who did give them back

---

[8] The poem from which this quotation comes has been lost.

5

– or who was even prepared to be completely truthful to someone in this condition – would not be doing the right thing.'

d   'Correct,' he said.

'This is not the definition of justice, then – that it is telling the truth, and returning what you have been given.'

'Yes, it is, Socrates,' Polemarchus interrupted. 'At least, it is if we are to believe Simonides.'

'I'd just like to say,' Cephalus put in, 'that this is where I hand the discussion over to you. It's time I was doing something about the sacrifices.'

'Well, am I not Polemarchus, your heir?'

'You certainly are,' he replied with a laugh, and went off to his sacrifices.

e   'Tell me then,' I said, 'you who have inherited the argument, what does Simonides say about justice that you think is correct?'

'That it is just to pay everyone what is owed to him.[9] That's what he says, and I think he's right.'

'Well,' I said, 'Simonides is a wise and inspired man. It is certainly not easy to disagree with him. But what on earth does he mean by this remark? You may well know, Polemarchus. I have no idea. He obviously doesn't mean what we were talking about just now. If one person gives something to another for safe keeping, and then asks for it back when he

332   is not in his right mind, Simonides doesn't mean that the other person should give it to him. And yet I imagine the thing which was given for safe keeping *is* owed to the person who gave it, isn't it?'

'Yes.'

'In that situation – when someone goes out of his mind, and then asks for it back – isn't returning it completely out of the question?'

'Yes, it is.'

'That isn't what Simonides means, apparently, when he says that it is just to pay back what is owed, or due.'

'No, it certainly isn't,' he said. 'What he thinks is due to friends is to do them good, not harm.'

'I understand,' I replied. 'If one person gives back to another money

b   which the other has given him for safe keeping, he is not giving what is due if his returning it and the other's receiving it are harmful, and if the two of them are friends. Isn't that what you think Simonides means?'

'Yes, it is.'

---

[9] Not a sentiment that is found in the little that survives of Simonides' poetry.

'What about enemies? Should you give them whatever is in fact due to them?''

'You certainly should,' he said. 'And what is due between enemies is what is appropriate – something harmful.'

'Simonides was speaking as a poet, then, apparently, and disguising his
c definition of justice. What he meant, it seems, was that justice was giving any individual what was appropriate for him, but he called it "what was owed."''

'Yes, that must have been what he meant.'

'Suppose, then, one of us had said to him: "Simonides, take the art or skill which is called medicine. What does it give that is due and appropriate, and to what does it give it?" What do you think his answer would have been?'

'Obviously,' he replied, 'he would have said it gives the body drugs and food and drink.'

'And the art of cookery? What does it give that is due and appropriate, and to what does it give it?'

d 'It gives flavour to cooked food.'

'Very well. Then what about the art or skill which we would call justice? What does it give, and to what does it give it?'

'Well, if we are to follow the previous definitions, Socrates, it gives benefits and injuries to friends and enemies.'

'Does he mean, then, that helping your friends and harming your enemies is justice?'

'I think so.'

'All right. When people are unwell, when it's a question of sickness and health, who is best at helping them if they are friends and harming them if they are enemies?'

'A doctor.'

e 'And when they're at sea? Who can best help or harm them amid the dangers of a sea voyage?'

'A ship's captain.'

'What about the just man? In what activity, and for what purpose, is he the one best able to treat his friends well and his enemies badly?'

'In war and alliances, I think.'

'Very well. Now, when people aren't ill, my dear Polemarchus, a doctor is no use to them.'

'True.'

'And when they're not at sea, a ship's captain is no use to them.'

'No.'

'Does that mean the just man is no use to them when they're not at war?'

'No, I'm sure it doesn't.'

'Justice is something useful even in peacetime, then?'

333   'Yes, it is.'

'But then so is agriculture, isn't it?'

'Yes.'

'For producing crops.'

'Yes.'

'And shoemaking?'

'Yes, that's useful.'

'For producing shoes, you would say, presumably.'

'Of course.'

'What about justice, then? When you say it's useful in peacetime, what is it useful *for*? What does it produce?'

'Contracts, Socrates.'

'And by contracts do you mean partnerships, or something else?'

'I mean partnerships.'

b   'All right. Is the just man a good and useful partner when it comes to making moves in draughts?[10] Or would someone who plays draughts be more use?'

'Someone who plays draughts would be more use.'

'And when it comes to bricklaying, or building in stone, is the just man a more useful and better partner than a builder?'

'Of course not.'

'Well, in what kind of partnership is the just man a better partner than a lyre player, in the way a lyre player is better at playing the notes?'

'In partnerships involving money, I think.'

'Unless by any chance, Polemarchus, it's a question of putting the
c   money to some use – if you have to buy or sell a horse jointly, for a sum of money. In that case, I imagine, someone who knows about horses is more use, isn't he?'

'Apparently.'

'And for buying or selling a ship, you'd want a shipbuilder or ship's captain.'

---

[10] 'Draughts' (American 'checkers') is a translation of convenience. The Greek word *petteia* seems to have applied to several board-games. The group includes but is not limited to strategic games of battle and capture.

'So it seems.'

'In what situation, then, requiring the joint use of silver or gold, is the just man more useful than anyone else?'

'When there's a need to deposit money, and have it kept safe.'

'You mean when there's no need to put it to any use. You just want it to stay where it is?'

'That's right.'

'So it's when money is useless that justice is useful for dealing with
d it?'[11]

'It looks like it.'

'And a pruning-knife? When you want to keep it safe, then justice is useful, both in public life and in private life. But when you want to use it, then the art of viticulture is what you want?'

'Apparently.'

'And are you going to say the same about a shield or a lyre? That justice is useful when you need to keep them safe and not use them? But that when you do need to use them, then you want the soldier's art and the art of music?'

'I shall have to say that.'

'And in all other examples, justice is useless when it comes to using any of them, and useful only when they are useless?'

'I suppose so.'

e   'In that case, my friend, justice might not seem to be of any great importance, if its only use is when things are useless. But let's look at a different question. In a fight – a boxing match, possibly, or a fight of some other sort – isn't the person who is cleverest at delivering a blow also the cleverest at guarding against one?'

'He certainly is.'

'And with disease? Is the person who is clever at guarding against it also the cleverest at implanting it secretly?'

'Yes, I think so.'

334   'And in warfare, the man who is good at guarding a military camp is also good at deception. He can steal the enemies' plans, or defeat their undertakings by stealth.'

'Certainly.'

'So whenever someone is clever at guarding something, he will also be clever at stealing it.'

---

[11] Money deposited with bankers or in temple treasuries did not gain interest.

'It looks like it.'

'So if the just man is clever at looking after money, he is also clever at stealing it.'

'Well, that's what the argument suggests,' he said.

'Then the just man, it seems, has turned out to be a kind of thief. You're probably thinking of Homer. He praises Autolycus, Odysseus' grandfather on his mother's side, and says that

> In swearing oaths and thieving he surpassed
> All men.[12]

Justice, according to you and Homer and Simonides, is apparently a kind of art of stealing – but with a view to helping one's friends and harming one's enemies. Wasn't that what you said?'

'No, I certainly didn't,' he said. 'Though personally, I don't any longer know what I was saying. But one thing I do think still, and that is that justice is treating your friends well and your enemies badly.'

'By friends do you mean the people each individual believes to be good, or those who really are good, even if he doesn't realise it? And the same with enemies?'

'In all probability,' he replied, 'people will like those they think are good, and dislike those they think are no good.'

'And do people ever make mistakes in this? Do they often think people are good when they are not, and vice versa?'

'Yes, they do make mistakes.'

'So for these people, are the good their enemies, and the bad their friends?'

'They certainly are.'

'Is it nevertheless just for these people, when this happens, to treat well those who are no good, and to treat the good badly?'

'It looks like it.'

'And the good are just. They're not the kind of people who do wrong.'

'True.'

'So according to your argument it is just to harm those who do no wrong.'

'Impossible, Socrates. It looks as if the argument is no good.'

'Then it must be right,' I said, 'to treat the unjust badly, and the just well.'

---

[12] *Odyssey* 19.395–396. Autolycus was a notorious trickster; his name includes the word for 'wolf'. The reference in 'swearing oaths' is to perjury for profit.

'That sounds better.'

'In that case, Polemarchus, there are many people for whom it will turn
e   out, if their judgment of people has been mistaken, that it is right to treat
their friends badly, since their friends are no good – and their enemies
well, since their enemies are good. In those circumstances we shall
end up saying the exact opposite of the definition we quoted from
Simonides.'

'Yes,' he said. 'It certainly can turn out like that. Let's change our
definition. We're probably not defining friend and enemy correctly.'

'How *are* we defining them, Polemarchus?'

'We said that the person who seemed to be good was a friend.'

'And now? How do you want to change that definition?'

335   'If someone both seems to be good and is, let's call him a friend. If he
seems to be, but isn't really, let's say that he seems to be a friend, but isn't
really a friend. And let the same definition apply to an enemy.'

'On this definition, it appears, the good man will be a friend, and the
one who is no good will be an enemy.'

'Yes.'

'Do you want us to make an addition to our definition of justice? Our
first definition was that it was just to help a friend and harm an enemy. Do
you want us now to add to that, and say that it is just to help a friend if he
is good, and harm an enemy if he is bad?'

b   'Yes,' he said, 'I think that would be an excellent definition.'

'But is it really in the nature of a just man,' I asked, 'to treat anyone in
the world badly?'

'It certainly is,' he said. 'He should treat badly those who are no good
– his enemies.'

'If you treat a horse badly, does it become better or worse?'

'Worse.'

'Worse by the standard we use to judge dogs, or the standard we use to
judge horses?'

'The standard we use to judge horses.'

'And dogs the same? If you treat *them* badly, they become worse by the
standard we use to judge dogs, not horses?'

'They must do.'

c   'What about humans, my friend? Are we to say, in the same way, that if
they are treated badly they become worse by the standard we use to judge
human excellence?'

'Certainly.'

11

'But isn't justice a human excellence?'[13]

'Again, it must be.'

'In which case, my friend, members of the human race who are treated badly must necessarily become more unjust.'

'It looks like it.'

'Are musicians able, by means of music, to make people unmusical?'

'No, that's impossible.'

'Can horsemen make people unskilled with horses by means of horse-manship?'

'No.'

d   'And can the just make people unjust by means of justice? Or in general, can the good use human excellence to make people bad?'

'No, that's impossible.'

'Yes, because it's not the property of heat, I assume, to make things cold. It's the property of its opposite.'

'Yes.'

'Nor is it the property of dryness to make things wet, but of its opposite.'

'Yes.'

'And it is certainly not the property of good to do harm, or treat people badly, but of its opposite.'

'Apparently.'

'And the just man is good?'

'Yes.'

'In that case, Polemarchus, it is not the property of the just man to treat his friend or anyone else badly. It is the property of his opposite, the unjust man.'

'I think you're absolutely right, Socrates,' he said.

e   'So if anyone says it is just to give everyone what is due to him, and if he means by this that what is due from the just man is harm to his enemies, and help to his friends, then whoever said this was not a wise man. What he said was wrong, since we have clearly seen that it is not just to treat anyone badly under any circumstances.'

'I agree,' he said.

'Shall we take up arms, then, you and I together, if anyone claims that this is what was said by Simonides, or Bias, or Pittacus, or any other of those wise and blessedly happy men?'

---

[13] The Greek could also mean 'isn't justice human excellence?'

'I certainly shall,' he said. 'I'm ready to play my part in the battle.'

336   'Do you know,' I asked, 'who I think was responsible for the saying that it is just to treat one's friends well, and one's enemies badly?'

'Who?'

'I think it was Periander, or Perdiccas, or Xerxes, or Ismenias the Theban, or some other rich man who thought he had great power.'

'You're absolutely right,' he said.

'Well, then,' I said, 'since this definition of justice – and of what is just – is clearly not right either, what other definition of it might be given?'

b   Even in the middle of our conversation Thrasymachus had repeatedly tried to take control of the discussion, but each time he had been prevented by those sitting round us, who wanted to hear the discussion through to the end. But when we reached this stopping-place in the argument, as I asked this question, he was incapable of remaining silent any longer. He gathered himself and sprang at us, like a wild beast at its prey. Polemarchus and I were alarmed and dismayed.

c   Speaking up loud and clear, Thrasymachus said: 'What's this nonsense that has got into you two, Socrates? Why be so obliging? Why keep giving way to one other? If you really want to know what justice is, then stop simply asking questions, and scoring points by proving that any answer given by anyone else is wrong. You know perfectly well it's easier to ask questions than to give answers. Come on, why don't you give some

d   answers yourself? Tell us what *you* say justice is. And don't go telling us that it's what's necessary, or what's beneficial, or what's advantageous, or what's profitable, or what's good for you. I won't take any of that stuff. No. Tell us please, quite clearly, exactly what you mean.'

I was dismayed by this intervention. I looked at him, and started to panic. And I'm sure, if I hadn't looked at the wolf before he looked at me, I'd have been struck dumb.[14] As it was, though, I had in fact looked at him

e   first – at the point where he began to be infuriated by the discussion. As a result, I was able to answer. 'Don't be angry with us, Thrasymachus,' I said, with some apprehension. 'If Polemarchus and I are making mistakes in our examination of the arguments, I assure you we're not making them on purpose. If we were looking for gold, we wouldn't deliberately give way to one another in our search, and so destroy our chances of finding it. So since what we are actually looking for is justice, a thing more valuable than a large quantity of gold, you can't imagine we are so stupid as to

---

[14] This was a popular superstition that became proverbial (as in our 'Cat got your tongue?').

make concessions to one another, and not be determined to bring it as
clearly as possible into view. Believe us, my friend. The trouble is, we lack
337   the ability. So when you clever people see our efforts, pity is really a far
more appropriate reaction than annoyance.'

This brought an unpleasant laugh from Thrasymachus. 'Oh my god,'
he said, 'I knew it. The irony of Socrates. I predicted it. I told these
people you'd refuse to give any answers, that you'd pretend to be
modest, that you'd do anything to avoid answering, if anyone asked you
a question.'

'Clever of you, Thrasymachus. Clever enough to know what would
b   happen if you were to ask someone what twelve was, but then give him a
warning before he answered: "Now look here, don't go telling us that
twelve is twice six, or three times four, or six times two, or four times
three. I'm not going to take any nonsense of that sort from you." It was
obvious to you, I imagine, that if you asked the question in that way, no
one could possibly answer it. Suppose the person you were asking had
objected: "What do you mean, Thrasymachus? Am I not to give any of
the answers you have forbidden? Are you serious? Even if one of them is
in fact true? Am I to give you some answer which is not the truth? Or
what?" What would your reply have been to his objection?'
c   'Oh, yes,' he said. 'Such a close analogy!'

'I don't see what's wrong with it,' I said. 'But even if it isn't close, it
may still seem to be, to the person being asked the question. Do you think
that will stop him giving the answer he thinks is right, whether we forbid
him to or not?'

'Is that just what you're going to do now? Are you going to give one of
the answers I told you not to give?'

'It wouldn't surprise me,' I said, 'if on reflection I came to that conclusion.'

'What if I give you an answer about justice which is quite different from
d   all those other answers, a much better answer than those? What do you
think should be your penalty?'[15]

'Well, obviously, the penalty appropriate to someone who doesn't
know. He should learn, I take it, from the person who does know.'

'You innocent,' said Thrasymachus. 'No, you must do more than learn.
You must pay me some money as well.'

'Very well. As soon as I have any, I will.'

[15] In Athenian legal procedure a defendant found guilty was given the opportunity to
propose to the jury a penalty different from that demanded by his accuser.

'You do have some,' said Glaucon. 'If it's money you're worried about, Thrasymachus, go ahead and speak. We will all pay up for Socrates.'

e   'I'll bet you will,' he said. 'Anything to allow Socrates to play his usual trick – not answer the question himself, but wait for someone else to answer it, and then take what he says and try to prove it wrong.'

'Really, my dear fellow!' I said. 'How could *anyone* answer the question if for a start he didn't know the answer – didn't so much as claim to know it – and on top of that, even supposing he *did* have some idea on the subject, if he'd been told by a man of some authority not to say any of the

338 things he thought? No, it makes much more sense for you to speak. You're the one who claims to know the answer and have something to say. So please, as a favour to me, don't keep your answer to yourself. Give Glaucon here and the others the benefit of your knowledge.'

After this appeal, Glaucon and the rest begged him to do as I asked. Thrasymachus clearly wanted to speak, to gain credit for the excellent answer he thought he had ready. But he pretended to argue, pretended

b   that he wanted me to be the one to answer. Finally he agreed, saying: 'There's the wisdom of Socrates for you. He refuses to do any teaching himself, just goes around learning from others, without so much as a thank you.'

'That I learn from others, Thrasymachus, is true. But when you say I give them no thanks, you are wrong. I give all the thanks in my power. And what is in my power is merely praise, since I have no money. How enthusiastic I can be, if I approve of what somebody says, you are about to find out, when you give your answer. I'm sure it will be a good one.'

c   'Hear it, then,' he said. 'I say that justice is simply what is good for the stronger. Well, where's all that praise? You're not going to give it, are you?'

'Yes, I will – as soon as I understand what you mean. At the moment I still don't know. What is good for the stronger, you say, is just. What do you mean by that, Thrasymachus? If Polydamas the all-in wrestler is stronger than us, and eating beef is good for building his body, you presumably

d   don't mean that this food is also good – and right[16] – for us who are weaker than him.'

'Socrates, you're beneath contempt. You're taking what I said in the way which makes it easiest to misrepresent my meaning.'

'Not at all, my friend. But you'll have to tell me more clearly what you mean.'

---

[16] 'Right' and 'just' both translate the Greek *dikaion*.

'All right,' he said. 'You must be aware that some cities are tyrannies, some are democracies, and others aristocracies?'

'Of course.'

'And what is in control in each city is the ruling power?'

'Yes.'

e   'Every ruling power makes laws for its own good. A democracy makes democratic laws, a tyranny tyrannical laws, and so on. In making these laws, they make it clear that what is good for them, the rulers, is what is just for their subjects. If anyone disobeys, they punish him for breaking 339 the law and acting unjustly. That's what I mean, "my friend," when I say that in all cities the same thing is just, namely what is good for the ruling authority. This, I take it, is where the power lies, and the result is, for anyone who looks at it in the right way, that the same thing is just everywhere – what is good for the stronger.'

'*Now* I understand what you mean,' I said, 'though whether or not it is true remains to be seen. So even your answer, Thrasymachus, is that what is good for a person is just, though that was an answer you told me firmly not to give. But you add the qualification "for the stronger."'

b   'A trivial addition, you may say.'

'That's not yet clear. It may well be an important one. What *is* clear is that we must examine whether what you say is true. Like you, I agree that justice is something that is good for a person, but while you qualify it as what is good for the stronger, I'm not so sure. We should examine the question.'

'Go on, then. Examine it.'

'I shall,' I said. 'Tell me, don't you also say that it is just for subjects to obey their rulers?'

'I do.'

c   'And are they infallible, the rulers in all these cities? Or are they capable of making mistakes?'

'They are certainly, I imagine, capable of making mistakes.'

'So when they set about enacting laws, do they enact some correctly, but a certain number incorrectly?'

'In my opinion, yes.'

'And "correctly" is enacting laws which are in their own interest, and "incorrectly" is enacting laws which are against their own interest? Is that what you mean?'

'Yes.'

'But whatever they enact, their subjects must carry it out, and this is justice?'

'Of course.'

'In that case, according to your definition, it is not only just to do what
d is good for the stronger, but also its opposite, what is not good for him.'

'What *do* you mean?' he said.

'I mean what you mean, I think. Let's look at it more closely. Haven't we agreed that the rulers, in giving orders to their subjects to do anything, sometimes make mistakes about what is in their own best interest, but that it is just for the subjects to carry out whatever orders their rulers give them? Isn't that what we have agreed?'

e   'Yes,' he said. 'I accept that.'

'Then you must also accept,' I said, 'that we have agreed it is just to do things which are not good for the rulers and the stronger, when the rulers inadvertently issue orders which are harmful to themselves, and you say it is just for their subjects to carry out the orders of their rulers. In that situation, most wise Thrasymachus, isn't the inevitable result that it is just to do the exact opposite of what you say? After all, the weaker have been ordered to do what is *not* good for the stronger.'

340 'Indeed they have, Socrates,' said Polemarchus. 'No question about it.'

'No question at all,' Cleitophon interrupted, 'if you are acting as a witness for Socrates.'

'Who needs a witness?' said Polemarchus. 'Thrasymachus himself agrees that rulers sometimes issue orders which are bad for themselves, but that it is right for their subjects to carry out these orders.'

'Yes, Polemarchus, because carrying out orders issued by rulers was what Thrasymachus defined as just.'

'Yes, Cleitophon, but in his definition he also said that what was good
b for the stronger was just. He gave both those definitions, and then went on to agree that those who are stronger sometimes tell those who are weaker, their subjects, to do what is bad for them, the stronger. It follows from these admissions that what is good for those who are stronger would be no more just than what is not good for them.'

'When he talked about what was good for the stronger,' said Cleitophon, 'he meant what the stronger thought was good for him. This is what the weaker must do, and that was his definition of justice.'

'Those weren't the words he used,' said Polemarchus.

c   'It's neither here nor there, Polemarchus,' I said. 'If those are the words

Thrasymachus is using now, let's take it in that sense. Tell me, Thrasymachus. Was that how you wanted to define justice, as what the stronger *thinks* is good for him, whether it really is good or not? Is that what we should take you to be saying?'

'Certainly not,' he said. 'Do you imagine I regard a person who makes a mistake, at the moment when he is making the mistake, as stronger?'

'That's certainly what I *thought* you meant, when you agreed that

d rulers are not infallible, that they sometimes make mistakes.'

'You're always trying to trick people, Socrates, in the way you argue. I mean, if someone makes a mistake in treating the sick, do you call him a doctor by virtue of the actual mistake? Or an accountant who makes a mistake, at the precise moment when he is making his mistake, by virtue *of* this mistake? No, I think that's just the form of words we use. We say "the doctor made a mistake," "the accountant made a mistake," "the

e teacher made a mistake." But the reality, I think, is that none of them, to the extent that he *is* what we call him, ever makes a mistake. In precise language, since you like speaking precisely, no one who exercises a skill ever makes a mistake. People who make mistakes make them because their knowledge fails them, at which point they are not exercising their skill. The result is that no one skilled, no wise man, no ruler, at the moment

341 when he is being a ruler, ever makes a mistake – though everyone would say "the doctor made a mistake" or "the ruler made a mistake." That's how you must take the answer I gave you just now. But the most precise answer is in fact that the ruler, to the extent that he *is* a ruler, does not make mistakes; and since he does not make mistakes, he *does* enact what is best for him, and this is what his subject must carry out. So as I said originally, my definition is that it is just to do what is good for the stronger.'

'Very well, Thrasymachus,' I said. 'So you think I'm a trickster, do you?'

'I certainly do.'

'You think I've been asking the questions I *have* been asking with the deliberate intention of winning the argument unfairly?'

'I'm quite sure of it. It won't do you any good, though. You can't use unfair arguments without my noticing, and once I notice what you are up

b to, you don't have the resources to defeat me in open argument.'

'As if I'd even dream of trying! But since we don't want this situation to arise again, could you make one thing clear? When you say it is right for the weaker to do what is good for the stronger, do you mean the ruler and the stronger in normal usage, or in the precise sense you were talking about just now?'

'I mean the ruler in the most precise sense possible,' he said. 'There you are. Do your worst. I make no special pleas. Try your tricks if you can. But you won't be able to.'

c   'Do you think I'm crazy? Do you think I want to beard the lion, and start playing tricks on Thrasymachus?'

'You certainly had a try just now, though you weren't much good at that either.'

'Well,' I said. 'Enough of all this. Now tell me. You were talking just now about the doctor in the precise sense. Is he a businessman? Or a healer of the sick? And make sure it's the true doctor you are talking about.'

'He's a healer of the sick.'

'What about a ship's captain? Is a ship's captain, in the correct sense, a master of sailors or a sailor?'

d   'A master of sailors.'

'It's not an objection, I take it, that he sails in the ship. Nor is he for that reason to be called a sailor, since the title "ship's captain" does not depend on his sailing, but on his art or skill, and his authority over the sailors.'

'True,' he said.

'And for each of these, is there something which is good for him?'[17]

'Certainly.'

'Doesn't the art or skill come into existence for just this reason, to seek out and provide what is good for each person?'

'Yes, it does.'

'For each of these skills, then, is there anything else which is good for it, apart from being as perfect as possible?'

'I don't understand your question.'

e   'Suppose you asked me if it was enough for the body to be the body, or whether it needed something else. I would reply: "It certainly does need something else. That's the reason why the art of medicine has come to be invented, because the body is defective, and therefore not self-sufficient. So the art of medicine was developed to provide it with the things which were good for it." Do you think I'd be right in giving that answer, or not?'

'Yes, I think you'd be right.'

---

[17] The reference could be either to the doctor and captain or to the sick and the sailors. So Thrasymachus could understand Socrates' next question as referring to the advantages that the artisan derives from his art.

342   'What about medicine itself? Is that defective? Does any art or skill, for that matter, stand in need of some virtue or excellence, in the way that eyes need sight and ears need hearing, and sight and hearing require an art or skill to preside over them, an art or skill which will think about and provide what is good for them? Is there any defect in the actual art or skill itself? Does each art or skill need a further art or skill, which will think about what is good for it? And this one which is thinking about it, does it in its turn need another of the same kind, and so on indefinitely, or does

b   it think for itself about what is good for it? Or does no art or skill have any need either of itself or of any other art or skill, for thinking about what is good for it in the light of its own defects? And is this because no art or skill contains any defect or fault, and because it is not appropriate for an art or skill to pursue the good of anything other than that of which it is the art or skill? Isn't any art or skill itself, in the precise sense, without fault or blemish if it is correct – so long as it is entirely what it is? And when you answer, use words in the precise sense you were talking about. Is it as I have described, or not?'

      'It is as you have described,' he said. 'Apparently.'

c   'In that case,' I said, 'the art of medicine does not think about what is good for the art of medicine, but what is good for the body.'

      'Yes.'

      'And horsemanship does not think about what is good for horsemanship, but what is good for horses. Nor does any art or skill think about what is good for itself – it has no need to. No, it thinks about what is good for the thing of which it is the art or skill.'

      'Apparently.'

      'But surely, Thrasymachus, arts and skills control, and have power over, the objects of which they are the arts and skills.'

      He conceded this, though with great reluctance.

      'In which case, there is no branch of knowledge which thinks about, or prescribes, what is good for the stronger, but only what is good for the weaker, for what is under its control.'

d   He agreed to this too, in the end, though he tried to resist it. And when he did agree, I continued: 'Isn't it a fact that no doctor, to the extent that he is a doctor, thinks about or prescribes what is good for the doctor? No, he thinks about what is good for the patient. After all, it was agreed that a doctor, in the precise sense, is responsible for bodies; he's not a businessman. Isn't that what was agreed?'

      Thrasymachus assented.

e   'And that the ship's captain, in the precise sense, was in command of sailors, not a sailor?'

'Yes, that was agreed.'

'So a ship's captain or commander of this type will not think about or prescribe what is good for the ship's captain, but what is good for the sailor, for the person under his command.'

He agreed, though reluctantly.

'And so, Thrasymachus,' I said, 'no one in any position of authority, to the extent that he *is* in authority, thinks about or prescribes what is good for himself, but only what is good for the person or thing under his authority – for whose benefit he himself exercises his art or skill. Everything he says, and everything he does, is said or done with this person or thing in mind, with a view to what is good and appropriate for the person or thing under his authority.'

343   At this point in the argument it was obvious to everyone that the definition of justice had changed into its opposite. Thrasymachus didn't try to answer. Instead he said: 'Tell me, Socrates, have you got a nanny?'

'I beg your pardon,' I said in some surprise. 'Shouldn't you be answering the question rather than asking things like that?'

'She takes no notice of your runny nose,' he said, 'and doesn't wipe it clean when it needs it. She can't even get you to tell the sheep from the shepherd.'

'What makes you say that?'

b   'You seem to imagine that shepherds, or herdsmen, are thinking about the good of their sheep or their cattle – that they are fattening them up and looking after them with some other end in view than the good of their masters and themselves. In particular, you don't seem to realise that rulers in cities – rulers in the true sense – regard their subjects as their sheep, and that the only thing they're interested in, day and night, is what benefit
c   they themselves are going to derive from them.[18] Such an expert are you in the just and justice, and in the unjust and injustice, that you haven't even grasped that justice and the just are actually what is good for someone else – good for the stronger, the ruler – while for the one who obeys and follows, they mean harm to himself. Injustice is the opposite.

---

[18] The comparison of ruler to shepherd goes back to Homer, who calls the supreme king Agamemnon 'shepherd of the peoples', using the term in a benign sense. Plato will develop the comparison beyond the confines of Book 1, in the relationship between the rulers of the ideal city and their sheepdog-like auxiliaries (440d, 459e). It is also important in the political theory of his *Statesman* or *Politicus* (271d–272b, 275a).

It rules over those who are truly simple-minded, the just, and its subjects
do what is good for that other person – the one who is stronger. They serve
d him, and make him happy. They don't make themselves happy at all.

'You can't avoid the conclusion, my simple-minded Socrates, that a
just man comes off worse than an unjust in every situation. Take contracts, for a start, where a just man goes into partnership with an unjust.
When the partnership is dissolved, you'll never find the just man better
off than the unjust. No, he'll be worse off. Or think about public life.
When there are special levies to be paid *to* the state, the just man
contributes more, and the unjust man less, from the same resources.[19]
When there are distributions to be made *by* the state, the just man receives
e nothing, while the unjust man makes a fortune. Or suppose each of them
holds some public office. The outcome for the just man, even if he suffers
no other loss,[20] is that his own financial position deteriorates, since he
cannot attend to it, while the fact that he is a just man stops him getting
anything from public funds. On top of this, he becomes very unpopular
with his friends and acquaintances when he refuses to act unjustly in
order to do them a favour. The outcome for the unjust man is the exact
344 opposite. I mean, of course, the man I was describing just now, the man
who has the ability to be selfish on a large scale. He's the one to think
about, if you want to assess the extent to which it is better for him, as a
private individual, to be unjust than just.

'The easiest place of all to see it is if you look at the most complete form
of injustice, the one which brings the greatest happiness to the person
who practises it, and the greatest misery to those who experience it, those
who would not be prepared to practise it themselves. By this I mean
tyranny, which takes other people's possessions – things which are sacred
and things which are not – both in secret and by open force. It does
b this not piecemeal but wholesale, though anyone who is caught committing one of these crimes on its own is punished and altogether disgraced.
Temple-robbers,[21] kidnappers, burglars, pickpockets and thieves, if they

---

[19] The *eisphora* was an emergency levy on capital wealth for military purposes. There
was no investigative bureaucracy to conduct audits.

[20] At Athens public offices were generally held by ordinary citizens in frequent rota-
tion rather than being the province of career politicians or bureaucrats. Most were
unpaid committee work. At the end of their term of office, magistrates submitted
their records to public scrutiny. Charges against them and complaints from any
citizen were considered by a special board and often led to penalties.

[21] Temples were not only sacred places but depositories of wealth. They served the
function of treasuries and, in some cases, banks.

carry out individual acts of wrongdoing, are known by the names of their crimes. But those who seize and enslave the citizens themselves, and not just their property, are not called by these terms of reproach. They are called blessed and happy, both by their fellow-citizens and by

c everyone else who hears about the wholesale injustice they have practised. Those who condemn injustice do so not through fear of practising it, but through fear of experiencing it. There you are, Socrates. Injustice is a thing which is stronger, more free and more powerful than justice, so long as it is practised on a large enough scale. So as I said in the first place,[22] justice is in fact what is good for the stronger, whereas injustice is what is profitable and good for oneself.'

d   Thrasymachus was planning to leave after this outburst, having deluged our ears, like some bath attendant, with this long, relentless explanation. But the people who were there wouldn't let him go. They forced him to stay and justify what he had said. And I too, for my part, was most insistent. 'My dear Thrasymachus,' I said to him, 'you can't be intending to chuck a speech like that at us, and then go away without properly telling us, or finding out, whether or not that is how things are.

e Do you think it's a trivial matter, this definition we are after? Far from it. We are trying to define the whole conduct of life – how each of us can live his life in the most profitable way.'

'Have I said anything to suggest that I disagree?' Thrasymachus asked.

'It doesn't *look* as if you agree,' I said. 'Either that or you have no concern for us, and don't care whether we live better or worse lives as a

345 result of our ignorance of what you claim to know. Please, my friend, enlighten us as well. It will be no bad investment for you to do a favour to a gathering as large as we are. For my own part, I have to say that I'm not convinced. I don't think injustice is something more profitable than justice, even if it's given a free hand and not prevented from doing what it wants. No, my friend, let him be unjust, let him have the power to act unjustly, whether in secret or in open warfare, still the unjust man cannot convince *me* that injustice is something more profitable than justice.

b Maybe someone else here feels the same. I may not be the only one. So please be so good as to convince us fully that valuing justice more than injustice is not the right strategy for us.'

'How am I to persuade you?' he asked. 'If you're not convinced by what I said just now, what more can I do for you? Do you want me to sit here and cram the argument in with a spoon?'

[22] 338e.

'God forbid,' I replied. 'No, but in the first place, if you say something, then stick by what you have said. Or if you change your ground, then do
c so openly. Don't try to do it without our noticing. At the moment, Thrasymachus, if we can take another look at our earlier discussion, you can see that though you started off by defining the doctor in the true sense, you didn't then think it necessary to keep strictly to the shepherd in the true sense. So you don't think of the shepherd, to the extent that he is a shepherd, as tending his flocks with a view to what is best for the sheep. You think he has a view to his own enjoyment – like a guest who has been invited out to dinner – or possibly again a view to their sale, like a busi-
d nessman, not a shepherd. The art of being a shepherd, however, is surely not concerned with anything other than making the best provision for what is under its direction. The question of its own excellence, I take it, is sufficiently provided for so long as it fully meets the requirements of the shepherd's art. That is why I thought, a moment ago,[23] that we must necessarily be agreed that any power or authority, to the extent that it is a power or authority, thinks about what is best only for what is under its
e control and in its care – and that applies to power or authority both in public life and in private life. You, on the other hand, think that rulers of cities – rulers in the precise sense – are keen to be rulers, don't you?'

'No,' he said. 'I don't *think* so. I'm quite sure of it.'

'What about other forms of power or authority, Thrasymachus? You must have observed that no one is prepared to exercise them of his own free will. They ask for pay, in the belief that the benefit from their power or authority will come not to them, but to those over whom they exercise
346 it. Tell me this. Don't we say that what makes each individual one of these arts or skills different from the others is the fact that it has a different function? And please be good enough to say what you really believe. That will help us to get somewhere.'

'Yes, that's what makes each one different,' he said.

'And does each one bring us its own individual benefit, rather than all bringing the same benefit? Does medicine bring health, for example, sea-manship safety at sea, and so on?'

'Yes.'

b 'And does the art of earning a living[24] bring payment? Is this its func-tion? Or are you saying that medicine and seamanship are the same?

---

[23] 342a–e.
[24] This sounds as odd in the Greek as it does in English. The word Socrates uses for it is probably a neologism.

Using words in their precise sense, please, as you instructed, if someone while acting as ship's captain recovers his health because sea voyages are good for him, is that any reason for you to call seamanship medicine?'

'Certainly not,' he said.

'You don't, I imagine, call the art of earning a living medicine, just because someone becomes healthy while earning a living?'

'Certainly not.'

'Nor do you call medicine the art of earning a living, do you, if someone earns a living practising medicine?'

c   He agreed.

'Right. Now, we agreed that each art or skill brought its own individual benefit?'

'What if we did?'

'Well, if there's any benefit which all practitioners of arts or skills receive alike, then clearly they're all making use of something else in addition, something which is the same for all of them, and benefits all of them.'

'It looks that way.'

'We say that they all have the practitioner's ability to benefit by earning a living, and that they do this by practising the art of earning a living in addition to their own.'

He conceded this, though unwillingly.

d   'In which case, none of them receives this benefit – earning a living – from his own art or skill. No, if we look at it in the precise sense, first medicine produces health, and then earning a living produces payment. First the art of building produces a house, and then earning a living comes along afterwards and produces payment. And the same with all the other arts or skills. Each performs its own function, and benefits the object of which it is the art or skill. If there is no payment in addition, does the practitioner get any benefit from his art or skill?'

'Apparently not,' he said.

e   'Does he then do no good when he works for nothing?'

'No, I should think he does do some good.'

'In that case, Thrasymachus, one thing is now clear. No art or skill, and no power or authority, provides what is beneficial for itself. They provide and prescribe, as we said originally, for what is under their authority. They think about what is good for it, the weaker, and not what is good for the stronger. That, my dear Thrasymachus, is why I said just now that no one was prepared, of his own free will, to exercise authority, to share in the

troubles of others, and try to put them right. No, they demand payment,
347 because the person who is going to be a good practitioner of an art or skill
never does or prescribes what is best for himself – if his prescription is in
accordance with his art or skill – but only what is best for the person under
his authority. That, I said, appeared to be the reason why, if people are
going to be prepared to rule, or exercise authority, there has to be payment
– either money, or prestige, or some penalty for not ruling.'

'Can you explain that, Socrates?' said Glaucon. 'I can see what you
mean by the two forms of payment. But the penalty you refer to, and how
you can put it in the category of a payment, that I don't understand.'

b   'Then you don't understand the payment the best rulers receive – the
one which persuades the most suitable people to rule, when they *are* prepared to rule. You're aware, aren't you, that ambition and greed are
regarded as, and indeed are, things to be ashamed of?'

'Yes, I am.'

'Well, that's the reason,' I said, 'why the good are not prepared to rule
in return for money or prestige. They don't want to make a legitimate
profit from their power, and be called mercenary. Nor do they want to
make use of their power to take money secretly, and be called thieves.
They won't rule for the prestige, because they're not ambitious. So if
c   they're going to agree to rule, there must be some additional compulsion
on them, some penalty. That's probably why it has always been regarded
as a disgrace for people to seek office voluntarily, rather than waiting until
they are forced to seek it. As for the penalty, it consists principally in being
ruled by someone worse, if they refuse to rule themselves. I think it's this
fear which makes decent people rule, when they *do* rule, and these are the
circumstances in which they seek power. They don't believe that they are
entering upon something good, or that it will bring them any benefit.
d   They approach it as something unavoidable, and because they have no one
better than themselves, or as good as themselves, to whom they can del-
egate the job. If there were ever a city of good men, there would probably
be as much competition *not* to rule as there is among us to rule. That
would be the proof that it really is not in the nature of the true ruler to
think about what is good for himself, but only about what is good for his
subject. The result would be that anyone with any sense would choose to
let someone else do good to him, rather than go to a lot of trouble doing
e   good to others.[25] This is where I completely disagree with Thrasymachus

---

[25] Not a conventional or readily declarable moral sentiment, if construed as condon-
ing the avoidance of effort on behalf of others. Generosity and benefaction were
praiseworthy and expected of those in a position to give it (*GPM* 175–180).

when he says that justice is what is good for the stronger. But we'll have another look at that question some other time. Much more important, I think, is what Thrasymachus is saying now, that the life of the unjust is better than the life of the just. What about you, Glaucon? Which do you choose? Which view do you regard as most accurate?'

'Personally,' he said, 'I prefer the view that the life of the just is more profitable.'

348   'Did you listen just now,' I said, 'to Thrasymachus' catalogue of the advantages in the life of the unjust?'

'Yes, I did,' he replied. 'But I don't find them convincing.'

'Do you want us to try and find some way of persuading him that he is wrong?'

'Of course I do,' he said.

'Well,' I said, 'if we make a speech in opposition to his speech, setting out the arguments in parallel, and saying what advantages there are, by contrast, in being just, and if he then speaks again, and then we make a second speech, we shall need to keep count of the advantages, and
b   measure them, as we both make our pairs of speeches. And we shall need judges of some sort, to come to a decision between us. But if we look at the question, as we did just now, on the basis of agreement with one another, we shall ourselves be at one and the same time both judges and advocates.'[26]

'We shall indeed.'

'Well, we'll do whichever you prefer.'

'The second way,' he said.

'Come on, then, Thrasymachus,' I said. 'Let's go back to the beginning, and you can give us our answers. Is it your claim that perfect injustice is more profitable than perfect justice?'

c   'That certainly is my claim, and I've told you why.'

'Very well, let me ask you a question about injustice and justice. Presumably you'd call one of them a virtue and the other a vice?'

'Of course.'

'You'd call justice a virtue, and injustice a vice?'

'Socrates, you're an innocent,' he said. 'Am I *likely* to say that, if I claim that injustice pays and justice doesn't?'[27]

---

[26] In some types of court-case the litigants were entitled to interleave two speeches each. This ABAB pattern is preserved for us in the *Tetralogies* of Antiphon.

[27] 'Virtue' as a translation of *aretē* must be understood to combine the connotation of superior functionality (as when e.g. a house is said to 'have the great virtue' of being cool in summer and warm in winter) with that of moral rectitude. Hence

'Then what *do* you call them?'

'The opposite,' he said.

'You call justice a vice?'

'No, I call it noble simplicity.'

d   'I see. And you call injustice duplicity, presumably?'

'No, I call it good judgement.'

'And you really think, Thrasymachus, that the unjust are wise and good?'

'Yes, if you mean those who are capable of perfect injustice, who can bring cities and nations under their control. You probably think I'm talking about stealing purses. Mind you,' he added, 'even that can be quite profitable, if you can get away with it. But it's trivial compared with the injustice I was describing just now.'

e   'Yes, I know which sort you mean,' I said. 'But I *was* surprised, before that, by your putting injustice with goodness and wisdom, and justice with their opposites.'

'Well, that's certainly where I do put them.'

'That's a much more awkward proposition, my friend. It makes it hard to know what to say. If you said that injustice was profitable, but nevertheless admitted, as most people do, that it was wickedness, or something to be ashamed of, we would be able to make some reply along conventional lines. As it is, however, you're obviously going to say that it is good and
349   strong, and credit it with all the qualities which we used to attribute to justice, since you didn't shrink from classifying it with goodness and wisdom.'

'That's an accurate prediction,' he said.

'Still, we mustn't hesitate, in our discussion, to pursue the object of our enquiry for as long as I take you to be saying what you think. My impression is, Thrasymachus, that this time you're not just trying to provoke us, but genuinely saying what you really believe about the truth of the matter.'

'Does it matter to you whether I really believe it or not? Why don't you try and disprove what I say?'

b   'No, it doesn't matter,' I replied. 'Now, I have a further question, on top of the ones I've asked already. Do you think one just man would be at all prepared to try and outdo another just man?'

footnote 27 (*cont.*)
Thrasymachus is reluctant to describe injustice – that masterful trait – as anything but a virtue. Hence too in the arguments at 335c and 353b–c the word is translated 'excellence'.

'No. If he did, he wouldn't be the polite simpleton we know him to be.'
'How about the just action?'
'No, he wouldn't try to do outdo the just action either,' he said.
'Would he think it right to outdo an unjust man? Would he think that was just, or would he think it was unjust?'
'He'd think it just and right – but he wouldn't be able to.'

c   'That isn't my question,' I said. 'My question is this. Does the just man think it wrong to outdo another just man? Does he refuse to do this, but think it right to outdo an unjust man?'
'Yes, he does.'
'What about the unjust man? Does he think it right to outdo the just man and the just action?'
'Of course he does. He thinks it right to outdo *everyone*.'
'Good. So the unjust man will try to outdo an unjust man and an unjust action, and will strive to take the largest share of everything for himself?'[28]
'Yes, he will.'
'Let's put it like this,' I said. 'The just man does not try to outdo what

d   is like him, but only what is unlike him, whereas the unjust man tries to outdo both what is like him and what is unlike him.'
'Admirably put.'
'The unjust man is wise and good, while the just man is neither of these things.'
'Right again,' he said. 'Well done.'
'And is the unjust man also like the wise and good, and the just man unlike?'
'Since the unjust man *is* wise and good, how could he not also be *like* the wise and good? And how could the just man not be unlike?'
'Good. So each of them has the qualities of the people he is like.'
'What else?'

e   'Well, Thrasymachus, do you agree that one person is musical and another unmusical?'
'I do.'
'Which of them do you think knows what he is doing, and which doesn't?'

---

[28] The verbal phrase translated as 'to outdo' literally means 'to have more', from which derives the range of meanings 'to be greedy', 'to take unfair advantage', as well as simply 'to have the advantage' in a situation, without connotations of unfairness. All these senses are brought into play in this argument. Thrasymachus introduced the term into the discussion at 344a when he described the unjust ruler as one who was capable of being 'selfish on a large scale'.

'I imagine I'd say the musical one knows, and the unmusical one doesn't.'

'Where the musical one knows, he is good, and where the unmusical one doesn't know, he is bad, would you say?'

'Yes.'

'What about someone with medical knowledge? Is that the same?'

'Yes, it is.'

'Do you think, then, my friend, that a musician tuning a lyre would want to outdo another musician – would think it right to get the better of him – in tightening and loosening the strings?'

'No, I don't.'

350 'What about someone unmusical? Would the musician want to outdo him?'

'He'd be bound to.'

'How about someone with medical knowledge? In prescribing food and drink, do you think he'd want to outdo a medical man or medical practice?'

'Of course not.'

'But he would want to outdo someone with no medical knowledge?'

'Yes.'

'Do you think it's the same for every branch of knowledge and ignorance? Do you think there is ever any knowledgeable person who would deliberately choose, either in action or in speech, to do more than another knowledgeable person would do? Wouldn't he do the same as someone like himself would do in the same situation?'

'I'm inclined to think that must be right,' he said.

b 'What about the person who is not knowledgeable? Wouldn't he try to outdo both equally – the person with knowledge *and* the person without knowledge?'

'He might.'

'And the knowledgeable person is wise?'

'Yes.'

'And the wise person is good?'

'Yes.'

'So the good and wise person will not be prepared to outdo the person like him, but only the person unlike him, his opposite.'

'Apparently,' he said.

'Whereas the bad and ignorant person will try to outdo both the person like him and his opposite.'

'It looks like it.'

'Now, Thrasymachus,' I said, 'doesn't our unjust man try to outdo both the person unlike him and the person like him? Isn't that what you said?'

c   'Yes, I did.'

'Whereas the just man will not try to outdo the person like him, but only the person unlike him?'

'Yes.'

'In that case,' I said, 'the just man is like the wise and good man, and the unjust man is like the bad and ignorant.'

'I suppose so.'

'But we agreed that each of them had the qualities of the person he was like.'[29]

'Yes, we did.'

'So our just man has turned out to be good and wise, and our unjust man ignorant and bad.'

Thrasymachus conceded all these points, but not in the easygoing way
d   I have just described. He had to be dragged every step of the way, sweating profusely, as you might expect in summer.[30] This was the occasion when I saw something I had never seen before – Thrasymachus blushing. Anyway, when we had agreed that justice was virtue and wisdom, and that injustice was vice and ignorance, I said, 'Well, let's leave that question. But we did also say that injustice was something powerful.[31] Or have you forgotten that, Thrasymachus?'

'No, I haven't,' he said. 'But as far as I'm concerned, I'm not happy with the argument you've just put forward. I have some comments I
e   would like to make on it. But if I made them, I know perfectly well you would say I was making a speech. So either let me say as much as I want to say, or if you want to go on asking questions, then carry on, and I'll behave as one does with old women telling stories. I'll say "Of course!" and nod or shake my head.'

'No,' I said. 'Not if it's not what you yourself think.'

'That way I'll please you,' he said, 'since you won't allow me to speak. What more do you want?'

'Nothing at all. If that's what you're going to do, go ahead. I'll ask the questions.'

'Ask away.'

'I'd like to ask the same question I asked before, so that we can pursue
351   our enquiry into what kind of thing justice actually is, compared with

---

[29] At 349d.   [30] By our calendar, the festival of Bendis took place in June.
[31] At 344c.

injustice, in an orderly way. The claim was, I believe, that injustice was
something more powerful, something stronger, than justice. Whereas in
fact,' I said, 'if justice is wisdom and goodness, it will easily be seen to be
something stronger than injustice, since injustice is ignorance. No one
could any longer fail to recognise that. But I don't just want a simple statement of that sort. I'm interested in a different approach. Would you say
b   a city can be unjust? Can it try to bring other cities into subjection, in an
unjust way? Can it succeed in bringing them into subjection, and having
subdued a large number of them, can it keep them under its control?'

'Of course it can,' he said. 'And the finest, the most perfectly unjust,
city will be best at it.'

'I can see why you say that,' I said. 'That *was* your position. But now I
have another question. When a city becomes more powerful than another
city, will it gain this power without the aid of justice, or must it necessarily use justice?'

c   'If your recent argument is valid,' he said, 'and justice is wisdom, then
with the aid of justice. If my theory was right, then with the aid of injustice.'

'I'm delighted to see, Thrasymachus, that you're not just nodding and
shaking your head, but giving proper answers.'

'Just to please you,' he said.

'Thank you. Can you do me one more favour? Tell me this. Suppose a
city, or an army, or pirates, or thieves, or any other group of people, are
jointly setting about some unjust venture. Do you think they'd be able to
get anywhere if they treated one another unjustly?'

d   'Of course not.'

'What if they didn't treat one another unjustly? Wouldn't they stand a
much better chance?'

'They certainly would.'

'Yes, because injustice, I imagine, Thrasymachus, produces faction and
hatred and fights among them, whereas justice produces co-operation and
friendship, doesn't it?'

'Let's say it does,' he said. 'I don't want to disagree with you.'

'Thank you, my friend. Now, another question. If it's the function of
injustice to produce hatred wherever it goes, then when it makes its
e   appearance among free men and slaves, won't it make them hate one
another, and quarrel with one another, and be incapable of any joint enterprise?'

'Yes, it will.'

'And if it makes its appearance in two people, won't they disagree, and hate one another, and be enemies both of each other and of the just?'

'They will,' he said.

'And if, my admirable friend, injustice appears in an individual, it surely won't lose its power. Won't it still retain it?'

'Let's say it will.'

'Clearly, then, its power is such that whatever it appears in – whether 352 city, nation, army, or anything else – it first renders incapable of concerted action, through faction and disagreements, and then makes an enemy to itself, to everything that opposes it, and to the just? Isn't that right?'

'It is.'

'And when it is present in an individual, too, I suspect, it will produce all these effects which it is its nature to bring about. In the first place, it will make him incapable of action, because he is at odds with himself, and in disagreement with himself. And in the second place it will make him an enemy both of himself and of those who are just, won't it?'

'Yes.'

'And are the gods, my friend, among the just?'

b   'They may as well be,' he said.[32]

'In that case, Thrasymachus, the unjust man will be an enemy of the gods as well, while the just man will be a friend.'

'Go on, have a party,' he said. 'Enjoy yourself. I'm not going to object. I don't want to make enemies of all these people.'

'Come on, then,' I said. 'If you want to give us a real treat, just carry on giving me the sort of answers you're giving now. I can see that the just are clearly wiser and better and more capable of action, whereas the unjust c are incapable of co-operating in anything; though when we speak of them as being unjust, and yet at times carrying out some vigorous joint action, we're not getting it exactly right. If they were completely unjust, they couldn't have resisted attacking one another. So there was obviously *some* justice among them, which stopped them acting unjustly against each other and their adversaries at the same time, and which enabled them to achieve what they did achieve. They set about their unjust actions in a d state of semi-injustice, since those who are wholly wicked, and completely unjust, are also completely incapable of doing anything. I am confident that this is how things are, and that your first statement is wrong.[33] But

---

[32] Given the activities attributed to the gods of the traditional Greek pantheon, the answer to this question would not go without saying.

[33] That is, the statement made at 344c and recalled at 350d.

whether the just live a better and happier life than the unjust – which was the second question we put forward for examination[34] – this has still to be examined. If you want my opinion, they certainly seem to, even from what we have said so far. All the same, we ought to look into it more closely. After all, our discussion is not about something incidental, but about how we ought to live our lives.'

'Look into it, then.'

'I will. Tell me this. Do you think a horse has something which is its function?'

'I do.'

e   'And would you define the function – of a horse or anything else – as that which you can only do – or can best do – with its help?'

'I don't follow,' he said.

'Look at it like this. Can you see with anything other than your eyes?'

'No.'

'What about hearing? Can you hear with anything other than your ears?'

'No.'

'So would we be justified in saying that these are their functions?'

'Yes.'

353   'What about pruning the stem of a vine? Could you use a carving knife, or an engraver's knife, or any number of things?'

'Of course.'

'But none of them would be as good, I take it, as a pruning knife made for that purpose.'

'True.'

'In that case, can't we define that as its function?'

'Yes, we can.'

'Now you may have a better understanding, I think, of the question I just asked you. I wanted to know whether the function of anything was that which it alone brought about, or which it brought about better than anything else.'

'Yes, I do understand,' he said. 'And I think this *is* the function of anything.'

b   'Right,' I said. 'And do you think that everything which has some function assigned to it also has an excellence?[35] Let's go back to the same examples. The eyes, we say, have a function?'

---

[34] 347e.
[35] See note 27 to 348c above explaining how *aretē* ranges between 'excellence' and 'virtue'.

'They do.'

'Do the eyes then also have an excellence?'

'They do.'

'What about the ears? Did we say they have some function?'

'Yes.'

'And an excellence as well?'

'Yes, they have an excellence as well.'

'And the same with everything else?'

'Yes, the same.'

'Well, then. Could the eyes ever perform their own function properly
c if they lacked their own specific excellence, if they had some defect
instead.'

'How could they? Presumably you mean blindness rather than
sight.'

'Whatever their excellence is,' I said, 'though so far that's not what I'm
asking. What I'm asking is whether it is their specific excellence which
makes them perform their function well, where they do perform it, and
their specific defect which makes them perform it badly.'

'Yes, that's true enough,' he said.

'And the same with the ears? Without their own excellence, will they
perform their function badly?'

'Yes.'

'And can we apply the same reasoning to everything else?'

d   'I think so.'

'Very well. Next question. Does your soul have a function, which
nothing else in the world could perform? Think about management, or
ruling, or decision-making, and all those sorts of things. Would we be
justified in attributing those functions to anything other than the soul?
Could we say they belonged to anything else?'

'No.'

'But then what about living? Shall we say that is a function of the soul?'

'Most definitely,' he said.

e   'And do we also say that there is an excellence of the soul?'

'We do.'

'In that case, Thrasymachus, will the soul ever perform its own functions well if it lacks its own specific excellence? Or is that impossible?'

'It's impossible.'

'So a bad soul necessarily results in bad ruling and bad management,
whereas a good soul results in the successful exercise of these functions.'

'Necessarily.'

'And we agreed that justice was excellence of soul, and that injustice was vice or defect of soul?'[36]

'We did.'

'In which case the just soul and the just man will have a good life, and the unjust man a bad one.'

354   'It looks like it,' he said, 'according to your argument.'

'But the person who has a good life is blessed and happy, while the person who doesn't is the opposite.'

'Of course.'

'So the just man is happy, and the unjust man is miserable.'

'They may as well be,' he said.

'But being miserable is not profitable, whereas being happy is.'

'Of course.'

'So injustice, my excellent Thrasymachus, is never more profitable than justice.'

'Go ahead, Socrates,' he said. 'It's Bendis' Day. Make a real feast of it.'

'Thanks to you, Thrasymachus,' I said, 'now that you've turned
b   friendly, and stopped being angry. And even then I haven't had a proper treat, though that's my fault, not yours. I think I've been like one of those gluttons who grab at everything that's carried past them, and taste it without ever properly enjoying what went before. Without waiting to find the first thing we were looking for – what justice actually is – I've dropped that, and gone charging off into asking questions about it – whether it's wickedness and ignorance, or wisdom and goodness. And then a little later, when the claim arose that injustice was more profitable than justice,
c   I couldn't resist going on from the earlier question to that one. So the result of our discussion is that I'm none the wiser. After all, if I don't know what justice is, I'm hardly going to know whether or not it is in fact some kind of excellence or virtue, or whether the person who possesses it is unhappy or happy.'

---

[36] At 350c–d.

Book 2

357 With these words I thought I had finished what I had to say. But I was wrong. Apparently it was only an introduction. Glaucon is an extremely determined character in everything he does, and on this occasion he
b refused to accept Thrasymachus' surrender. 'Socrates,' he said, 'do you really want to convince us that it is in every way better to be just than unjust, or is it enough merely to seem to have convinced us?'

'I would prefer,' I said, 'really to convince you, if I had a choice.'

'In that case,' he said, 'you are not achieving your aim. Tell me this. Do you think there is a good of the kind we would choose to have because we value it for its own sake, and not from any desire for its results? Enjoyment, for example, and pleasures which are harmless and produce no consequences for the future beyond enjoyment for the person who possesses them.'

c 'Yes,' I said, 'I do think there is a good of this kind.'

'What about the sort we value both for itself and for its consequences? Things like thinking, seeing, being healthy. We value goods of this sort, I imagine, for both reasons.'

'Yes,' I said.

'And can you distinguish a third class or category of good,' he asked, 'a class which contains physical exercise, undergoing medical treatment when we are ill, practising medicine, and earning a living in general?
d These we would describe as unpleasant but beneficial. We would not choose to have them for their own sakes, but only for the payment or other benefits which result from them.'

'Yes,' I said, 'there is this third class as well. What of it?'

'In which of these classes,' he asked, 'do you put justice?'

37

358   'In my opinion,' I replied, 'it is in the finest class, which is to be valued
by anyone who wants to be happy, both for itself and for its consequences.'

'That's not what most people think,' he said. 'Most people would put
it in the unpleasant class, which we should cultivate in return for payment
and reputation, on account of public opinion, but which purely for itself
is to be avoided like the plague.'

'I know that's what they think,' I said. 'Thrasymachus criticised it –
and praised injustice – on those grounds some while back. But I'm a slow
learner, apparently.'

b   'Well,' he said, 'listen to me as well, and see if you agree with what
I suggest. I think Thrasymachus too readily allowed himself to be
bewitched by you, like a snake being charmed by a snake-charmer. As far
as I'm concerned, the proof is not yet convincing, either for justice or
injustice. I want to be told what each of them is, and what effect it has,
just by itself, when it is present in the soul. I want to forget about the
rewards and results it brings. So here's what I am going to do, if you have
c   no objection. I'm going to revive Thrasymachus' argument. First I shall
say what kind of thing people reckon justice is, and how they think it
arises. Secondly I shall claim that all those who practise it do so as something unavoidable, against their will, and not because they regard it as a
good. Thirdly I shall say that this is a rational way for them to behave,
since the unjust man, in their view, has a much better life than the just
man. These are not my own opinions, Socrates. But I am dismayed by the
d   unending sound in my ears of Thrasymachus and thousands like him,
whereas I have never yet heard from anyone, in the form I would like to
hear it, the argument *for* justice, the argument that it is something better
than injustice. I want to hear it praised simply for itself, and I have high
hopes that you, if anyone, can do this for me. So I am going to make the
most powerful speech I can in defence of the unjust life, and in my speech
I shall show you how I want to hear you, in your turn, criticising injustice
and defending justice. There you are. See if you approve of my suggestion.'

e   'I'd like nothing better,' I replied. 'What else would anyone with any
sense prefer to make a habit of talking about or hearing about?'

'That's good,' he said. 'Now, listen to the first thing I said I was going
to talk about – what sort of thing justice is, and how it arises. Doing
wrong, men say, is by its nature a good – and being wronged an evil – but

the evil of being wronged outweighs the good of doing wrong. As a result,
359 when people wrong one another and are wronged by one another, and get
a taste of both, those who are unable to avoid the one and achieve the other
think it will pay them to come to an agreement with one another not to
do wrong and not to be wronged. That's how they come to start making
laws and agreements with one another, and calling lawful and just that
which is laid down by the law. They say that this is the origin and essential nature of justice, that it is a compromise between the best case, which
is doing wrong and getting away with it, and the worst case, which is being
b wronged and being unable to retaliate. Justice, being half-way between
these two extremes, is not prized as a good; it finds its value merely in
people's want of power to do wrong. The person who does have the power
to do wrong – the true man – would never make an agreement with
anyone not to do wrong and not to be wronged. It would be lunatic for
him to do that. That, more or less, is the nature of justice, Socrates. That
is what it is like, and those are the kinds of causes which gave rise to it,
according to this theory.[1]

   'As for the claim that people who practise justice do so reluctantly,
being too weak to do wrong, the easiest way to see that it is true is to
c imagine something like this. Suppose we gave each of them – the just and
the unjust – the freedom to do whatever he liked, and then followed them
and kept an eye on them, to see which way his desire would take each of
them. We would soon catch the just man out. Led on by greed and the
desire to outdo others, he would follow the same course the unjust man
follows, the course which it is everybody's natural inclination to pursue
as a good, though they are forcibly redirected by the law into valuing
d equality. Roughly speaking, they would have the freedom I am talking
about if they had the kind of power they say the ancestor of Gyges the
Lydian once had. They say he was a shepherd, and that he was a serf of
the man who was at that time the ruler of Lydia. One day there was a great
rainstorm and an earthquake in the place where he grazed his sheep. Part
of the ground opened up, and a great hole appeared in it. He was aston-
ished when he saw it, but went down into it. And the legend has it that
among many marvels he saw a hollow horse made of bronze, with

---

[1] The passage is an early appearance of the concept of a social contract imposed on a
state of nature, which was to have great importance in the classic political and moral
theories of the enlightenment. It is unclear whether Plato has any particular contemporary version of this concept in mind.

e   windows in it. Peeping through them, he saw inside what appeared to be
    a corpse, larger than human, wearing nothing but a golden ring on its
    hand. They say he removed the ring, and came out.

    'The shepherds were having one of their regular meetings, so that they
    could give the king their monthly report on the flocks. And the man
    turned up as well, wearing the ring. As he sat with the rest of them, he
360 happened to twist the setting of the ring towards him, into the palm of his
    hand. When he did this, he became invisible to those who were sitting
    with him, and they started talking about him as if he had gone. He was
    amazed, and twisted the ring again, turning the setting to the outside. As
    soon as he did so, he became visible. When he realised this, he started
    experimenting with the ring, to see if it did have this power. And he found
    that that was how it was. When he turned the setting to the inside, he
    became invisible; when he turned it to the outside, he became visible.
b   Once he had established this, he lost no time arranging to be one of those
    making the report to the king. When he got there, he seduced the king's
    wife, plotted with her against the king, killed him and seized power.

    'Imagine there were two rings like that, and that the just man wore one,
    while the unjust man wore the other. People think that no one would be
    sufficiently iron-willed to remain within the bounds of justice. No one
    could bring himself to keep his hands off other people's possessions, and
    steer clear of them, if he was free to take whatever he liked without a
c   second thought, in the market-place, or go into people's houses and sleep
    with anyone he liked; or if he could kill or release from prison anyone he
    chose, and in general go round acting like a god among men. If he behaved
    like this, the just man would be acting no differently from the unjust. Both
    would be following the same course.

    'This is a strong argument, you might say, for the claim that no one is
    just voluntarily, but only under compulsion. Justice is not thought to be
d   a good thing for individuals, since wherever anyone thinks he *can* do
    wrong, he does do wrong. Every man believes injustice to be much more
    profitable for the individual than justice. And he will be right to think this,
    according to the person putting forward this view. Anyone who came into
    possession of the kind of freedom I have described, and then refused ever
    to do anything wrong, and did not lay a finger on other people's posses-
    sions, would be regarded by observers as the most pathetic and brainless
    of creatures – though of course in public they would praise him, lying to
    one another because of their fear of being wronged.

e   'That's all I have to say about that claim. As for the choice between the lives of the people in question, the only way we can make it properly is by contrasting the completely just man with the completely unjust man. How shall we contrast them? Like this. We will subtract nothing either from the injustice of the unjust man or from the justice of the just man. We will assume that each is a perfect example of his particular way of behaving. So for a start let's make the unjust man's behaviour like that of a skilled practitioner of a profession. A really good ship's captain or

361 doctor, for example, can distinguish in the exercise of his skill between what is not feasible and what is feasible. He attempts what is feasible, and avoids what is not feasible. What is more, if he makes a false move somewhere, he is capable of correcting it. That's how it can be with our unjust man. Let's assume, if he is going to be *really* unjust, that he goes about his wrongdoings in the right way, and gets away with it. The one who gets caught is to be regarded as incompetent, since perfect injustice consists in appearing to be just when you are not. We must credit the completely unjust man, then, with the most complete injustice. To the person who

b commits the greatest wrongs we must not deny – in fact, we must grant – the enjoyment of the greatest reputation for justice. If he makes a false move, we must allow him the ability to put it right. He must be capable of using persuasion – so that if any evidence of his wrongdoings is brought against him, he can talk his way out of it – but capable also of using force where force is needed, relying on his courage and strength, and the possession of friends and wealth.

'That is our model of the unjust man. Beside him let us put our imaginary just man, a simple and honourable man who wants, in Aeschylus' words, not to appear to be good, but to be good.[2] We must deprive him of

c the appearance, since if he appears to be just, the appearance of justice will bring him recognition and rewards, and then it will not be clear whether his motive for being just was a desire for justice or a desire for the rewards and the recognition. So we must strip him of everything but justice; we must put him in a situation which is the opposite of our previous example. Despite doing nothing wrong, he must have the worst possible reputation for injustice. Then, if it is unaffected by disgrace and its consequences, the purity of his justice will have been tested in the fire. Let

d him live out his life like this, without any change, until the day of his death, appearing to be unjust though actually being just. That way they

---

[2] Part of the description (*Seven against Thebes* 592) of the wise and god-fearing seer Amphiaraus, explaining why he chooses to put no blazon on his shield.

can both attain the extreme – one of justice, the other of injustice – and the judgment can be made, which of them is happier.'

'Help!' I said. 'That's a pretty vigorous job you've done, my dear Glaucon, cleaning up each of our contestants to get them ready for judgment. Like scouring a statue.'

'I've done my best,' he said. 'And if both their situations are as I have described, it shouldn't be beyond us, I imagine, to give a full account of e the kind of life which awaits each of them. So that is what I must do now. And if my language is rather crude and uncivilised, Socrates, don't imagine it's me talking. No, it's the people who recommend injustice in preference to justice. They will claim that in this situation the just man will be whipped and put on the rack, will be thrown into chains and have his eyes burnt out. Finally, after all these injuries, he will be crucified, and

362 realise that the important thing to aim for is not *being* just, but *appearing* to be just.[3] So what Aeschylus said turns out to be a much more accurate description of the unjust man, who wants not to appear to be unjust, but to be unjust, living his life in touch with reality rather than trying to satisfy appearances and public opinion,

> In his mind enjoying the deep furrow's fruit,
> b   From which good counsel grows.[4]

In the first place, they will say, he can be a ruler in his city, because of his reputation for justice; secondly, he can marry where he likes, give his daughters in marriage to whom he chooses, and make contracts and partnerships with anyone he wishes. Besides all this he finds it easy to make himself a rich man, since he has no compunction about acting unjustly. That is why, they say, he is successful in political and legal disputes – both c public and private – and why he gets the better of his enemies. By getting the better of them he grows rich, and can help his friends and harm his enemies. He can make full and generous sacrifices and offerings to the gods, and is much better able than the just man to serve the gods and that part of mankind whom he chooses to serve. As a result, they claim, he is

---

[3] Glaucon is exaggerating. Although a type of crucifixion was one of the methods by which criminals were executed in Athens, torture and mutilation was not a standard form of punishment. It is rather what a tyrant would inflict on his enemies.

[4] These lines are also part of the description of Amphiaraus and follow on immediately from the line adapted (but not directly quoted) at 361b. In their original context they referred to his intelligence and his attempt to prevent bloodshed between the two brothers Eteocles and Polynices; in their new context the 'good counsel' becomes the careful scheming of the unjust man.

in all probability more likely than the just man to be the gods' favourite. Those are the ways, Socrates, in which they say the unjust man gets a better deal, both from gods and men, than the just man.'

d   When Glaucon finished, I was all set to reply. But his brother Adeimantus intervened. 'I hope you don't think, Socrates,' he said, 'that that is the whole of their case.'

'Why? What more is there?' I asked.

'We have left out the part,' he said, 'which most needs to be included.'

'Well,' I said, 'let brother stand by brother, as the saying goes.[5] By all means join in, and come to his assistance, if he has left anything out – though as far as I am concerned, even what he did say was enough to throw me, and make me incapable of coming to the defence of justice.'

e   'Nonsense,' he said. 'You must listen to this second instalment as well. To make it clearer what I think Glaucon wants, we must go through the contrary arguments to his – the ones which recommend justice and

363 criticise injustice. Fathers giving advice to their sons, and all those who are responsible for others, encourage them to be just – not, I take it, because they value justice by itself, but because they value the approval it brings. If they appear to be just, they argue, then this reputation will bring them public office, marriage and all the benefits Glaucon has just enumerated, which the just man gains from being well thought of. And that isn't all they have to say about the benefits of reputation. Once they start adding in the approval of the gods, they have an abundance of rewards to

b   offer the pious – gifts of the gods, they say. The admirable Hesiod and Homer[6] say the same thing. Hesiod says that for the just, the gods make oak trees

> Bear acorns on their lofty tops, and bees
> Beneath, on lower branches. Weight of wool
> Burdens their fleecy sheep.

And many other benefits of the same kind.[7] Homer says much the same:

---

[5] Not a proverb attested before Plato. A contemporary variant runs: 'There is pardon for helping a brother.'

[6] As authors of the Greeks' most ancient poems describing their gods, Hesiod and Homer functioned as theological authorities.

[7] *Works and Days* 232–234. The other benefits mentioned by Hesiod are: absence of war and famine, women bearing children who are like their fathers, abundance rendering trade by sea unnecessary.

> Or like some worthy king who, fearing god,
> Supports the right. For him the rich dark earth
c > Bears wheat and barley, while with fruit his trees
> Bow down. Unfailingly his flocks bear lambs.
> For him the sea yields fish.[8]

Musaeus and his son make the just receive rewards of a more exciting
kind from the gods.[9] In their account, they conduct them to Hades, sit
d them down, and organise a party for the pious. They crown them, and
make them spend the whole of time getting drunk, regarding perpetual
drunkenness as the finest reward for human goodness. Others again grant
rewards from the gods which are more extensive even than these. They
say that children's children and a tribe of descendants are the posterity of
the pious man, the man who keeps his oaths. That, and some more like it,
is what they say in praise of justice. As for the impious and unjust, they
e bury them in Hades, in mud of some kind. They make them carry water
in a sieve;[10] and they bring them into disgrace while they are still alive.
They impose on the unjust all Glaucon's list of penalties for those just
people who have the reputation of being unjust; these are all the penalties
they can think of. That, then, is their recommendation and criticism of
each of the two ways of life.

'Apart from that, Socrates, you should take into account another
common way of talking about justice and injustice – both in everyday
364 speech and in the poets. In their praise of self-discipline and justice, they
all sing with one voice. They regard them as a good, but as one which is
difficult and laborious, whereas self-indulgence and injustice are pleasant
and easy to follow; they are shameful only in the reputation they bring,
and by convention. They say that for the most part unjust actions are
more profitable than just ones. They are quite happy to congratulate the

---

[8] *Odyssey* 19.109–113, omitting line 110 ('and ruling over many powerful men'), and
breaking off in mid-sentence ('. . . yields fish because of his good leadership, and
under him his people flourish').

[9] A reference to 'mystic' cults and their associated body of poetry – cults which distinguished themselves from the common run of religious ritual by requiring a special
regimen and/or purificatory initiation in this life in order to gain rewards in the
afterlife. By Musaeus' son is probably meant Eumolpus, founder of the clan which
had charge of the most famous of the mystic rites engaged in by Athenians – the
Eleusinian. For general information on these cults see W. Burkert, *Greek Religion*
(Cambridge, Mass.: Harvard University Press, 1985), ch. 6.

[10] The traditional punishment of the daughters of Danaus. In the *Gorgias* (493a–c)
their fate is used as an allegory for the consequences of self-indulgence in the
absence of purificatory initiation.

wicked, if they possess wealth and exercise power, and to pay them
b respect in both public life and private life. The others they despise and
ignore – any of them who are weak and poor – though they admit they are
better people than the wicked. However, the most remarkable statements
of all on this subject are those about the attitude of the gods to human goodness. They say the gods give many good people unhappiness and a
wretched life, while to their opposites they give a life which is quite
different. Mendicant priests and seers knock at the rich man's door, and try
c to persuade him that they have a power, bestowed on them by the gods in
return for sacrifices and incantations, to use the delights of feasting to put
right any wrong done by him or his ancestors.[11] And that if anyone wants
to harm an enemy, for a small charge they can injure just and unjust alike
with charms and spells. They say they can persuade the gods to act for
them. To all these claims they call the poets as witnesses. Some quote
them on the ease of wrongdoing.

> There is much wickedness; it is never hard
d > To make that choice. The way is smooth, the goal
> Lies near at hand. Virtue is out of reach
> Without much toil. That is the gods' decree.[12]

It's a long, uphill road. Others, talking about the way men can influence
the gods, call Homer to witness, with his claim that

> Even the gods themselves
> Will hear our prayers. Men who do wrong, and sin,
e > Can thus dissuade them from their purposes
> With fair entreaty or with sacrifice,
> With incense or the fat of offered meat.[13]

They bring forward a host of books by Musaeus and Orpheus, the children of Selene and the Muses, so they claim. These are what govern their
sacrificial rituals, and they persuade cities as well as individuals that
sacrifices and pleasurable amusements can win release and purification
365 from injustice both for those still alive and for those who have passed

[11] The victims of animal sacrifice in Greek religious ritual were made the centrepiece
of a feast.

[12] Hesiod, *Works and Days* 287–289. Hesiod goes on to mitigate the 'long, uphill road'
with the thought that once you get to the top it becomes easy to follow.

[13] The words spoken to Achilles by his childhood guardian Phoenix in *Iliad* 9.497–501,
omitting line 498: '[the gods] who are our superiors in excellence, honour and
might'.

away. Passing through the rites, they call it, which can release us from evils in the afterlife. And if we don't sacrifice, then horrors await us.

'That's the nature and force, Socrates, of all the things that are said about goodness and wickedness, and the value put on them by men and gods. What effect do we think they have on the minds of the young when they hear them – the able ones, those capable of flitting, as it were, from
b opinion to opinion, gathering information on what sort of person to be, and which way to go, in order to live the best possible life? A young man might well ask himself, using Pindar's words, "How climb the highest wall? Will justice help? Or devious deception?"[14] And so live my life to its end, in the safety of the citadel? To judge by the poets, if I am just without also seeming to be just, I can expect nothing out of it but hardship and clear loss. If I am unjust, but have gained a reputation for justice, then I
c am promised a wonderful life. Therefore, since "Appearance," as the wise men have pointed out to me, "overpowers truth" and controls happiness,[15] I must turn all my attention to that. I must draw an exact likeness of goodness around myself, as a front and façade, bringing along behind it the wise Archilochus' crafty and subtle fox.[16]

'"The trouble with that," someone will say, "is that it is hard to be evil and get away with it for ever." "Well," we shall say, "nothing great was
d ever easy. But if we are going to be happy, we must follow where the trail of our argument leads us. And to get away with it, we shall form secret clubs and societies,[17] and there are teachers of persuasion to give us the wisdom of the assembly and the lawcourts. With their help we shall sometimes use persuasion, and at other times force, and so come out on top without paying for it."

'"But it's impossible to use stealth or force against the gods." "Well, if the gods don't exist, or if they are not at all interested in men, why should
e we in our turn be interested in keeping what we do a secret? If they *do* exist, and *are* interested in men, our only knowledge or hearsay of them comes from custom and the poets who sing of the gods' family histories.

---

[14] The quotation is adapted to fit seamlessly into the young man's thought. Other sources give us a fuller version of the fragment: 'How climb the highest wall? Will justice help the race of men that dwells on earth to scale it? Or devious deception? My mind is divided and cannot say for certain.'
[15] A fragment of a lost poem by Simonides.
[16] The cunning fox of animal fable was a frequent figure in the poems of Archilochus.
[17] In the absence of formal political parties, private clubs were important in launching the politically ambitious. In the fifth century they became notorious hives of oligarchic conspiracy against the institutions of democratic Athens.

But these are the writers who tell us that it is in the gods' nature to be moved and won over 'with fair entreaty and with sacrifice'.[18] We must either believe both the claims made by the poets or neither of them. And if we believe them, the best policy will be to act unjustly, and use the

366 proceeds to pay for sacrifices. If we act justly, we shall avoid punishment by the gods, but also lose the rewards of injustice, whereas if we are unjust we shall get the rewards, and by means of prayers when we overstep the mark and do wrong we can persuade the gods to let us off without penalty."

"'Ah, but we shall have to pay in the next world – either we ourselves or our descendants – for the wrongs we do here." "Not so, my friend," he

b will say, with a calculating air. "There is great power in the mystic rites, and the gods who give absolution. So say the greatest cities, and the children of the gods, those who become the poets and mouthpieces of the gods; they assure us these things are so."

'What reason remains, then, for us to choose justice in preference to the most complete injustice? If we can have injustice coupled with counterfeit respectability, then we shall be following our own inclinations in our dealings with gods and men alike, both in our lifetime and after our death. That is the opinion of most people and of the experts. In the light

c of all these arguments, Socrates, what could induce anyone with any force of personality, any financial resources, any physical strength or family connections, to be prepared to respect justice, rather than laugh when he hears it being recommended? If anyone can show that what we have said is false, and is fully satisfied that justice is a good thing, then I imagine he is very forgiving towards the unjust, and does not get angry with them.

d He knows that apart from those who are born with a kind of divine aversion to injustice, or who gain the knowledge to refrain from it, no one really wants to be just. People condemn injustice as a result of cowardice, or old age, or weakness of some other kind, and from an inability to practise it. It's quite obvious. The minute one of these people comes into a position of power, he immediately starts acting as unjustly as he possibly can.

'The reason for all this is simply the observation which prompted the two of us to inflict these long speeches on you, Socrates. It is this. There

e is no shortage of people like you, my admirable friend, who claim to be supporters of justice, starting with the heroes of early days, whose words

---

[18] Referring back to 364e.

have come down to us, right up to people of the present day. None of you has ever condemned injustice or recommended justice except in terms of the reputation, prestige and rewards they bring. Nobody has ever yet, either in poetry or in private discussion, given a sufficiently detailed account of each of them in itself, when it is present with its own force in the soul of the person possessing it, undetected by gods or by men. No one has shown that injustice is the greatest of the evils the soul has within it, or 367 that justice is the greatest good. If that were what you had all been saying right from the start, and if you had been persuading us from our earliest years, we would not now be keeping an eye on one another, to guard against injustice. Each man would be keeping an eye on himself, afraid that by doing wrong he might admit the greatest of evils to share his abode.

'This, Socrates, and perhaps even more than this, is what Thrasy-machus, or anyone else for that matter, might say on the subject of
b justice and injustice. They assign the wrong value to each – a gross mistake, in my view. The reason – and I will be quite open with you – why I have set out their position as vigorously as I can is that I want to hear the opposite view from you. Don't just demonstrate to us by argument that justice is something more powerful than injustice.[19] Tell us what effect each of them has, just by itself, on the person possessing it, which makes one of them something bad and the other something good. You must strip them of their reputations, as Glaucon recommended. You must remove from each its true reputation, and give it a false reputation. Otherwise we
c shall say that you are not defending justice, but the appearance of justice, and that you are not condemning injustice, but the appearance of injus-tice. We shall say you are encouraging us to be secretly unjust, and that you agree with Thrasymachus when he says that justice is what is good for someone else – what is good for the stronger – whereas injustice is what is good and profitable for oneself – what is bad for the weaker. You agreed that justice was one of those great goods which are worth having partly for their consequences, but much more so for their own sake,
d goods such as sight, hearing, intelligence – and health, for that matter – and the rest of that finest class of goods, those which are good by their very nature, and not because of the reputation they bring.[20] That is the

---

[19] As in the argument with Thrasymachus (351a).
[20] The Greek is ambiguous, and could also mean 'and the rest of that class of goods which are productive by their very nature, and not because of the reputation they bring'.

praise of justice I want you to make. Just by itself, how does it help – and
how does injustice harm – the person who possesses it? You can leave the
praise of rewards and reputation to others. I'm prepared to accept other
people praising justice in these terms, and condemning injustice, and
listen to them extolling or criticising the reputation and rewards associated with them. But I won't accept it from you, unless you tell me I must,
since this is precisely the question you have spent your whole life
e studying. So please don't just demonstrate to us by argument that justice
is something more powerful than injustice. Tell us the effect each of them
has, just by itself, on the person possessing it – whether or not gods and
men know about it – the effect which makes one of them good and the
other bad.'

I had always had a high opinion of Glaucon's and Adeimantus' characters, but when I heard what they had to say I was particularly delighted
368 with them. 'So, children of the great man,'[21] I said, 'Glaucon's lover was
right, when you distinguished yourselves in the battle at Megara, to begin
his poem in your honour with the words:

> Ariston's sons, great father's godly line . . .[22]

A fair description, I think, my friends. There was certainly something
inspired about your performance just now – to be able to speak like that
in favour of injustice without being convinced it is a better thing than
b justice. And judging by the evidence of your whole way of life, I believe
you when you say you are really not convinced, though from what you
actually said I wouldn't have believed you. The trouble is, the more firmly
I believe you, the less certain I am what to do next. I can't defend justice.
I don't think I have the ability. I say that because you have rejected the
arguments by which I thought I had proved to Thrasymachus that justice
c was something better than injustice. On the other hand, I can't *not* defend
her, since I can't help feeling it is wrong to stand idly by when I hear

---

[21] An obscure phrase. It could be a playful address between intimates (compare 'you
son of a gun'); an ironic allusion to the brothers' inheritance of the argument from
Thrasymachus (compare 358b, 331d); or an anticipation of the mention of their
father Ariston in the verse that Socrates proceeds to quote.

[22] The identity of Glaucon's lover is not known, although Critias (see pp. xi–xiii of the
introduction) has been thought a likely candidate. A pattern of homosexuality in
which an older man would act as social mentor to a youth in return for sexual favours
was standard in Athens (see K. J. Dover, *Greek Homosexuality*, Cambridge, Mass.:
Harvard University Press, 1978). It is unclear which of the many battles between
Athens and Megara is meant. Ariston's name means 'Best'.

justice coming under attack, and not come to her defence for as long as I have breath in my body and a tongue in my head. So the best thing is to make what defence I can.'

Well, Glaucon and the rest of them insisted that they wanted me to make a defence, and not abandon the argument. They wanted me to make a full investigation into what justice and injustice both were, and what the true position was concerning the benefit they both brought. So I adopted what seemed to me the best approach. 'The enquiry we are undertaking
d is not a simple matter. If you ask me, it requires sharp eyesight. And since we are not clever people, I think we should conduct our search in the same sort of way as we would if our eyesight were not very good, and we were told to read some small writing from a bit of a distance away, and then one of us realised that a larger copy of the same writing, apparently, was to be found somewhere else, on some larger surface. We would regard it as a stroke of luck, I think, to be able to read the large letters first, and then turn our attention to the small ones, to see if they really did say the same thing.'

e 'We certainly would,' said Adeimantus. 'But where can you see anything like that in our search for justice?'

'I'll tell you,' I said. 'We say that there is justice in an individual; but also, I take it, justice in a whole city?'

'Yes.'

'And a city is something bigger than an individual?'

'Yes, it is.'

'In that case, maybe justice will be on a larger scale in what is larger,
369 and easier to find out about. So if you approve, why don't we start by finding out what sort of thing it is in cities? After that we can make a similar inquiry into the individual, trying to find the likeness of the larger version in the form the smaller takes.'

'I think that's a good idea,' he said.

'Suppose then,' I said, 'we were to study the theoretical origin of a city, would we also see the origin in it of justice and injustice?'

'We might,' he said.

'And if we do that, is there a chance that what we are looking for will be easier to find?'

b 'Yes, much easier.'

'You think, then, that this is a task we should attempt to complete? I suspect it is a fairly major undertaking, so you decide.'

'We have decided,' said Adeimantus. 'Go ahead.'

'Very well,' I said. 'The origin of a city lies, I think, in the fact that we are not, any of us, self-sufficient; we have all sorts of needs. Can you think of any other reason for the foundation of a city?'

'No, I can't.'

c   'Different individuals, then, form associations with one person to meet one need, and with another person to meet a different need. With this variety of wants they may collect a number of partners and allies into one place of habitation, and to this joint habitation we give the name "city," don't we?'

'Yes, we do.'

'Does one person share with another, when he *does* share – or does he accept a share – because he thinks it is better for him personally?'

'Yes, he does.'

'Right then,' I said. 'Let's construct a hypothetical city, from the beginning. It is the product, apparently, of our needs.'

'Of course.'

d   'And the first and most important of those needs, if we are to exist and stay alive, is the provision of food.'

'Unquestionably.'

'Second comes the need for housing, and third the need for clothing and things like that.'

'That is right.'

'Well then,' I said, 'how will our city be equal to meeting these requirements? Won't it just be one farmer, plus a builder, plus a weaver? Or should we add a shoemaker as well, and anyone else who provides for physical needs?'

'Yes, we should.'

'So the most basic city would have to consist of four or five men.'

'It looks like it.'

e   'Next question. Should each one of them make what he produces available to all alike? Should the one farmer, for example, provide food for four? Should he put four times the hours, and four times the effort, into the production of food, and then share it with the others? Or should he

370 forget about them and provide for himself alone, producing only a quarter of the amount of food in a quarter of the time – and of the remaining three-quarters, devote a quarter each to the provision of housing, of clothing, and of footwear? That way he would save himself the trouble of sharing with others, and provide for his own needs by his own individual efforts.'

'No, Socrates,' Adeimantus replied, 'the other way is probably easier.'

'That's certainly what you'd expect,' I said. 'And one thing immedi-
b ately struck me when you said that, which is that one individual is by
nature quite unlike another individual, that they differ in their natural
aptitudes, and that different people are equipped to perform different
tasks. Don't you think so?'

'I do.'

'Well, then. Will a single individual do better exercising a number of
skills, or will each do best concentrating on one?'

'Concentrating on one,' he replied.

'And another thing. It is clear, I think, that if you let the right moment
for a task pass by, the task suffers.'

'Yes, that is clear.'

'That is because the task in hand will not wait for the person doing it
c to have a spare moment. So it is essential that whoever is doing it should
concentrate on it, and not regard it as a hobby.'

'Yes, it is essential.'

'It follows from this that in any enterprise more is produced – and that
it is better and more easily produced – when one person does a single task
which is suited to his nature, and does it at the right time, keeping himself
free from other tasks.'

'It certainly does.'

'Then it will take more than four citizens, Adeimantus, to provide for
the needs we were talking about. The farmer, it appears, will not make
d himself a plough with his own hands – not if it's going to be a good plough
– nor a hoe, nor any of his other farming implements. No more will the
builder, who also needs a number of tools. And the same goes for the
weaver and the shoemaker.'

'True.'

'So carpenters, and blacksmiths, and a whole lot of skilled workers of
that kind, will become partners in our little city, and make the place quite
crowded.'

'They will.'

e   'All the same, it still won't be all that large, even if we add cattlemen,
shepherds and other herdsmen, so that the farmers can have oxen for
ploughing, and so that builders as well as the farmers will be able to use
animals for carrying materials, and so that weavers and shoemakers can
have hides and wool.'

'It certainly won't be a small city,' he said, 'if it contains all that.'

'That's not all,' I said. 'It will be more or less impossible to locate the city itself in a place where it won't need imports.'

'Quite impossible.'

'So it will require yet more people in addition, to bring it the things it needs from some other city.'

'It will.'

371 'What is more, if their agent goes empty-handed, taking nothing which meets the needs of the people from whom they are importing the things they are short of, then he will come back empty-handed, won't he?'

'I think so.'

'So in their own economy the citizens must not only provide adequately for themselves; they must also produce the right kind of goods – and in large enough quantities – for the people they need to trade with.'

'Yes, they must.'

'So our city needs more farmers, and more workers in other occupations.'

'Yes.'

'And more agents as well, presumably, the ones who are going to do all the importing and exporting. These people are merchants, aren't they?'

'Yes.'

'So we shall need merchants as well.'

'Definitely.'

b 'And if our trade is by sea, we shall need a large number of other people as well – experts on seafaring.'

'Yes, a large number.'

'What about trade in the city itself? How will each group share its production with others? That after all was our reason for forming an association and establishing a city.'

'Obviously,' he said, 'by buying and selling.'

'That will give rise to a market-place and a currency, a unit of exchange for transactions.'

'Undoubtedly.'

c 'But when the farmer, or member of one of the other occupations, brings to market part of what he produces, he may not arrive there at the same moment as those who need to exchange goods with him. Is he going to sit around in the market-place, taking time off from his work?'

'Certainly not,' he said. 'There are people who identify this need, and

make themselves available for this activity. In a well-run city they tend to
d be the weakest physically, those who are useless for any other kind of
work. They have to wait around there in the market-place, receiving
goods in exchange for money from those who have something to sell, and
then again money in return for goods from all those who want to buy.'

'So this is the need,' I said, 'which brings dealers into our city. Don't
we call people dealers, if they sit there in the market-place offering a
selling and buying service, whereas those who travel round the cities we
call merchants?'

'We do.'

'And there is still another group of people, I think, offering a service.
e We certainly would not want them as partners or associates for their
mental attributes, but they possess physical strength suitable for manual
labour. This they offer for sale, and the price they put on it they call their
hire. That, I imagine, is why they in turn are called hired labourers. Isn't
that right?'

'Yes.'

'So hired labourers, it seems, will also go to fill up our city.'

'I think they may.'

'Well then, Adeimantus, is our city now large enough? Is it complete?'

'Maybe it is.'

'In which case, where exactly are justice and injustice to be found in it?
In which of the elements we have examined have they made their appearance?'

372 'Speaking for myself, Socrates,' he said, 'I have no idea – unless, I
suppose, it is in some sort of need which those elements have of one
another.'

'I think that may be the right answer,' I said. 'We must examine it
without hesitation. Let's look first at the way people will spend their time
in an economy of this kind. Won't it be that they produce bread and wine
and clothing and shoes? They will build themselves houses. In summer
they will go about their work lightly clad, and barefoot, and in winter they
b will be properly clothed and shod. They will live on barley-meal and
wheat flour. Kneading and baking these, they will have fine barley cakes
or wheat loaves served on reeds or fresh leaves. They will eat lying on
straw beds covered with bryony and myrtle. They can live very well like
this – they and their children. Drinking wine after their meals, wearing
garlands on their heads, and singing the praises of the gods, they will live

c quite happily with one another. They will have no more children than
   they can afford, and they will avoid poverty and war.'[23]

   At this point Glaucon interrupted. 'No art of cookery, apparently, for
   these people you describe as living so well.'

   'That's a good point,' I said. 'I forgot that they will have the art of
   cookery. Obviously they will use salt, and olives, and cheese, and they will
   boil the usual country dishes of wild roots and vegetables. And for dessert
d we can offer them figs and chickpeas and beans; and they will roast myrtle
   berries and acorns in front of the fire, with a modest amount to drink. In
   this way, living lives which are peaceful and in all probability healthy, they
   will die in old age, handing down the same way of life to their descendants.'

   'If you were organising a city of pigs, Socrates, isn't that just how you
   would feed them?'[24]

   'Well, what sort of meals *should* we give them, Glaucon?' I asked.

   'The usual kind. If they are going to eat in comfort, they should lie on
e couches, eat off tables, and have the cooked dishes and desserts which
   people today have.'

   'I see,' I replied. 'So we are not just looking at the origin of a city, apparently. We are looking at the origin of a luxurious city. Maybe that's not
   such a bad idea. If we look at that sort of city too, we may perhaps see the
   point where justice and injustice come into existence in cities. I think the
   true city – the healthy version, as it were – is the one we have just
   described. But let's look also at the swollen and inflamed city, if that is
   what you prefer. We can easily do that. What's to stop us?'

373   'All this, and this way of life, will not, it seems, be enough for some
   people. They will have couches and tables, and other furniture in addition, and cooked dishes of course, and incense, perfumes, call-girls, cakes
   – every variety of all these things. As for those needs we talked about at
   the beginning, we can no longer prescribe only the bare necessities –
   houses, clothing and shoes. We must introduce painting and decoration,
   and start using gold and ivory and all those sorts of things, mustn't we?'

   ---

   [23] The picture borrows some of its effect from that of the primeval golden age in
   Hesiod's *Works and Days* (109–126), notably the absence of war and the relative simplicity of life; but it owes much more to a sentimental view of the life of the small
   farmer or peasant in the Athenian countryside. The contempt Glaucon is about to
   show for it is accordingly that of the sophisticated city-dweller.

   [24] Pigs were considered slow and stupid (compare 535e) as well as dirty and greedy –
   the emblem of all that was uncouth.

b   'Yes.'

'So once again we must enlarge our city, since our first, healthy city is
no longer big enough. We must fill it with a great mass and multitude of
things which are no longer what cities must have as a matter of necessity.
For example, we must have hunters of all kinds, artists, all those using
figure and colour for their imitations, and those using music, poets and

c   their assistants – reciters, actors, dancers, producers – and the makers of
all sorts of goods, especially those used for making women look beautiful.
What's more, we shall need more people in service. Don't you think we
shall need attendants for our sons, wetnurses, nannies, hairdressers,
barbers, not to mention cooks and chefs? And besides those, we shall need
people to keep pigs as well. We didn't have them in our earlier city, since
there was no need for them. But in this city there *will* be a need for them,
as also for all sorts of other livestock, in case anyone wants them to eat.
Isn't that right?'

d   'Of course.'[25]

'And living like this, will we have much greater need of doctors than we
did before?'

'Yes. Much greater.'

'What is more, I imagine the territory which was originally adequate to
feed the original population will no longer be adequate. It will be too
small. Do we accept that?'

'Yes.'

'Do we need, then, to carve ourselves a slice of our neighbours' territory, if we are going to have enough for pasturage and ploughing? And do
they in turn need a slice of our land, if they too give themselves up to the
pursuit of unlimited wealth, not confining themselves to necessities?'

e   'They are bound to, Socrates.'

'And will the next step be war, Glaucon? Or what?'

'War.'

'Let us say nothing for the moment,' I said, 'about whether the effect
of war is harmful or beneficial. Let us merely note that we have discovered, in its turn, the origin of war. War arises out of those things which
are the commonest causes of evil in cities, when evil does arise, both in
private life and public life.'

'Yes.'

---

[25] Meat was a luxury, and the rural diet was of necessity mainly vegetarian. There were
also deliberate vegetarians, notably the Pythagorean communities, who practised
vegetarianism for philosophic reasons.

374   'Our city needs to be even bigger, my friend. And not just a bit bigger;
we must add to it a whole army, which can go out and fight against
invaders, and defend all our wealth and the other things we were talking
about just now.'

'What about the citizens themselves? Aren't there enough of them?'

'No,' I said, 'not if we were right, you and the rest of us, in what we
agreed earlier, when we were forming our city. Surely we agreed, if you
remember, that no individual was capable of practising several arts or
skills properly.'

'True.'

b   'Well, how about fighting in battle?' I asked. 'Don't you think that is
essentially an art or skill?'

'Very much so,' he said.

'And should we regard the art of shoemaking as more important than
the art of war?'

'No.'

'Well then. We didn't allow our shoemaker to try and be a farmer as
well – or a weaver or builder. He had to be a shoemaker, to make sure the
business of shoemaking was carried out properly. In the same way we
assigned a single task to each member of the other occupations – the task
he was naturally suited to, and for which he would keep himself free from
c   other tasks, working at it throughout his life, and taking every opportunity to produce good results. Isn't it of the highest importance that
warfare should be carried on as efficiently as possible? Or is war so easy
that any farmer, any shoemaker, or any practitioner of any art or skill, can
be a soldier as well?[26]

'Even to be a decent draughts or dice player, you have to have been
d   playing since you were a child. It can't be done in your spare time. So how
can you pick up a shield – or any other weapon or instrument of war – and
immediately be equipped to take your place in the battle-line, or in any of
the other sorts of fighting which occur in time of war? Think of other
instruments: there isn't one of them that will turn a person into a craftsman or athlete simply by being picked up, or that will be of any use to him
if he has no expertise or has not had enough practice in handling it.'

'No,' he said, 'they'd be extremely valuable instruments if you could.'

---

[26] It was a point of pride among the general citizenry of most of the Greek states of the
fifth and (to a lesser degree) the fourth centuries to fight their own battles; there were
no standing armies of professional soldiers. For further background consult ch. 12e
('Warfare') of *CAH* 6.

e   'Since the guardians' job, then,' I said, 'is the most important, it must
correspondingly call for the greatest freedom from other activities, together
with the highest level of expertise and training.'

'That's certainly my opinion,' he said.

'And also, of course, a natural disposition suited to precisely this way
of life?'

'Of course.'

'And it would be our job, apparently, if we are capable of it, to choose
which dispositions, and which kinds of dispositions, were suited to the
defence of the city.'

'That would indeed be our job.'

'Heavens,' I said, 'that's a major responsibility we have taken upon
375 ourselves. All the same, as far as our abilities permit, we must try not to
back out of it.'

'Yes, we must.'

'Well, then,' I said, 'when it comes to acting as a guardian, don't you
think that in his disposition a young man of good birth is like a young
pedigree hound?'

'In what way?'

'Well, for example, each of them needs acute senses, speed in pursuit
of what they detect, and strength as well, in case they catch it and have to
fight with it.'

'Yes,' he said, 'they need all these qualities.'

'Plus courage, of course, if he is to fight well.'

'Of course.'

'But is any living creature likely to be brave – whether horse or dog or
b anything else – if it doesn't have a spirited and energetic nature? Haven't
you noticed what an irresistible and unconquerable thing spirit is? With
spirit, any living creature is fearless and invincible in the face of any
danger.'

'Yes, I have noticed that.'

'As for the physical characteristics required of a guardian, then, they
are obvious.'

'Yes.'

'And the mental requirement is that he should be spirited, or energetic.'

'Yes. That too.'

'In that case, Glaucon,' I said, 'if their natural disposition is as we have
described, what is to stop them being aggressive towards one another and
the rest of the citizens?'

'Precious little,' he said.

c   'But we want them to be gentle in their dealings with their own people, and fierce in their dealings with the enemy. Otherwise they won't need to waste time looking for someone else to come along and destroy their city; they'll be in there first, doing it for themselves.'

'True,' he said.

'What shall we do, then?' I asked. 'Where can we find a natural disposition which is both gentle and full of spirit? After all, I take it that a gentle disposition is the opposite of spirit.'

'It appears to be.'

'And yet if someone is deficient in either of these qualities, he cannot
d   possibly be a good guardian. The combination of them looks like an impossibility, which means that a good guardian is an impossibility.'

'Perhaps it is.'

I didn't know what to say then. I thought over what we had said, and then tried again. 'No wonder we can't find the answer, my friend. We have forgotten the example we set up for ourselves.'

'Explain.'

'We forgot that there actually are natural dispositions of the kind we have just decided don't exist, dispositions which do contain these opposite qualities.'

'Where?'

'Well, you can find them in a number of animals, but especially in the
e   one we compared with our guardian. You are aware, presumably, that it is the natural disposition of pure-bred dogs to be as gentle as possible to those they know and recognise, and the exact opposite to those they don't know.'

'Yes, I am.'

'So such a thing is possible,' I said. 'And in looking for a guardian of this kind, we are not looking for something unnatural.'

'Apparently not.'

'In that case, do you think the person who is going to be guardian material needs another quality as well? Do you want him, as well as being spirited and energetic, to be also by temperament a lover of wisdom, a philosopher?'[27]

376   'What do you mean? I don't understand.'

---

[27] *Philosophia* in Greek derives from two words meaning 'love of wisdom'. It is largely at Plato's hands that it comes to mean something closer to 'philosophy'. See pp. xviii–xxii of the introduction.

'It's another thing you see in dogs,' I replied.' Something which makes you wonder at the animal.'

'What is that?'

'When it sees someone it doesn't know, a dog turns nasty, even though it hasn't been badly treated by him in the past. When it sees someone familiar, it welcomes him, even if it has never been at all well treated by him. Haven't you ever found that rather remarkable?'

'I'd never really thought about it, up to now,' he said. 'But I think there's no doubt a dog does behave like that.'

'It seems clever, this side of its nature. It seems to show a true love of wisdom.'

b   'In what way?'

'Because,' I replied, 'it classifies what it sees as friendly or hostile solely on the fact that it knows one, and doesn't know the other. It must be a lover of knowledge if it defines friend and enemy by means of knowledge and ignorance.'

'Yes,' he said, 'it must.'

'And are love of knowledge and love of wisdom the same thing?'

'They are.'

'So can we say with some confidence of a man too, that if he is going to
c   be someone who is gentle towards those he knows and recognises, he must by his nature be a lover of knowledge and of wisdom?'

'We can.'

'Then will the person who is going to be a good and true guardian of our city be a lover of wisdom, spirited, swift and strong?'

'He certainly will.'

'Well, so much for his nature. But what about the upbringing and education of our guardians? What form will those take? Will looking into
d   that question be of some use to us in finding the answer to our main enquiry, which is how justice and injustice arise in a city? We want to cover the subject properly, without going on at enormous length.'

Glaucon's brother answered. 'Speaking for myself,' he said, 'I'm quite sure that looking into it will be useful in our main aim.'

'In that case, my dear Adeimantus,' I said, 'we must certainly not leave it out, even if it takes longer than we expect.'

'No, we mustn't.'

'Very well, then. Let's imagine we are telling a story, and that we have all the time in the world. Let's design an education for these men of ours.'
e   'Yes, that's what we should do.'

'What should their education be, then? Isn't it hard to find a better education than the one which has been developed over the years? It consists, I take it, of physical education for the body, and music and poetry[28] for the mind or soul.'

'It does.'

'And shouldn't we start their education in music and poetry earlier than their physical education?'

'We should.'

'Do you count stories as part of music and poetry, or not?'

'Yes, I do.'

'And are stories of two kinds – one true, the other false?'

'Yes.'

'Should we educate them in both, starting with the false?'

377   'I don't understand what you mean,' he said.

'You mean you don't understand that we start off by telling children legends? These, I take it, are broadly speaking false, though there is some truth in them. And we start children on these legends before we start them on physical education.'

'That is right.'

'That was what I meant when I said we should start their education in music and poetry before their physical education.'

'You were right,' he said.

b   'Very well, then. You are aware that it is the beginning of any undertaking which is the most important part – especially for anything young and tender? That is the time when each individual thing can be most easily moulded, and receive whatever mark you want to impress upon it.'

'Yes, of course.'

'Shall we be perfectly content, then, to let our children listen to any old stories, made up by any old storytellers? Shall we let them open their minds to beliefs which are the opposite, for the most part, of those we think they should hold when they grow up?'

'No. We shall certainly not allow that.'

'For a start, then, it seems, we must supervise our storytellers. When c   they tell a good story, we must decide in favour of it; and when they tell a

---

[28] Instrumental music, at least until the end of Plato's life, directly accompanied or otherwise complemented song, chant and declamation rather than being developed for its own sake. The single word *mousikē* can therefore denote accomplishment in both music and poetry.

bad one, we must decide against it.[29] We shall persuade nurses and mothers to tell children the approved stories, and tell them that shaping children's minds with stories is far more important than trying to shape their bodies with their hands.[30] We must reject most of the stories they tell at the moment.'

'Which ones?'

d 'If we look at our greatest stories, we shall see how to deal with lesser examples as well,' I replied. 'Greater and lesser must have the same standard, and the same effect. Don't you think so?'

'Yes, I do,' he said. 'But I'm not even sure which these "great" stories are you talk about.'

'The ones Hesiod and Homer both used to tell us – and the other poets. They made up untrue stories, which they used to tell people – and still do tell them.'

'Which stories? What is your objection to them?'

e 'The one which ought to be our first and strongest objection – especially if the untruth is an ugly one.'

'What is this objection?'

'When a storyteller gives us the wrong impression of the nature of gods and heroes. It's like an artist producing pictures which don't look like the things he was trying to draw.'

'Yes,' he said, 'it is right to object in general to that sort of story. But what exactly do we mean? Which stories?'

'I'll start,' I said, 'with an important falsehood on an important subject. There is the very ugly falsehood told of how Ouranos did the things Hesiod says he did, and how Kronos in his turn took his revenge on him.[31]
378 As for what Kronos did, and what his son did to him, even if they were true I wouldn't think that in the normal course of events these stories should be told to those who are young and uncritical. The best thing

---

[29] While there was no state supervision in Athens of the stories children heard in the course of their education, the state did control the poetic works that adult citizens witnessed at the dramatic festivals, since it was the responsibility of various magistrates to select, from a pool of applicants, the dramatists who could take part each year.

[30] The reference is to the use of massage and swaddling clothes for directing the growth of infants.

[31] Hesiod, *Theogony* 154–182, 453–506. The sky god Ouranos prevented the children conceived for him by the earth mother Gaia from emerging into the light. Gaia's son Kronos avenged them by castrating his father with a sickle of his mother's manufacture. Kronos in his turn swallowed the children borne him by his consort Rhea and succumbed likewise to the wiles of the mother and of one of those children, Zeus, who thereby became king of the gods.

would be to say nothing about them at all. If there were some overriding
necessity to tell them, then as few people as possible should hear them,
and in strict secrecy. They should have to make sacrifice. Not a pig, but
some large and unobtainable sacrificial animal, to make sure the smallest
possible number of people heard them.'

'Yes,' he said. 'Those stories are pretty hard to take.'

b   'We will not have them told in our city, Adeimantus. When the young
are listening, they are not to be told that if they committed the most
horrible crimes they wouldn't be doing anything out of the ordinary, not
even if they inflicted every kind of punishment on a father who treated
them badly. We won't tell them that they would merely be acting like the
first and greatest of the gods.'

'Good heavens, no. Personally, I don't think these are at all the right
stories to tell them.'

c   'Nor, in general, any of the stories – which are not true anyway – about
gods making war on gods, plotting against them, or fighting with them.
Not if we want the people who are going to protect our city to regard it as
a crime to fall out with one another without a very good reason. The last
thing they need is to have stories told them, and pictures made for them,
of battles between giants, and all the many and varied enmities of gods
and heroes towards their kinsmen and families. If we do intend to find
some way of convincing them that no citizen has ever quarrelled with

d   another citizen, that quarrelling is wrong, then this is the kind of thing
old men and women must tell our children, right from the start. And as
the children get older, we must compel our poets to tell stories similar to
these. As for the binding of Hera by her son, the hurling of Hephaestus
out of heaven by his father, for trying to protect his mother when she was
being beaten, and the battles of the gods which Homer tells us about,[32]
whether these stories are told as allegories or not as allegories, we must
not allow them into our city. The young are incapable of judging what is

e   allegory and what is not, and the opinions they form at that age tend
to be ineradicable and unchangeable.[33] For these reasons, perhaps, we

---

[32]   The son who bound Hera and the son who came to her defence against Zeus are one
and the same: Hephaestus. The story is that he was rejected by his mother at birth
and in revenge made a trick throne for her which caught her fast when she sat in it.
The incident with Zeus is narrated by Homer, *Iliad* 1.586–594. Battles of the gods
in Homer: *Iliad* 20.1–74, 21.385–513.

[33]   At school, Athenian youngsters would memorise rather than interpret poetry, but it
was characteristic of the professional intellectuals who offered the elite a higher education to find hidden meanings in the poets, especially Homer.

should regard it as of the highest importance that the first things they hear should be improving stories, as beautiful as can be.'

'That makes sense,' he said. 'But suppose someone were to go on and ask us what these things are, and what stories we should tell, which ones should we say?'

'Adeimantus,' I said, 'we are not acting as poets at the moment, you and 379 I. We are the founders of a city. It is the founders' job to know the patterns on which poets must model their stories, or be refused permission if they use different ones. It is not their job to start creating stories themselves.'

'True,' he said. 'But what about this question of patterns for stories about the gods? What should these patterns be?'

'Something like this, I should think. They should always, I take it, give a true picture of what god is really like, whether the poet is working in epic, or in lyric, or in tragedy.'

'Yes, they should.'

'Well then, isn't god in fact good? Shouldn't he be represented as such?'

b   'Of course.'

'The next point is that nothing that is good is harmful, is it?'

'No, I don't think so.'

'Does what is not harmful do any harm?'

'No.'

'Can what does no harm do any evil?'

'No, it can't do that either.'

'But if something does no evil, it couldn't be the cause of any evil, could it?'

'Of course not.'

'Very well. Now, is the good beneficial?'

'Yes.'

'Responsible for well-being, in other words?'

'Yes.'

'In that case the good is not responsible for everything. It is responsible for what goes well, but not responsible for what goes badly.'

'Absolutely.'

c   'In which case,' I said, 'god, since he is good, could not be responsible for everything, as most people claim. Some of the things that happen to men are his responsibility, but most are not; after all, we have many fewer good things than bad things in our lives. We have no reason to hold anyone else responsible for the good things, whereas for the bad things we *should* look for some other cause, and not blame god.'

'I think you are absolutely right.'

d   'In that case,' I said, 'we should not allow Homer or any other poet to make such a stupid mistake about the gods, and tell us that two jars

> Stand in the hall of Zeus, full filled with fates.
> One of the two holds good, the other ill.

Nor that the person to whom Zeus gives a mixture of the two

> Sometimes encounters evil, sometimes good,

whereas for the person to whom he does not give a mixture, but gives evil in its pure form,

> Dread famine drives him over earth's fair face.[34]

e   Nor describe Zeus as

> Of good and evil steward and dispenser.[35]

As for Pandarus' violation of the oaths and the truce, we shall dis-

380   approve of anyone who says that Athena and Zeus were the cause of it,[36] or that Themis and Zeus were the cause of the quarrel of the goddesses, and the judgment between them.[37] Nor again must we let the young hear the kind of story Aeschylus tells, when he says:

> For god implants the fatal cause in men,
> When root and branch he will destroy a house.

If anyone writes about the sufferings of Niobe – as here[38] – or about the house of Pelops,[39] or the Trojan War, or anything like that, we must either not allow them to say that these events are the work of a god, or if the poet claims that they *are* the work of a god, then he must find more or less the

---

[34] A mixture of quotation and description of *Iliad* 24.527–532. The words are spoken by Achilles to Priam.

[35] Where this line comes from is not known.

[36] Homer, *Iliad* 4.30 ff. Despite the piety of the Trojans towards him, Zeus succumbs to cajoling by Hera and Athena, who support the Greeks, and agrees to permit Athena to beguile the Trojan archer Pandarus into breaking the truce currently holding between the two sides in the war.

[37] The Trojan prince Paris judged in favour of Aphrodite in the contest for beauty between her and the goddesses Hera and Athena – a decision that eventually led to the Trojan War.

[38] Aeschylus' *Niobe* has not been preserved. Niobe boasted of having finer children than those of the goddess Leto – Apollo and Artemis. As a result, these gods were sent by their mother to destroy the children of Niobe.

[39] The lurid travails of the descendants of Pelops – including adultery, child killing, cannibalism, and multiple murder between kin – were a frequent topic of tragic drama.

b sort of explanation we are looking for at the moment. He must say that
what god does is right and good, and that these people's punishments
were good for them. We must not allow the poet to say that those who paid
the penalty were made wretched, and that the person responsible was a
god. If poets said that the wicked were made wretched because they
needed punishment, and that in paying the penalty they were being
helped by god, then we should allow that. But the claim that god, who is
good, is responsible for bringing evil on anyone, is one we must oppose
with every weapon we possess. We must not let anyone make this claim in

c our city, if it is to be well governed, nor should we let anyone hear it,
whether the hearer be young or old, and whether or not the storyteller
tells his story in verse. These claims, if they were made, would neither be
holy, nor good for us, nor consistent with one another.'

'You have my vote for this law,' he said. 'I thoroughly approve.'

'There you are, then,' I said. 'That would be one of the laws about the
gods, one of the patterns on which storytellers must base their stories, and
poets their poems – that god is not responsible for everything, but only
for what is good.'

'Yes,' he said, 'that should do it.'

d 'What about a second law, or pattern? Do you think god is a magician?
Would he deliberately appear in different guises at different times? Are
there times when he really becomes different, and changes his shape into
many forms, and other times when he deceives us into thinking that is
what he is doing? Or do you think he has a single form, and is of all creatures the least likely to depart from his own shape?'

'I'm not sure I'm in a position to answer that, just at the moment.'

'How about a different question? When things do depart from their
own shape, isn't it necessarily true that they either change themselves or
are changed by something else?'

e 'Yes, it is.'

'Doesn't an external cause of change or motion have least effect on the
finest specimens? Think of a body, for example, and the effect on it of
food, drink and exertion. Or plants, and the effect of sun and wind and
things like that. Isn't the healthiest and strongest specimen least affected?'

381 'Yes, of course.'

'And wouldn't the bravest and wisest soul be least disturbed and altered
by an outside influence?'

'Yes.'

'The same, presumably, goes for anything manufactured – furniture, houses and clothes. What is well made and in good condition is least affected by time and other influences.'

'That is so.'

b   'So anything which is a fine example, whether by its nature or its design, or both, is the most resistant to being changed by an external agency.'

'It looks like it.'

'But god and his attributes are in every way perfect.'

'Of course.'

'So god would be most unlikely to take many shapes as a result of external causes.'

'Most unlikely.'

'Could he, in that case, change and transform himself?'

'Obviously he does,' he said. 'If he changes at all, that is.'

'Does he then turn himself into something better and more beautiful, or into something worse and uglier than himself?'

c   'If he does change, it must necessarily be into something worse. I don't imagine we are going to say that god is lacking in beauty or goodness.'

'No, you are quite right,' I said. 'And that being so, do you think that anyone, Adeimantus, whether god or man, is prepared to make himself worse in any way at all?'

'No, that's impossible,' he said.

'In which case,' I replied, 'it is also impossible for god to have any desire to change himself. No, each of the gods, it appears, is as beautiful and good as possible, and remains for ever simply in his own form.'

'Yes,' he said, 'I think that must undoubtedly follow.'

d   'Well, then, my friend, we don't want any of the poets telling us,' I said, 'that

> Disguised as strangers from afar, the gods
> Take many shapes, and visit many lands.[40]

We don't want any of their falsehoods about Proteus and Thetis,[41] nor do we want tragedies or other poems which introduce Hera, transformed into the guise of a priestess, collecting alms for

---

[40] Homer, *Odyssey* 17.485–486.
[41] Both were divinities of the ocean who slipped from the grasp of mortals by changing into a multitude of different creatures.

The life-giving sons of Argive Inachus.[42]

e And there are many other falsehoods of the same sort which we don't want them telling us – any more than we want mothers to believe them, and terrify their children with wicked stories about gods who go round at night, taking on the appearance of all sorts of outlandish foreigners. That way we can stop them from blaspheming against the gods, and also stop them turning their children into cowards.'

'No, we don't want any of that.'

'Well then,' I suggested, 'though the gods would not themselves change, maybe they nevertheless make it seem to us that they appear in all sorts of different guises? Perhaps they deceive us, and play tricks on us.'

'Possibly.'

382 'What! Would a god be prepared to deceive us, in his words or his actions, by offering us what is only an appearance?'

'I don't know.'

'You don't know,' I said, 'that the true falsehood – if one can call it that – is hated by god and man alike?'

'What do you mean?'

'I mean this. No one deliberately chooses falsehood in what is surely the most important part of himself, and on the most important of subjects. No, that is the place, more than any other, where they fear falsehood.'

b 'I still don't understand,' he said.

'That's because you think I'm talking about something profound,' I said. 'But all I mean is that the thing everyone wants above all to avoid is being deceived in his soul about the way things are, or finding that he has been deceived, and is now in ignorance, that he holds and possesses the falsehood right there in his soul. That is the place where people most hate falsehood.'

'I quite agree,' he said.

'As I was saying just now, this ignorance in the soul, the ignorance of the person who has been deceived, can with absolute accuracy be called true falsehood, whereas verbal falsehood is a kind of imitation of this

c condition of the soul. It comes into being later; it is an image, not a wholly unmixed falsehood. Don't you agree?'

'I do.'

---

[42] We do not know why Hera was collecting alms for the sons of Inachus. The line quoted comes from a lost play of Aeschylus.

'The real falsehood is hated not only by gods but also by men.'

'Yes, I think so.'

'What about verbal falsehood? When is it useful, and for whom? When does it not deserve hatred? Isn't it useful against enemies, or to stop those who are supposed to be our friends, if as a result of madness or ignorance

d   they are trying to do something wrong? Isn't a lie useful in those circumstances, in the same way as medicine is useful? And in the myths we were discussing just now, as a result of our not knowing what the truth is concerning events long ago, do we make falsehood as much like the truth as possible, and in this way make it useful?'

'Yes,' he said, 'that is exactly how it is.'

'In which of these ways, then, is falsehood useful to god? Does he make falsehood resemble the truth because he doesn't know about events long ago?'

'No, that would be absurd,' he said.

'So there is nothing of the false poet in god.'

'I don't think so.'

e   'Is he afraid of his enemies? Would he tell lies for that reason?'

'Far from it.'

'Or because of the ignorance or madness of his friends, perhaps?'

'No,' he said. 'No one who is ignorant and mad is a friend of the gods.'[43]

'There is no reason, then, for god to tell a falsehood.'

'No, none.'

'So the supernatural and the divine are altogether without falsehood.'

'Absolutely.'

'In that case, god is certainly single in form and true, both in what he does and what he says. He does not change in himself, and he does not deceive others – waking or sleeping – either with apparitions, or with words, or by sending signs.'

383   'That's how it seems to me too,' he said, 'as I listen to what you say.'

'Do you agree then,' I asked, 'that this should be the second pattern for telling stories or writing poems about the gods? They are not magicians who change their shape, either in their words or their actions, and they do not lead us astray with falsehoods.'

'Yes, I agree.'

'So while there is much in Homer we approve of, we shall not approve

---

[43] Adeimantus gives full weight to a term (*theophilēs*) that usually means simply 'favoured by the gods', i.e. 'fortunate'.

b of Zeus' sending a dream to Agamemnon;[44] nor of Aeschylus, when
   Thetis says that Apollo, singing at her wedding, "dwelt upon the children" she would have,

> Their length of life, their freedom from disease,
> And summing up, sang me a hymn of blessing
> For my good luck and favour with the gods.
> My hope was high, for Phoebus was a god,
> And Phoebus' mouth, brimming with mantic art,
> Must speak the truth, I thought. But he who sang,
> He who was present at the feast, the one
> Who said these things, is now the one who killed
> My son.[45]

c When anyone talks in this way about the gods, we shall get angry with
   him, and not grant him a chorus.[46] Nor shall we allow teachers to use his
   works for the education of the young – not if we want our guardians to
   become god-fearing and godlike, to the greatest extent possible for a
   human being.'
      'I entirely agree,' he said, 'with these patterns, and I would want to see
   them made law.'

---

[44] *Iliad* 2.1–34: Zeus sends a dream to Agamemnon promising him victory over the
Trojans if he leads an immediate assault against them, but his real intention is to
bring about a Greek defeat that will salve Achilles' wounded pride.
[45] The goddess Thetis was the mother of Achilles. Achilles was killed by an arrow from
the Trojan Paris, guided by Apollo (also known as Phoebus). We have lost the play
of Aeschylus from which these lines come.
[46] That is, not allow him to stage his play.

Book 3

386 'When it comes to stories about the gods, then,' I said, 'this is apparently the sort of thing which from their earliest childhood people must be told – and not told – if they are to show respect for the gods and their parents, and put a high value on friendship with one another.'[1]

'Yes, I think our views on this are correct,' he said.

'What about courage? If we want them to be brave, aren't these the
b stories we should be telling them, plus the kind of stories which will minimise their fear of death? Do you think anyone can ever get to be brave if he has this fear inside him?'

'Good heavens, no.'

'How about belief in the underworld and its horrors? Do you think that makes people fearless in the face of death, makes them choose death in preference to defeat or slavery?'

'Of course not.'

'This is another branch of storytelling, then, where it looks as if we must keep an eye on those who want to tell these stories. We shall have to
c ask them to stop being so negative about the underworld, and find something positive to say about it instead. What they say at the moment is neither true, nor helpful to those we want to become warlike.'

'Yes, we shall have to keep an eye on them,' he said.

'Then we shall eliminate all descriptions of that sort, starting with:

> I had rather labour as a common serf,
> Serving a man with nothing to his name,
> Than be the lord of all the dead below.[2]

---

[1] Respect for parents: 378b; friendship with one another: 378c–d.
[2] Homer, *Odyssey* 11.489–491. The ghost of Achilles is speaking to Odysseus in the underworld.

71

Or:

d
> His halls revealed to mortals and immortals,
> Grim, dank, abhorrent even to the gods.[3]

Or:

> Alas, there is then, in the house of Hades,
> A spirit and a phantom, but no mind
> Within it dwells.[4]

Or:

> Alone possessed of thought, the rest but shadows.[5]

Or:

> Leaving his limbs, his soul to Hades flew,
> Its fate lamenting, and lost youth and strength.[6]

387 Or:

> Like smoke his soul departed, crying shrill,
> Beneath the earth.[7]

Or:

> As in dark corners of mysterious caves
> The squeaking bats take flight when, from the bunch
> That clings together on the rock, one falls –
> So, shrilly crying, did these souls depart.[8]

b We shall ask Homer and the rest of the poets not to be angry with us if we strike out these passages, and any others like them. Not that they lack poetic merit, or that they don't give pleasure to most people. They do. But the more merit they have, the less suitable they are for boys and men who are expected to be free, and fear slavery more than death.'

'Absolutely.'

'So we must also discard all the weird and terrifying language used

---

[3] Homer, *Iliad* 20.64–65. The 'halls' are the realm of Hades, god of the dead.
[4] *Iliad* 23.103–104. This is Achilles' lament after he has tried and failed to grasp hold of the ghost of his friend Patroclus.
[5] *Odyssey* 10.495: a description of the soul of the wise prophet Tiresias in the under- world, the single exception to the rule voiced by Achilles in the previous quote.
[6] *Iliad* 16.856–857: a description of Patroclus slain by Hector.
[7] *Iliad* 23.100–101: again of Patroclus, as he slips from Achilles' grasp.
[8] *Odyssey* 24.6–9: a description of the souls of the suitors slain by Odysseus.

c   about the underworld. No more wailing Cocytus, or hateful Styx,[9] or food
for worms, or mouldering corpses, or any other language of the kind
which makes all who hear it shudder. It may be fine in some other context,
but when it comes to our guardians, we are worried that this shuddering
may make them too soft and impressionable for our needs.'

'We are right to be worried,' he said.

'That sort of language must go, then?'

'Yes.'

'And our storytellers and poets should use language which follows the
opposite pattern?'

'Obviously.'

d   'Then we shall get rid of weeping and wailing by famous men.'

'We shall have to,' he said, 'We can't get rid of the other things, and not
that.'

'What you *should* ask yourself, though,' I said, 'is whether or not we
shall be right to get rid of them. Our view is that a good man does not
regard it as a disaster when death comes to another good man, his friend.'

'Yes, that is our view.'

'So he certainly wouldn't lament on his friend's account, as if something awful had happened to him.'

'No, he wouldn't.'

'But we also say that when it comes to living a good life, a good man is
e   the most capable of meeting his own needs, and has less need of other
people than anyone else has.'

'True.'

'So he least of all will regard it as a misfortune to lose a son, or a brother,
or some money, or anything like that.'

'Yes.'

'And he least of all will grieve over the loss. He more than anyone can
take it in his stride when an accident of this kind happens to him.'

'He can indeed.'

'We shall be right, then, to get rid of the heroes' songs of lamentation,
388   putting them in the mouths of women — and not even the best women, at
that — and cowards. We want the people we say we are bringing up to be
guardians of our country to be appalled at the idea of behaving like this.'

'Yes, we shall be right,' he said.

---

[9]   'Wailing' and 'hateful' are the etymological meanings of these names of underworld
rivers.

'So we have another request to make to Homer and the rest of the poets: not to show us Achilles, the son of a goddess,

> First lying on his side, then on his back,
> Then on his front,

and then when he gets up,

> Drifting, distraught and aimless, on the shore
> Of the unharvested sea.[10]

b Nor, as he puts it, "taking the black, burnt dust in both his hands, and pouring it o'er his head".[11] We shall ask him to spare us all the rest of those tears and laments he makes him utter. We shall ask him not to show Priam, close kinsman of the gods, in his entreaties:

> Rolling in dung, calling each man by name.[12]

Much more important, we shall ask him not to show the gods lamenting, and saying:

c
>   Ah! Woe is me,
> Unhappy mother of a noble son.[13]

If he must show the gods behaving like this, let him at least not have the nerve to give us such a false picture of the greatest of the gods, when he makes him say:

> How dear to me the man my eyes now see
> Pursued around the city. My heart grieves.[14]

Or:

> And must Sarpedon, that most dear of men,
d
> Fall to Patroclus, son of Menoetius?[15]

---

[10] *Iliad* 24.10–12: Achilles is unable to sleep for missing the dead Patroclus and remembering their experiences together.

[11] *Iliad* 18.23–24: Achilles' reaction on being brought the news of Patroclus' death.

[12] *Iliad* 22.414–415. Priam, king of Troy, was seventh in line from Zeus, the king of the gods. Here he implores his people to allow him to go to Achilles to beg back the corpse of his son Hector, slain by Achilles in revenge for Patroclus.

[13] *Iliad* 18.54: Thetis' reaction on hearing the grief of her son Achilles at Patroclus' death, from which comes the quotation at 388b.

[14] *Iliad* 22.168–169: Zeus expresses his sadness on behalf of Hector, about to be slain by Achilles.

[15] *Iliad* 16.433–434: Sarpedon was a mortal son of Zeus, who here grieves that Patroclus is about to slay him.

If our young men take these kinds of things seriously, my dear Adeimantus, if they don't laugh at them as the unworthy offerings of storytellers, then, since they are only human, they are hardly going to think it beneath them to behave like this themselves. They won't be appalled at the very idea of speaking or acting in this way. No, they'll be quite unashamed, making not the slightest effort to put a brave face on it, as they give voice to great songs of grief and lamentation over trivial misfortunes.'

e   'You're absolutely right,' he said.

'But that isn't how they should be behaving, as our reasoning just now showed. And until someone gives us a good reason for believing something different, we must have faith in our reasoning.'

'No, it isn't how they should be behaving.'

'On the other hand, they must not be too fond of laughter either. Abandonment to violent laughter, generally speaking, is a violent agent for change.'

'I agree,' he said.

'So we must not accept it if we are shown men of any importance – still
389 less gods – being overcome by laughter.'

'Particularly not the gods.'

'So we won't accept this sort of thing about the gods from Homer:

> Unquenchable the laughter that arose
> Among the blessed gods. They sat and watched
> Hephaestus bustling up and down the hall.[16]

We mustn't accept this, according to your reasoning.'

b   'Call it mine, if you like,' he said. 'We certainly mustn't accept it, anyway.'

'Then again, truth is another thing we must value highly. If we were right just now,[17] if lies really are useless to the gods, and useful to men only in the way medicine is useful, then clearly lying is a task to be entrusted to specialists. Ordinary people should have nothing to do with it.'

'Clearly.'

'So if anyone is entitled to tell lies, the rulers of the city are. They may do so for the benefit of the city, in response to the actions either of enemies
c   or of citizens. No one else should have anything to do with lying, and for

[16] *Iliad* 1.599–600. Hephaestus, the lame and ugly god, is clowning in the role of wine-pourer, a role typically assigned to the youthful and attractive, in order to amuse and pacify his fellow-gods.

[17] 382c.

75

an ordinary citizen to lie to these rulers of ours is as big a mistake – bigger, in fact – as telling your doctor or trainer lies about the condition of your body when you are ill or in training, or giving a ship's captain misleading information about the ship and its crew, and how you or your fellow-sailors are getting on.'

'Very true,' he said.

d   'So if a ruler catches anyone else in the city lying – any of those "who work as artisans,"

> A prophet, healer of ills, or worker of wood,[18]

he will punish him for introducing a practice which is as subversive and destructive in a city as it is in a ship.'

'Yes, if actions are going to be true to words,' he said.

'And then what about self-discipline? Won't our young men need that?'

'Of course they will.'

'For the general population, doesn't self-discipline consist principally e   in being obedient to their masters, and being themselves masters of the pleasures of drink, sex and food?'

'Yes, I think it does.'

'We shall approve, I think, of the kind of thing Diomedes says in Homer:

> Be seated, friend, in silence. Hear my advice.[19]

And the lines which come next:

> The Achaeans now moved forward, breathing fire.
> Silent they marched, in awe of their commanders.[20]

And any other passages like these.'

'Yes, we shall approve of them.'

'What about lines like this?

> You wine-dulled dolt,
> With spaniel eyes, and courage of a deer.[21]

---

[18] *Odyssey* 17.383–384. The sentence concludes: 'or an inspired poet, who pleases with his song'.

[19] *Iliad* 4.412: the hero Diomedes rebukes his companion Sthenelus.

[20] In fact these two lines neither follow the previous quotation nor each other, but are from different descriptions contrasting the silence of the Greek advance with the racket made by the Trojans (*Iliad* 3.8 and 4.431).

[21] *Iliad* 1.225: Achilles is insulting Agamemnon, commander-in-chief of the Greek army.

390 And the speech which follows? Shall we approve of them, and any other
piece of insolence, in the works of the storytellers or the poets, addressed
by an ordinary citizen to his rulers?'

'No, we shan't.'

'No. If we want the young to develop self-discipline, I don't think these
are the right things for them to hear – though it's no surprise if they are
entertaining in other ways. Do you agree?'

'Yes,' he said.

'How about making a very wise man say he thinks the finest of all sights
is this:

> With bread and meat the tables laden full,
b > And pourers drawing wine from mixing-bowls
> To fill the waiting cups.[22]

Do you think hearing that is going to help a young man be master of
himself? Or this?

> Nothing so wretched as to meet one's fate
> Dying of hunger.[23]

And what about showing Zeus remaining awake all alone while the other
c gods and mankind sleep, but then happily forgetting all his plans in his
desire for sex, and being so carried away with the sight of Hera that he
refuses to go inside, and wants to make love right there on the ground?
He is gripped, he says, by desire greater even than when they first slept
with one another, deceiving their dear parents.[24] Nor do we want to show
the binding of Ares and Aphrodite by Hephaestus for the same kind of
behaviour.'[25]

'No, I certainly don't think that is the right sort of thing to show,' he
said.

---

[22] *Odyssey* 9.8–10: a selective quotation of the proverbially clever Odysseus' actual
remark after hearing the bard Demodocus sing, which is rather that no situation is
more delightful than when banqueters sit listening happily to a singer, among laden
tables.

[23] *Odyssey* 12.342. The speaker is one of Odysseus' shipwrecked crew, Eurylochus,
urging his fellows to eat the sacred cattle of the Sun god. Odysseus has just commanded them to resist their hunger.

[24] The episode is narrated in *Iliad* 14.292–353. Hera, consort of Zeus, protests at the
shameless behaviour, but she has in fact planned the seduction all along.

[25] *Odyssey* 8.266–366. Hephaestus punishes his consort Aphrodite and her lover Ares
by trapping them under an invisible mesh while they are in bed together, then calling
on the other gods to witness their embarrassment

'On the other hand,' I said, 'if there are any examples, in the speeches
d   or actions of distinguished men, of endurance in the face of everything,
then these are models for them to observe and listen to. For example:

> He smote his chest, and thus rebuked his heart.
> Bear up, my heart. You have borne yet worse than this.'[26]

'Yes, those are unquestionably the right models,' he said.

'Then again, we must not allow our citizens to be corrupt or avaricious.'

'No.'

e   'We won't let them hear this recited, then:

> With gifts can gods, with gifts can noble kings
> Be swayed.[27]

We shall not praise Achilles' tutor Phoenix for giving sound advice to him,
to come to the defence of the Achaeans if he was rewarded with gifts, but
not lay aside his anger if there were no gifts.[28] Nor shall we think it right
391   – in fact, we shall not believe it – for Achilles himself to be so avaricious,
taking gifts from Agamemnon, or on another occasion refusing to release
Hector's body for burial except in return for payment.'[29]

'No,' he said, 'it would be quite wrong to praise this kind of behaviour.'

'It's only my high opinion of Homer,' I said, 'which stops me calling it
impious to talk like this, or give ear to people when they talk like this,
about Achilles. Or to suggest that he said to Apollo:

> Thou most destructive out of all the gods,
> Archer Apollo, thou hast injured me.
> I'd swiftly take revenge, had I the power.[30]

b   Or that he refused to obey the river-god, and offered to fight him.[31] Or
that he wanted to offer Patroclus, after his death, the locks of his hair
which were sacred to the other river, Spercheius:

[26] *Odyssey* 20.17–18. Odysseus, hearing his maidservants flirting with the suitors the
night before he is to take his vengeance on them all, banishes thoughts of immediate
slaughter.

[27] The quotation may be from Hesiod. The sentiment is cited as proverbial in
Euripides, *Medea* 964.

[28] *Iliad* 9.515–523. The gifts are from king Agamemnon, with whom Achilles has his
quarrel.

[29] *Iliad* 24.501–2, 552–562, 592–595.

[30] *Iliad* 22.15, 20. Apollo has tricked Achilles into allowing the Trojans to slip back
inside their city walls.

[31] Achilles challenges the river-god Scamander in *Iliad* 21.222 ff.

> Now let me give Patroclus, noble hero,
> This lock of hair, to take with him.[32]

We should not believe Achilles did this. As for his dragging Hector round
the tomb of Patroclus, and slaughtering live prisoners on his funeral

c pyre,[33] we shall not admit that any of these are true stories. Achilles was
the son of a goddess and of Peleus – a most sensible man and a grandson
of Zeus – and he was brought up by the wise Cheiron. We're not going to
have our people believing that he was so utterly disturbed as to possess
two completely contradictory faults – an avaricious meanness of spirit,
and great arrogance towards gods and men.'

'You are right,' he said.

'In which case,' I said, 'let us not believe either – and let us not allow

d people to say – that Theseus the son of Poseidon and Peirithous the son
of Zeus set off to carry out those disgraceful abductions, or that any other
hero and child of a god could bring himself to do terrible godless deeds
of the kind which nowadays are falsely attributed to them.[34] Let us
require poets to say either that these were not their actions or that they
were not the children of gods. They must not say both, and they must not

e try to persuade our young men that gods can father evil deeds, or that
heroes are no better than men. As we said earlier, these beliefs are both
impious and untrue. We proved, didn't we, that it is impossible for evil to
come into being from the gods?'[35]

'We did.'

'What is more, these beliefs are damaging to those who hear them.
Anyone will forgive himself for doing wrong if he believes that this sort
of thing was and is typical even of:

> The gods' close kin, those near to Zeus, who have
> An altar sacred to ancestral Zeus
> On Ida's mountain, high among the clouds,
> And in their veins the blood of demigods
> Has not run dry.[36]

[32] *Iliad* 23.151. Since he is now doomed to die at Troy, Achilles releases himself from
the vow made by his father to reserve the lock for a sacrifice to Spercheius, the river
of Achilles' homeland, upon his return.

[33] Dragging Hector: *Iliad* 24.14–21; slaughtering the prisoners: *Iliad* 23.175–176.

[34] In collusion with his cousin Peirithous, Theseus, king of Athens, abducted Helen
from Sparta to be his bride, thus provoking a war with Sparta. The pair then
attempted to abduct the goddess Persephone from the underworld to be bride to
Peirithous.   [35] 379a–380c.

[36] A fragment of Aeschylus' lost play *Niobe*. Niobe is speaking of her divine ancestry.
Her father Tantalus was son of Zeus.

That's why we must put a stop to stories of this kind, before they produce a totally casual attitude in our young men toward wickedness.'

392   'Yes, we must,' he said.

'Well, then,' I asked, 'in our definition of the kind of stories which may and may not be told, what class of stories is left? We have dealt with stories about the gods, and about demigods, heroes and the dead.'

'We have.'

'The final class, then, would be stories about mankind.'

'Clearly.'

'And we are not in a position to lay down rules for that just at the moment, my friend.'

'Why not?'

'Because we shall say, I imagine, that writers of poetry and prose both
b   make very serious errors about mankind. They say that lots of people are unjust but happy, or just but miserable, and that injustice pays if you can get away with it, whereas justice is what is good for someone else, but damaging to yourself. We shall stop them saying things like this, and tell them to say just the opposite in their poems and stories. Don't you think so?'

'I'm quite sure we shall,' he said.

'But if you admit I'm right about that, can't I claim that you have admitted what we have been trying to prove all along?'

'Yes,' he said, 'I see how the argument would go.'

c   'So we can't reach an agreement about mankind, and the kind of stories which should be told, until after we have discovered what sort of thing justice is, and shown that its nature is to be profitable for the person who possesses it, whether or not people *think* he is just.'

'Very true.'

'Let that be enough on the stories. The telling of them, I suggest, is the next thing for us to think about. Then we shall have completely covered both what should be told and how it should be told.'

'I don't understand,' said Adeimantus at this point. 'What do you mean?'

d   'It's important that you do understand, though,' I said. 'Here's a way of looking at it which may give you a better idea. Aren't all stories told by storytellers and poets really a narrative – of what has happened in the past, of what is happening now, or of what is going to happen in the future?'

'Well, obviously.'

'Don't they achieve their purpose either by simple narrative, or by narrative expressed through imitation, or by a combination of the two?'

'There again, I'm afraid, I still need a clearer explanation.'

'As a teacher,' I said, 'I seem to have a laughable inability to make my meaning clear. I'd better do what people who are no good at speaking do – avoid generalisations, take a particular example, and try to use that to
e show you what I mean. You know the beginning of the *Iliad*, where the poet says that Chryses asks Agamemnon to let his daughter go, and Agamemnon loses his temper, and then Chryses, when his request is
393 turned down, utters a prayer to Apollo against the Achaeans?'

'Yes. I do.'

'In that case, you must be aware that down as far as the lines

> He implored the Achaean lords, but most of all
> Atreus' two sons, the marshals of the host,[37]

the poet speaks in person. He does not attempt to direct our imagination towards anyone else, or suggest that someone other than himself is
b speaking. But in the lines which follow he talks as if he himself *is* Chryses, and does everything he can to make us imagine it is not Homer speaking, but the priest. He talks like an old man. The whole of the rest of his narrative is constructed along more or less the same lines – not only events at Troy, but also events in Ithaca, and the whole of the *Odyssey*.'

'Exactly,' he said.

'But it's all narrative – both the individual speeches he delivers and the bits he says in between the speeches?'

'Yes, of course.'

c 'And when he makes a speech in the character of someone else, can we say that he always makes his own style as close as possible to that of the person he tells us is speaking?'

'No question of it.'

'But making yourself resemble someone else – either in the way you speak or in the way you look – isn't that imitating the person you make yourself resemble?'

'Of course it is.'

'In passages like this, apparently, Homer and the rest of the poets use imitation to construct their narrative.'

'Yes.'

'If there were no passages where the poet concealed his own person,

---

[37] *Iliad* 1.15–16. The passage Socrates is discussing runs from line 8 to line 42. Chryses, a priest of Apollo, comes to ransom his daughter. She has been captured in a raid by the Greeks (Achaeans) and is in the possession of the supreme commander Agamemnon, son of Atreus.

d then his whole work, his whole narrative, would have been created without using imitation. To save you telling me again that you don't understand how this can be, I will explain. Imagine Homer told us that Chryses came, bringing his daughter's ransom, as a suppliant to the Achaeans, and in particular to their kings, but then went on to tell the story not in the person of Chryses, but still as Homer. You realise that would be simple narrative, not imitation. The story would go something

e like this. I'm no poet, so I won't tell it in verse: "The priest came and prayed that the gods might grant to the Achaeans that they should capture Troy, and return home safely, but he asked them to release his daughter in return for the ransom, and out of reverence for the god. When he had finished, the rest of the Achaeans showed him respect, and would have agreed to his request, but Agamemnon lost his temper, telling him to depart immediately, and not come back again; otherwise his priest's staff and the god's garlands would be no protection to him. The priest's

394 daughter would be an old woman living in Argos with him before there was any question of releasing her. He told the priest to go away and stop bothering him, if he wanted to get home safely. The old man was alarmed by Agamemnon's threats, and went away in silence. But after he had left the camp he addressed many prayers to Apollo, calling on the cult-names of the god, reminding him of past favours, and asking his help in return if he had ever, in the building of temples or the sacrifice of victims, given the god a gift which had been a source of pleasure to him. In return for these favours, he prayed that Apollo's arrows might make the Achaeans

b pay for his tears." That, my friend, is the simple narrative, without imitation.'

'I see,' he said.

'In that case,' I said, 'you can also see that you get just the opposite if you omit what the poet says between the speeches, and leave the dialogue.'

'Yes, I can see that too,' he said. 'That's the kind of thing you get in tragedy.'

'Exactly,' I said. 'Now I think I can make clear to you what I couldn't make clear before, that one type of poetry and storytelling is purely

c imitative – this is tragedy and comedy, as you say. In another type, the poet tells his own story. I imagine you'd find this mainly in dithyramb. The third type, using both imitation and narrative, can be found in epic poetry, and in many other places as well.[38] Are you following me?'

---

[38] Tragedy and comedy were in Socrates' and Plato's day the pre-eminent forms of literature. The dithyramb was a type of choral lyric, originally connected with the cult

'Yes. I see now what you were getting at.'

'Now, let me remind you what we have just been saying. We said we had decided *what* stories should be told, but still had to look into the question *how* they should be told.'

'Yes, I remember that.'

d   'So the thing I was really trying to say we should make up our minds about was this. Shall we permit poets to use imitation in their works? Or partly imitation and partly narrative? In which case, when should they use one, and when the other? Or should they not use imitation at all?'

'Let me make a prediction,' he said. 'You're going to ask whether or not we should allow tragedy and comedy into our city.'

'Possibly,' I said. 'Possibly more than that, even. I don't know yet. But we have set sail, and must go where the wind, or the argument, blows us.'

e   'You are right,' he said.

'Here's a question for you, then, Adeimantus. Do we want our guardians to be given to imitation, or not? Or does the same principle apply here as applied earlier?[39] The principle was that each individual can only do one thing well. He can't do lots of things. If he tries, he will be jack of all trades, and master of none.'

'Yes, it does apply. Why shouldn't it?'

'Does it apply to imitation as well? Is the same person incapable of imitating many things as well as he can imitate one?'

'Of course.'

395   'So he's unlikely both to follow one of the worthwhile occupations and also to be a versatile imitator, and given to imitation. After all, the same people aren't even able to be successful in two apparently quite similar forms of imitation such as comedy and tragedy. You did classify both of those, just now, as types of imitation?'

'I did. And you're right. The same people can't be good at both.'

'Nor as reciters and actors either.'[40]

'True.'

b   'The same people can't even be actors in comedy as well as tragedy. These are all examples of imitation, aren't they?'

'Yes, they are.'

---

of Dionysus. The 'other places' in which both imitation and narrative are found would include the victory odes of Pindar and much other lyric poetry.

[39]   369e–370c, 374a–d.

[40]   'Reciters' (or 'rhapsodes') specialised in the performance of epic poetry, that of Homer above all. They did not act in drama.

'What's more, Adeimantus, I think man's nature is a currency minted into even smaller denominations than these. This means he can't be good at imitating many different things, nor good at doing the many real things of which the imitations are copies.'

'Very true,' he said.

'So if we stick to our original plan, which was that our guardians should
c be released from all other occupations, and be the true architects of freedom for our city, and that everything they do must contribute to this end, it is essential that they do not do or imitate anything else. If they do imitate anything, then from their earliest childhood they should choose appropriate models to imitate – people who are brave, self-disciplined, god-fearing, free, that sort of thing. They should neither do, nor be good at imitating, what is illiberal, nor any other kind of shameful behaviour, in case enjoyment of the imitation gives rise to enjoyment of the reality. Have you
d never noticed how imitation, if long continued from an early age, becomes part of a person's nature, turns into habits of body, speech and mind?'

'I certainly have,' he said.

'So imitating a woman, young or old, maybe abusing her husband, or
e competing with the gods and boasting about her good fortune, or in the grip of disaster, or grief, or mourning, will not be a legitimate activity for the people we say we are interested in – the ones we wanted to grow up into the right sort of men. They are, after all, men. And still less do we want them imitating a woman who is ill, or in love, or in childbirth.'

'Absolutely not,' he said.

'Nor should they imitate female or male slaves behaving in the way slaves behave.'

'No. Not that either.'

'Nor the wrong sort of men, presumably: cowards, and those whose behaviour is the opposite of what we said just now they *should* imitate –
396 men who insult or ridicule one another, or use bad language, drunk or for that matter sober, and all the other faults which people of this sort are guilty of in their language and behaviour towards themselves and others. Nor, in my opinion, should they get in the habit of modelling themselves, in their language or behaviour, on people who are mad. They must recognise madness and wickedness in men and women, but none of this is behaviour for them to adopt or imitate.'

'Very true,' he said.

'What about people working in bronze?' I asked. 'Or practising some

other art or skill? Or rowing triremes, or calling the time to the rowers,[41] or any other activity of this type? Should our guardians
b imitate them?'

'How can they,' he said, 'if they are not even allowed to be interested in any of them?'

'What about horses neighing and bulls bellowing? Will they imitate those? Or the sound of rivers, or the sea breaking on the shore, or thunder, or anything of that sort?'

'No. They are forbidden either to be mad or to behave like those who are mad.'

'If I understand you rightly, then,' I said, 'there is a form of speech and
c of narrative which is the one the right sort of man would employ when he needed to say something, and then again a second form of speech, quite unlike the first, which would appeal to a man with the opposite kind of nature and upbringing, and which he would employ.'

'What are these forms of speech?'

'I think the decent man, when he comes in his narrative to some saying or action of a good man, will be prepared to report it as if he himself really were the person concerned. He will not be ashamed of an imitation of this sort. He will imitate the good man most when he acts in a responsible and
d wise manner, and will imitate him less, and less fully, when the good man is led astray by disease or passion, or by drunkenness or misfortune of some kind. When he comes to someone who is unworthy of him, I think he'll refuse to make any serious attempt to resemble one who is his inferior – except perhaps briefly, when the character is doing something good
e – both because he has had no training in imitating people like this, and because he resents shaping and modelling himself on the pattern of his inferiors. Inwardly he treats behaviour of this sort as beneath him – unless of course it's in jest.'

'Very likely,' he said.

'So he'll use the kind of narrative we described a few moments ago, when we were talking about Homer's epics. The way he tells stories will combine both styles, imitation and the other kind of narrative, but with only a small amount of imitation even in a long story. Or have I got it wrong?'

'No,' he said, 'this is bound to be the style of a speaker of this sort.'

[41] These military tasks were performed by the poorest class of Athenian society.

397   'Now, as for the speaker who is not of this sort, the worse he is, the more prepared he will be to use imitation all the time.[42] There is nothing he will regard as beneath him, and so he will take it upon himself, in all seriousness, and at public performances, to imitate all the things we were talking about just now – thunder, the din of wind and hail, of wheels and pulleys,

b   the sound of trumpet, pipe, panpipe, and every musical instrument, even the noise of dogs, or sheep, or birds. Will the way this man tells stories consist entirely of imitation, in word and gesture, with maybe a small element of narrative?'

'Again, it's bound to.'

'There you are, then,' I said. 'That's what I meant when I said there were two styles of storytelling.'

'I accept that,' he said. 'There *are* two.'

'Of these two styles the first involves only slight variations. If he uses a musical mode and rhythm which are right for his style, it is pretty well possible for the person who tells stories in the right way – since the vari

c   ations in his style are very slight – to achieve musical consistency, using a single mode and of course a similarly appropriate rhythm.'

'That is certainly true.'

'What about the style of the other storyteller? Because of the enormous range of variations it contains, won't it need just the opposite treatment – all the musical modes, and every kind of rhythm – if it too is to be told in a way appropriate to it?'

'Undoubtedly.'

'Do all poets, then, and storytellers of all kinds, hit upon one or other of these styles, or some combination of the two?'

'They must,' he said.

d   'In that case,' I asked, 'what shall our policy be? Shall we allow them all into our city? Or one or other of the pure styles? Or the mixed style?'

'If my view prevails,' he said, 'we shall allow only the pure imitator of the good man.'

'And yet the mixed style is enjoyable as well, Adeimantus. In fact, the one which is the exact opposite of the one you are selecting is by far the most enjoyable, in the opinion of children and their attendants, and of the population at large.'

'Yes, it is the most enjoyable.'

'Possibly, however, you would say that this style is not in tune with our

---

[42] An alternative version of Plato's text yields the translation: 'the more prepared he will be to narrate anything and everything'.

e regime. Our men do not have a dual or manifold nature, since each of
   them performs only one task.'

   'No, it is not in tune.'

   'Is this the reason, then, why ours is the only city in which we shall
   find a shoemaker who is only a shoemaker, and not a ship's captain as
   well as a shoemaker, a farmer who is only a farmer, and not a juryman
   as well as a farmer, a soldier who is only a soldier, and not a businessman
   as well as a soldier, and the others the same?'

   'Yes,' he said.

398 'Suppose, then, there were a man so wondrous wise as to be utterly versatile, able to imitate anything. If he came to our city wanting to perform
   his poems in person, it looks as if we would fall down before him, tell him
   he was sacred, exceptional and delightful, but then explain to him that we
   do not have men like him in our city, that it is not right for them to be
   there. We would pour myrrh over his head, garland him with woollen garlands, and send him on his way to some other city.[43] For our own good,

b we would content ourselves with a simpler, if less enjoyable, poet and
   storyteller, who can imitate the decent man's way of speaking, and model
   his stories on those patterns which we laid down at the beginning of our
   attempt to provide an education for our soldiers.'

   'Yes, that is certainly what we should do, if it were up to us.'

   'Well, my friend,' I said, 'on the poetic and musical side of our education it looks as if we have dealt pretty fully with the section on stories
   and myths. We have laid down both what stories are to be told and how
   they are to be told.'

   'Yes, I agree,' he said. 'I think we have dealt with that.'

c 'Well then, does that leave the question of styles of songs and music?'

   'Obviously it does.'

   'Presumably anyone could now work out the kind of character we need
   to prescribe for those, to be in harmony with what has been laid down
   already.'

   Glaucon laughed. 'It looks, in that case, Socrates, as if I'm not
   "anyone." I'm not sure I'd trust myself to make a guess, on the spur of
   the moment, about the sort of thing we ought to prescribe. Though I have
   a pretty good idea.'

---

[43] Lavish treatment with myrrh and garlands was given to statues of a deity. But these
statues were not then expelled from the city; this suggests rather the expulsion of a
sacred scapegoat in order to remove impurities from the community, as in the annual
festival of the Thargelia.

'What you certainly can say with some confidence, I imagine, is that
d music is essentially composed of three elements: words, harmonic mode[44]
and rhythm.'

'Yes, I can say that,' he said.

'As far as the words go, then, they are no different from words which
are not set to music. Shouldn't they conform to the same patterns we laid
down just now, and be in the same style?'

'Yes, they should.'

'What is more, the mode and rhythm must follow from the words.'[45]

'Of course.'

'And mourning and lamentation were things we said we could do
without in our stories.'

'They were.'

e   'Which then are the mourning modes? You're musical. You tell me.'

'The Mixolydian,' he said. 'The Syntonolydian. That sort of thing.'

'Should these be banned, then?' I asked. 'After all, they are no use even
to women – if we want them to be good women – let alone to men.'[46]

'They certainly should.'

'Drunkenness is also something quite unsuitable for our guardians.
And so are luxury and laziness.'

'Of course they are.'

'Which of the modes, then, are appropriate to luxury and parties?'

'There are some Ionian modes,' he said, 'and again Lydian, which are
called relaxed.'

399   'Will these be any use to men of a warlike disposition?'

'No,' he said. 'So it looks as if that leaves you with the Dorian and
Phrygian.'

'I don't know about modes,' I said. 'Leave me the mode which can most
fittingly imitate the voice and accents of a brave man in time of war, or in
any externally imposed crisis. When things go wrong, and he faces death

---

44 The several harmonic modes (*harmoniai*) of Greek music are literally 'attunements'.
     The chief component of each mode was a fixed series of tonal intervals, but other
     matters beyond the bare notes of the scale seem also to have been specified, such as
     the relative frequency of the notes to be used, and the tessitura (the degree of high
     or low singing required). Thus the choice of mode could determine the style of the
     musical piece, and from early times differences in mode went with differences in
     poetic genre, occasion and mood. For further details consult M. L. West, *Ancient
     Greek Music* (Oxford: Oxford University Press, 1992).
45 A conventional but conservative opinion, which came under increased pressure
     during the fourth century from the rise of virtuoso instrumental playing.
46 Ritualised keening at funerals was the province of women rather than men.

b   and wounds, or encounters some other danger, in all these situations he
holds out to the end in a disciplined and steadfast manner. Plus another
mode for someone engaged in some peaceful, voluntary, freely chosen
activity. He might be trying to persuade someone of something, making
some request – praying to a god, or giving instructions or advice to a man.
Or just the opposite. He might be listening patiently to someone else
making a request, or explaining something to him, or trying to get him to
c   change his mind, and on that basis acting as he thinks best – without arrogance, acting prudently and calmly in all these situations, and being
content with the outcome. These two modes, then. One for adversity and
one for freely chosen activity, the modes which will best imitate the voices
of the prudent and of the brave in failure and success. Leave me those.'

'Leave you, in other words, with precisely the two I suggested just
now,' he said.[47]

'That means we shan't want an enormous range of strings, and every
possible mode, in our songs and melodies.'

'No, I think not,' he said.

d   'In which case we shan't produce any makers of those triangular harps,
or regular harps, or all those many-stringed instruments which can play
many modes.'[48]

'Apparently not.'

'What about the makers and players of reed instruments? Will you
allow them into your city? Isn't playing a reed instrument more "many-
stringed" than anything else? And aren't the instruments which can play
many modes in fact just imitations of the reed-pipe?'

'Yes, obviously they are.'

'That leaves you the lyre and the cithara,' I said.[49] 'They'll be right for
the city. In the countryside, by contrast, there could be some sort of
panpipe for our herdsmen.'

---

[47] The classification of the Dorian mode as dignified and manly was long established,
but the standard association of the Phrygian was rather with the freedom shown in
excitement, as in ecstatic religious ritual.

[48] Harps were of Lydian origin and retained associations of foreignness.

[49] The reed-pipe (*aulos*) was nothing like a flute (the traditional translation of the word)
but more like an oboe or clarinet. It had a strong and uncompromising tone, and was
the favoured instrument of the wilder sorts of religious ritual. Many notes could be
produced from manipulation of a single hole, whereas each string of a lyre produced
only a single note. The lyre and the cithara were the fundamental stringed instruments. Their principal service was that of duplicating the sung melody. The reed
pipe, by contrast, lent itself to solos.

e   'Well, that's certainly the way our reasoning points,' he said.

'There's nothing very radical,' I said, 'in our preferring Apollo and Apollo's instruments to Marsyas and his instruments.'

'Good heavens, no,' he said. 'I'm sure there isn't.'

'Ye dogs!' I said.[50] 'Without meaning to, we have purged the city we said was too luxurious.'

'That was sensible of us,' he said.

'Come on, then,' I said. 'Let's purge the rest of it. Our next concern after mode will be rhythm. We should not pursue complexity, nor do we
400   want all kinds of metres. We should see what are the rhythms of a self-disciplined and courageous life, and after looking at those, make the metre and melody conform to the speech of someone like that. We won't make speech conform to rhythm and melody. Which these rhythms are is for you to say, as it was with the modes.'

'I really don't know what to say about that,' he said. 'In my experience, there are three types of rhythm from which metres are woven together, just as when it comes to tones, there are four elements from which all the modes are derived. But I have no idea which types imitate which lives.'

b   'That's something we can ask Damon about,' I said. 'He can tell us which metres are appropriate to meanness of spirit, arrogance, madness and other faults of character, and which rhythms should be left for those whose character is the opposite. I seem to remember, though I can't be sure, hearing him use terms like "composite enoplion"; then there were "dactyls," and "heroic metre," which he arranged, somehow or other, so that upbeat and downbeat were made equal as it turns into short or long
c   at the end. Then there was the "iambic," I seem to remember, and another he called "trochaic," with their long and short syllables. For some of them, I think he condemned or approved the pulse of the metrical feet as much as the rhythms themselves.[51] Or possibly it was the two together, I can't be sure. All these questions, as I say, can be referred to Damon. It

---

[50] It is characteristic of Socrates to swear 'by the dog' – a euphemistic oath, comparable to our substitution of 'gosh!' for 'God!'

[51] Greek metre was based on length of syllable rather than stress-accent. One long syllable was the equal of two short. The three types of rhythm fundamental to poetic metre correspond to different proportions between the divisions (upbeat and downbeat) of the metrical foot: 2:2 or equal as in dactyl ($\bar{\ } \breve{\ }\breve{\ }$), spondee ($\bar{\ }\bar{\ }$) and anapaest ($\breve{\ }\breve{\ }\bar{\ }$); 2:1 or double as in iamb ($\breve{\ }\bar{\ }$) and trochee ($\bar{\ }\breve{\ }$); 3:2 as in cretic ($\bar{\ }\breve{\ }\bar{\ }$). The enoplion (or 'martial') was a rhythm used for processional and marching songs; heroic metre is the dactylic hexameter of Homeric epic, in which dactyl and spondee can be substituted for each other.

would take us a long time to decide them. Or do you think we should try?'

'God forbid.'

'But that gracefulness and want of grace can follow on from what is
d rhythmical and unrhythmical, that is something you *can* decide.'

'Of course.'

'But then if rhythm and mode follow language, as we said just now, and
not the other way round, what is rhythmical must follow and imitate fine
language, while what is not rhythmical follows the opposite. The same
with harmony and discord.'

'Yes, rhythm and mode certainly should follow language,' he said.

'What about manner of speaking,' I asked, 'and what is actually said?
Don't they follow from the nature of the speaker's soul?'

'Of course.'

'And the other things follow from manner of speaking?'

'Yes.'

'In that case, all these things – the right way of speaking, the right
e attunement, grace and rhythm – follow from a good nature. I don't mean
the good nature which is the polite name we give to stupidity,[52] but the
true intelligence which consists in a character which is rightly and properly constituted.'

'Exactly,' he said.

'So if the young are to perform their proper function, aren't these the
qualities they should be everywhere aiming at?'

'They are.'

401 'Painting is full of these qualities, I imagine, as is any skill of the same
sort. So are weaving, embroidery, building – the manufacture of any
household object, in fact – even the condition of our bodies and of all
things that grow. All these contain gracefulness and want of grace. Want
of grace or rhythm, and wrong attunement, are close relatives of wrong
speech and a wrong nature, while their opposites are close relatives and
imitations of the opposite, the self-disciplined and good nature.'

'Precisely,' he said.

b 'Is it only the poets we have to keep an eye on, then, compelling them
to put the likeness of the good nature into their poems, or else go and write
poems somewhere else? Don't we have to keep an eye on the other craftsmen as well, and stop them putting what has the wrong nature, what is
undisciplined, slavish or wanting in grace, into their representations of

---

[52] *Eu-ētheia*, 'good nature', more usually meant 'simplicity' in the disparaging sense.

living things, or into buildings, or into any manufactured object? Anyone who finds this impossible is not to be allowed to be a craftsman in our city.

c That way our guardians will not be brought up among images of what is bad, like animals put out to graze on bad pasture. We don't want them browsing and feeding each day – taking in a little here and a little there – and without realising it accumulating a single large evil in their souls. No, we must seek out the craftsmen with a gift for tracking down the nature of what is fine, what has grace, so that our young can live in a healthy environment, drawing improvement from every side, whenever things which are beautifully fashioned expose their eyes or ears to some whole-

d some breeze from healthy regions and lead them imperceptibly, from earliest childhood, into affinity, friendship and harmony with beauty of speech and thought.'

'Yes, that would be by far the best way for them to be brought up,' he said.

'Aren't there two reasons, Glaucon, why musical and poetic education is so important? Firstly because rhythm and mode penetrate more deeply into the inner soul than anything else does; they have the most powerful

e effect on it, since they bring gracefulness with them. They make a person graceful, if he is rightly brought up, and the opposite, if he is not. And secondly because anyone with the right kind of education in this area will have the clearest perception of things which are unsatisfactory – things which are badly made or naturally defective. Being quite rightly disgusted by them, he will praise what is beautiful and fine. Delighting in it, and

402 receiving it into his soul, he will feed on it and so become noble and good. What is ugly he will rightly condemn and hate, even before he is old enough for rational thought. And when rationality does make its appearance, won't the person who has been brought up in this way recognise it because of its familiarity, and be particularly delighted with it?'

'Yes,' he said. 'If you ask me, that certainly is the point of a musical and poetic education.'

'It's just like learning to read,' I said. 'We could do it as soon as we realised that there are only a few letters, and that they keep recurring in all the words which contain them. We never dismissed them as unworthy of our attention, either in short words or in long, but were keen to

b recognise them everywhere, in the belief that we would not be able to read until we could do this.'

'True.'

'Well, then. We shan't recognise copies of the letters – supposing reflections of them were to appear in water, or in a mirror – until we can recognise the letters themselves. Don't both involve the same skill and expertise?'

'Of course they do.'

c 'And isn't it, as I say, exactly the same with musical and poetic education? There's not the remotest chance of becoming properly educated – either for ourselves or for the people we say we must educate to be our guardians – until we recognise the sort of thing self-discipline is. Likewise courage, liberality and generosity of spirit, which keep recurring all over the place, plus all the qualities which are closely related to them, and their opposites. We must see the presence both of them and of their likenesses in all the things they are present in, and we must learn never to dismiss them, be the context trivial or important, but to regard them as part of the same skill and expertise.'

'Yes,' he said, 'it is absolutely essential that we learn this.'

d 'So if someone is lucky enough to possess a soul containing a good character, and a physical form which matches and harmonises with that character, which is modelled on the same pattern, wouldn't that be the fairest of sights for anyone with eyes to see it?'

'Very much so.'

'But what is fairest is most desirable.'

'Naturally.'

'So the well educated man will fall in love with people as much like this as possible. But he will not fall in love with someone whose soul and body are out of tune.'

'Not if the defect is in the soul,' he said. 'If it is in the body, he might put up with it, and be prepared to love him.'

e 'Ah, yes, of course,' I said. 'Am I right in thinking you are – or were – the lover of a boy like this? Anyway, be that as it may, I think you're right. Now, the next question. Does too much pleasure have anything to do with self-discipline?'

'How could it? Too much pleasure makes you as irrational as pain does.'

'Does it have anything to do with any other good quality?'

'No.'

403 'How about arrogance and indiscipline? Does it have anything to do with those?'

'Yes, everything.'

'Can you think of any pleasure greater or keener than sexual pleasure?'

'No,' he said. 'Nor a more insane pleasure, either.'

'Whereas the right sort of love is by its nature the self-controlled and harmonious love of what is self-disciplined and beautiful?'

'Precisely,' he said.

'So we must not offer the right sort of lover what is insane, or what is related to lack of discipline?'

'No, we mustn't.'

b　'In which case we mustn't offer him sexual pleasure, must we? Neither lover nor boy must have anything to do with it, if they are loving and being loved in the right way.'

'Good heavens, no, Socrates. We certainly mustn't offer them that.'

'You will pass a law to that effect, presumably, in this city you are founding. A lover can kiss his boy friend, spend time with him and touch him, as he would a son – for beauty's sake, and if the boy says "yes." Apart

c　from that, his relationship with the boy he is interested in should never allow anyone to imagine he has gone any further than that. Otherwise he will be condemned as uneducated, and blind to beauty.'

'Yes, I shall pass a law to that effect,' he said.

'Well, then, do you think our discussion of musical and poetic education has come to an end?' I asked. 'It has certainly ended where it *ought* to end. Music and poetry ought, I take it, to end in love of beauty.'

'I agree,' he said.

'And after musical and poetic education, our young men must be given a physical education.'

'Naturally.'

d　'Here, too, from their earliest childhood and throughout their lives, they must be brought up very carefully. The situation is something like this, I believe, but see what you think. It's my opinion that if the body is in good shape, it does not by its own excellence make the soul good. On the other hand, a good soul *can* by its own excellence make a body as good as it is capable of being. What is your opinion?'

'I agree with you,' he said.

'Let's assume we have made adequate provision for the mind. If we

e　were now to entrust it with making detailed prescriptions for the body, contenting ourselves for brevity's sake with providing general guidelines, would we be going about things in the right way?'

'We would.'

'Well, drunkenness was one thing we said they should avoid. A guard is the last person who can be allowed to get drunk, and not know where on earth he is.'

'Yes,' he said, 'it's absurd for a guardian to need a guardian.'

'What about their food? After all, these men are competing for us, aren't they, in the most important of all competitions?'

'Yes.'

'In that case, would the diet of present-day athletes be the right thing
404 for them?'

'It might well be.'

'It's a pretty soporific diet,' I said, 'and unreliable from a health point of view. Haven't you noticed that these athletes spend most of their lives asleep, and that if they depart even slightly from their prescribed regime, they contract serious and acute diseases?'

'Yes, I have noticed that.'

'We need something a bit less crude as a regimen for our warrior-athletes. It's vital that they should be alert, like hounds, as keen of sight and
b hearing as possible, and capable, when they are on active service, of tolerating a variety of drink and food, extremes of heat, storms, without any adverse effect on their health.'

'Yes, I think I agree.'

'Well, then, won't the best physical education be sister, in a way, to the musical and poetic education we have just outlined?'

'How do you mean?'

'It will be physical education, I take it, of a simple and judicious type – especially since it is intended for those who are soldiers.'

'Simple and judicious in what way?'

'This is the sort of thing you could learn from Homer, actually. In the
c heroes' feasts when they are on campaign, you remember, he does not feast them on fish – despite the fact that they are on the Hellespont, right by the sea – nor on stewed meat, but only on roast, which is what soldiers would find easiest to cope with. Wherever you are, more or less, it is easier just to use fire than to carry pots and pans around with you.'

'It certainly is.'

'As for seasonings, Homer never, as far as I remember, says anything about them. All athletes know, don't they, that if you want your body to be in good shape you must avoid anything like that?'

'They are right about this,' he said, 'and they do well to avoid that kind of thing.'

d   'Then if you think this is right, my friend, Syracusan cuisine and the
Sicilian *à la carte* are apparently not things you approve of.'[53]

'No, I don't think I do approve of them.'

'Then you disapprove also of Corinthian girl friends for men who are
going to be in good shape physically.'[54]

'Definitely.'

'How about the delights, so-called, of Attic pastries?'

'I have no choice but to condemn those too.'

'I suspect that if we likened these foods, and this whole regimen, to the
e   music and song that uses every mode and all the rhythms, that would be
an accurate comparison.'

'Indeed it would.'

'There, variety and luxury bred indiscipline. Here it breeds disease.
And as simplicity in music and poetry gave souls self-discipline, so simplicity in physical training gives bodies health, doesn't it?'

'That is absolutely right,' he said.

405   'As lawlessness and disease multiply in a city, don't lawcourts and
clinics start opening up all over the place? And when even free men, in
large numbers, start taking them seriously, don't these disciplines become
extremely self-important?'

'How can they fail to?'

'You won't be able to find any clearer evidence of bad, inferior education in a city, will you, than the need for skilled doctors and judges. And
b   not just among ordinary manual workers, but even among those with pretensions to a free and enlightened upbringing? Don't you think it's a disgrace, and a sure sign of poor education, to be forced to rely on an
extraneous justice – that of masters or judges – for want of a sense of
justice of one's own?'[55]

'The greatest disgrace possible,' he said.

'And yet, is it really any more disgraceful, would you say, than the
person who in addition to spending the greater part of his life in the law-

---

[53] Sicily in general, and the court of Dionysius at Syracuse in particular, were noted
for elaborate cuisine.

[54] Corinth was a noted supplier of *hetairai* – female dining companions, professionals
something like the Japanese geisha, except that sex was taken for granted as part of
the service.

[55] Athenian lawcourts were in fact staffed by amateurs – jurymen chosen by lot from a
pool of citizen volunteers, and a judge who was no more than a presiding magistrate,
also chosen by lot, and held office only for a year. Hence the word translated as
'judges' at 405a also means 'jurors'.

courts as defendant or plaintiff, is also convinced, such is his ignorance
c of what is good, that his cleverness at committing crimes, and his subsequent ability to use every evasion and loophole to escape conviction and
avoid paying the penalty, is actually a matter for self-congratulation? And
all for the sake of what is trivial and of no importance, because he does
not realise how much finer and better it is to see to it that his life does not
depend on finding a juror who is half-asleep.'

'You're right,' he said. 'That is worse than the previous example.'

'And don't you think it's a disgrace,' I asked, 'to need medical
d attention, not as a result of injuries or the onset of some seasonal illness,
but because our inactivity, and a routine such as we have described, have
filled us up with gas and ooze, like a marsh, and compelled those clever
doctors of the school of Asclepius to invent names like "wind" and "flux"
for our diseases?'

'Yes, they really do have some extraordinary new names for diseases,'
he said.

e 'It wasn't so, I believe, in Asclepius' time. I am thinking of his sons, at
Troy. When Eurypylus is wounded, and is given Pramnian wine with a lot
406 of barley sprinkled over it and cheese grated on to it – which does indeed
seem likely to cause a fever – they do not criticise the woman who gives
him the drink, nor do they find fault with Patroclus, who is responsible
for the treatment.'

'Yes, it certainly is a surprising drink to give someone in that con
dition.'

'Until you remember,' I said, 'that it was not until the time of
Herodicus, or so they say, that the school of Asclepius took up the modern
medicine which is a slave to the disease. Herodicus was an athletics coach
b who became an invalid. With a combination of physical regimen and
medicine, he started off by making his own life a misery, and then gradu
ated to making other people's lives a misery as well   lots of them.'

'How did he do that?'

'By making his own death such a long-drawn-out business,' I said. 'He
devoted himself to his terminal illness – without ever really managing to
cure himself – and spent his whole life completely wrapped up in the
business of being a patient. He had a wretched time if he departed in any
way from his normal routine, but using his knowledge to give himself a
hard death, he did reach old age.'

'A fine reward for his skill,' he said.

c 'No more than he deserved, for not realising that Asclepius' failure to explain this branch of medicine to his sons was not the result of ignorance or lack of experience. It was because he knew that in any well–run society each citizen has his own appointed function to perform in the state, and that no one can afford to spend his whole life being ill and being an invalid. We recognise this when it's the man in the street, but then rather absurdly fail to recognise it in the case of those who are rich and supposedly fortunate.'

'What do you mean?'

d   'When a carpenter falls ill,' I said, 'he has no objection to taking some medicine from the doctor to purge the disease, or to getting rid of it by means of an emetic, or cauterisation, or surgery. But if he is prescribed a long course of treatment, and has to wear special caps,[56] with all that involves, he'll soon tell you he can't afford to be ill, and that life is not worth living if he has to spend all his time thinking about his illness, and

e neglecting his business. Then he'll bid a doctor of this kind good day, and resume his normal routine. If he regains his health, he can get on with his life, and do his work. If he is too weak physically, he will die, and so escape his troubles.'

'Yes, I think that's the right kind of attitude towards medicine for someone like that.'

407   'Because he had a certain function to perform,' I said, 'and his life was worth nothing to him if he couldn't perform it?'

'Clearly.'

'Whereas the rich man, in our view, has no prescribed function of the kind which makes life not worth living if he is forced to give it up.'

'Not if we're to believe what people say.'

'You're obviously not aware of Phocylides' saying, that once you have the means of subsistence you should start to practise goodness.'

'I am aware of it,' he said, 'but I don't think people should wait that long.'

'Well, we won't argue with him about that,' I said. 'However, here's a

b question we *can* settle for ourselves. Is practising goodness something the rich man should devote himself to, and is life not worth living for a rich man who can't devote himself to it? Or is being an invalid a handicap to carpentry, or any other art or skill, because it stops people concentrating on them, and yet not an impediment to following Phocylides' advice?'

---

[56] Felt caps for the head, typically worn by long-term invalids – not a treatment, but something like staying on the couch all day in one's dressing-gown.

'It certainly is an impediment,' he said. 'In fact, this exaggerated concern for the body, going beyond normal physical exercise, is just about the greatest impediment of all. It creates difficulties when you are running a household, or on military service, or even in some sedentary job holding public office.'

c 'Worst of all,' I said, 'it is a problem when it comes to any form of learning, thought or self-development. Concern for the body is for ever imagining headaches or dizziness, and saying they are caused by philosophy, so that wherever it appears, it is in every way an impediment to the practice and study of virtue. It makes people spend their whole time thinking they are ill. They can't stop worrying about their bodies.'

'That wouldn't surprise me,' he said.

'Are we going to say, then, that this too is something Asclepius was aware of? There are some people whose constitution and regimen give

d them good physical health, but who have contracted some identifiable illness. It was for their benefit, and for people in their situation, that he taught the art of medicine, using drugs and surgery to rid them of their diseases, but then prescribing their normal daily routine, to avoid disruption to civic life, whereas he did not try to prescribe for those whose bodies are internally riddled with disease. He didn't try to draw off a little bit here, pour in a little bit there, and in this way give men long and unpleasant lives, and enable them to produce children, in all probability, no

e different from themselves. He thought it wrong to treat those who were unable to take their place in the daily round, on the grounds that they were worth nothing either to themselves or to the city.'

'A bit of a statesman, your Asclepius.'

'He obviously was. And as for his children – with a father like that –

408 you can see both that they distinguished themselves at Troy on the field of battle, and that they employed medicine in the way I have described. Do you remember how they treated Menelaus for the wound he received from Pandarus?

> They sucked the blood,
> And to the wound applied their soothing herbs.[57]

They did not try to tell him what he should eat or drink afterwards, any more than they tried to tell Eurypylus. They thought that for men who had been in good health and living a sober life before they were wounded,

b their drugs were a sufficient cure. They could even drink a posset of

[57] *Iliad* 4.218.

barley and cheese immediately afterwards. But if someone was naturally unhealthy, and leading a dissolute life, they regarded his life as of no value either to himself or to anyone else. They did not believe their art was intended for people like this, and they refused to treat them, even if they were richer than Midas.'

'Very enlightened, the way you describe them, these sons of Asclepius.'

'So they should be,' I said. 'All the same, Pindar and the tragedians do
c not believe us. They say that Asclepius was the son of Apollo, that in return for gold he cured a rich man who was at death's door, and that for this he was struck by lightning. What we have said so far does not allow us to believe both parts of their story. If he was the son of a god, we shall say, then he was not mercenary. If he was mercenary, then he was not the son of a god.'

'I quite agree with you,' he said, 'as far as that goes. But there's another question I'd like to ask you, Socrates. We need good doctors in our city,
d don't we? And I imagine the best doctors will be the ones who have treated the greatest number of healthy and sick people. Similarly, the best judges will be those who have associated with all kinds of characters.'

'We certainly do need doctors,' I said. 'Good ones, that is. And do you know who I think the good ones are?'

'I will if you tell me,' he said.

'I'll try. But you're asking about two quite different things in the same question.'

'Why is that?'

'Doctors will become most skilled,' I said, 'if from their earliest years they not only learn the art of medicine, but also come into contact with
e the largest possible number of the most diseased bodies, and if they have themselves suffered from all illnesses, and are by their nature far from healthy. The reason for this, I believe, is that they do not use the body to treat the body. If they did, it would not be allowable for a doctor's body ever to be, or get itself into, a bad condition. No, they use the mind to treat the body, and it is not permitted for a mind which has become diseased, and is still in bad shape, to treat anything successfully.'

'True,' he said.

'A judge, on the other hand, uses the mind to rule the mind. So it is not
409 allowable for a judge's mind, from its earliest years, to be brought up in close contact with minds which are no good, or for it to have done a complete course in all forms of wrongdoing for itself, so that it can readily draw on its own experience in dealing with the wrongdoings of others,

like a doctor drawing on his experience of the body when he treats disease. No, if it is to be fine and noble, and able to judge questions of right and wrong in a healthy way, it must have had no experience – no taint – of evil natures when it was young. That's why, when they are young, people who
b   are morally good strike us as naïve, and easily fooled by wrongdoers. They have no internal model corresponding to the behaviour of people who are no good.'

'Yes, that's exactly what happens to them,' he said.

'For that reason,' I said, 'the good judge must be old, not young, a late developer when it comes to discovering the nature of injustice. He will not have seen it as something internal, in his own soul, but as something external, in the souls of others. He will have trained himself over a long period of time to see the kind of evil injustice is, relying on theoretical knowledge, not on personal experience.'

c   'Yes, that certainly seems the noblest kind of judge.'

'And a *good* judge, what is more. That was your question. After all, a good soul makes a good person. The person who is knowing and distrustful, with a long history of wrongdoing of his own, who regards himself as a criminal, but a clever one, can cope with people like himself when he meets them. His wariness makes him seem knowing, because he has the model of his own behaviour to refer to. But when he comes into
d   contact with people who are good, older people, then he looks pretty silly. He is distrustful without reason, and cannot recognise a healthy nature, because he has no model of it. But because he encounters more people who are no good than good, he is regarded, by himself and by others, as wise rather than foolish.'

'That is absolutely true,' he said.

'In that case,' I said, 'if we are looking for a good and wise judge, he is not our man. We want the other sort. Evil can never understand either
e   goodness or itself, whereas goodness, if its natural gifts are improved by education, will in time gain a knowledge both of itself and of evil. So though the good man can become wise, in my view, the bad man cannot.'

'That's my view, too,' he said.

'In which case, this is the kind of art of judging you will legislate for in your city, isn't it, together with an art of medicine of the kind we
410   described earlier? Between them they will care for the souls and bodies of those citizens who are naturally good. As for the ones who are not good, they will allow the physically defective to die, whereas those who have incurable faults of the soul they will themselves put to death.'

'Yes. After all, it has been shown to be the best thing both for the individuals concerned and for the city.'[58]

'Of course, our young people will clearly be reluctant to resort to the law, if they receive the simple musical and poetic education we described, the one we claimed bred self-discipline.'

'Yes. What of it?'

b 'Well, won't the person with the right musical and poetic education take the same approach in his hunt for a physical education? Won't he end up, if he so chooses, gaining independence from medicine except in emergencies?'

'Yes, I think he will.'

'His actual physical training, his exercises, are things he will do with a view to arousing the spirited part of his nature rather than developing his strength – unlike most athletes, whose diet and exercise is aimed at improving their physique.'

'Exactly,' he said.

'In that case, Glaucon,' I said, 'when people establish a system of c artistic and physical education, isn't their reason for doing so different from the one usually attributed to them – that one cares for the body, and the other for the soul?'

'What *is* the reason, then?' he asked.

'I suspect both are established principally for the benefit of the soul.'

'Explain.'

'Have you never observed the mentality of those who spend all their time on physical education, to the exclusion of musical and poetic education? Or those whose way of life is the opposite?'

'What have you in mind?'

d 'Savagery and hardness, in the one case. Weakness and gentleness, in the other.'

'Yes,' he said, 'I have noticed that those whose education is purely physical turn out more savage than they should. Those who have only a musical and moral education, on the other hand, do become softer than is good for them.'

'What is more,' I said, 'the fierce element comes from the spirited part of their nature. Correctly brought up, it would be brave, but when it is developed to a higher pitch than is necessary, it is likely to become harsh and unmanageable.'

---

[58] At 407e this conclusion was drawn concerning those whose physical ill-health precluded useful activity of either a manual or intellectual sort. There has been no previous discussion, however, of the treatment of the incurably criminal.

'Yes, I think that's right,' he said.

e   'What about the gentle element? Isn't it a property of the wisdom-loving or philosophical nature? Undue relaxation makes it too soft, doesn't it, whereas the right upbringing makes it gentle and well-behaved.'

'Yes.'

'The guardians must have both these natural attributes, we say.'[59]

'Yes, they must.'

'And these must be harmonised with one another?'

'Of course.'

'The soul of someone who is harmonised in this way is self-disciplined and brave, isn't it?'

'Yes.'

411 'Whereas the soul of someone discordant is cowardly and uncivilised?'

'Exactly.'

'So if you give music the chance to play upon your soul, and pour into the funnel of your ears the sweet, soft, lamenting modes we were talking about a little while ago, if you spend your whole life humming them,

b   bewitched by song, then the first effect on a nature with any spirit in it is to soften it, like heating iron, making it malleable instead of brittle and unworkable. But if you press on regardless, and are seduced by it, the next stage is melting and turning to liquid – the complete dissolution of the spirit. It cuts the sinews out of your soul, and turns it into a "feeble warrior."'[60]

'Yes,' he said.

'If you start with a soul which is not very spirited by nature,' I said, 'this happens quite quickly. If you do have a spirited soul, you weaken the

c   spirit and make it unstable – easily roused by trivial things, and as easily extinguished. People like this become hot-tempered and quick to anger rather than spirited; they are full of discontent.'

'They certainly do.'

'What about the person who puts a lot of effort into his physical training, and eats like a horse, but has nothing to do with music or philosophy? At first, because his body is in good shape, isn't he full of decision and spirit? Doesn't he become braver than he was before?'

'Much braver.'

'But suppose that is all he does. Suppose he has no contact with the

d   Muse. Even if he did have some love of learning in his soul, it gets no taste

___

[59] 375c–376c.   [60] Said of Menelaus in Homer (*Iliad* 17.588).

of learning or enquiry, and has no experience of rational argument or any artistic pursuit. As a result, since it never wakes up and has nothing to feed on, and since there is nothing to purify its senses, it becomes weak, and deaf, and blind, doesn't it?'

'Yes, it does,' he said.

'Someone like this becomes an enemy of rational argument, I suspect, and an enemy of music and literature. He abandons any attempt at
e persuasion using rational argument, and does everything with savage violence, like a wild animal. He lives his life in ignorance and stupidity, without grace or rhythm.'

'Yes,' he said, 'that's exactly what he is like.'

'If you want my opinion, then, the two elements for which some god has given mankind two arts – one musical and poetic, the other physical – seem to be not the mind and the body, or only incidentally, but the
412 spirited part of their nature and the philosophical part, so that these can be brought into harmony with one another through the appropriate tension and relaxation.'

'Yes, those do seem to be the two elements,' he said.

'In that case, we would be entitled to describe as perfectly musical and harmonious the person who best combines physical with musical and poetic education, and who introduces them into his soul in the most balanced way. Far more musical and harmonious than the person who tunes the strings of an instrument.'

'Very likely, Socrates.'

'Well then, Glaucon, won't we always need someone like this in our city
b to keep an eye on things, if our state is to be secure?'

'Yes, we shall. It will be our greatest need.'

'So much for the patterns of education and upbringing. We don't have to go through the dances, modes of hunting and coursing, athletic events or horse races that go with them. It's pretty obvious these must follow from the patterns, so there can't now be any difficulty in discovering them.'

'No, it probably wouldn't be too difficult,' he said.

'Very well, then,' I said. 'What is the next question we have to decide? Isn't it which of these people are to rule, and which be ruled?'

'Unquestionably.'

c 'Is it obvious the rulers should be older, and those who are ruled younger?'

'Yes, it is.'

'And that the rulers should be the best among them?'

'That too.'

'Among farmers, aren't the best ones the ones who most possess the attributes of a farmer?'

'Yes.'

'So in this context, since we are looking for the best of the guardians, must they not be the ones who most possess the attributes of a guardian of the city?'

'Yes.'

'And for this purpose, do they have to be wise, powerful and above all devoted to the city?'

d   'They do.'

'And people are most devoted to whatever it is they love.'

'Bound to be.'

'And they love most what they believe to have the same interests as themselves, the thing whose success or failure they think results in their own success or failure.'

'True,' he said.

'Then we must select from the guardians the kind of men who on

e examination strike us most strongly, their whole lives through, as being utterly determined to do what is in the city's interests, and as refusing to act in any way against its interests.'

'Yes, they should be the people we want.'

'I think we should observe them at all ages, to make sure they are the guardians and defenders of this belief, and that neither magic nor force can make them forget, and jettison their conviction that they should do what is best for the city.'

'What do you mean by this jettisoning?' he asked.

'I'll tell you,' I said. 'I think our minds can lose a belief either with or

413 without our consent. With our consent when it's a false belief and we learn better. Without our consent in the case of all true belief.'

'I understand the loss which is with our consent, but the loss which is without our consent I need to have explained to me.'

'Really? Don't you agree with me that what is good can be taken away from people only without their consent, whereas what is bad is taken away with their consent? Isn't being deceived about the truth something bad, and knowing the truth something good? And don't you think that having a belief which agrees with the way things are is knowing the truth?'

'You're right. When people lose a true belief, it is without their consent.'

b   'And is that a question of theft, or magic, or force?'

'Once again, I'm afraid, I don't see what you mean.'

'I seem to be making myself about as clear as a tragic poet,' I said. 'By theft I mean people who are talked into changing their minds, and people who forget. Either the passage of time or some process of argument takes away their belief without them realising it. You do see what I mean now, I hope?'

'Yes.'

'By force I mean those whom pain or grief causes to change their beliefs.'

'Yes, I understand that as well,' he said. 'And I agree.'

c   'As for magic, you would also accept, I imagine, that there are people whose beliefs change because they are seduced by pleasure, or because there is something they are afraid of.'

'Yes, all the things which deceive us do look like a form of magic.'

'So as I said just now,[61] we must look for those who are the best defenders of their conviction that in any situation they must do what they think is in the city's best interests for them to do. From their earliest childhood we must watch them, and set them the kind of tasks which could most

d easily make them lose sight of this aim, and lead them astray. Then we must choose the ones who remember their aim and are not easily led astray. Those who are led astray we must reject, mustn't we?'

'Yes.'

'As a second type of test we must give them hardship, pain, and trials, and in all of them look for the characteristics we want.'

'Correct,' he said.

'Then we must have a third type of test – a test for magic – and watch their reactions to that. Just like people taking young colts close to loud and confused noises, to find out if they are easily frightened, we must expose

e our guardians, when they are young, first to danger and then to pleasure. We must test them like gold in the fire, only more so. Does this one stand out in every situation as immune to magic and endowed with grace? Is he a good guardian of himself and the musical education he has received? Does he show qualities of rhythm and harmony in all the tests we set him? Is he the kind of person who would be the greatest use to himself and the

[61] 412e.

city? From our children, from our young and grown men, the one who
414   under constant testing emerges as pure is the one who should be
appointed as a ruler and guardian of our city. We should heap honours on
him, in life and in death, and when it comes to burial and other memorials he should receive the greatest tributes. The one who fails the tests we
should reject. Well, Glaucon, so much for my views on the selection and
appointment of the rulers and guardians. It's only a general outline, of
course, not a precise specification.'

'I think my views are pretty much the same as yours,' he said.

b   'In that case, aren't these really the people who can most accurately be
called full guardians – making sure friends within do not *want* to harm it,
and enemies without are not *able* to harm it? The young people whom we
have been calling guardians up to now we can call auxiliaries,[62] the defenders of the rulers' beliefs.'

'I agree.'

'In that case,' I said, 'how can we contrive to use one of those necessary
falsehoods we were talking about a little while back? We want one single,
c   grand lie which will be believed by everybody – including the rulers,
ideally, but failing that the rest of the city.'[63]

'What kind of thing do you mean?'

'A very familiar story, of Phoenician origin. It has happened in the past,
in several places. So the poets tell us, and they have found believers. But
it has not happened in our time, and I don't even know if it *could* happen.
People would take a lot of persuading.'

'You seem a bit reluctant to tell your story,' he said.

'With good reason – as you will see when I do tell you.'

d   'Don't worry,' he said. 'Tell it.'

'Very well. I will. Though I don't know how I shall have the nerve, or
find the right words. I have to try and persuade first of all the rulers themselves and the soldiers, and then the rest of the city, that the entire
upbringing and education we gave them, their whole experience of it happening to them, was after all merely a dream, something they imagined,
and that in reality they spent that time being formed and raised deep

---

[62] In addition to its general meaning, the term can be used to refer to mercenary troops
(compare Adeimantus' complaint at 419a), as well as to a tyrant's bodyguard, which
was typically composed of such mercenaries.

[63] The need for falsehoods was explained at 382c–d. The lie is grand or noble (*gennaios*)
by virtue of its civic purpose, but the Greek word can also be used colloquially, giving
the meaning 'a true-blue lie', i.e. a massive, no-doubt-about-it lie (compare the term
'grand larceny').

e   within the earth – themselves, their weapons and the rest of the equip-
ment which was made for them. When the process of making them was
complete, the earth their mother released them, and now it is their duty
to be responsible for defending the country in which they live against any
attack – just as they would defend their mother or nurse – and to regard
the rest of the citizens as their brothers, born from the earth.'

'No wonder you were so embarrassed about telling us your lie.'

415   'Yes, I had good reason,' I said. 'But you must listen to the second half
of the story as well. "You are all brothers," our story will tell them, "all of
you in the city. But when god made you, he used a mixture of gold in the
creation of those of you who were fit to be rulers, which is why they are
the most valuable. He used silver for those who were to be auxiliaries, and
iron and bronze for the farmers and the rest of the skilled workers. Most

b   of the time you will father children of the same type as yourselves, but
because you are all related, occasionally a silver child may be born from a
golden parent, or a golden child from a silver parent, and likewise any type
from any other type. The first and most important instruction god gives
the rulers is that the thing they should be the best guardians of, the thing
they should keep the most careful eye on, is the compound of these metals

c   in the souls of the children. If their own child is born with a mixture of
bronze or iron in him, they must feel no kind of pity for him, but give him
the position in society his nature deserves, driving him out to join the
skilled workers or farmers. On the other hand, any children from those
groups born with a mixture of gold or silver should be given recognition,
and promoted either to the position of guardian or to that of auxiliary.
There is a prophecy, god tells them, that the end of the city will come
when iron or bronze becomes its guardian."[64] Well, that's the story. Can
you think of any possible way of getting people to believe it?'

d   'No,' he said. 'Not the actual people you tell it to. But their children
might, and *their* children after them, and the rest of the population in later
generations.'

'Even that might help them to care more about the city and one
another. I think I see what you're getting at. Anyway, let that turn out as
popular belief and tradition will have it. Our job now is to arm these
earth-born warriors of ours, and lead them forth, with the rulers at their

---

[64] This part of the story makes use of a different mythical tradition, that found in
Hesiod's story of the different races of men – gold, silver, and so on (*Works and Days*
109–201). But Hesiod's races are successive generations, and his story is one of decay
over time. This aspect of the tradition will come to the fore in Book 8 (546a–547a).

head. Let them go and look for the best place in the city to put their camp,
e   a place from which they can most easily control their own citizens, if any
of them refuse to obey the laws, or repel any external threats, in the event
of some enemy coming down on them "like a wolf on the fold." When
they have set up their camp, they can sacrifice to the appropriate gods, and
then organise their sleeping accommodation. Does that sound right?'

'Yes,' he said.

'Should it be the kind of accommodation which will give them adequate shelter both in winter and summer?'

'Of course. This is their home you are talking about, I take it.'

416   'Yes,' I said. 'But a home fit for soldiers, not for businessmen.'

'What is the difference, in your view?'

'I'll try and tell you. When shepherds are breeding dogs as protectors
of their flocks, the worst possible disaster and disgrace, I imagine, is to
breed dogs whose nature and training are such that lack of discipline,
hunger or some fault of character leads them to try to attack the sheep
themselves, and start behaving like wolves instead of dogs.'

'Yes, of course that is a disaster.'

b   'In that case we must guard in every way we can against our auxiliaries
doing the same sort of thing to the citizens. After all, they are stronger
than the citizens. We don't want them behaving like savage masters
instead of friendly allies.'

'Yes, we must guard against that,' he said.

'Won't the best insurance against this be for them to have received a
really good education?'

'But they *have* received one,' he said.

And I said, 'We can't be sure of that, my dear Glaucon. What we *can*
c   be sure about is what we have just been saying, which is that when it
comes to gentleness – both to themselves and to those under their protection – then the right education, whatever that may be, is the key.'

'Yes, we are right to be sure of that.'

'In addition to this education, an intelligent observer may say, the
guardians should be furnished with housing and a general standard of
d   living which will not hinder them from becoming the best possible
guardians, and which will give them no encouragement to do wrong in
their dealings with the rest of the citizens.'

'He may say that. And he will be quite right.'

'Well, then,' I said, 'do you agree with some suggestions about the way
they should live and be housed if this is what we want them to be like? In

the first place, no one is to have any private property beyond what is absolutely essential. Secondly, no one is to have the kind of house or store-room which cannot be entered by anyone who feels like it. For their sub-sistence, which should meet the needs of self-disciplined and courageous

e warrior-athletes, they should impose a levy on the rest of the citizens, and receive an annual payment for their role as guardians which leaves them with neither a surplus nor a deficiency. They should live a communal life, eating together like soldiers in camp. As for gold and silver, they should be told they already have in their souls, all the time, the divine gold and silver given to them by the gods. They have no need of human gold in addition, and it is sacrilege to contaminate the divine gold they possess by adding to it a mixture of the perishable gold, since the gold in circulation

417 among ordinary people has been the cause of much evil, whereas their own gold is pure. To them alone, out of the city's population, is it forbid-den to handle or touch gold or silver, or be beneath the same roof, or wear it as jewellery, or drink from gold or silver cups. In this way they will be kept safe, and they will keep the city safe. Once they start acquiring their own land, houses, and money, they will have become householders and farmers instead of guardians. From being the allies of the other citizens they will turn into hostile masters. They will spend their whole lives

b hating and being hated, plotting and being plotted against. Their fears of enemies inside the city will be much more numerous and more acute than their fears of enemies outside the city. Both they themselves and the city will be heading at full speed towards imminent destruction. For all these reasons, shall we say that our guardians are to be provided with the housing and way of life we have described? Are these the laws we should enact, or not?'

'They certainly are,' said Glaucon.

Book 4

419 At this point Adeimantus interrupted us. 'How will you defend yourself,
Socrates, against the charge that you are not making these men very
happy, and that they have only themselves to blame? The city in fact
belongs to them, yet they derive no benefit from it. Other people have
acquired land, built themselves beautiful great houses, and are now
collecting the furniture to go with them; they make their own sacrifices to
the gods; they entertain foreign visitors; and they are also the owners of
the things you've just been talking about – gold, silver and everything
420 which is regarded as necessary for people who are going to be happy. Our
men just seem to sit there in the city, like hired bodyguards. All they do
is guard it.'

'Yes,' I said, 'and working just for their keep at that. Unlike the others,
they receive no pay over and above their food, so if they feel like going
abroad as private individuals, they won't be able to. They can't give presents to mistresses, or spend money on anything else they choose, on the
things people who are generally regarded as happy spend money on. You
left that, and a whole lot more along the same lines, out of your accusation.'

'Very well,' he said, 'you can take those as being part of the accusation
as well.'

b   'What is our defence, then? Is that your question?'
'Yes.'

'We shall find our answer, I think, if we carry on down the same road.
We shall say that we wouldn't be at all surprised if even our guardians
were best off like this, but that in any case our aim in founding the city is
not to make one group outstandingly happy, but to make the whole city

as happy as possible. We thought we would be most likely to find justice
in a city of this kind, and most likely to find injustice in the city with the
c   worst institutions, and that looking at these would give us the answer to
our original question. What we are doing at the moment, we believe, is
not separating off a few of the inhabitants, and making *them* happy, but
constructing a complete city, and making that happy. We'll have a look at
its opposite later. Imagine we were putting the colours on a statue of a
man, and someone came along and told us we were doing it wrong, since
we weren't using the most beautiful colours for the most beautiful parts
d   of the living creature.[1] The eyes, the most beautiful feature, had been
coloured black, not purple. We would regard it as a quite reasonable
defence to say to him: "Hang on a minute. You surely don't think, do you,
that we should make the eyes – or any of the other parts of the body – so
beautiful that they don't even look like eyes. The thing to ask yourself is
whether by giving the right colours to everything we are making the whole
e   thing beautiful." It's the same with us. You mustn't start forcing us to give
the guardians the kind of happiness which will turn them into anything
other than guardians. We could perfectly easily dress our farmers in
purple robes, and give them gold jewellery to wear, and tell them to work
the land when they feel like it. We could let our potters recline on ban-
queting couches, passing the wine to the right and feasting in front of
their fire, with their potters' wheels beside them for when they really felt
like doing some pottery. We could make everyone else happy in the same
421   kind of way, so that the whole city would be happy. You mustn't ask us to
do that. If we do as you suggest, the farmer will not be a farmer, the potter
will not be a potter, nor will anyone else continue to fulfil any of the roles
which together give rise to a city.

'For most of the population it is not that important. If our cobblers are
no good, if they stop being proper cobblers and only pretend to be when
they are not, the city won't come to much harm. But if the guardians of
our laws and our city give the impression of being guardians, without
really *being* guardians, you can see that they totally destroy the entire city,
since they alone provide the opportunity for its correct management and
b   prosperity. If we are making real guardians, people who are incapable of
harming the city, whereas the person who criticises us is making them into
farmers of some kind, who are not so much running a city as presiding

---

[1] Our image of Greek statues is one of unpainted stone. This, however, is the fault of
time, which has left the stone but removed the paint.

over a jolly banquet at a public festival, then he is not talking about a city
at all. The question we have to ask ourselves is this. What is our aim in
appointing the guardians? Is it to provide the greatest possible happiness
for them? Or does our aim concern the whole city? Aren't we seeing if we
can provide the greatest degree of happiness for that? Isn't that what
c we should be compelling these auxiliaries and guardians to do? Shouldn't
we be persuading them – and everyone else likewise – to be the best possible practitioners of their own particular task? And when as a result the
city prospers and is well established, can't we then leave it to each group's
own nature to give it a share of happiness?'

'I'm sure you're right,' he said.

'In that case,' I said, 'I want to ask another question, closely related to
the last one. Are you going to think that reasonable as well?'

'What question, exactly?'

d   'I wonder if there aren't some things which can corrupt other skilled
workers as well, so that they too turn bad.'

'What sort of things?'

'Wealth and poverty,' I said.

'And how do they corrupt them?'

'Like this. Do you think a potter who becomes rich will still be prepared to practise his craft?'

'No.'

'Does he grow more lazy and careless than he was before?'

'Yes. Much more.'

'He becomes a worse potter, in fact?'

'Again, much worse.'

'On the other hand, if poverty stops him equipping himself with tools
e or anything else he needs for his business, will what he produces suffer?
And will his sons, or anyone else he teaches, turn out worse craftsmen as
a result of his teaching?'

'Of course.'

'So both these things, poverty and wealth, have a damaging effect both
on what craftsmen produce and on the craftsmen themselves.'

'It looks like it.'

'We've found another class of things, apparently, for our guardians to
watch out for. They must do everything they can to prevent them creep-
ing into the city without their noticing.'

'What sort of things do you mean?'

422   'Wealth and poverty,' I said. 'One produces luxury, idleness and

revolution, the other meanness of spirit and poor workmanship – and of course revolution as well.'

'Exactly. But here's a question for you, Socrates. Since our city has no money, how will it be capable of fighting a war – especially if it is forced into war with a large, wealthy city?'

'Well, obviously fighting one large, wealthy city will be more difficult than fighting two.'

b   'What do you mean?' he said.

'Well, for a start,' I said, 'if they have to fight, I take it their opponents will be rich men. They by contrast will be warrior-athletes, won't they?'

'Yes,' he said. 'For what that's worth.'

'Think about boxing, Adeimantus. Don't you think a single boxer, with the finest possible training, could easily fight two rich, fat people who were not boxers?'

'Possibly not both at the same time,' he said.

'Even if he were allowed to take to his heels, and then turn round and
c   hit whichever of them was nearer to him at the time? Even if he kept on doing this repeatedly, on a sunny day, in stifling heat? Don't you think a boxer like this could even beat a larger number of opponents of that sort?'

'It would certainly be no surprise if he did.'

'And don't you think the rich have greater knowledge and experience of the art of boxing than of the art of war?'

'I certainly do,' he said.[2]

'So our trained warriors will probably have no difficulty in fighting against two or three times their own numbers.'

'I'm not going to argue with you,' he said. 'I think you're right.'

d   'What if they sent an embassy to one of the other two cities, and said to them, quite truthfully, "Gold or silver are no use to us. We are not allowed them. But you are. Be our allies in this war, and you can have our opponents' wealth." Do you think anyone who heard this offer would choose to make war on dogs who are lean and fit, rather than side with the dogs against the fat, tender sheep?'

'No, I don't. But if the wealth of the other cities is concentrated in the
e   hands of one city, you'd better be careful it doesn't pose a threat to the one that has no wealth.'

'Well, if you think there's any point in calling anything "a city" other than the one we are establishing, the best of luck to you.'

---

[2] Sports were the man of leisure's regular concern, whereas it was a controversial question whether the handling of weapons required special training.

'What *should* we call them?' he asked.

'The others need some grander name,' I said. 'Each of them is "cities upon cities, but no city," as the quip goes.[3] At the very least two, opposed
423 to one another. A city of the poor, and a city of the rich. Each of these contains many more, and if you treat them as a single city, you will achieve nothing, whereas if you treat them as several cities, offering one group the money and power – or even the people themselves – of another group, you will always have plenty of allies and few enemies. As long as your city lives the disciplined life we have just laid down for it, it will be a great city. Not in reputation, I don't mean, but great in fact, even if it is a city with only
b a thousand men to fight for it. You will have a job to find a single city which is great in this way, either among Greeks or non-Greeks, though you will find plenty, many times the size of this one, which give the illusion of greatness. Don't you agree?'

'Emphatically,' he said.

'In that case,' I said, 'this could also be an excellent marker, or limit, for our rulers, to show them how big they should make the city, and the amount of land they should mark out for a city this size, before saying "no" to any more.'

'What is the limit?' he asked.

'This, I would guess. As long as any increase in size is unlikely to stop the city remaining united, they should let it go on increasing. But not beyond that point.'

'Yes, that's a good approach,' he said.
c 'In which case we shall give our guardians one further instruction. They are to guard in every way against the city being small, but also against its giving the appearance of greatness. It should be no more than adequate in size, and united.'

'A trivial task for them, no doubt.'

'Yes,' I said. 'Almost as trivial as the requirement we mentioned earlier,[4]
d for an inferior child of the guardians to be sent to join the other classes, and for an outstanding child from those classes to join the guardians. This was intended to show that among the rest of the citizen body they should assign each individual to the one task he is naturally fitted for, so that by applying himself to his own one task each may become a single person

---

[3] It is likely that this obscure proverbial expression had its origin in a board game of the *petteia* family (see note 10 to 333b, p. 8 above), a game of battle between cities, itself called 'Cities'.

[4] 415b–c.

rather than many people, and in this way the entire city may grow to be a single city rather than many cities.'

'Oh, fine,' he said. 'Even simpler than our first directive.'

'You may be thinking, my dear Adeimantus, that we give them a great
e long list of weighty instructions. But we don't do that. The instructions are all trivial, provided they keep a careful eye on the "first and great commandment."[5] Though "great" isn't really the right word. More of a minimum requirement.'

'And what is that requirement?' he asked.

'Education and upbringing,' I said. 'If the guardians are well educated, and grow up into men of sound judgment, they will have no difficulty in seeing all this for themselves, plus other things we are saying nothing
424 about – such as taking wives, marriage, and having children. They will see the necessity of making everything as nearly as possible "shared among friends," in the words of the proverb.'[6]

'Yes, that would be best,' he said.

'Once it gets off to a good start,' I said, 'our regime will be a kind of virtuous circle. If you can keep a good system of upbringing and education, they produce naturally good specimens. These in their turn, if they receive a good education, develop into even better specimens than their
b predecessors. Better in general, and better in particular for reproduction. The same is true in the animal kingdom.'

'I'm sure you're right,' he said.

'To put it briefly, then, the overseers of our city must keep a firm grip on our system of education, protecting it above all else, and not allowing it to be destroyed accidentally. They must reject any radical innovation in physical or musical education, preserving them as far as they can unchanged. They should regard with apprehension anyone who tells them that

> The latest song, fresh from the singer's lips,
> Has most appeal to men.[7]

c People who approve of this might easily think the poet meant a new style of song, rather than just new songs. But that is not the sort of thing they

---

[5] Said with reference to the proverb 'the fox knows many things, the hedgehog one great thing'.
[6] The proverb was 'friends will hold things in common', and is said to have originated in the unusually close-knit Pythagorean communities of southern Italy.
[7] An adaptation of Homer, *Odyssey* 1.351–352.

should approve of, and they should not think that was what the poet meant. They should beware of new forms of music, which are likely to affect the whole system of education. Changes in styles of music are always politically revolutionary. That's what Damon says, and I believe him.'

'In which case, you can count me among the believers as well,' said Adeimantus.

d   'Presumably this is where we think the guardians should build their watchtower. In music.'

'It's certainly a place where breaking rules can easily become a habit without anyone realising,' he said.

'Yes, people don't see how breaking rules in the realm of entertainment can do any harm.'

'It can't,' he said. 'Except that once the idea of breaking rules has gradually established itself, it seeps imperceptibly into people's characters and habits. From there it brims over, increasing as it goes, into their contracts

e   with one another. And from contracts, Socrates, it extends its course of wanton disruption to laws and political institutions, until finally it destroys everything in private and public life.'

'I see. So that's how it is, is it?'

'I think so,' he said.

'In that case, as we were saying at the beginning, our children must have entertainment of a more disciplined kind.[8] When entertainment is

425 undisciplined – and children likewise – it's impossible for the children to grow up into disciplined and responsible men.'

'Of course,' he said.

'If they start off as children with the right sort of entertainments, they will acquire discipline through their musical education. This discipline has the opposite effect on them to the effect you were describing just now. It accompanies them in all their actions, and helps them grow, correcting any part of the city which may earlier have gone wrong.'

'That is true,' he said.

'When this happens,' I said, 'these people find out for themselves the apparently trivial rules which were all destroyed by their predecessors.'

'What rules are those?'

b   'Things like the young keeping quiet in the presence of their elders, as

---

[8] The reference is to the austerity of the literary and musical reforms proposed in Books 2 and 3, and first remarked upon at 399e.

they should; giving up their seats to them; standing up when they come in; respect for their parents; their hair-styles, clothes, shoes and general appearance. All those sorts of things. Don't you agree?'

'Yes, I do.'

'I think it's absurd to make laws about these things. They aren't the result of spoken or written rules. And even if they were, they wouldn't last.'

'Of course not.'

c   'It certainly looks, Adeimantus, as if everything follows from the direction a person's education takes. Like always produces like, doesn't it?'

'Naturally.'

'And I imagine we'd say the final result, for better or worse, is something unique, complete and vigorous.'

'What else?'

'Well, for my part,' I said, 'in this situation I wouldn't go so far as to try and pass laws about this kind of thing.'

'I'm sure you're right,' he said.

'But then what on earth are we to do about business dealings?' I asked.

d 'The contracts various parties make with one another in the market-place, for example? Or contracts with builders, cases of slander or assault, the bringing of lawsuits and the selection of juries, the payment or collection of any tariffs due in markets or ports, and the general regulation of markets, city or harbours? Can we really bring ourselves to legislate for any of these?'

'No,' he said. 'If we've got the right sort of citizens, it's a waste of time telling them what to do. I imagine they can easily develop most of the nec-

e essary legislation for themselves.'

'Yes, my friend,' I said. 'Provided, that is, god grants them the safe preservation of the laws we have described so far.'

'The alternative,' he said, 'is for them to spend their whole lives enacting and amending detailed legislation of this kind, in the belief that they will hit on the ideal solution.'

'You mean their lives will be like those of people who are ill, and who lack the self-discipline required to give up their unhealthy way of life.'

'Precisely.'

426   'What a delightful life those people lead! Their medical treatment achieves nothing, except to increase the complications and severity of their ailments, yet they live in constant hope that each new medicine recommended will be the one which will make them healthy.'

'Yes, that's exactly what life is like for patients of that sort,' he said.

'And what about their equally charming habit of reserving their greatest hostility for the person who tells them the truth, which is that until
b they give up drinking, over-eating, sex and idleness, no medicine, cauterisation or surgery, no charms, amulets or anything of that kind, will do them the slightest good.'

'It's not a charming habit in the least,' he said. 'There's nothing charming about getting angry with people who tell you the truth.'

'You don't seem to be a great admirer of people like this,' I said.

'Emphatically not.'

'So you won't be impressed if, as we were just saying, the city as a whole
c behaves like this. Don't you think this is just what cities are doing when they are badly governed, and yet forbid their citizens to make any change at all in the constitution, telling them they will be put to death if they do? Rather it is the person who takes the city as it is, who is the people's most beguiling servant and flatterer, who creeps into their good graces, who anticipates their wishes and is adept at satisfying them – this person they will declare a fine man, a man profoundly wise. This man they will honour.'[9]

'Yes, I think it's exactly what cities are doing. And I can see nothing to be said for it.'

d 'How about those who are willing and eager to be the servants of cities like this? Don't you admire their courage and readiness?'

'Yes, I do,' he said. 'Apart from the ones who let the approval of the majority fool them into thinking they really are statesmen.'

'Are you saying you can't find any excuse for these people? If a man knows nothing about measurement, and lots of people who also know nothing tell him he is six feet tall, do you suppose it is possible for him to
e avoid thinking that's what he is?'

'No, I don't.'

'Don't let it annoy you, then. After all, surely people like this are the most entertaining of all, passing and amending the kind of laws we were describing just now, in the constant belief that they will find an answer to

---

[9] Although the Athenian political system made it quite easy for citizens to propose new laws or decrees for action, it hedged the procedure by making liable to prosecution and severe penalty anyone whose proposal was found to contravene existing law. The rhetoric used in such cases tended to present the laws as ancestral and permanent. In practice, new laws and decrees were most often proposed by the leading politicians, who became adept at surviving the legal hazards.

dishonesty in business dealings and all the areas I have just been talking about. They don't realise they are cutting off the Hydra's head.'

427   'Though that's exactly what they *are* doing,' he said.

'Well, if it were up to me,' I said, 'I wouldn't have thought the true law-giver should concern himself with these details of the laws and the con-stitution – either in a badly-governed or a well-governed city. In one it is pointless, and achieves nothing; in the other, some of the legislation can be devised by absolutely anyone, while the rest follows automatically from our previous arrangements.'

b   'In that case,' he asked, 'what area of lawmaking have we still got left?'

And I said, '*We* haven't got any. But Apollo at Delphi has – the most important, the finest and the most fundamental pieces of legislation.'

'What are those?'

'The foundation of temples. Sacrifices. Other acts of service per-formed for gods, demigods and heroes. The burial places of the dead, and the observance which must be paid to those below to keep them

c   favourable. We do not know about this kind of thing, and when we found our city, if we have any sense, the only advice we shall follow, the only authority we shall recognise, is the traditional authority. And I take it that in these matters Apollo, making his pronouncements seated on the stone which forms the earth's navel, is the ancestral authority for the whole of mankind.'[10]

'You are right,' he said. 'That must be our approach.'

d   'In that case, son of Ariston, your city can now be regarded as founded. The next step is to look inside it, and for that you are going to need a pretty powerful light. You can provide your own, or get your brother and Polemarchus and the others to help you. Then perhaps we shall find some way of seeing just where in the city justice is, where injustice is, what the difference is between the two, and which of them people who are going to be happy must possess, whether all the gods and all mankind realise they possess it or not.'

e   'Oh, no, you don't,' said Glaucon. 'You told us *you* were going to look for justice. You said it was impious not to do everything you possibly could to support justice.'

---

[10] The oracle of Apollo at Delphi was authoritative on religious questions for the entire Greek world – questions which were not as a rule so sharply differentiated from other kinds of political questions as they are in this passage. It was also consulted before the founding of any colony. The sanctuary contained a stone, the 'navel-stone', which was thought to mark the centre of the earth.

'That's true,' I said. 'Thank you for reminding me. I must do what I promised. But you must do your bit as well.'

'We will.'

'In that case,' I said, 'here's how I hope to find the answer. I take it our city, if it has been correctly founded, is wholly good.'

'It can't help being.'

'Clearly, then, it is wise, courageous, self-disciplined and just.'

'Clearly.'

'Then as we find each of these elements in it, those we have not yet found will constitute the remainder.'

'Of course.'

428   'With any four things, if we were looking for one of them in some place or other, and it was the first thing we caught sight of, that would be enough for us. But if we identified the other three first, then the one we were looking for would *ipso facto* have been identified as well, since clearly it could then only be whatever was left.'

'You are right,' he said.

'It's the same for us now. Since there actually are four elements, should we conduct our search in the same way?'

'Yes. Obviously.'

b   'Well, I think the first one to catch the eye is wisdom. And it seems to have an unusual feature.'

'What is that?'

'It is truly wise, I think, this city we have described. It has good judgment, doesn't it?'

'Yes.'

'Now this thing, judgment, is clearly knowledge of some sort. Good decisions, I take it, are the result of knowledge, not ignorance.'

'Obviously.'

'But our city contains many types of knowledge, of very different kinds.'

'Of course it does.'

'Is it the knowledge possessed by its carpenters which entitles us to call c   our city wise, and say it possesses good judgment?'

'Certainly not,' he said. 'That merely entitles us to call it good at carpentry.'

'So a city is not to be called wise because of its knowledge and judgment in making the best possible wooden furniture.'

'Absolutely not.'

'How about its knowledge of making things out of bronze, or any other knowledge of that kind?'

'No, nothing like that,' he said.

'Nor the knowledge of how to grow crops from the soil, since that's called farming.'

'So I believe.'

'Is there, then,' I asked, 'among any of the citizens of this city we have
d just founded, *any* branch of knowledge which makes decisions about the city as a whole – deciding on the best approach to itself and to other cities – and not about one particular element in the city?'

'There most certainly is.'

'What is this knowledge, and in which group is it to be found?'

'It is the knowledge possessed by the guardians,' he said. 'And it is to be found in the rulers, whom we have just been calling the perfect guardians.'[11]

'And what is the label you give your city on the strength of this knowledge?'

'I call it sound in judgment, and truly wise.'

e   'So which do you think our city will have more of? Metalworkers, or these true guardians?'

'Metalworkers,' he said. 'Far more.'

'Of all the groups which have a branch of knowledge of their own, and which are identified as a group, wouldn't the guardians be the smallest?'

'Easily the smallest.'

'In which case, the wisdom of a city founded on natural principles depends entirely on its smallest group and element – the leading and
429 ruling element – and the knowledge that element possesses. The class which can be expected to share in this branch of knowledge, which of all branches of knowledge is the only one we can call wisdom, is by its nature, apparently, the smallest class.'

'That's very true,' he said.

'Well, that's one of the four things we were looking for. And we've not only found it, I'm not quite sure how, but also found whereabouts in the city it is located.'

'Nothing much wrong with the way it was found as far as I'm concerned,' he said.

'Courage, next. It is not hard to see both the thing itself and the part of

---

[11] They were distinguished as 'full guardians' at 414b.

the city in which it is located, the part which gives the city the name
"courageous."'

'Explain.'

b   'No one classifying a city as cowardly or brave would look at any other
part of it than the part which makes war in the city's defence, and serves
in its army.'

'Yes, that's the only part anyone would look at,' he said.

'I think the reason for that,' I said, 'is that the cowardice or bravery of
the rest of the population would not be enough to make the city itself
cowardly or brave.'

'No, it wouldn't.'

'Does that mean a city's courage, as well as its wisdom, lies in a part of
c itself, because it has in that part a power capable of preserving, in all situations, the opinion that what is to be feared is just what the lawgiver listed
and classified as such in the course of their education? Or isn't that what
you call courage?'

'I didn't altogether follow that. Say it again.'

'I mean that courage is a kind of preservation,' I said.

'Preservation? Of what?'

'Of the opinion formed by education, under the influence of law, about
which things are to be feared. When I talked about its preservation in all
d situations, I meant keeping it intact, through pains, pleasures, desires and
fears, without rejecting it. I can give you an analogy, if you would like.'

'I would.'

'When dyers want to dye wool purple,' I said, 'you know they start by
selecting, from wools of various colours, the ones which are naturally
white. They give these a lengthy preliminary preparation, so that they will
e absorb as much of the colour as possible. Only then do they do the dyeing.
Anything dyed in this way is colour-fast. No washing, with or without
detergent, can remove the colour from it. But when things are dyed in
some other way, whether the wool is some other colour, or whether it is
white but dyed without preparation, you know what happens.'

'Yes,' he said. 'They look faded and ridiculous.'

'That's the kind of thing you must imagine we too were doing, to the
430 best of our ability, when we selected our soldiers and gave them their
musical, poetic and physical education. You must realise that all we were
trying to do was organise things so that they would absorb our laws as
completely as possible, like a dye. We wanted them to possess the right
character and upbringing, so that their views on danger and other things

would be colour fast, incapable of being washed out by any of the de-
b tergents which are such good solvents. Not by pleasure, which is a better
solvent than any soda or lye. Nor by pain, fear or desire, which are
stronger than any other detergent. This kind of power and preservation
I call courage – the preservation, in all situations, of correct and lawful
belief about what is to be feared and what is not. That's my definition,
unless you have some objection to it.'

'No, I have no objection,' he said. 'I take it that when a slave or an
animal has a correct opinion on these subjects, an opinion which is not the
result of education, you do not regard this as properly lawful,[12] and you
c give it some name other than courage.'

'Precisely,' I said.

'In that case, I accept your definition of courage.'

'Take it as a definition of courage *in a city*,' I said, 'and you will be right.
We can give a better account of courage some other time, if you like. At
the moment, though, we are investigating justice, not courage. And for
that purpose I think this is enough.'

'Yes. You are right.'

d 'That leaves two things to for us to identify in our city,' I said. 'One is
self-discipline. The other is the object of our entire investigation, justice.'

'Yes.'

'Well, is there some way we can find justice without having to bother
about self-discipline?'

'I don't know,' he said. 'I wouldn't want it to make its appearance too
soon, if that means giving up the search for self-discipline. If I have any
say in the matter, please examine self-discipline first.'

'Well, if it's not wrong of me, I'm quite happy to do that?'

e 'Start looking, then.'

'I shall have to,' I said. 'My first impression is that it is more like a
harmony or musical mode than the other two.'

'In what way?'

'Self-discipline, I take it, is a kind of order. They say it is a mastery of
pleasures and desires, and a person is described as being in some way or
other master of himself. And there are other clues of the same sort in the
way it is talked about, aren't there?'

'Indeed there are,' he said.

'But isn't the phrase "master of himself" an absurdity?[13] The master of

---

[12] A less secure manuscript reading would be translated 'not properly permanent'
rather than 'not properly lawful'.

[13] The literal meaning of the phrase translated 'master of himself' here and through-

431 himself must surely also be slave to himself, and the slave to himself must
     be master of himself. It's the same person being talked about all the time.'
         'Of course.'
         'What this way of speaking seems to me to indicate is that in the soul of
     a single person there is a better part and a worse part. When the naturally
     better part is in control of the worse, this is what is meant by "master
     of himself." It is a term of approval. But when as a result of bad upbring-
     ing or bad company the better element, which is smaller, is overwhelmed
   b by the mass of the worse element, this is a matter for reproach. They call
     a person in this condition a slave to himself, undisciplined.'
         'Yes, I think that is what it indicates,' he said.
         'Now, if you take a look at this new city of ours, you will find one of
     these situations prevailing. You will admit that it can quite legitimately be
     called master of itself, if something in which the better rules the worse
     can be called self-disciplined and master of itself.'
         'Yes, when I take a look at our city,' he said, 'you are right.'
   c   'But you do also find the whole range and variety of desires, pleasures
     and pains. Particularly in children, women, slaves, and among so-called
     free men, in the majority of ordinary people.'
         'You certainly do.'
         'Whereas simple, moderate desires, which are guided by rational cal-
     culation, using intelligence and correct belief, are things you come across
     only among a few people, those with the best natural endowment and the
     best education.'
         'True,' he said.
         'Well, do you see the same qualities in your city? And are the desires of
   d the ordinary majority controlled by the desires and wisdom of the dis-
     cerning minority?'
         'Yes, they are.'
         'So if any city can be called the master of its pleasures and desires, and
     master of itself, this one can.'
         'It certainly can,' he said.
         'In which case, can't we also call it self-disciplined in all these respects?'
         'Very much so.'
         'What is more, if agreement is to be found among rulers and ruled in
   e any city about which of them is to rule, it is to be found in this one, don't
     you think?'

         out this passage is 'stronger than himself', which is an idiom in Greek but not in
         English. Correspondingly, the phrase translated 'slave of himself' has the literal
         meaning 'weaker than himself'.

'I couldn't agree more.'

'Well then, when they agree in this way, in which of the two groups of citizens will you say the self-discipline is located? In the rulers? Or in the ruled?'

'In both, I suppose.'

'See what a plausible prediction we made just now,' I said, 'when we compared self-discipline to a harmony of some sort?'[14]

'Explain.'

'It is not the same as courage and wisdom. Each of those was located in a particular part, and yet one of them made the whole city wise, and the other made it brave. Self-discipline does not operate in the same way. It extends literally throughout the entire city, over the whole scale, causing those who are weakest – in intelligence, if you like, or in strength, or again in numbers, wealth or anything like that – together with those who are strongest and those in between, to sing in unison. So we would be quite justified in saying that self-discipline is this agreement about which of them should rule – a natural harmony of worse and better, both in the city and in each individual.'

b   'I quite agree,' he said.

'Very well. Three of the qualities have been identified in our city. Or such is our impression, at any rate. What can the remaining quality be, which allows a city to share in excellence? Because clearly, this is going to be justice.'

'Clearly.'

'Now, Glaucon, this is the moment for us to position ourselves, like huntsmen, in a ring round the thicket. We must concentrate, and make

c   sure justice does not escape. We don't want it to vanish and disappear from view. It's obviously here somewhere, so keep your eyes open, and try your hardest to see where it is. If you see it first, give me a shout.'

'Some hope,' he said. 'No, I'm afraid the only help I'm going to be to you is if you want a follower, someone who can see things when they are pointed out to him.'

'Say a prayer, then, and follow me.'

'I will. Just you lead the way,' he said.

'The place is impenetrable,' I said, 'and full of shadows. And it's certainly dark. Not an easy place to dislodge our quarry from. Still, we must go on.'

'Yes, we must.'

d   And then I caught sight of it. 'Aha! Over here, Glaucon,' I cried. 'This looks like the trail. I think our quarry is not going to escape us, after all.'

[14] At 430e.

'That's good news,' he said.

'We've been complete idiots.'

'In what way?'

'We're fine ones! It's been lying here under our noses all this time. Right from the start, though we couldn't see it. We've been making fools

e of ourselves. You know how sometimes you look for a thing when you're holding it in your hand. Well, that's what we've been doing. We haven't been looking in the right direction. We've been looking miles away in the opposite direction, and that's probably why we haven't seen it.'

'What do you mean?'

'All I mean,' I said, 'is that I think we've been talking about it, and listening to ourselves talking about it, without realising it was in some way what we were talking about.'

'This is a very long introduction,' he said. 'Your audience is getting impatient.'

433   'Very well. See if I'm talking sense, then. The principle we laid down right at the start, when we first founded our city, as something we must stick to throughout – this, I think, or some form of it, is justice. What we laid down – and often repeated, if you remember – was that each individual should follow, out of the occupations available in the city, the one for which his natural character best fitted him.'[15]

'Yes, we did say that.'

'And we have often heard others say, and have often said ourselves, that

b doing one's own job, and not trying to do other people's jobs for them, is justice.'[16]

'Yes, we have said that.'

'Well, it looks, my friend, as if in some way or other *justice* is this business of everyone performing his own task. Do you know what makes me think that?'

'No. Tell me.'

'I think the remaining element in the city, besides the virtues we have been looking at – self-discipline, courage and wisdom – is the thing which gave all the others the power to come into being, and the thing whose

---

[15] Laid down at 370a–c; repeated or alluded to at 374a–e, 395b, 406c, 421a.

[16] Credit for not trying to do other people's jobs was typically claimed by or awarded to citizens who avoided litigiousness or aggressive politicking, and to states which respected the autonomy of other states (see *GPM* 188). It therefore accrued also to the contemplative life of the philosopher who shunned political ambition. On the other hand, non-interference could be given the coloration of apathy, aggressiveness that of dynamism, as famously in Pericles' funeral oration in Thucydides (2.40).

continued presence keeps them safe once they *have* come into being. We

c said earlier that justice would be the one left over, if we could only find the other three.'[17]

'Yes, it would have to be,' he said.

'Now, if we had to decide,' I said, 'which of these elements would do most to make our city good by its inclusion, that would be a difficult decision. Is it the agreement of the rulers and the ruled? Or the preservation, in the ranks of the warriors, of an opinion approved by law about which things are to be feared and which are not? Or the wisdom and protectiveness we find in the rulers? Or does the largest contribution to making the

d city good come from the presence, in child and woman, slave and free man, in skilled craftsman, ruler and ruled, of the principle that each single individual is to perform his own task without troubling himself about the tasks of others?'

'Yes, that would be a difficult decision,' he said. 'Bound to be.'

'So as a means of producing an excellent city, the ability of everyone to perform his own function is apparently a strong competitor with the city's wisdom, self-discipline and courage.'

'Very much so.'

'And would you not say that the thing which is a strong contender with them when it comes to producing an excellent city is justice?'

e 'Definitely.'

'Here's another way of looking at it. See if you still agree. Will you give the rulers in your city the task of hearing cases in the lawcourts?'

'Of course.'

'When they hear cases, will their main aim be to make sure no class either takes what belongs to another, or has what belongs to it taken away by somebody else?'

'Yes, that will be their main aim.'

'Because this is just?'

'Yes.'

434 'So from this point of view as well, people's ownership and use of what belongs to them, and is their own, can be agreed to be justice.'

'That is so.'

'Now, see if you agree with me about the next step. If a carpenter tried to do the job of a shoemaker, or a shoemaker the job of a carpenter, either because they exchanged tools and positions in society, or because one

---

[17] 427e–428a.

person tried to do both jobs, do you think in general that changes of this sort would do much harm to the city?'

'No, not really,' he said.

'But I imagine it's different when someone who is naturally a craftsman
b or moneymaker of some other kind is puffed up by wealth, popularity, strength, or something like that, and tries to enter the warrior class, or when one of the warriors tries to enter the decision-making and guardian class, without being up to it. If these people exchange tools and positions in society, or if one person tries to do all these jobs at the same time, then I think you will agree with me that this change and interference on their part is destructive to the city.'

'Yes, it certainly is.'

c   'It is the interference of our three classes with one another, then, and interchange between them, which does the greatest harm to the city, and can rightly be called the worst crime against it.'

'Absolutely.'

'Isn't "injustice" the name for the greatest crime against one's own city?'

'Of course.'

'That, then, is what injustice is. Conversely, its opposite – the ability of the commercial, auxiliary and guardian classes to mind their own business, with each of them performing its own function in the city – this will be justice, and will make the city just.'

d   'Yes, I think that's exactly how it is,' he said.

'I don't think we can be too sure about it just yet,' I said. 'If the same characteristic turns up in each individual human being, and is agreed to be justice there too, then we shall accept it, since there will be no alternative. If not, we shall have to look for something else. For the moment, though, let's complete our original enquiry. We thought if we started with some large object which had justice in it, and tried to observe justice there,
e that would make it easier to see what justice was like in the individual.[18] We chose a city as this large object, and that's why we founded the best city we could, in the confident belief that it is in the good city that justice is to be found. Now let us apply our findings there to the individual. If they agree, well and good. If we come to some other conclusion about the
435 individual, then we shall go back to the city again, and test it on that. If we look at the two side by side, perhaps we can get a spark from them.

---

[18] See 368e.

Like rubbing dry sticks together. If that makes justice appear, we shall have confirmed it to our satisfaction.'

'You're on the right road,' he said. 'That is what we must do.'

'Very well, then,' I said. 'If you have two things – one larger, one smaller – and you call them by the same name, are they like or unlike in respect of that which gives them the same name?'

'Like,' he said.

b   'So the just man in his turn, simply in terms of his justice, will be no different from a just city. He will be like the just city.'

'He will.'

'In the case of the city, we decided it was just because each of the three types of nature in it was performing its own function. And we decided it was self-disciplined, brave and wise as a result of other conditions and states of the same three types.'

'True.'

c   'In that case, my admirable friend, if the individual too has these same elements in his soul, we shall feel entitled to expect that it is because these elements are in the same condition in him as they were in the city that he is properly titled by the same names we gave the city.'

'Yes, inevitably,' he said.

'Well! Here's another simple little question we seem to have blundered into,' I said. 'About the soul, this time. Does it contain these three elements within it? Or doesn't it?'

'Not such a little question, if you ask me. Maybe, Socrates, there is some truth in the saying that the good never comes easily.'

d   'So it seems. And I have to tell you, Glaucon, that in my view we are certainly not going to find a precise answer to our enquiry by the kind of methods we are using at the moment in our argument. There *is* a way of getting there, but it is longer and more time-consuming.[19] Still, we may be able to get an answer which is no worse than our earlier answers and investigations.'

'Can't we be content with that?' he said. 'For my part, I would reckon that was enough to be going on with.'

'Yes,' I said, 'I'd be more than satisfied with that, too.'

'No weakening, then,' he said. 'Carry on with the enquiry.'

e   'Very well. Do we have no choice but to agree that in each of us are found the same elements and characteristics as are found in the city? After

---

[19] The allusion is explained in Book 6, 504a–d.

all, where else could the city have got them from? It would be ludicrous
to imagine that the spirited element in cities has come into being from
anywhere other than the individual citizens – where the citizens in fact
possess this reputation. People in Thrace, for example, or Scythia, or
pretty well anywhere in the North. The same goes for love of learning,
which can be regarded as the outstanding characteristic of our region.[20]
Or the commercial instinct, which you could say was to be found principally among the Phoenicians and people in Egypt.'

'Yes, it would be totally ludicrous to imagine these qualities came from
anywhere else.'

'That's the way it is, then,' I said. 'No problem in recognising that.'

'None at all.'

'What *is* a problem, though, is this. Do we do each of these things with
the same part of ourselves? Or, since there are three elements, do we do
different things with different elements? Is there one element in us for
learning, another for feeling spirited, and yet a third for our desire for the
pleasures of food, sex, and things like that? Or do we do each of these
things, when we embark upon them, with our entire soul? Those are questions to which it will be hard to give a convincing answer.'

'I agree,' he said.

'So, let us try to ascertain whether they are the same as each other or
different. And let's go about it like this.'

'Like what?'

'It's obvious that nothing can do two opposite things, or be in two
opposite states, in the same part of itself, at the same time, in relation to
the same object. So if this is what we find happening in these examples,
we shall know there was not just one element involved, but more than
one.'

'Fair enough.'

'Now, concentrate.'

'I am,' he said. 'Carry on.'

'Is it possible,' I asked, 'for one thing to be at the same time, and with
the same part of itself, at rest and in motion?'

'No.'

'Can we be even more precise about what we are agreeing, to avoid
argument later on? Imagine a man standing still, but moving his head and

---

[20] Both because the clear, dry air of the place was thought to promote clarity and acute-
ness in its inhabitants, and because Athens was an international magnet for intellectuals and had an especially well-developed cultural life.

his hands. If anyone said the same man was at the same time both at rest and in motion, then I don't think we would regard that as a legitimate
d   claim. What he should say is that one part of him is at rest, and another part is in motion, shouldn't he?'

'Yes, he should.'

'He could amuse himself with an even more ingenious example. If he said, of a spinning top with its centre fixed in one place, or of anything
e   else rotating on the same spot, that the whole thing is both at rest and in motion, we would not accept that. In cases like this, the parts in respect of which they are both stationary and in motion are not the same parts. We would say they possess both a vertical axis and a circumference. With respect to the axis they are at rest, since they remain upright. With respect to the circumference they are rotating. And if, while they are still revolving, the vertical axis inclines to right or left, or front or back, then they can't be at rest at all.'

'True,' he said.

'So we're not going to be at all intimidated by examples of this kind. It will do nothing to persuade us that it is in any way possible for one thing,
437   in the same part of itself, with respect to the same object, to be at the same time in two opposite states, or to be or do two opposite things.'

'It certainly won't persuade me,' he said.

'All the same,' I said, 'we don't want to have to work our way through every objection of this kind, spending hours establishing that they are not valid. So let us proceed from here on the assumption that this *is* the situation, with the proviso that if this isn't how things turn out to be, all our conclusions based on this assumption will have been destroyed.'

'Yes, that is what we should do,' he said.
b   'Very well. Now, think about things like saying "yes" and saying "no", desire and rejection, or attraction and repulsion. Wouldn't you classify all those as pairs of opposites? Whether they are activities or states will be irrelevant for our purposes.'

'Yes, as opposites.'

'What about hunger and thirst,' I said, 'and desires in general? Or
c   wanting and being willing? Wouldn't you find all those a place among the categories we just mentioned? Won't you say, for example, that the soul of the person who desires something either reaches out for what it desires, or draws what it wants towards itself? Or to the extent that it is willing to have something provided for it, that it mentally says "yes" to it, as if in reply to a question, as it stretches out towards the realisation of its desire?'

'Yes.'

'What about not wanting, being unwilling, and not desiring? Won't we classify them with rejection and refusal, with all the corresponding opposites, in fact?'

'Of course.'

d   'That being so, can we say that the desires form a class, and that the most striking of them are the ones we call thirst and hunger?'

'We can.'

'And that one is a desire for drink, the other a desire for food?'

'Yes.'

'Well, then, is thirst, considered simply as thirst, a desire in the soul for anything more than we have just said? For example, is thirst thirst for a warm drink or a cold drink? For a large drink or a small one? Or, to put it
e   briefly, is it for any particular kind of drink at all? Or does the addition of a little bit of warmth to the thirst produce the desire for cold as well? And does the addition of cold produce desire for warmth? If the presence of largeness makes the thirst a large one, will it produce the desire for a large drink? And will a small thirst produce the desire for a small one? But thirst itself cannot possibly be a desire for anything other than its natural object, which is purely and simply drink – any more than hunger can be a desire for anything other than food.'

'That's right,' he said. 'Each and every desire, in itself, is a desire only for the thing which is its natural object. The additional element in each case is what makes it a desire for this or that particular *kind* of object.'

438   'We don't want to be interrupted by objections we haven't considered,' I said. 'So here's one. No one desires drink, but rather good drink. No one desires food, but rather good food, since everyone desires good things. So if thirst is a desire, it must be a desire for something good. Either a drink, or whatever else it is a desire for. The same goes for the other desires.'

'Well,' he said, 'you might think there was something in this objection.'

b   'Yes,' I said, 'but if you take all the things which are such as to be related to something else, I think that qualified instances are related to qualified objects, whereas the things themselves are each of them related only to an object which is just itself.'

'I don't understand,' he said.

'What don't you understand? That it is the nature of what is greater to be greater than something?'

'No, I understand that.'

'Greater than what is smaller?'

'Yes.'

'And what is much greater than what is much smaller?'

'Yes.'

'And what was once greater than what was once smaller, and what will be greater than what will be smaller?'

'Obviously,' he said.

c   'And the same with more in relation to less, double in relation to half, and all those sorts of things? Or heavier in relation to lighter, faster in relation to that which is slower? Or hot in relation to cold, for that matter, or anything of that sort?'

'Certainly.'

'What about branches of knowledge? Doesn't the same principle apply? There is knowledge in itself, which is knowledge simply of that which can be learnt – or of whatever it is we are to suppose that knowledge is knowledge of. Then there is this or that branch of knowledge,

d which is knowledge of this or that specific subject. The kind of thing I mean is this. When a knowledge of housebuilding came into being, did it differ from other branches of knowledge? Was that why it was called knowledge of building?'

'Yes, of course.'

'Because it was a specific branch of knowledge, different from all the other branches?'

'Yes.'

'And was it not because it was knowledge of some specific subject that it became a specific branch of knowledge? And the same with the other branches of skill and knowledge?'

'True.'

'Well, if you understood it this time,' I said, 'that is what you must take me to have meant just now. I said that when things are such as to stand in some relation to something else, the things just by themselves are related to objects just by themselves, while qualified instances are related to

e qualified objects. That's not in any way to say they *are like* the things they are in relation to – that the knowledge of health and disease is healthy or diseased, or that the knowledge of good and bad is good or bad. Rather, since the knowledge here is not of that which just is the object of knowledge, but of some qualified object – in this case what is healthy or diseased – the knowledge itself turned out to be a specific branch of knowledge as well. This is why it was no longer simply called knowledge, but rather, because of this specific addition, medical knowledge.'

'I understand,' he said. 'And I think you're right.'

439   'Let's go back to thirst, then,' I said. 'Won't you put that in the category of things which are what they are in relation to something else? Thirst, then, is of course thirst . . .'

'Yes. For drink.'

'So for any particular kind of drink, isn't there also a particular kind of thirst? Whereas thirst as such is not thirst for a large drink or a small drink, nor for a good drink or a bad drink – nor, to put it briefly, for any specific drink at all. No, the object of thirst as such is, in the nature of things, simply drink as such, isn't it?'

'Absolutely.'

'Then all the thirsty person's soul wants, in so far as he is thirsty, is to drink. That's what it reaches out for, and makes for.'

b   'Clearly.'

'And if there is anything at all holding it back when it is thirsty, would this have to be a different element in it from the actual part which is thirsty, and which drives it like an animal to drink? After all, the same thing cannot, in our view, do two opposite things, in the same part of itself, with respect to the same object, at the same time.'

'No, it cannot.'

'In the same way, I think it's wrong to say of an archer that his hands are pushing and pulling the bow at the same time. What we should say is that one hand is pushing, while the other is pulling.'

'Precisely,' he said.

c   'Now, can we say that some thirsty people sometimes refuse to drink?'

'Yes, lots of them,' he said. 'Often.'

'What can be said about these people, then? Can't we say there is something in their soul telling them to drink, and also something stopping them? Something different from, and stronger than, the thing telling them they *should* drink?'

'Yes, I think we can say that,' he said.

'The thing which stops them in these cases – doesn't it arise, when it

d   does arise, as a result of rational calculation, whereas the things which drive or draw them towards drink are the products of feelings and disorders?'

'Apparently.'

'It will be a reasonable inference, then,' I said, 'that they are two completely different things. The part of the soul with which we think rationally we can call the rational element. The part with which we feel sexual desire, hunger, thirst, and the turmoil of the other desires can be called the irrational and desiring element, the companion of indulgence and pleasure.'

e   'Yes,' he said, 'that would be a perfectly natural conclusion for us to come to.'

'Let's take it, then, that we have established the presence of these two elements in the soul. How about spirit, the thing which makes us behave in a spirited way? Is that a third element? If not, its nature must be the same as one of the others. Which?'

'The second, maybe. The desiring element.'

'As against that,' I said, 'there's a story I once heard which I think can guide us here. Leontius, the son of Aglaeon, was on his way up to town from the Piraeus. As he was walking below the north wall, on the outside, he saw the public executioner with some dead bodies lying beside him. He wanted to look at the bodies, but at the same time he felt disgust and

440 held himself back. For a time he struggled, and covered his eyes. Then desire got the better of him. He rushed over to where the bodies were, and forced his eyes wide open, saying, "There you are, curse you. Have a really good look. Isn't it a lovely sight?"'

'Yes, I've heard that story, too,' he said.

'It shows that anger can sometimes be at war with the desires, which implies that they are two distinct and separate things.'

'Yes, it does show that,' he said.

'Aren't there lots of other situations as well – whenever people are

b   forced into doing things by their desires against the advice of their reason – when they curse themselves, and are furious with the bit of them which forces them to do these things? It's as if there's a civil war going on inside someone like this, with spirit acting as an ally of reason. Spirit siding with the desires, on the other hand, when reason has declared its opposition, is not the kind of thing I imagine you'd ever claim to have seen, either in yourself or in anybody else.'

'No, I certainly haven't,' he said.

c   'Think about someone who realises he is in the wrong. Isn't it the case that the better his character, the less he is capable of feeling anger at having to endure hunger, or cold, or anything like that at the hands of someone he regards as entitled to inflict these things on him? Isn't it his spirit, as I say, which refuses to raise any objection?'

'Yes, that's true.'

'How about someone who thinks he is *being* wronged? While this is

d   going on, doesn't he boil with rage at hunger, cold and any hardships of this kind? Doesn't he ally himself with what he thinks is just, and endure all these things until he wins through, refusing to give up his justified indignation until he either achieves his aim, or dies, or is called back and pacified by the reason within him, like a dog being recalled by a shepherd?'

'Yes, that's a very close parallel with what you were talking about. What is more, in our city we specified that the auxiliaries should be obedient dogs to the city's shepherd rulers.'[21]

'Good,' I said. 'You understand exactly what I'm talking about. But there's another point too you might notice about it.'

'What is that?'

e   'It's the opposite of our suggestion about the spirited element a few moments ago. We thought then it was desirous in character, whereas now we regard it as anything but. In the civil war of the soul, it is far more likely to take up arms on the side of the rational part.'

'Absolutely,' he said.

'Is it something independent of the rational element as well, or is it some form *of* the rational element? Are there not three elements in the soul, but only two, the rational and the desiring? Or is the soul like the city? The city was held together by three classes, commercial, auxiliary
441 and decision-making. Does the soul also contain this third, spirited, element, which is auxiliary to the rational element by nature, provided it is not corrupted by a poor upbringing?'

'Yes, it does contain a third element,' he said. 'It must do.'

'Yes, provided this can be shown to be something distinct from the rational element, just as it was shown to be something distinct from the desiring element.'

'That's easily shown,' he said. 'You can see it in young children. Right
b   from the time they are born, they are full of spirit, though most of them, if you ask me, only achieve some degree of rationality late in life. And some never at all.'

'How right you are. Even in animals you can see that what you are talking about applies. And apart from these examples, there is the evidence of Homer, in the line I think we quoted earlier:

He smote his chest, and thus rebuked his heart.[22]

---

[21] 416a.

[22] *Odyssey* 20.17, quoted together with line 18 at 390d. The citation develops the comparison of spirit to a dog, since Odysseus is quieting the heart that bays like a dog within him and longs for revenge.

In that passage Homer clearly portrays two different elements. The
c part which has reflected rationally on what is better and what is worse has
some sharp words to say to the element which is irrationally angry.'

'You are certainly right,' he said.

'There we are, then,' I said. 'We have made it to dry land – not without
difficulty – and we are pretty well agreed that the soul of each individual
contains the same sorts of thing, and the same number of them, as a city
contains.'

'True.'

'The immediate and inescapable conclusion is that the individual is
wise in the same way, and using the same part of himself, as the city when
it was wise.'

'Of course.'

d   'Also that the thing which makes the individual brave, and the way in
which he is brave, is the same as the thing which makes the city brave, and
the way in which it is brave. That in everything to do with virtue the two
of them are the same.'

'Yes, that is inescapable.'

'So a just man is just, I think we shall say, Glaucon, in the same way a
city was just.'

'That too follows with complete certainty.'

'We haven't at any point forgotten, I hope, that the city was just when
each of the three elements in it was performing its own function.'

'No, I don't think we have forgotten that,' he said.

e   'In that case, we must also remember that each one of us will be just,
and perform his own proper task, when each of the elements within him
is performing *its* proper task.'

'Yes, we must certainly remember that.'

'Isn't it appropriate for the rational element to rule, because it is wise
and takes thought for the entire soul, and appropriate for the spirited
element to be subordinate, the ally of the rational element?'

'Yes.'

'Won't a combination, as we said,[23] of musical and physical education
442 make these two elements concordant? They will bring the rational part to
a higher pitch, with their diet of improving stories and studies, while at
the same time toning down the spirited part by gentle encouragement,
calming it by means of harmony and rhythm.'

---

[23] 411a–412a.

'They certainly will,' he said.

'When these two elements are brought up on a diet of this kind, when they truly receive the teaching and education appropriate to them, then the two of them will exercise control over the desiring element, which in any individual is the largest element in the soul and, left to itself, the most insatiable where material goods are concerned. They will keep a close eye on it, to make sure the satisfaction of the body's so-called pleasures
b doesn't encourage it to grow great and strong, stop performing its own function, and throw the life of all of them into confusion by its attempt to enslave and rule over elements which it is not naturally equipped to rule over.'

'They will indeed,' he said. 'A very close eye.'

'Aren't these two elements also the best defenders, for body and soul in their entirety, against external enemies? One makes the decisions, the other does the fighting, under the leadership of the ruling element, using its courage to put those decisions into effect.'

'True.'

c 'The title "brave," I think, is one we give to any individual because of this part of him, when the spirited element in him, though surrounded by pleasures and pains, keeps intact the instructions given to it by reason about what is to be feared and what is not to be feared.'

'Rightly so,' he said.

'And the title "wise" because of that small part which acted as an internal ruler and gave those instructions, having within it a corresponding knowledge of what was good both for each part and for the whole community of the three of them together.'

'Exactly.'

'What about "self-disciplined"? Isn't that the result of the friendship
d and harmony of these three? The ruling element and the two elements which are ruled agree that what is rational should rule, and do not rebel against it.'

'Yes. That's exactly what self-discipline is,' he said, 'both for a city and for an individual.'

'And a person will be just, finally, by virtue of the principle we have several times stated.[24] It determines both the fact and the manner of his justice.'

'Yes, inevitably.'

---

[24] The principle of doing one's own job, last mentioned at 441d. See also 433b, with note 14.

'In that case,' I said, 'do we find justice looking at all blurred round the edges? Does it seem any different to us from what it was when it showed up in the city?'

'Not to me it doesn't.'

e   'If there *is* anything in our soul which is still inclined to dispute this,' I said, 'we can appeal to everyday life for final confirmation.'

'What do you mean, everyday life?'

'Well, imagine we were discussing this city and the man who by his nature and upbringing resembles it, and we had to agree whether we thought a man like this would embezzle a sum of gold or silver deposited with him for safe keeping. Could anyone, do you suppose, possibly

443   imagine such a man to be more likely to do this than people who were different from him?'

'No,' he said. 'I don't suppose anyone could.'

'Would this man have anything to do with temple-robbery, theft and betrayal? Either of his friends in private life, or of his city in public life?'

'No, he wouldn't.'

'What is more, he would be utterly reliable in keeping oaths and other sorts of agreement.'

'Of course.'

'Then again adultery, neglect of parents, failure in religious observance – he'd be the last person you'd expect to find with those faults.'

'Absolutely the last,' he said.

b   'Is the reason for all this that when it comes to ruling and being ruled, each of the elements within him performs its own function?'

'Yes, that is the reason. The sole reason.'

'In which case, do you still want justice to be anything more than this power which can produce both men and cities of this calibre?'

'No, that's more than enough for me,' he said.

'In that case, we have seen the final realisation of our dream – our

c   suspicion that our very first attempt at founding our city might possibly, with a bit of divine guidance, have hit upon both the origin, and some sort of model, of justice.'

'Yes, we certainly have seen its realisation.'

'So this principle, Glaucon – that if you are a shoemaker by nature, you should confine yourself to making shoes, if you are a carpenter you should confine yourself to carpentry, and so on – really was a kind of image of justice. Which is why it was so useful to us.'

'Apparently so.'

'But the truth is that although justice apparently *was* something of this
d kind, it was not concerned with the external performance of a man's own
function, but with the internal performance of it, with his true self and
his own true function, forbidding each of the elements within him to
perform tasks other than its own, and not allowing the classes of thing
within his soul to interfere with one another. He has, quite literally, to put
his own house in order, being himself his own ruler, mentor and friend,
and tuning the three elements just like three fixed points in a musical scale
e – top, bottom and intermediate. And if there turn out to be any intervening elements, he must combine them all, and emerge as a perfect unity
of diverse elements, self-disciplined and in harmony with himself. Only
then does he act, whether it is a question of making money, or taking care
of his body, or some political action, or contractual agreements with
private individuals. In all these situations he believes and declares that a
just and good action is one which preserves or brings about this state of
444 mind, and that wisdom is the knowledge which directs the action. That
an unjust action, in its turn, is any action which tends to destroy this state
of mind, and that ignorance is the opinion which directs the unjust
action.'

'You are absolutely right, Socrates.'

'Well then,' I said, 'if we were to say we had found the just man and the
just city, and what justice really was in them, we couldn't be said to be
totally wide of the mark, in my view.'

'We most certainly couldn't,' he said.

'Is that what we are going to say, then?'

'We are.'

'Let's leave it at that, then,' I said, 'since the next thing we have to look
into, I imagine, is injustice.'

'Obviously.'

'Injustice, on this definition, must be some sort of civil war between
b these three elements, a refusal to mind their own business, and a determination to mind each other's, a rebellion by one part of the soul against
the whole. The part which rebels is bent on being ruler in it when it is not
equipped to be, its natural role being that of slave to what is of the ruling
class. Something like this is what we shall say, I think. And we shall add
that the disorder and straying of the three elements produce injustice,
indiscipline, cowardice, ignorance – evil of every kind, in fact.'

c 'We shall not say something *like* this,' he said. 'We shall say exactly
this.'

'Very well,' I said. 'Now that we have a clear picture of injustice and justice, do we also have a clear picture of unjust actions and acting unjustly? And similarly of just actions?'

'Explain.'

'Well,' I said, 'the effect on the soul of actions which are just and unjust is really no different from the effect on the body of actions which are healthy and unhealthy.'

'In what way?'

'Things which are healthy produce health, presumably. And things which are unhealthy produce disease.'

'Yes.'

d   'So does acting justly produce justice, and acting unjustly produce injustice?'

'It's bound to.'

'Producing health is a question of arranging the elements in the body so that they control one another – and are controlled – in the way nature intends.[25] Producing disease is a question of their ruling and being ruled, one by another, in a way nature does not intend.'

'True.'

'Does it follow, then,' I asked, 'that producing justice in its turn is a question of arranging the elements in the soul so that they control one another – and are controlled – in the way nature intends? Is producing injustice a question of their ruling and being ruled, one by another, in a way nature does not intend?'

'Indeed it is,' he said.

e   'In which case, virtue would apparently be some sort of health, beauty and vigour in the soul, while vice would be disease, ugliness and weakness.'

'That is so.'

'Doesn't it follow also that good behaviour leads to the acquisition of virtue, and bad behaviour to the acquisition of vice?'

'Inevitably.'

'The only question now remaining for us to answer, it seems, is which 445 is more profitable. Just actions, good behaviour and being just – whether the just person is known to be just or not? Or unjust actions, and being unjust – even if the unjust person gets away with it, and never reforms as a result of punishment?'

---

[25] It was common in medical theory to attribute health to the right balance between the constituents of the body, disease to a disruption of this balance.

'Now that justice and injustice have turned out to be the kinds of things we have described, that seems an absurd question, if you want my opinion, Socrates. When the body's natural constitution is ruined, life seems not worth living, even with every variety of food and drink, and all manner of wealth and power. Is someone's life going to be worth living

b when the natural constitution of the very thing by which he lives is upset and ruined, even assuming he can then do anything he likes – apart from what will release him from evil and injustice, and win him justice and virtue?'

'You're right,' I said, 'It's an absurd question. Still, now that we've got to the point of being able to see as clearly as possible that this is how things are, this isn't the moment to take a rest.'

'No,' he said. 'The last thing we should do is show any hesitation.'

c 'This way, then, if you want to see what I believe to be the forms taken by vice. The ones worth looking at, anyway.'

'I'm right behind you,' he said. 'Speak on.'

'Well, now that we've got this far in our discussion,' I said, 'it looks from my vantage-point as if there is a single form of virtue, and any number of forms of vice, of which four are worth mentioning.'

'Please explain,' he said.

'If you think how many types of political regime there are with their own specific form,' I said, 'that's probably how many types of soul there are.'

'And how many is that?'

d 'Five types of political regime,' I said, 'and five types of soul.'

'Tell me which they are,' he said.

'All right. I would say that one type of regime is this one we have just described, though there are two names it might be given. It might be called monarchy, if one exceptional individual emerges among the rulers, or aristocracy if several emerge.'

'True.'

e 'This one, then, I class as a single form,' I said. 'It makes no difference whether it is several who emerge, or an individual. Given the upbringing and education we have described, they would not disturb any of the important laws of the city.'

'No. That wouldn't be sensible,' he said.

Book 5

449 'Very well, then. "Good" and "correct" are the labels I attach to a city and political regime of this kind, and to a man of this kind. And if this city is correct, then I call other cities bad and faulty, both in the way they are run and when it comes to forming the character of the individual soul. The bad ones fall into four categories.'

'What are they?'

b I was about to embark on a systematic account of the way I thought the various categories developed out of one another, when Polemarchus, who was sitting a little bit away from Adeimantus, reached out a hand and took hold of his cloak up at the shoulder. Drawing Adeimantus towards him, he leaned forward and started whispering to him. All we could hear of it was: 'What shall we do? Shall we let it go?'

'No,' Adeimantus replied, out loud.

'What in particular,' I asked, 'do you not want to let go?'

'You.'

c 'What in particular that I have said?'

'We think you're taking the lazy way out. Short-changing us out of a whole line of thought – and an important one – in the argument, to save yourself the trouble of explaining it. You think that when it comes to women and children you can get away with a casual remark to the effect that friends will hold things in common, as if no one could be in any doubt about this.'[1]

'Wasn't what I said correct, then, Adeimantus?'

'Yes, it was,' he said. 'But like the rest of our correct statements, it

---

[1] The reference is to 423e–424a.

144

needs some explanation. What do you mean by "common"? There are
d lots of possibilities, and you're not going to get away without telling us
which one you mean. We've been sitting around here patiently, assuming
you were bound to say something about the production of children – what
their practice will be in this regard, and how they will bring the children
up once they are born, and this whole business you've suggested of
women and children being "in common." We think it's of great, indeed
crucial, importance for our state whether this is done in the right way or
the wrong way. So when you started to deal with another regime before
450 settling these questions in a satisfactory way, we made the decision you
heard us making, not to let you go until you have given a full description
of this topic, like the other topics.'

'Count me in as well,' said Glaucon, 'as a joint proposer of this motion.'

'Take it as a unanimous decision, Socrates,' Thrasymachus added.

'I hope you realise,' I said, 'what you're doing in taking me to task.
You're taking us right back to square one, to begin a second major discussion about our state, just as I was starting to congratulate myself on
having completed my account of it. I'd have been only too pleased if those
b remarks had been accepted as they stood. Instead of which you've
brought them up for examination, without the slightest idea what a verbal
hornet's nest you are stirring up. I could see it earlier on, which was why
I thought I would save us a lot of trouble back then by avoiding the question.'

'Do you think,' Thrasymachus asked, 'that all these people have come
here to look for the rainbow's end?[2] Or have they come to listen to a discussion?'

'To listen to a discussion. But it has to be of a reasonable length.'

'Well, Socrates,' said Glaucon, 'for people with any sense a reasonable
length of time to listen to a discussion of this kind is their whole life. So
c don't worry about us. Worry about the question we are asking you. You
are going to have your work cut out to explain to us what you think this
business of things being "in common" among our guardians will be like,
as it affects women and children and the children's upbringing while they
are still young, in the intervening period between birth and formal education. That is generally regarded as the most demanding part of their
upbringing, so you must try and tell us what form it ought to take.'

'What an innocent request! But it's not an easy matter to explain. It's

---

[2] The Greek expression used by Thrasymachus, meaning 'to prospect for gold', was
similarly proverbial of engaging in a wasteful task with little chance of success.

open to objection at a number of points – even more so than the suggestions we have made so far. There may be doubts whether it is practicable, and however possible it may be, there will be doubts about its
d wisdom. Hence my reluctance to get involved with it, in case my suggestions strike you, my dear friend, as just wishful thinking.'

'No need for reluctance. Your audience is neither ignorant, nor scept-
ical, nor hostile.'

'Do you really think,' I asked him, 'that you're encouraging me by
saying that?'

'Yes,' he replied.

'Because the effect is exactly the opposite. If I thought I knew what I
e was talking about, then your encouragement would be welcome. In a
gathering of intelligent and congenial people, talking about important
and congenial topics, the knowledge that what one is saying is true gives
grounds for security and confidence. But if you're not sure of the answer
and are still looking for it when you start talking – as I am now – that's an
451 alarming and unsettling experience. It's not the fear of making a fool of
myself – that would be childish. No, I'm worried that if I make a false step
on the path of truth, I shan't just fall myself, but shall drag my friends
down with me as well – and in a place where a false step is most disastrous.
So I make my apologies to Adrasteia for what I am about to say, Glaucon,
since I believe that when it comes to involuntary crimes, homicide is less
serious than giving wrong directions on the subject of fine, good and just
b institutions, and that it is better to take chances of that sort with one's
enemies than with one's friends. So thanks a lot for your encouragement.'

Glaucon laughed. 'Well, Socrates, if what you say does us any harm,
we'll treat it like a homicide case. We acquit you of misleading us, and you
can leave the court without a stain on your character. So relax. Tell us
what you have to say.'

'Well, the law says if you are acquitted, then you are free from pollution. The chances are if it's true in the case of homicide, it's true here as
well.'[3]

'That's all right, then. Say on.'

c 'In that case,' I said, 'I'd better go back and deal now with something I
should perhaps have dealt with earlier, in its rightful place. Though
maybe this is the right way to do it. Get the men's performance well and

---

[3] In Athenian law the relatives of a murder victim could pardon the murderer and so
acquit him – that is, free him of penalties – if it was determined at trial that the
murder was involuntary.

truly finished first, before going on to the women's.[4] All the more so as that is what you are so keen on. For people whose nature and education are as we have described, then, the only correct way of possessing and dealing with women and children, in my opinion, is one based on the orig-inal starting-point we gave them at the beginning. Our intention, I take it, was to make the men in our hypothetical city into some kind of guardians of the herd.'[5]

d   'Yes.'

'Shall we follow that up then by giving them a birth and upbringing consistent with this role? Shall we see whether or not that suits our purpose?'

'What do you mean?'

'I mean this. Do we think female watchdogs should do their share of watching, in the same way as male watchdogs? Should they do their share of hunting, and join in other activities? Or do we think that bearing and raising puppies makes them incapable of doing their share? Do we expect the females to stay at home indoors while the males do the work and have the whole responsibility for the flocks?'

'We think they should join in everything,' he said. 'We treat the females

e   as weaker, though, and the males as stronger.'

'Well then, is it possible to employ one animal for the same tasks as another without giving it the same upbringing and training?'

'No, it's not possible.'

'So if we're going to employ women for the same tasks as men, we must give them the same teaching.'

'Yes.'

452 'The education we gave men had a musical and poetic element, and a physical element.'

'Yes.'

'So women too should receive these two disciplines, plus military train-ing. And they should be treated in the same way.'

'It looks like it,' he said, 'from what you've been saying.'

'Much of what we are saying now is pretty unconventional. It may well seem absurd, if our suggestions are really going to be put into practice.'

---

[4] There may be an allusion to the classification of mimes (dramatised scenes from everyday life) as 'men's performances' and 'women's performances', according to whether the fictional characters were male or female. Plato's dialogues are thought to have been influenced by the mimes of the fifth-century Sicilian writer Sophron, which were so classified.

[5] The comparison was introduced in Book 2, 375a, and developed at 416a and 440d.

'Indeed it may.'[6]

'What do you find the most absurd thing about it? Isn't it obviously the
b idea of women taking exercise naked, along with men, in the wrestling-
schools?[7] Not just young women, but older ones as well, like the old men
you find in the gymnasiums. They're all wrinkled, and by no means a
pretty sight, but they still retain an enthusiasm for taking exercise.'

'Yes,' he replied. 'That would certainly look pretty absurd – at least the
way things are at present.'

'Well, now that we've brought the subject up, we mustn't be afraid of
c all the standard jokes we'd hear from humorists if we introduced changes
of that sort in physical exercise, in musical and poetic education, and particularly in carrying arms and riding on horseback.'

'You are right,' he said.

'And since we *have* brought it up, we must get on to the difficult business of legislation, with a request to these comedians to be serious. We
don't mind *them* not performing their own proper function. We can
remind them that it is not so very long since the Greeks thought it
immoral and absurd, as most foreigners still think it, for men to be seen
d naked. When first the Cretans, and then the Spartans, started exercising
naked, all that became a legitimate target for the humorists of the day.
Don't you agree?'

'I do.'

'I take it that once experience showed that you can do all these activities
better stripped than wearing clothes, then too the perception of absurdity
evaporated in the face of what rational calculation had revealed to be best.
It became clear that only a fool regards as laughable anything other
e than what is bad. Anyone who tries to be amusing by pointing at any
spectacle other than the spectacle of folly and wickedness must quite
seriously have set himself some standard of beauty other than that of the
good.'

---

6 Although women of the Athenian elite had at least basic literacy, girls were not normally given the education of boys. As in most other Greek states, they were trained
for the dual roles of household management and raising children, and had no political rights as individuals. Spartan women, exceptionally, were given a gymnastic
training equivalent to that of males. This is the first of a number of ways in which
Socrates' proposals for social reform in Book 5 resemble, with much exaggeration,
existing social arrangements at Sparta: see pp. xiv–xvi of the introduction. Some
women apparently managed to participate in the philosophic life – two women are
reported to have been students at Plato's Academy, and Pythagorean communities
may have included them as equals.

7 Since the late sixth or early fifth century it had become standard in the Greek world
for men to take their physical exercise naked.

'Exactly,' he said.

'In that case, don't we have to start by agreeing whether our suggestions are feasible or not? Let's give anyone who wants to challenge us
453 either in jest or in earnest – the opportunity to raise the questions: Is the
human female naturally capable of sharing all the activities of the male?
Or none of them? Or is she capable of some but not others? If so, in which
class does military activity come? Isn't that the best way for us to start –
and probably the best way to finish as well?'

'Much the best.'

'Would you like us to mount our own challenge, then?' I asked. 'We
don't want the other side's position abandoned without a struggle.'

b   'Why not? There's nothing to stop us.'

'All right. Let's speak for them. "Socrates and Glaucon, there's no need
for anyone else to challenge you. You yourselves agreed, when you first
started founding your city, that in the natural order of things each individual should carry out one task, the one for which he was fitted."[8]

'Yes, I think we did agree that. How could we disagree?'

'"Can you deny that a woman's nature is completely different from a
man's?"'

'No. Of course it's different.'

'"In that case, shouldn't each also be assigned a task appropriate to his
or her nature?"'

c   'Of course.'

'"Then you must be wrong now. You must be contradicting yourselves
when you say that men and women should perform the same tasks,
despite having widely differing natures." That's what they will say. And
what will you say? Will you have any defence against this objection?'

'It's very hard,' he said, 'to think of one just like that. No, I shall ask
you – in fact, I do ask you now – to present our side of the argument,
whatever it is, as well.'

'This is what I was afraid of, Glaucon. I could see this kind of question
d   coming up – and a whole lot of others like it. That's why I was reluctant
to touch upon the law relating to the acquisition and upbringing of
women and children.'

'I don't blame you,' he said. 'It doesn't look easy.'

'No, it doesn't. But whether you fall into a small swimming-pool or into
the middle of the largest sea, you still have to swim just the same. That's
a fact of life.'

'It certainly is.'

[8] 369e–370c.

'So we're going to have to swim too, and try and save ourselves from this objection. Let's hope we get picked up by a dolphin, or some equally unlikely agent of rescue.'[9]

e   'Yes, it does look as if we shall have to swim for it.'

'Come on then,' I said. 'Let's see if we can find an escape route. We agreed that different natures ought to pursue different occupations, and that a woman's nature was different from a man's nature. But now we are saying that these different natures ought to pursue the same occupations. Is that what we are being accused of?'

'It is indeed.'

454   'Extraordinary, Glaucon, isn't it, the power disputation has?'

'Why?'

'Because I think lots of people fall into it quite involuntarily. They believe they are holding a discussion, whereas in fact they are having a competition. Because they're incapable of examining what they are talking about by drawing distinctions, they look instead for purely verbal contradictions of what has been said. It's a competition they are having with one another, not a discussion.'

'True,' he said. 'That does happen to a lot of people. Does it apply to us as well, in what we are talking about now?'

b   'Very much so,' I replied. 'It looks as if we have lapsed into disputation.'

'In what way?'

'In our thoroughly courageous and competitive, but literal-minded way, we are pursuing the statement that different natures should not engage in the same occupations. We have not begun to ask ourselves what *kind* of natural difference or sameness we were specifying, or what our distinction applied to when we assigned different occupations to different natures, and the same occupations to the same natures.'

c   'No,' he said, 'we didn't ask ourselves that.'

'In which case there is nothing, as far as I can see, to stop us asking ourselves whether bald men and men with hair have the same nature or different natures. And when we agree that they have different natures, we can say that if bald men are shoemakers, then men with hair should not be allowed to make shoes. Or if men with hair are shoemakers, then bald men should not be allowed to.'

[9] The tale of the minstrel Arion's ride to safety on a dolphin after being made to jump overboard by a corrupt crew is the most famous account of such an incident to have come down from antiquity. See Herodotus 1.24.

'That would be ludicrous.'

'Yes, it would be ludicrous – for one very simple reason. When we made our rule, we weren't talking about natures which were the same or
d different in every possible way. We confined ourselves to the one kind of difference and sameness which was relevant to the occupations in question. We meant, for example, that two people with a talent for medicine both had the same nature.'

'Yes.'

'Whereas people who are good at medicine and people who are good at carpentry have different natures?'

'Absolutely.'

'So if either the male sex or the female sex is clearly superior when it comes to some skill or occupation, then we shall say this occupation should be assigned to this sex. But if the only difference appears to be that the female bears the children, while the male mounts the female, then we
e shall say this in no way proves that for our purposes a woman is any different from a man. We shall still think the guardians and their women should follow the same occupations.'

'And rightly.'

455 'The next step is to tell those who disagree with us to answer one simple question. For which skill or occupation associated with the running of a city are women's and men's natures not the same, but different?'

'A fair question.'

'And they might say, as you did a few moments ago, that it is not easy to find a satisfactory answer just like that, though with a bit of thought it wouldn't be so hard.'

'They might.'

'Do you want us to ask our opponent on this issue to follow us, and see
b if we can somehow demonstrate to him that in the management of a city there is no occupation which is the exclusive preserve of women?'

'Yes.'

'Come on then, we shall say to him. Tell us this. When you said that one man was naturally suited for something, and another naturally unsuited, did you mean that one learnt it easily, and the other with difficulty? Was one capable, after a brief period of instruction, of discovering a lot for himself about the thing he was learning, while the other, with any amount of instruction and practice, couldn't even remember the things he had been taught? For one of them, was the body the mind's useful

c assistant, while for the other it was its opponent? When you talked of
people being well or ill suited for various things, did your distinction
amount to anything other than this?'

'No. I don't think anyone will challenge that.'

'Can you think of any human activity in which the male sex is not superior to the female in all these ways? Or do we have to give a long account

d of weaving, cookery and baking cakes – things the female sex is thought
to be pretty good at, and where it is particularly absurd for them to be
second-best?'

'No,' he said. 'If you are saying that one sex is better than the other at
practically everything, then you are right. It's true there are plenty of
individual women who are better at all sorts of things than individual
men, but in general you are right.'

'In that case, my friend, none of the activities connected with running
a city belongs to a woman because she is a woman, nor to a man because
he is a man. Natural attributes are evenly distributed between the two

e sexes, and a woman is naturally equipped to play her part in all activities,
just as a man is – though in all of them woman is weaker than man.'

'Exactly.'

'Does that mean we should entrust everything to men, and give
nothing to a woman?'

'Of course not.'

'No. We shall say, presumably, that one woman is a natural doctor, while
another is not, that one is naturally musical, and another unmusical.'

'Certainly.'

456 'Isn't one warlike and fitted for physical training, while another is
unwarlike and no lover of training?'

'That's certainly my belief.'

'What about wisdom-loving and wisdom-hating? Or spirited and
lacking in spirit?'

'Yes, those also.'

'In which case, there are women who are suited to be guardians, and
women who are not. Weren't those the attributes we chose for the men
who were suited to be guardians?'

'They were.'

'So when it comes to guarding a city, both a woman and a man possess
the same natural attributes. They differ only in strength and weakness.'

'That's the way it looks.'

b 'It follows that women with these abilities should also be selected to live

with the men who have these abilities, and be fellow-guardians with them.
They are quite capable of it, and their natures are closely related to those
of the men.'

'Precisely.'

'And the same natures should be given the same occupations, shouldn't
they?'

'Yes, they should.'

'We have come right round in a circle, back to where we started.[10] We
agree there is nothing unnatural in giving those of the guardians who are
women a musical education and a physical education.'

'We certainly do.'

c   'So it was not an impossibility, some sort of dream, this lawgiving of
ours. There was a natural justification for the law we passed. It is society
today, apparently, which is out of step and unnatural.'

'Apparently.'

'Very well. Now, our question was whether our proposals were feasible
and for the best.'[11]

'It was.'

'Has it been agreed that they are feasible?'

'Yes.'

'So should the next step be to agree that they are for the best?'

'Obviously.'

'Well then, if we want a woman to become guardian material, we shall
not have one education for making men guardians, and another for
d making women guardians, shall we? Particularly when they have the same
natural attributes to start with.'

'No, we shall have the same education for both.'

'Now, here's another point I'd like your opinion about.'

'What is that?'

'Whether you feel, in your own mind, that one man is better and
another man is worse. Or do you think all men are the same?'

'No, I certainly don't.'

'Well, then. In the city we founded, which do you think we shall find
turn out the better men? The guardians who have received the education
we described? Or the shoemakers trained in the art of shoemaking?'

'That's a fatuous question,' he said.

e   'I see. What about the rest of the citizens? Aren't the guardians better
than all of them?'

---

[10] 451e.   [11] 450c.

'Much better.'

'What about the women? Won't the women guardians be the best of the women?'

'Again,' he said, 'much the best.'

'Is there anything better for a city than for it to have its women and its men alike become as good as possible?'

'No, there isn't.'

457 'And will this be brought about by the availability of musical and physical education of the kind we described?'

'Of course.'

'So our arrangements are not only feasible, but also in the best interests of our city.'

'Yes.'

'They must strip, then, the women among our guardians. Virtue will be their cloak. They must play their part both in war and in being the guardians of the city in general. That, and nothing else. And of those

b tasks, women should be given lighter ones than men, because their sex is weaker. Any man who laughs at the idea of naked women, if they are exercising naked in pursuit of excellence, is "plucking the unripe fruit of laughter."[12] He has no idea, apparently, what he is laughing at, or what he is doing. It is a good saying – and always will be – that what is good for us is beautiful, and what is bad for us is ugly.'

'Absolutely.'

'Can we say, then, that in our provisions for the legal position of women we have survived the first wave of criticism? In laying down that our male

c and female guardians should in all respects lead a common life, we have not been completely overwhelmed. There is some consistency in the argument that this is both feasible and beneficial.'

'That's certainly no small wave you have survived,' he said.

'You won't think so when you see the next one.'

'Go on, then. Let me see it.'

'I believe that this law, and the others which preceded it, imply a further law.'

'What law?'

d 'That all these women shall be wives in common for all these men. That none of them shall live as individuals with any of the men. That children

---

[12] The quotation adapts a fragment of the poet Pindar that was originally directed against the philosophic speculation of his day, with its unripe *wisdom*, rather than against satire.

in turn shall belong to all of them. That no parent shall know its own child, no child its own parent.'

'Yes,' he said. 'When it comes to scepticism about the feasibility or utility of this proposal, that is a much larger wave than the first.'[13]

'I don't imagine there could be any disagreement about its utility. No one would deny that if it is possible, having wives in common and children in common is a major benefit. But on the question of its feasibility or otherwise I suspect there would be a lot of disagreement.'

e   'There would be plenty of disagreement,' he replied, 'on both counts.'

'Two arguments going into partnership, you mean, I thought I was going to escape one of them. If you agreed that it was useful, I would merely be left with the argument about its feasibility or otherwise.'

'Well, you didn't get away with it, and you haven't escaped. So you must defend yourself on both counts.'

458   'Yes, I must pay that penalty. But do me one favour, please. Allow me a small break. Like those people with idle minds who entertain themselves with daydreams when they are out for a walk on their own. People like this, I believe, don't bother to find out *how* something they want can happen. That's something they forget about, to save themselves the trouble of thinking about what is feasible or otherwise. They assume that what they want can be had easily, and go straight on to planning the future, and enjoying the rehearsal of the things they are going to do once they have got what they want, so making an already lazy mind even lazier.

b   I'm feeling a bit short of energy myself at present, so I want to postpone the question of feasibility, and consider it later. For the moment I'll assume our proposals are feasible. With your permission, I want to examine the way the rulers will organise these things when they do happen, and show that putting them into practice would be of the greatest possible benefit to the city and its guardians. I want you to help me make a thorough examination of those questions first, and leave the other questions until later, if that's all right with you.'

'It is all right,' he said. 'Begin your enquiry.'

c   'Very well. If our rulers are to be worthy of the name, and their auxiliaries likewise, then I think the auxiliaries will be prepared to carry out

---

[13]   Various forms of communal sexuality and family life among exotic non-Greek tribes are noted already by the early fifth-century historian Herodotus, but the Greek world could offer, as a distant parallel, only the custom at Sparta that men who lacked heirs were permitted to produce them from others' wives, or from their own wives but using other men as fathers.

orders, and the rulers will issue those orders either in obedience to the
letter of the law, or, in places where we have left the interpretation of the
law to them, in obedience to its spirit.'

'That's fair enough,' he said.

'It will be your job, then, as their lawgiver, just as you selected the men,
so now to select the women as well, as similar as possible in nature,
and allocate them to the men. Since houses and dining-halls will be
d communal, and no one will possess any private property of this kind, the
sexes will live in close proximity, and in this state of universal proximity,
both in their physical education and in the rest of their upbringing, their
natural instincts will inevitably, I think, lead them into having sex with
one another.[14] Or don't you regard that as inevitable?'

'Well, it's not a mathematical inevitability. But it is a sexual inevitability, and for the majority of people that is probably a keener agent of
persuasion and attraction.'

'Much keener,' I said. 'Now for the next point, Glaucon. In the city
e of the blessed, haphazard sexual intercourse is unholy. Like haphazard
behaviour of any kind. The rulers will not allow it.'

'No, because it is wrong.'

'Clearly the next step is for us to do everything we can to make marriages as sacred as possible. And it will be the most useful marriages which
are the sacred ones.'[15]

'Absolutely.'

459 'What will make them the most useful? Tell me something, Glaucon.
I've noticed that as well as hunting dogs you have a fair number of pure-
bred birds in your house. Isn't there one thing you surely must have
noticed about their unions and production of offspring?'

'What sort of thing?' he asked.

'For a start, though they are all pure-bred, aren't some of them – don't
they prove themselves to be – the best?'

'Yes, they do.'

---

14 The communal dwellings and mess halls of the guardians, and their lack of private
property, were discussed at the end of Book 3 (416d–417b). Communal mess halls
were a distinctive feature of domestic life at Sparta, as also in Crete. But they were
reserved for men, and were not residences.

15 The Greek word for 'marriage' could also be used to refer to sexual liaisons in
general. Throughout the Greek world, legitimate marriage was sanctified by a religious ritual. There may also be an allusion to the Athenian festival of the Sacred
Marriage, held in honour of the union of the king of the gods, Zeus, and his consort,
Hera.

'Do you in that case breed from all of them alike? Or are you careful to breed as much as possible from the best?'

'I breed from the best.'

b   'What about age? Do you breed from the youngest? Or the oldest? Or do you breed, as far as possible, from those in their prime?'

'From those in their prime.'

'If the breeding is not handled like this, do you think your stock of birds and dogs will greatly deteriorate?'

'Yes, I do.'

'What about horses, and other animals?' I asked. 'Do you think they're in any way different?'

'No. That would be absurd.'

'Help!' I exclaimed. 'We're going to need some extremely expert rulers, my dear friend, if the same applies to the human race as well.'

c   'Well, it certainly does apply. But why do they have to be expert?'

'Because they are going to have to use some pretty strong medicine,' I replied. 'With doctors, I take it that when your body is ready to respond to a prescribed regimen, and doesn't need medicines, a second-rate doctor will do. But if it's a question of prescribing medicines as well, then we know a more resolute physician is needed.'

'True. But why is that relevant?'

'I'll tell you. The probability is that our rulers will need to employ a

d   good deal of falsehood and deception for the benefit of those they are ruling. And we said, if I remember rightly, that useful things of that kind all came in the category of medicine.'[16]

'How right we were,' he said.

'Well, it looks as if one place where it really matters whether we were right over this is when we come to their unions, and production of children.'

'In what way?'

'On the principles we have agreed, the best men should have sex with the best women as often as possible, whereas for the worst men and the

e   worst women it should be the reverse. We should bring up the children of the best, but not the children of the worst, if the quality of our herd is to be as high as we can make it. And all this has to happen with no one apart from the actual rulers realising it, if our herd of guardians is also to be as free as possible from dissension.'

---

[16] 382c–d, 389b–d, 414b–c.

'Quite right.'

'In that case we must legislate for some festivals, at which we shall bring together the brides and their grooms. We must have sacrifices, and our 460 poets must compose hymns appropriate to the unions which are taking place. We shall leave the number of marriages to the rulers, so they can keep the number of men as nearly as possible at the same level, taking war, disease and things like that into account. That will stop our city getting either too large or too small, if it can be prevented.'

'That's right,' he said.

'We must have lotteries, I think – and pretty ingenious ones – so that every time there is a marriage the inferior type we want to exclude will blame chance rather than the rulers.'

'They'll have to be extremely ingenious, these lotteries of yours.'

b   'Presumably those among the young men who are outstanding in war or any other sphere are to be given various prizes and rewards, and in particular more generous permission to sleep with the women, so that as many of the children as possible can plausibly be fathered by young men of this sort.'

'That's right.'

'As for the children who will be born from time to time, they will be taken away by the officials responsible for these things. These officials may be men or women, or men *and* women, since offices, I take it, are open to women and men alike.'

'Yes.'

c   'The children of good parents will be taken, I think, and transferred to the nursing-pen, where there will be special nurses living separately, in a special part of the city. The children of inferior parents, on the other hand, or any deformed specimen born to the other group, will be removed from sight into some secret and hidden place, as is right.'[17]

'Yes,' he said, 'at any rate if the breed of guardians is going to remain pure.'

'Will these officers also be in charge of feeding? They will bring the mothers to the nursing-pen when their breasts are full, though using d   every means they can think of to prevent any of them recognising her own child, and they will make sure there are other women with milk, in case the actual mothers do not have enough. Will they keep an eye on the

---

[17] The cryptic phrase would doubtless have suggested to Plato's contemporaries the not uncommon practice of infanticide by exposure, as a way of dealing with unwanted births.

mothers themselves, to make sure they suckle for a moderate time, and that the broken nights, and the rest of the hard work, are delegated to nurses and nannies?'

'This is a very relaxed way of raising children you are proposing for our women guardians.'

'That's as it should be,' I said. 'Now, let's continue in a systematic way with the task we set ourselves. We said children should be born to those in their prime.'

c   'True.'

'Well, do you agree that a reasonable span for a woman's prime is twenty years, and for a man's thirty?'

'Which twenty? And which thirty?' he asked.

'For a woman it means starting at twenty, and going on bearing children for the city until forty. For a man, when his days as a sprinter are behind him, then he should father children for the city from that age until fifty-five.'

461   'Yes,' he agreed. 'For both of them that is the prime of life, both physically and mentally.'

'If someone older or younger than this takes part in producing children for the state, we shall call it an offence against the gods and against justice, since the child he is fathering for the city, if it escapes detection, will come into being without the sacrifices and prayers which the priestesses and priests and the entire city will offer at every marriage festival – that from good parents may come forth ever better children, and from useful
b   parents still more useful children. The child will be born in darkness, the product of a dangerous lack of self-control.'

'Yes, we shall be right to call that an offence.'

'And the same law applies,' I said, 'if a man who is still entitled to father children gets access to a woman of the appropriate age without a ruler promoting the union. We shall say he is presenting the city with an illegitimate, unauthorised and unholy child.'

'And we shall be absolutely right,' he said.

'Of course, when women and men pass the age for producing children,
c   we shall declare them free, presumably, to have sex with anyone they like, apart from a daughter, or a mother, or their daughters' daughters or their mother's mothers. For a woman, anyone other than a son or father, or their sons' sons or father's fathers. And all this only when we have first impressed upon them how careful they must be. If there is a pregnancy, then ideally the embryo should never see the light of day. If one does force

its way into existence, the parents must deal with it on the understanding that they cannot bring up a child of this sort.'

d   'That all seems quite reasonable,' he said. 'But this business of fathers and daughters, and the relationships you were talking about just now – how will they tell their own from anyone else's?'

'They won't. When a man takes part in a marriage, he will regard as his children all those born in the tenth – or indeed the seventh – month from the day of the festival. He will call the male children his sons, and the female children his daughters. They will call him father. Similarly he will call the children's offspring his grandchildren, and they in turn will call his generation grandfathers and grandmothers. Those born during the period when their mothers and fathers were producing children they will

e   call their sisters and brothers. In this way they can avoid one another, as we were suggesting just now. However, the law will allow unions between brothers and sisters, if that is how the lot falls out, and if the Pythian priestess gives her consent as well.'

'Quite right.'

'There you are, Glaucon. That's what it is for women and children to be "in common" among the guardians of your city. That's what it is like. The next thing we have to do is establish from what has been said that it is consistent with the rest of the constitution, and that it is by far the best arrangement. Or should we go about things in some other way?'

462   'No, let's go about it that way. By all means.'

'If we want to settle this, isn't it a good starting-point to ask ourselves what is the greatest good we can think of in the organisation of our city – the thing the lawgiver should be aiming at as he frames his laws – and what is the greatest evil? Then we can ask "Do the proposals we have just described match the features of this good? Do they fail to match the features of this evil?"'

'Yes, that's the best possible starting-point,' he said.

b   'Well, then, can we think of any greater evil for a city than what tears it apart and turns it into many cities instead of one? Or any greater good than what unites it and makes it one?'

'No, we can't.'

'Is it community of pleasure and pain which unites it, when as far as possible all the citizens are equally affected by joy or grief over any particular gain or loss?'

'It certainly is.'

'And is individual variation in these feelings divisive? Things happen to the city or to its inhabitants which make some people distraught and
c   others delighted?'

'Of course it's divisive.'

'Is this because words like "mine" and "not mine" are not applied by people in the city to the same things? The same with "somebody else's"?'

'It certainly is.'

'Does that mean the best-regulated city is the one in which the greatest number of people use this phrase "mine" or "not mine" in the same way, about the same thing?'

'Much the best.'

'And the one which is most like an individual person? Take the example of someone hurting his finger. It is the whole community extending through the body and connecting with the soul, the soul being the ruling
d   element that organises the community into a single system – this entire community notices the hurt and together feels the pain of the part that hurts, which is why we say "the man has a pain in his finger." The same applies to any other part of the human body, to the pain felt when a part of it is hurt or the pleasure felt when the part gets better.'

'Yes,' he said, 'the same does apply. And in reply to your question, the city with the best constitution is organised in a very similar way to this.'

'When anything at all – good or bad – happens to one of its citizens, a
e   city of this kind will be most inclined to say that what is affected is a part of itself. The whole city will rejoice together or grieve together.'

'Yes, it's bound to. A city with good laws, that is.'

'This is the moment for us to return to our city,' I said, 'and look for the characteristics our argument has led us to agree on. We want to know if this city possesses them to an outstanding degree, or if some other city does.'

'Yes, we do need to go back and do that.'

463   'Very well. Presumably there are rulers and common people, aren't there, in other cities as well as in our city?'

'There are.'

'Do they all call one another citizens?'

'Of course.'

'But in other cities, what else do the common people call the rulers, apart from calling them citizens?'

'In most cities they call them their masters. In democratic cities they just call them rulers.'[18]

'What about the common people in our city? What do they say their rulers are, apart from being citizens?'

b   'Saviours and defenders,' he said.

'And what do the rulers call the common people?'

'Paymasters and providers.'

'What do the rulers in other cities call their common people?'

'Slaves.'

'And what do the rulers call each other?'

'Fellow-rulers.'

'What do ours call each other?'

'Fellow-guardians.'

'Can you answer this, then? Would any of the rulers in the other cities find it possible to address one of his fellow-rulers as a relative, and another as unrelated?'

'Yes. Plenty of them would find that possible.'

c   'Doesn't such a person think and speak of his relative as "his," and one who is unrelated as "not his"?'

'Yes.'

'What about your guardians? Could any of them think of one of his fellow-guardians, or address him, as if he were unrelated?'

'No,' he said. 'Every time he meets any of them, he will assume he is meeting his brother, or sister, or father, or mother, or son, or daughter – or the child or parent of one of these.'

'That puts it very clearly. Now, here is another question. Will your laws

d merely require them to use these names of relationships, or will you also require all the behaviour that goes with the name? When it comes to their fathers, will you not require everything from them that law and custom enjoin in the way of respect, care, and the duty of obedience to parents? Otherwise it will be the worse for them both in the eyes of gods and in the eyes of men, since their behaviour will be irreligious and unjust. Is that the sort of thing you want ringing in their ears from earliest childhood, with a chorus of citizens pointing out their duty towards their fathers, or the people they are taught to think of as their fathers, and their other relatives? Or do you want them to hear something different?'

---

[18] At Athens the term 'ruler' was also the title for the nine 'archons', high officials of state, appointed annually by lot from among the citizens, but in no sense a ruling class.

e   'No, just that. It would be ridiculous for them merely to use the names
      of relationships, as a verbal convention, without the corresponding be-
      haviour.'
          'In that case, there will be greater agreement in this city than in any
      other about the terms we were referring to a moment ago. They will say,
      of the success or failure of any individual, "this success is mine," or "this
      failure is mine."'
          'Very true,' he said.

464   'And did we say that feeling pleasures and pains in common followed
      from this way of thinking and speaking?'
          'We did. And we were right.'
          'Then will our citizens, more than any others, hold one and the same
      thing – which they will call "mine" – in common? And because they
      feel the same about it, will they feel the greatest community of pain and
      pleasure?'
          'Yes, much the greatest.'
          'And the reason for this, over and above the general organisation of the
      city, is the business of women and children being in common among our
      guardians?'
          'Yes, that's the main reason,' he said. 'Far more important than any-
      thing else.'

b   'But we also agreed that this is the greatest good for a city. We said
      a well-regulated city was like a body in the way it relates to the pain or
      pleasure of one of its parts.'
          'Rightly.'
          'In which case the greatest good of our city has been proved to result
      from women and children being in common among the defenders of our
      people.'
          'Precisely.'
          'This of course ties in with what we said originally. Our view was, I
      think, that if they were going to be true guardians they should not have
c   private houses, or land, or property of any kind, but that they should
      receive their livelihood from the other citizens as payment for their
      guardianship, and all make use of these resources jointly.'[19]
          'It was. And we were correct.'
          'Well, then, as I say, won't those arrangements we agreed earlier, when
      combined with these present ones, be even more effective in turning them

---

[19] 416d–417b.

163

into true guardians? Won't it make them give the name "mine" to the same things, rather than all applying it to different things, and so tearing the city apart? It will stop one of them carting off to his own house, inde-pendently of the others, whatever he can get for himself; and another

d doing the same, to *his* own house, along with a wife and children, and the private pleasures and pains they bring with them in private matters. Won't our arrangements give them a single opinion about what belongs to them, give them the same goal to aim at, and make them all as nearly as possible subject to the same pains and pleasures?'

'They certainly will,' he said.

'How about lawsuits and prosecutions directed at one another? Won't those virtually disappear among them, since they have no private prop-

e erty apart from their own bodies, everything else being jointly owned? Won't this free them from all the disputes people run into through the possession of money, children and families?'

'Yes, they are absolutely certain to be rid of those.'

'Nor will there be any justification for legal actions for violence or assault among them. Presumably we shall say that it is right and proper for people to fight their own battles against their peers, since this will compel them keep in good shape physically.'

'Quite right, too.'

465 'Yes,' I said, 'and there's another benefit in this law, too. If one of them gets angry with another, and can find an outlet for his anger in this kind of way, it will be less likely to lead to a serious dispute.'

'Much less likely.'

'An older person will of course be entitled to give orders and punish-ments to all those who are younger.'

'Obviously.'

'And it's equally obvious that without the authority of the rulers there is very little chance of a younger person trying to do violence to an older, or strike him. Nor will he treat him disrespectfully in any other way, I

b suspect, since there will be two guardians – fear and shame – quite capable of stopping him. Shame will keep him from laying a finger on those he regards as parents. The fear will be that others will come to the aid of his victim – some in their capacity as sons, others as brothers, and others as fathers.'

'Yes, that is what tends to happen,' he said.

'So will our laws result in the men living at peace with one another in all situations?'

'Very much so.'

'And if these people do not fall out among themselves, there will be no danger of the rest of the city being divided, either against them or against each other.'

c   'No, there won't.'

'I am embarrassed even to mention the more trivial of the evils they will be released from. I mean the flattery of the rich by the poor, the difficulties and hardships they experience in bringing up children and earning a living because of the need to maintain a household – now borrowing, now defaulting on their debts, now providing in any way they can, handing the money over to their wives and slaves, and entrusting the management of it to them. All the difficulties people have over this kind of thing, my friend, are familiar, demeaning and not worth mentioning.'

'Yes, they are familiar,' he said. 'A blind man couldn't miss them.'

'Our guardians will be free from all these worries, and live a life happier than any Olympic victor.'

'Happier in what way?'

'Victors in the Olympics are regarded as happy with only a fraction of what is offered to our guardians, whose victory is finer and whose maintenance at the public expense is more complete.[20] The victory they win is the safety of the entire city, and the crown of victory, for them and their children, is their upkeep and all the necessities of life. From the city which belongs to them they receive privileges while they are alive and an honourable burial when they die.'

'Very fine privileges, too.'

'Do you remember,' I asked, 'how dismayed we were a little while ago[21] by the suggestion – I can't imagine who made it – that we were not making our guardians happy, since they had the opportunity to possess all the property of the citizens, and yet possessed nothing? We said, if I remember rightly, that this was a question we would consider later, if the opportunity arose. For the time being we were making our guardians guardians, and the city as happy as we were capable of making it. We were not looking at one class within the city, with a view to shaping the happiness of that class.'

'Yes, I do remember that.'

'Good. If it now turns out that the life of our defenders is clearly finer

---

[20] Winners of major athletic competitions, then as now, tended to become celebrities. Among the privileges accorded by Athens to victors in the Olympic games were meals at public expense.   [21] 419a.

b and better by far than the life of victors in the Olympic games, then it clearly isn't in any way on a par with the life of our shoemakers, the members of any other skilled occupation, or our farmers, is it?'

'No, I think not.'

'All the same, it's worth repeating now what I said then. If a guardian attempts to become happy in a way which stops him being a guardian, if he is not satisfied with this restrained and secure way of life – the best way of life, in our view – if he gets some idiotic adolescent notion of happiness into his head, which drives him, simply because he has the power, to c start getting his hands on all the property in the city, then he will realise the true wisdom of Hesiod's saying that the half is in some sense greater than the whole.'[22]

'If he takes my advice,' he said, 'he will stick to the way of life we have outlined.'

'Does that mean,' I asked, 'that you agree with the partnership we have described between women and men – in education, raising children and acting as guardians to the other citizens? Do you agree that whether they remain in the city or go out to war, women should act as joint guardians d and joint hunters, the way dogs do, and that so far as possible they should share in every way in all the men's duties? Do you agree that this behaviour of theirs will be for the best, and will not conflict with the nature of a woman as compared with a man, the natural partnership of the sexes with one another?'

'Yes, I do agree.'

'Then what remains is for us to decide whether in that case it is possible for this partnership to exist among men as well as among other animals – and in what way it is possible. '

'That's exactly what I was just going to suggest.'

e 'After all, when it comes to making war, I think it's obvious how they will go about it.'

'How?'

'They will go on campaign together, bringing the most robust of the children with them on active service, so that like the children of people in other skilled occupations they can observe the occupation they will have 467 to follow when they grow up. Besides observing, they should act as assistants and servants in everything to do with war, and be some help to their fathers and mothers.[23] Haven't you noticed how people learn a skill? The

[22] *Works and Days* 40.
[23] There was no parallel for such a practice in Greek ways of warfare. Greek soldiers did not take their families with them on campaign.

children of potters, for example, spend a long time as assistants, watching, before they are allowed anywhere near a pot.'

'A very long time.'

'And are potters going to be more careful than our guardians when it comes to educating their own children, giving them the necessary experience and opportunity to observe?'

'No, that would be ludicrous,' he said.

b   'What is more, any living creature will fight better in the presence of its own young.'

'That's true. But if they are defeated – and these things do happen in time of war – there's a very real danger, Socrates, that along with the guardians themselves the children will be lost as well, and that this will make recovery impossible for the rest of the city.'

'True,' I said. 'But what is *your* view on that? Do you think, for instance, that the aim should be to avoid all possible risk?'

'No.'

'Well then, if they *are* going to take risks, shouldn't it be in situations where success will make them better people?'

'Obviously.'

c   'Do you think that for men who are going to be warlike it makes very little difference – and is therefore not worth the risk – whether or not they can observe the art of war as children?'

'No, it does make a difference, in the way you suggest.'

'What we want to bring about, then, is a way of making the children observers of war, while at the same time thinking of some clever means of ensuring their safety. That would be ideal, wouldn't it?'

'Yes.'

'Well then,' I said, 'for one thing their fathers will not be without
d   experience. They will be as expert as human beings can be at judging which campaigns are dangerous and which are not.'

'Fair enough.'

'So they will take them on some campaigns, but think twice about others.'

'Yes, that will be the right approach.'

'And to command them their fathers will presumably not give them those who are least able, but those well qualified by age and experience to be guides and tutors.'[24]

'Yes, those will be the right people.'

---

[24] At Athens the task of the *paidagōgos* bore no relation to 'pedagogy' but was limited to that of attendant or chaperone (as at 373c, 397d). It was a task assigned to slaves.

'Will this be enough?' I asked. 'After all, events are unpredictable, as all sorts of people are constantly finding out.'

'They certainly are.'

'So to meet unpredictable situations we must give them wings, my friend, from their earliest childhood. Then they can take to flight if they have to.'

'What do you mean?'

e   'We must put them on horseback at the youngest possible age. Once we have taught them to ride, we can take them as observers, mounted on horses which are not spirited and warlike, but the swiftest and most obedient we can find. In this way they can get an excellent view of what will be their occupation, and still make their escape safely, if the need arises, by following guides who are older than they are.'

468   'I think that is a good suggestion,' he said.

'What about the actual fighting?' I asked. 'What do you think the behaviour of the soldiers towards each other and the enemy should be? Do you agree with my ideas, or not?'

'Tell me your ideas.'

'Let's start with their behaviour towards each other. Anyone who out of cowardice leaves his place in the line, throws away his weapons, or does anything of that sort should be reduced to the rank of skilled worker or farmer, shouldn't he?'

'He certainly should.'

'Anyone who falls alive into the hands of the enemy can be handed over

b   as a gift to those who capture him. They can do what they like with their catch.'

'By all means.'

'As for someone who wins a prize for valour, and distinguishes himself, don't you think that in the first place he should be crowned, there in the field, by the adolescents and children – every one of them in turn – who are on campaign with him?'[25]

'I do.'

'How about being shaken by the hand?'

'Yes, that too.'

'You won't agree with my next suggestion, I don't suppose.'

'What is it?'

'That he should kiss, and be kissed by, each of them.'

[25] The crown would be a garland, and was a traditional award for distinguished military service, as medals are nowadays.

c   'That above all. And I propose an amendment to this law. For the dur-
ation of the campaign no one he wants to kiss shall be allowed to refuse.
That should make anyone who is in fact in love with someone else –
whether that someone is male or female – all the more determined to win
a prize.'

'Excellent,' I said. 'After all, it has already been decided that the good
man is to get more marriages than other people, and that the good should
be selected more frequently than the rest – so that as many children as
possible may be born to parents of this kind.'

'Yes, we did decide that.'[26]

'In Homer, too, it is right to give the same kind of rewards to those of
d   the young who excel. Homer says that Ajax, when he distinguished
himself in battle, "was rewarded with the best cuts of meat from the
fillet"[27] – an appropriate reward for someone young and courageous,
allowing him to be honoured and increase his strength at the same time.'

'Quite right, too,' he said.

'On this point at least, then, we shall follow Homer. In our sacrifices
and everything of that sort, we too shall honour the good men in proportion to the excellence they have shown, both with songs of praise and in
the ways we have described, and on top of that with

e   The seats of honour, cuts of meat, and cups
                    More often filled.[28]

In this way we shall hope to train our good men and women as well as
rewarding them.'

'An excellent plan.'

'Very well. Then we come to those killed on active service. If anyone
dies after covering himself with glory, shall we not say first of all that he
is a member of the golden class?'

'We certainly shall.'

'We shall accept Hesiod's view, shan't we? When people of this class die,

469   They dwell upon the earth as noble spirits,
                    Holy, averters of evil, guardians
                    Of humans blessed with speech articulate.'[29]

---

[26] 460b.   [27] Iliad 7.321.

[28] The Homeric phrase occurs twice: Iliad 8.162, 12.311.

[29] The transmitted text of Hesiod is different (Works and Days 122–123): 'They dwell
upon the earth as noble spirits through the designs of mighty Zeus, averting evil,
guardians of humans who must die.'

'Yes, we shall accept Hesiod's view.'

'Shall we in that case enquire of Apollo how we ought to bury these superhuman, these divine people, and what mark of distinction we should give them? And shall we then bury them in the way he recommends?'

'We certainly shall.'

'For the rest of time, shall we look after their graves as those of
b superhumans, and bow down before them? Shall we follow this same observance on the death of anyone who is judged to have been outstandingly good in his life, whether he dies from old age or any other cause?'[30]

'Yes,' he said, 'that will be the right thing to do.'

'Now, what about the enemy? How will our soldiers treat them?'

'What do you mean?'

'Take enslavement, for a start. Do you think it is right for Greeks to enslave Greek cities? Or should they rather do everything they can to stop
c any other city doing so? Should they encourage other cities always to spare the Greek race, and so protect themselves against enslavement by the barbarians?'

'Yes. Sparing them is far and away the best policy.'

'Is the best thing, then, for them both to avoid owning Greek slaves themselves, and also to advise other Greeks not to own them?'

'It certainly is,' he said. 'That way they are likely to turn their attention more towards the barbarians, and leave one another alone.'[31]

'How about plundering the dead,' I asked, 'after a victory? Apart from their weapons, that is. Is that the right thing to do? Doesn't it give cowards
d an excuse not to go after those who are offering resistance? As if they were performing some useful task in grubbing round the body on their hands and knees? Haven't armies often been lost as a result of this kind of looting?'

'Yes. Very often.'

'Besides, doesn't plundering corpses strike you as demeaning and mercenary? Isn't it petty and womanish to go on regarding the body of the

---

[30] It was the practice of Greek communities to worship their important ancestral figures as 'heroes' or demigods. The authority of Apollo's oracle was often involved in conferring the status of hero on the dead person.

[31] The enslavement of fellow-Greeks defeated in war continued in the fourth century over a rising swell of protest and despite the fact that a characteristic political position of the age was 'panhellenism' – the belief that Greek states would not co-exist peacefully unless united against a common barbarian enemy, Persia (compare 470c–e). Other consequences of panhellenism come into play in the paragraphs that follow.

dead person as hostile once the enemy has flown, leaving behind the
c instrument he was fighting with? Can you see any difference at all between
a person behaving like this and dogs which get angry with the stones they
are hit by, but show no interest in the person throwing them?'

'No,' he said. 'No difference at all.'

'Should we then put a stop to plundering corpses? And refusing to
allow an enemy to take up the dead for burial?'

'We most certainly should.'

'We shan't, I imagine, take their weapons to our temples to present
as offerings. Particularly not the weapons of Greeks, if we are at all
470 interested in maintaining good relations with the rest of Greece. We are
more likely to be afraid there may be some pollution in bringing offerings
of this kind to a temple from our fellow-Greeks — unless of course the god
tells us something different.'

'Quite right.'

'What about laying waste Greek territory, and burning houses?' I
asked. 'How will your soldiers behave to the enemy when it comes to this?'

'What do *you* think? I'd be glad to hear your opinion on the subject.'

b 'My opinion is that they shouldn't do either of those things. They
should take only the current year's crop. Do you want me to tell you why?'

'By all means.'

'It seems to me that just as we have these two names, war and civil war,
so there are two realities, corresponding to two kinds of conflict in two
different areas. The first area I am talking about is what is one's own, or
related. The second is what is not one's own, or alien. "Civil war" is the
name for conflict with what is one's own. "War" is the name for conflict
with what is not one's own.'

'Nothing wide of the mark there,' he said.

c 'Do you think my next shot is on target as well? I maintain that to a
Greek, the whole Greek race is "his own," or related, whereas to the barbarian race it is alien, and "not its own."'

'A fair claim.'

'When Greeks fight barbarians, then, and barbarians Greeks, we shall
say they are at war. We shall say they are natural enemies, and that hostilities of this sort are to be called a war. But in cases where Greeks fight
d Greeks, we shall say they are natural friends, but that in this situation
Greece is sick, and divided against itself. We shall say that hostilities of
this kind are to be called a civil war.'

'Personally,' he said, 'I am content to take this view.'

'Now think about the thing we call civil war at the moment, where something of this sort arises in a city, which becomes divided against itself. If each side lays waste the land of the other, and burns their houses, then the civil war is regarded as an abomination, and both sides as unpatriotic. Otherwise they could never have brought themselves to savage

e their nurse and mother. What is thought to be reasonable is for the winners to take the crops of the losers, treating them as people with whom they will one day settle their differences, not as people with whom they will always be at war.'

'Yes, that is a much more humane attitude.'

'What about the city you are founding?' I asked. 'Won't it be a Greek city?'

'Yes, it must be.'

'In which case, will the citizens be good and humane people?'

'Very much so.'

'Won't they be lovers of Greece? Won't they regard Greece as belonging to them? Won't they share in the religion of all the Greeks?'

'Again, very much so.'

471   'In which case, won't they regard a dispute with Greeks as civil war, given that Greeks are their own people? Won't they refuse even to give it the name "war"?'

'They will.'

'Won't they handle their disagreement like people who will one day settle their differences?'

'Unquestionably.'

'The correction they employ will be of a gentle kind. Since they are agents of correction, not enemies, they won't use slavery or death as punishments.'

'Exactly,' he said.

'And because they are Greeks, they will not lay waste to Greece, or burn houses, or accept that all the inhabitants of a city – men, women and

b children alike – are their enemies.[32] They will regard their enemies at any particular time as few, the ones responsible for the dispute. For all these reasons they will refuse to lay waste the land, or destroy the houses, of people whom they mostly regard as their friends. They will pursue their dispute only up to the point where those responsible are compelled by

---

[32] The Peloponnesian War offered notorious cases in which the victorious power put to death the males of military age and sold into slavery the remainder of the population of a city.

those who are not responsible, and who are suffering as a result, to make
amends.'

'For my part,' he said, 'I agree that this is how our citizens should treat
their enemies. As for the barbarians, they should treat them in the way
Greeks at the moment treat one another.'

c   'Should we then lay down another law for our guardians, forbidding
them to devastate land or burn houses?'

'Yes, we should. And let us by all means lay it down that we're satisfied
both with these arrangements and with our earlier ones. The fact is,
Socrates, if you're allowed to go on talking about this kind of thing, I don't
think you'll ever come back to the question you originally postponed in
order to go into all these details, the question whether it is possible – and
just *how* it is possible – for political arrangements of this kind to be introduced.[33] That their introduction would be a great benefit to the city in
d which they were introduced – well, I might even add one or two points
which you didn't mention. They would be outstanding in time of war
because of their refusal to desert one another. They would regard themselves as brothers, fathers and sons, and call themselves by these names.
If the women served in the army with them, either in the front line or in
reserve to unnerve the enemy and meet any possible need for reinforce-
ments, I'm sure the army would be totally invincible. And I can see
e benefits you haven't mentioned at home as well. So you can take it I agree
that introducing these political arrangements would bring them all these
benefits, and countless others. You needn't go on discussing the arrangements. Instead we can concentrate on giving ourselves a convincing
answer to the questions, *are* they possible and *how* are they possible? We
can forget about the rest.'

472   'That's a very direct assault,' I said, 'on my way of explaining things.
You don't have a great deal of sympathy with my misgivings. What you
perhaps don't realise, after I have narrowly escaped the first two waves of
criticism, is that you are now exposing me to a third – the largest and most
threatening of the three. But you will have a lot of sympathy when you
see it and hear it. You will see why I hesitated, why I was afraid to put
forward such an unlikely-sounding answer for examination.'

b   'The more excuses you make, the less chance there is that we shall let
you off telling us how these political arrangements are possible. Stop
playing for time, and tell us.'

[33] 458a–b, 466d–e.

'Well, the first thing to remember,' I said, 'is that we have reached this point in the course of an enquiry into the nature of justice and injustice.'

'Fair enough. What follows from that?'

'Only this. If we do discover what sort of thing justice is, are we then
c   going to decide that the just man must be in no way different from justice itself, but in every way like justice? Or will we be content if he comes as close to it as possible, and has a larger measure of it than anyone else?'

'We shall be content with that,' he said.

'So when we asked what sort of thing justice was by itself, and looked for the perfectly just man, if he existed, and asked what he would be like if he did exist, what we were looking for was a model. The same with injustice and the unjust man. We wanted to look at the perfectly just and unjust man, see
d   how we thought they were placed in respect of happiness and its opposite, and be compelled to agree, for ourselves as well, that whoever came closest to those examples would have a share of happiness which came closest to theirs. It wasn't our aim to demonstrate that these things were possible.'

'True enough.'

'Suppose a painter paints a picture which is a model of the outstandingly beautiful man. Suppose he renders every detail of his painting perfectly, but is unable to show that it is possible for such a man to exist. Do you think that makes him any the worse a painter?'

'Good heavens, no.'

e   'Then what about us? Aren't we in the same position? Can't we claim to have been constructing a theoretical model of a good city?'

'We certainly can.'

'In which case, do you think our inability to show that it is possible to found a city in the way we have described makes what we have to say any less valid?'

'No,' he said.

'Well, that's how things are. So if you want me, as a favour to you, to do my best to show how, exactly, and under what circumstances, it would be most possible, then you in return, for the purposes of this demonstration, must make the same allowances for me.'

'What allowances?'

473   'Is it possible for anything to be put into practice exactly as it is described? Or is it natural for practice to have less hold on truth than theory has? I don't care what some people may think. What about you? Do you agree, or not?'

'I agree,' he said.

'Then don't keep trying to compel me to demonstrate that the sort of thing we have described in a theoretical way can also be fully realised in practice. If we turn out to be capable of finding how a city can be run in a way pretty close to what we have described, then you can say that we have discovered how what you are asking for can be put into practice. Or won't you be satisfied with that? I know I would.'

'So would I.'

'The next step, apparently, is for us to try to discover, and point out, what the failings are in cities nowadays, which stop them being run in this way, and what is the minimum change which could help a city arrive at political arrangements of this kind. Ideally a single change. Failing that, two. And failing that, as few as possible in number and as small as possible in impact.'

'Absolutely,' he said.

'All right, then. There is one change which I think would allow us to show that things could be different. It is not a small change or an easy one, but it is possible.'

'What is it?'

'We've been using the analogy of waves. Well, now I'm coming to the largest wave. But I'll make my suggestion anyway, even if it is literally the laughter of the waves which is going to engulf me in ridicule and humiliation. Listen carefully to what I am about to say.'

'Tell me.'

'There is no end to suffering, Glaucon, for our cities, and none, I suspect, for the human race, unless either philosophers become kings in our cities, or the people who are now called kings and rulers become real, true philosophers – unless there is this amalgamation of political power and philosophy, with all those people whose inclination is to pursue one or other exclusively being forcibly prevented from doing so. Otherwise there is not the remotest chance of the political arrangements we have described coming about – to the extent that they can – or seeing the light of day. This is the claim which I was so hesitant about putting forward, because I could see what an extremely startling claim it would be. It is hard for people to see that this is the only possible route to happiness, whether in private life or public life.'

And Glaucon said, 'Really, Socrates! Here's what you can expect after a suggestion like that. You're facing a large and ugly crowd. The cloaks come off – practically hurled off. They're stripped for action. All that's needed is a weapon, any weapon, and they'll have launched themselves at you, bent on mayhem. Can you hold them off, find an argument to escape by? If you can't, you'll get what you deserve: utter humiliation.'

'It's your fault. You got me into this.'

'I'm glad I did,' he said. 'But I won't abandon you. I'll give you what help I can – which means support, encouragement, and maybe answers
b which are more sympathetic than someone else would give you. So in the knowledge that you have an ally of this kind, try to convince the sceptics that the truth is as you say.'

'Well, with such an ally,' I said, 'I must needs try. It's essential, I think, if we are to find some way of escaping the opponents you are talking about, that we should give them a definition of these philosophers, and tell them who these people are we have the nerve to say ought to be rulers. This portrait of them will make possible a defence which demonstrates that some people are naturally fitted both to grasp philosophy
c and to be leaders in a city, whereas other people are not equipped to grasp it. For them it is better to follow a leader.'

'Yes,' he said, 'this would be a good moment for a definition.'

'Come on, then. Follow me. Let's see if somehow or other we can give a satisfactory explanation.'

'Lead on.'

'Do I need to remind you – or do you remember – that when we say someone is a lover of something, he must not, strictly speaking, love one bit and not another bit? It must be clear that he loves the whole thing.'
d 'It looks as if I do need reminding,' he said. 'I don't quite remember that.'

'That might be a reasonable position for some people, Glaucon, but not for a lover. You of all people shouldn't need reminding that in one way or another a lover, or an admirer of young boys, is smitten and aroused by anyone of the right age. He finds them all worthy of his attention and affection. Isn't that the attitude you all have to beautiful boys? One has a snub nose, so you call him cute, and praise him for that. The one with a
e beak you say is kingly. The one who is a cross between the two you say is perfectly proportioned. The dark ones you say have a manly look. The white are children of the gods. And as for the honey-pale – even the name is no more than a euphemism dreamed up by a lover who is quite happy
475 to put up with pallor, provided it is on the cheek of youth. In short, you

will make any excuse, use any turn of phrase, in order to avoid rejecting a single one of those who are in the bloom of youth.'

'If you want to take me as your example, and say of lovers that that is how they behave, then for the sake of argument I agree.'

'How about lovers of wine?' I asked. 'Don't you find them behaving in just the same way? Don't they love any wine, for any reason?'

'They certainly do.'

'And you see the same thing, I think, with those who are ambitious and
b love honour. If they can't get to be generals, they become captains. If they can't win recognition from the great and the good, then they are happy to win recognition from those who are lesser and inferior, since it is recognition, in short, that their hearts are set on.'

'Absolutely.'

'Tell me this, then. Yes or no. When we say someone desires something, shall we say he desires that whole class of things? Or does he desire one particular example of it, but not another?'

'The whole class of things,' he said.

'Shall we say, then, that the philosopher is a lover of all wisdom? He's not a lover of one kind of wisdom, but not of another.'[34]

'True.'

c 'So if a man is choosy about what he studies – especially if he is young, and has not yet developed principles on which to judge what is worthwhile and what is not – we shall not call him a lover of learning or a lover of wisdom, any more than we say that the man who is choosy about his food is hungry, or that he wants food. We don't call him a good eater. We call him a poor eater.'

'And we are quite right.'

'Whereas the man who is wholeheartedly ready to taste all learning, who approaches learning gladly and with an insatiable appetite – this man we shall be justified in calling a philosopher, wouldn't you say?'

d 'In that case,' Glaucon said, 'a lot of surprising people will come in this category. All those who love to be spectators, for example – I think the reason they love to be spectators is because they enjoy learning. And people who love to be members of an audience are an unlikely group to find in the ranks of the philosophers. They behave as if they had rented

---

[34] The Greek word *philosophos*, 'philosopher', is a compound of two words meaning 'lover of wisdom', and is formed in the same way as the terms describing the lovers of boys, of honours, and of wine.

out their ears to listen to every chorus they can find. So they do their round of the festivals of Dionysus, never missing one, either in town or country.[35] But they wouldn't willingly go anywhere near a philosophical discussion or any activity of that sort. Shall we say that all these people,
e and anyone else who is a student of anything similar, or of the handicrafts – shall we say that all these are philosophers?'[36]

'No,' I said. 'But we *can* say they bear some resemblance to philosophers.'

'Who are the real philosophers, then, in your view?'

'They *are* spectators, but spectators of the truth.'

'That's all very well as far as it goes,' he said. 'But in what sense do you mean it?'

'It's not at all easy to explain – to anyone else. But you, I think, will accept the following argument.'

'How does it go?'

476 'Since beautiful is the opposite of ugly, they form a pair.'

'Of course.'

'And since they form a pair, you will agree also that each of them is one.'

'Yes. That too.'

'The same applies to just and unjust, good and bad, and all the forms or characters of things.[37] Each is in itself one, but because they appear all over the place, through their association with various activities and bodies and with one another, each gives the appearance of being many.'

'Correct,' he said.

---

[35] Choral and theatrical performance (including what we know as Greek tragedy and comedy) was characteristic of the various festivals honouring the god Dionysus – both the major celebrations held in the city of Athens and the smaller ones in the villages around Athens and elsewhere.

[36] The terms translated 'all those who love to be spectators' and 'people who love to be members of an audience' are Platonic coinages formed on the analogy of the words labelling the lovers of boys, honour, wine, wisdom.

[37] The expression 'forms or characters of things' – the form or character of the just, of the good, and so on – is one by which Socrates designates what he will also call e.g. '(the) beautiful itself', '(the) good itself' (507b), or in general 'what each thing (itself) is' (490b, 507b). The usual translation is simply '(the) forms'. See p. xxx of the introduction for more about their role in the *Republic*. The disjunctive expression 'forms or characters of things' is intended to reflect something of the range of meaning in the single Greek word *eidos*, as well as the fact that a phrase like 'the form of the good', unlike the Greek phrase to which it corresponds, and unlike 'the character of the good', has no non-technical meaning. Although the translation will sometimes use the simple expression 'forms' and sometimes the disjunctive 'forms or characters (of things)', in all instances the Greek uses a single term, either *eidos* or its synonym *idea*.

'That, then, is how I distinguish those you were talking about just now
b – those who enjoy being spectators, those who take pleasure in any art or
skill, people who are active – from the subjects of our present discussion,
the people whom alone we could truly call philosophers.'

'Explain.'

'Well, I imagine that audiences and spectators can take pleasure in
beautiful sounds and colours and shapes, and in everything which is
created from these elements, but that their minds are incapable of seeing,
and taking pleasure in, the nature of beauty itself.'

'True.'

'Whereas those who are capable of approaching beauty itself, and
c seeing it just by itself, would be few in number, wouldn't they?'

'Very few.'

'Take the man who believes in beautiful objects, then, but does not
believe in beauty itself, and cannot follow if you direct him to the knowledge of it. Is his life a dream, do you think, or is he awake? Think about
it. Isn't dreaming like this? Suppose one thing, A, resembles another
thing, B. Isn't dreaming the state, whether in sleep or waking, of thinking
not that A resembles B, but that A is B?'

'Well, *I* would certainly say that someone who made a mistake like that
was dreaming.'

d 'What about the person who is just the opposite, who believes in beauty
itself, who can look both at it and at the things which share in it without
mistaking them for it or it for them? Does his life, in its turn, strike you
as waking or dreaming?'

'Waking,' he said. 'Very much so.'

'In that case, would we be justified in claiming that this man's state of
mind, because he knows, is knowledge, and the other man's state of mind,
because he merely believes, is opinion or belief?'[38]

'Yes, we would.'

'Suppose the second man gets angry with us, the man we say believes
e and does not know. Suppose he challenges us, and says we are wrong. Will
we have any way of winning him over and gently persuading him, without
telling him how unhealthy he is?'

'We ought to be able to,' he said.

---

[38] A single word in the original (*doxa*), which when contrasted with knowledge would
typically carry the connotation that the grounds of the belief are insecure, whether
or not the belief is true.

'Come on, then, think what we can say to him. Do you want us to question him, like this? We could tell him we have no objection to his knowing things. If he did know anything, we could say to him, we would be delighted to see it. At the same time we could ask him this question. "Does the man who knows know something or nothing?" Will you answer for him, please?'

'My answer is that he knows something.'

'Something that is? Or something that is not?'

'Something that is. How could anything be known, if it were something that is not?'[39]

477   'Do we regard it as certain, then, however often we re-examine the question, that what altogether *is* something is altogether knowable, while what is not something in any way at all is wholly unknowable?'

'Absolutely certain.'

'Very well. But suppose there is something whose nature is both to be and not to be. Wouldn't it occupy an intermediate position between what purely and simply *is* something and what, by contrast, is not something in any way at all?'

'Yes, it would.'

'So if knowledge is directed at what *is* something, and ignorance, necessarily, at what is *not* something, then we must also look for what is

b directed at this intermediate class – what occupies an intermediate position between ignorance and knowledge – if indeed there is such a thing.'

'We must.'

'Do we say there is such a thing as opinion or belief?'

'Of course.'

'Is it a capacity different from knowledge, or the same?'

'Different.'

'So belief is directed at one object, and knowledge at another, each according to its own particular capacity.'

'Yes.'

---

[39] The single Greek verb *einai*, 'to be', can mean (i) to be something, i.e. to be there, to exist, (ii) to be something, i.e. to be qualified in a certain way ('to be Athenian'), (iii) to be something, i.e. to be some one thing ('this person is Plato'), (iv) to be the case, to be true, to be a fact. Throughout this argument the translation 'to be something', as the closest match for the ambiguity of the Greek, is often, but not invariably, chosen. In all cases, however, the Greek uses a single but – from our perspective, at least – multiply ambiguous verb. Whether a single concept is in play at all times, or whether the argument depends on shifts among the various senses of the verb, and if so, whether such shifts are illegitimate, and how many of those senses are involved – all these are controversial matters.

'So whereas knowledge is by its nature directed at what is, at knowing how things are . . . Or rather, I think there is an important distinction we should make first.'

'What is that?'

c 'Shall we say that capacities are a class of things which make us capable of doing whatever we are capable of doing, and make anything else capable of doing whatever *it* is capable of doing? For example, I would classify sight and hearing as capacities, if you understand what I mean by the category.'

'Yes, I do understand,' he said.

'Then let me tell you what I think about them. A capacity has no colour or shape for me to see, nor any such property that I would normally refer to in other situations in order to distinguish one class of things from another in my own mind. The only element of a capacity I consider is what it is directed at and what its effect is.[40] That is how I classify each

d capacity. Any capacity which is directed at the same object and has the same effect, I call the same capacity, and any capacity which is directed at a different object and has a different effect, I call a different capacity. How about you? Is that your method?'

'Yes,' he said.

'Then let us resume the argument where we left off, my good friend.

e Would you say that knowledge is a capacity? If not, what category would you put it in?'

'I would put it in this category. I would say it is the most powerful capacity of all.'

'What about belief? Shall we call it a capacity, or give it some other description?'

'No, a capacity. The thing which makes us capable of forming beliefs must be belief.'

'And a moment ago you agreed that knowledge and belief were not the same thing.'

'Of course. How could anyone with any sense ever regard what is infallible as the same as what is not infallible?'

'Excellent,' I said. 'Clearly we agree that belief is something different

478 from knowledge.'

---

[40] It is not clear whether these are two independent criteria, or two different but mutually entailing criteria, or whether this is a compound phrase expressing a single criterion. In the last case one would understand the 'object' to which the capacity is directed as its task or purpose. More literally, the phrase in Greek runs 'directed at the same (thing)'.

'Yes.'

'So these capacities, having different capabilities, are each of them by their nature directed at different objects.'

'Necessarily.'

'Knowledge, I take it, is directed at what is, and consists in knowing things as they are?'

'Yes.'

'Whereas belief, according to us, is a matter of forming opinions, isn't it?'

'Yes.'

'Will its opinions be about the same thing as knowledge knows? Will the object of knowledge and the object of belief be the same thing? Or is that impossible?'

'Yes, it is impossible, from what we have agreed – that is, if it is the
b nature of different capacities to be directed at different objects, and if knowledge and belief are both capacities, and if each is different from the other, as we claim. On these premises it is a contradiction for the object of knowledge and the object of belief to be the same thing.'

'So if what *is* something is the object of knowledge, then the object of belief must be something else?'

'Yes, it must.'

'Does belief, then, form an opinion about what is *not* something? Or is it impossible even to have an opinion about what is not something? Look at it like this. When a man has an opinion, isn't his belief directed towards something? Or is it possible to have a belief which is not a belief about anything?'[41]

'No, it is not possible.'

'So when he has a belief, it is a belief about some one thing?'

'Yes.'

c 'But what is not something cannot properly be called some one thing. It would most properly be called nothing.'

'Quite true.'

'And we necessarily associated ignorance with what is not something, and knowledge with what is something.'

'Rightly so,' he said.

'So belief does not form opinions either about what is or about what is not something.'

---

[41] The Greek phrase translated as 'what is not something', is (like the English) sufficiently ambiguous to permit, although it does not require, the equation with 'what is not anything at all', 'nothing'.

'No.'

'So belief cannot be either ignorance or knowledge.'

'Apparently not.'

'Is it then beyond the limits set by these two? Does it surpass knowledge in clarity, or ignorance in lack of clarity?'

'No.'

'Do you think, then,' I asked, 'that belief is something more obscure than knowledge, but clearer than ignorance?'

'That's exactly what I think.'

d   'It lies within those limits?'

'Yes.'

'So belief would be between the other two.'

'It certainly would.'

'Very well. Did we say a few moments ago that if there were anything whose nature was both to be something and not to be something, such a thing occupied an intermediate position between what purely and simply is something and what is not something in any way at all? We said that neither knowledge nor ignorance could be directed at such an object, but only something which clearly occupied an intermediate position between ignorance and knowledge.'

'We did. And we were right.'

'And now it turns out that what we call belief, or opinion, clearly does occupy this intermediate position.'

'Yes, it clearly does.'

e   'It remains for us to discover, apparently, what it is that has a share in both – in being something, and in not being something – but cannot properly be called either in its pure form. Then if it *does* make its appearance, we will be justified in calling it the object of belief or opinion. We can assign extremes to extremes, and intermediates to intermediates, can't we?'

'We can.'

479   'Having established these definitions, I have a question to put to that fine fellow who thinks there is no beauty in itself, no form or character of beauty which remains always the same and unchanging, who thinks that beauty is plural – that born spectator who cannot tolerate anyone saying that beauty is one, or justice is one, or anything like that. "Well, my friend," we shall ask him, "is there any of these numerous beautiful things which cannot on occasion appear ugly? Anything just which cannot appear unjust? Anything holy which cannot appear unholy?"'

b   'No,' he said. 'They must necessarily appear to be both beautiful and
ugly. And the same with all the other examples you ask about.'

'What about all those things we call "double"? Don't they seem to be
half as often as they seem to be double?'

'They do.'

'And big things and small things, light things and heavy things? They
won't be called by these names we give them any more than by their opposites, will they?'

'No,' he said. 'Each of them can always lay claim to both labels.'

'All these examples, then – are they what they are described as any more
than their opposites?'

c   'That's like people who play with ambiguities at dinner parties. Or the
child's riddle, the one about the eunuch, about throwing something at a
bat, what the riddle says he threw at it, and what it was sitting on.[42] Your
examples are all ambiguous, in that it is impossible to form any definite
conception of them either as being something, or as not being something,
or as both, or as neither.'

'Do you have any way of dealing with them, then?' I asked. 'Do you
have anywhere better to put them than at the mid-point between being
something and not being something? They are not more obscure than
what is not something, I take it, so they can't *not be* something to a greater
degree than that. Nor are they clearer than what *is* something, so they
d   can't *be* something any more than that.'

'Very true.'

'So we have discovered, apparently, that most people's varying stan-
dards of beauty and things like that are rattling around somewhere in the
middle, between what is *not* something and what purely and simply *is*
something.'

'We have.'

'And we agreed earlier that if anything of this kind made its appearance, we must call it an object of belief, not an object of knowledge. It is
for the intermediate capacity to grasp what shifts about in the intermediate position.'

---

[42] The scholia (comments written in the margins of manuscripts) give two versions of
this riddle: the shorter version has a man, yet not a man (a eunuch), throwing a stone,
yet not a stone (a pumice stone), at a bird, yet not a bird (a bat), sitting on a perch,
yet not a perch (a reed); the longer version adds that he saw yet did not see the bird,
and threw yet did not throw the stone at it, but does not solve these two elements of
the puzzle.

'Yes, that is what we agreed.'

c   'So shall we say that the people who look at lots of beautiful things, but fail to see beauty itself, and who cannot follow someone else who directs them to it – or who look at lots of just things, but fail to see justice itself, and the same with all the other examples – shall we say that they have beliefs or opinions about all these things, but no knowledge of the things their beliefs are about?'

'Yes, that is what we must say.'

'What about the people who in each case look at the things themselves, at what is always the same and unchanging? Won't we say that they have knowledge, and not merely belief?'

'Again, we must.'

'Well, then. Shall we say that these people take pleasure in and enjoy the things knowledge is directed at, while the others take pleasure in and enjoy the things belief is directed at? Don't we remember saying that these people enjoy beautiful sounds and colours, and that sort of thing, that this is what they look at, but that they cannot cope with the idea that there might be such a thing as beauty itself?'

'We do.'

'So we shan't be giving offence if we call them lovers of opinion or belief, rather than lovers of wisdom? It won't make them very angry if we describe them like that?'

'Not if they listen to me,' he said. 'After all, no one should ever get angry at the truth.'

'And those who in each case take pleasure in what is something, just by itself, should be called lovers of wisdom or philosophers, not lovers of opinion, shouldn't they?'

'They certainly should.'

Book 6

484 'Well, Glaucon,' I said, 'it's been a long discussion, and not without its difficulty. But it is now clear which are the lovers of wisdom, the philosophers, and which are not.'

'Not easy in a short discussion either, perhaps.'

'Apparently not. Personally, though, I think it could still be made a lot clearer if it were the only thing we had to talk about, and if there weren't a large number of topics still needing explanation before we can see how the just life differs from the unjust.'

b 'All right. What do we have to look at next?'

'The question which naturally follows, of course. Given that those who are capable of grasping what is always the same and unchanging are philosophers, while those who are not capable of it, who drift among things which are many and widely varying, are not philosophers, which of the two groups ought to be leaders in a city?'

'Well, what would be a reasonable answer to that question?'

'Whichever group is clearly able to protect a city's laws and way of life should be made its guardians.'

c 'Correct.'

'Take a different question,' I said. 'If a guard is keeping an eye on something, is it obvious whether he should be blind or have good eyesight?'

'Of course it's obvious.'

'Can you see any difference between those who are blind and those who are genuinely lacking in knowledge of everything that is? They have no clear pattern or model in their soul. They can't look at what is most real

d the way painters do, making constant comparisons with it and observing it as closely as possible, and in this way establish rules about beauty, justice

and goodness in everyday life – if they need establishing – or defend and
preserve rules which already exist.'

'No, I can't,' he said. 'There is no difference to speak of between these
people and the blind.'

'Are these the people we shall appoint as guardians, then? Or the ones
who do know about each thing that is, who are the equal of the others in
experience of practical affairs, and not inferior in any other area of human
excellence?'

'If they *are* equal in other matters, then it would be absurd not to
choose this second group, since on grounds of knowledge – which is the
single most important thing – they come out on top.'

485   'Shouldn't we explain, then, how it can be possible for the same people
to have not just philosophical knowledge, but also practical experience
and the rest of human excellence?'

'Yes, we should.'

'In that case, as we said at the beginning of this discussion,[1] their
natural character is the first thing we have to find out about. If we can
come to a satisfactory conclusion about that, then I think we shall agree
that the same people can possess all these qualities, and that these are the
only people who should be rulers of cities.'

'Explain.'

'Let's assume that one element of the philosopher's nature is agreed
b between us. He is always in love with any learning which helps to reveal
that reality which always is, and which is not driven this way and that by
becoming and ceasing to be.'

'Yes, let's take that as agreed.'

'Further, he is in love with the whole of that reality. He will not readily
give up any part of it, whether small or large, more valuable or less valuable. We explained that earlier when we were talking about those who are
ambitious or those who are lovers.'[2]

'That's right,' he said.

'Ask yourself, in that case, whether there is a second, additional,
attribute which those who are going to be the kind of people we were
talking about must possess.'

c   'What sort of attribute?'

'Truthfulness. Not willingly accepting falsehood in any form. A hatred
of falsehood, and a love of truth.'

---

[1] 474b.   [2] 474d–475b.

'Yes, that probably is a second attribute,' he said.

'Not just "probably," my friend. If you are a lover by nature, then you necessarily love everything related to, or belonging to, the boy you love.'

'Correct.'

'Can you think of anything which belongs to wisdom more than truth does?'

'Of course not.'

'In which case, is it possible for the same nature to be both a lover of

d wisdom and a lover of falsehood?'

'No.'

'The genuine lover of learning, then, must make every possible effort, right from earliest childhood, to reach out for truth of every kind.'

'Absolutely.'

'Besides, we can be sure, I take it, that the stronger a person's desires are in one direction, the weaker they will be in other directions. Like a stream when it gets diverted.'

'True. What of it?'

'In someone whose stream flows in the direction of learning and everything like it, I imagine the desires will be concerned with the pleasure of the mind alone, just by itself. They will give up the pleasures arising out of the body. That's assuming the person is a true philosopher, a genuine lover of wisdom, not a pretend lover.'

e 'That must necessarily be so.'

'A person like this will be self-disciplined, and he certainly won't be avaricious. The things which make people interested in money, and the lavish expenditure that goes with it, may well be of interest to other people, but they won't be of interest to him.'

'True.'

486 'And I suppose there's one other question to ask when you come to decide what is a philosophical nature and what is not.'

'What is that?'

'You should be on the lookout for a nature which is mean-spirited. Small-mindedness, I would imagine, is the last thing you want in a soul which is going to spend all its time reaching out for the wholeness and totality of things – divine and human.'

'That's very true,' he said.

'Do you think, then, that the mind which is not afraid of great things, and can contemplate the whole of time and the whole of reality, is likely to regard human life as of any great importance?'

b   'No, that's impossible.'

'Even death won't seem frightening to someone like this, will it?'

'Certainly not.'

'A cowardly and mean-spirited nature can have nothing to do with true philosophy, apparently.'

'No, I don't think it can.'

'Well, then, is there any way this well-ordered person – who is not avaricious, not mean-spirited, not a charlatan or a coward – could turn out to be a contract-breaker, or unjust?'

'No, there isn't.'

'So if you want to know whether a soul is a lover of wisdom or not, another thing to look at, right from its earliest years, is whether it is just and gentle or unsociable and savage.'

'Very much so.'

'And I'm inclined to think there's something else you will do well not to overlook.'

c   'What is that?'

'Is he quick or slow to learn? You wouldn't expect anyone ever to show a great deal of enthusiasm for an activity which he found unpleasant, and in which he had difficulty ever accomplishing anything.'

'No, that's not something that could happen.'

'What if he had a hopeless memory, and could retain nothing of what he learnt? How could he help being empty of knowledge?'

'He couldn't.'

'And if he is toiling away to no purpose, don't you think that in the end he will be driven to hate himself and the whole enterprise?'

'Of course he will.'

d   'In which case, when we are deciding which souls are truly philo-sophical, let's leave out any soul with a poor memory. Let's insist that it should have a good memory.'

'By all means.'

'Now, think about a soul with an unmusical or unrefined nature. This can only lead, we would say, to lack of proportion.'

'Of course.'

'And do you think truth is akin to proportion, or lack of proportion?'

'To proportion.'

'In that case, a natural proportion and a pleasant nature are additional qualities we should look for in a mind whose innate disposition will be easily led in every case towards the character of what is.'

e   'Unquestionably.'

'What do you reckon? For a soul which is going to share fully and completely in what is, aren't all the qualities we have outlined essential and interconnected?'

487   'Absolutely essential,' he said.

'In which case, can you find any fault with an activity which no one could ever follow properly without having a naturally retentive memory, an aptitude for learning, a willingness to undertake great things, a pleasant nature – and without being a friend and kinsman of truth, justice, courage and self-discipline?'

'Momus himself[3] could not object to an activity of that kind.'

'And once they have grown up and completed their education, you are going to entrust your city to people like this – and to no one else – aren't you?'

b   At this point Adeimantus intervened. 'No one could possibly argue against what you've said so far, Socrates. But I know what happens to people who at one time or another have listened to the things you've just been saying. As they see it, their lack of experience of question and answer allows them to be led just a little astray by the argument at each stage. But then when all the little things they've said are collected together at the end, it reveals a major error and contradiction of what they said originally.

c   They are like beginners playing draughts against experts. By the end of the game they find they are trapped, and have no move they can make. In the same way these people find, by the end of the argument, that they are trapped and have nothing they can say in this rather different kind of draughts which uses words instead of pieces. But it does nothing to convince them that the truth is as you say. I say this with our present discussion in mind. I can imagine someone saying at this point that although he can't challenge the answer to any particular step in your questioning, in

d   real life he can see that the majority of those who go in for philosophy – not the ones who dabble with it as part of their education and then give it up at an early age, but the ones who spend much longer on it – turn out to be extremely odd, not to say thoroughly bad. Even for those we regard as the best of them, the effect of the way of life you recommend is to make them useless to their cities.'

I listened to this, and then said: 'Do you think what they say is wrong?'

'I don't know. I'd be glad to hear your opinion.'

---

[3] Momus: the personification of blame or censure.

e   'The answer you'd get is that I think what they say is true.'

'In that case,' he asked, 'how can it be right to say that cities will find no release from their troubles until philosophers, who we agree are useless to them, become their rulers?'

'That question calls for an answer by means of an analogy.'

'Something you've never been much in the habit of using, of course.'

'I see. First you let me in for proving something which is extremely
488   difficult to prove. Then you make fun of me. Well, if you need any further proof of how firmly I cling to analogies, then listen to this one. The best of the philosophers find themselves, *vis-à-vis* their cities, in a situation so awkward that there is nothing in the world like it. To construct an analogy in their defence, you have to draw on a number of sources, like painters painting composite creatures – half-goat, half-deer – and things like that. Imagine some ships, or one ship, and a state of affairs on board something
b   like this.[4] There's the shipowner, larger and stronger than everyone in the ship, but somewhat deaf and rather short-sighted, with a knowledge of sailing to match his eyesight. The sailors are quarrelling among themselves over captaincy of the ship, each one thinking that he ought to be captain, though he has never learnt that skill, nor can he point to the person who taught him or a time when he was learning it. On top of which they say it
c   can't be taught. In fact they're prepared to cut to pieces anyone who says it can. The shipowner himself is always surrounded by them. They beg him and do everything they can to make him hand over the tiller to them. Sometimes, if other people can persuade him and they can't, they kill those others or throw them overboard. Then they immobilise their worthy shipowner with drugs or drink or by some other means, and take control of the ship, helping themselves to what it is carrying. Drinking and feasting, they sail in the way you'd expect people like that to sail.
d   More than that, if someone is good at finding them ways of persuading or compelling the shipowner to let them take control, they call him a real seaman, a real captain, and say he really knows about ships. Anyone who can't do this they treat with contempt, calling him useless. They don't even begin to understand that if he is to be truly fit to take command of a ship a real ship's captain must of necessity be thoroughly familiar with the

---

[4] The comparison seems to be intended as an image of the Athenian democracy, in which the authority of the people (the shipowner/captain) is subverted by those leading figures on the political stage (the crew) who know best how to secure the people's compliance with their own designs. The metaphor of the ship of state was common in Greek poetry.

e seasons of the year, the stars in the sky, the winds, and everything to do
with his art. As for *how* he is going to steer the ship – regardless of
whether anyone wants him to or not – they do not regard this as an additional skill or study which can be acquired over and above the art of being
a ship's captain.[5] If this is the situation on board, don't you think the
489 person who is genuinely equipped to be captain will be called a stargazer, a
chatterer, of no use to them, by those who sail in ships with this kind of crew?'

'Absolutely,' Adeimantus replied.

'I don't imagine you need to have the similarity with the attitude of
cities towards true philosophers spelled out in detail. You can probably
see what I'm getting at.'

'Indeed I can.'

'So your first response to this character who expresses surprise that
philosophers are not treated with respect in cities might be to suggest this
analogy to him. You might try to persuade him that it would be far more
b surprising if they *were* treated with respect.'

'I will suggest it,' he said.

'Yes, and you can also suggest to him that what he says is true. To the
majority of people the best of those doing philosophy *are* useless. You
must point out to him, however, that the blame for their uselessness lies
not with the philosophers, but with those who make no use of them. It is
unnatural for the captain to beg the sailors to come under his command,
or for the wise man to go to the rich man's door. Whoever dreamed up
that saying was wrong.[6] The truth is that neither a rich man who is ill nor
a poor man who is ill has any choice but to go to the doctor's door, and
that anyone who wants to be ruled has no choice but to go to the door of
c the person who knows how to rule. It's not up to the ruler, if he really is
any good, to beg those he is ruling to *be* ruled. You won't go far wrong if
you compare our present political leaders to sailors of the kind we have
just described, and the people described by politicians as useless star-
gazers to true ship's captains.'

'Quite right,' he said.

'For these reasons, and under these conditions, it is not easy to value the
best way of life – not with all those people following a completely different

---

[5] The sense of the Greek is unclear. It could also mean, for example, 'Nor do they
accept the possibility that, along with the art of navigation, he could gain, by instruction or practice, the skill to keep control of the helm whether anyone wants him to
or not.'

[6] Simonides is reported to have said that it is better to be rich than wise, because wise
men are found at the courts of the rich.

d way of life. But by far the greatest and most powerful objection to philosophy is provided by those who claim they *are* following this way of
life. You said about them that the opponent of philosophy would describe
most of those who go in for it as villains, while the best were useless. And
I agreed that you were right, didn't I?'

'Yes.'

'Well, then, have we explained the reason why the good ones are
useless?'

'We have. Very clearly.'

'Do you want us to go on to explain why it's inevitable that most of
those who go in for philosophy will turn out to be villains? Shall we try
e and demonstrate, if we can, that philosophy is not to blame for this
either?'

'Yes, please.'

'Let's begin our discussion by reminding ourselves of the point where
we were describing the nature which anyone who was going to be an outstanding individual must necessarily be born with.[7] He was guided, if you
490 recall, in the first place by the truth, which he had to follow in every way,
in all circumstances. Otherwise he would be a charlatan, and wholly out
of touch with true philosophy.'

'Yes, that is what we said.'

'Isn't this one characteristic which runs completely counter to the
opinions normally held about him?'

'Yes, completely,' he said.

'Won't it be reasonable for us to defend him by saying that it was, after
all, the nature of the true lover of learning to keep struggling towards
what is, and that he did not waste time on what opinion sees, in each case,
b as many? Never losing his edge, never abandoning his passion, he kept on
going until he had grasped the nature of what each thing itself is with that
part of his soul – the part akin to it – which is equipped to grasp this kind
of thing. And it was only when he used this part of his soul to get close to
and be intimate with what really is, so engendering understanding and
truth, that he found knowledge, true life, nourishment, and relief from
the pains of the soul's childbirth?'

'That will be the most reasonable defence imaginable,' he said.

'Very well. Will a love of falsehood form any part of this person's character? Or its exact opposite – a hatred of falsehood?'

---

[7] 485a–487a.

c   'A hatred of falsehood.'

'And where truth led, we could not possibly say, I imagine, that a chorus of evils followed.'

'Of course not.'

'What did follow was a healthy and just character, with self-discipline close behind.'

'Correct.'

'And the rest of the chorus making up the philosophic cast? Is there any need to insist on putting them on parade again? You remember, presumably, that the appropriate companions of the virtues I have mentioned were going to be courage, greatness of spirit, a disposition to learn and a good memory. And your objection to this was that although we could make everyone agree in theory with what we said, as soon as we turned

d   from the argument to the people the argument was about, what they would say was that some philosophers were useless, while most of them were as bad as bad could be. It was asking the reason for this accusation that brought us to the question which occupies us at the moment – why are most philosophers bad? That is why we have once again taken up the nature of those who are true philosophers, and felt obliged to define it.'

e   'That is so,' he said.

'We must examine the ways in which this nature gets corrupted and in most cases destroyed – though a small number escape, the ones we call useless rather than wicked. The next step after that is to look at the natures which imitate the philosophical nature and adopt the philo-

491 sophical way of life. We must ask ourselves what kinds of soul they are that finish up in an unsuitable way of life which is too much for them, and that by constantly striking the wrong note have given philosophy everywhere, and in the eyes of everyone, the reputation you are talking about.'

'What are the ways they get corrupted?'

'I'll try and explain, if I can. There is one point where I think we can count on general agreement. Among the human race, natures of this kind, possessing all the qualities we have just laid down as essential to the devel-

b   opment of the true philosopher, are few and far between. Don't you agree?'

'Absolutely.'

'And for these few, think how many fatal dangers there are.'

'Such as?'

'The one which will sound most surprising is that each of the qualities we praised in the philosophical nature – I mean courage, self-discipline and all the virtues we described – can corrupt the soul which possesses it, and distract it from philosophy.'

'Yes, that does sound odd,' he said.

c   'And apart from these, everything which is generally regarded as a good can also have a corrupting and distracting influence. Things like beauty, wealth, physical strength, influential family connections, and all the advantages they bring with them. You know the kind of thing I mean.'

'Yes, I do. But I wouldn't mind hearing you spell it out in more detail.'

'Once you get the general idea,' I said, 'you'll find it quite straight-forward. What I've just said won't strike you as odd at all.'

'All right, then. Tell me how to go about it.'

d   'Take any seed or living thing, plant or animal. We know that if it cannot find the nourishment, climate and habitat appropriate to it, then the stronger it is, the more completely it fails to develop its potential. In other words, the bad is a worse enemy of what is good than of what is not good.'

'Obviously.'

'So it stands to reason that in an adverse environment the best nature will come off worse than an inferior nature.'

'Yes, it does.'

e   'Doesn't the same apply to souls, Adeimantus? Can we say that the nat-urally best souls will turn out particularly badly if they get a bad educa-tion? Don't you think great crimes and sheer wickedness are the product of a vigorous nature corrupted by its upbringing, not of an inferior nature? Do you think a weak nature can ever be responsible for anything great – good or evil?'

'No,' he said, 'I think it's the vigorous nature, as you say.'

492   'So if what we defined as the philosophical nature gets the course of study it requires, I assume it can't help growing and coming to all manner of excellence. But if the seed falls in the wrong place, if that is where it grows and is nourished, then without the assistance of some god it will turn out the exact opposite. Or do you too go along with the general view? Do you think some young people are corrupted by sophists? Are there any individual sophists who do any corrupting worth talking about? Don't you think the people who say this are themselves the worst sophists of all? Don't they offer the most complete education? Can't they turn young and

b   old, men and women, into anything they choose?'

'When do they do this?' he asked.

'When they're all sitting together in large numbers,' I replied. 'In the assembly, or in the lawcourts, the theatre, or on active service, or any other general gathering of a large number of people. They make a tremendous din, shouting or hammering their disapproval and approval – grossly exaggerated, in either case – of the things that are said and done. Added to them you get the rocks and the place they are in echoing the din of

c approval and disapproval, and making it twice as loud.[8] In those surroundings a young man "hath no stomach," as the saying goes, to the fight. What individual tuition can stand firm against it without being swept away by this torrent of disapproval and approval, and disappear, swept away wherever the flood takes it? How can he avoid agreeing with the crowd about good and bad, following the same way of life as the crowd, and being like the crowd?'

d 'He can't, Socrates. He's bound to agree with them.'

'Yes,' I said, 'and we still haven't mentioned the strongest compulsion they use.'

'What is that?'

'The compulsion they apply by their actions – these teachers and sophists – if they fail to convince him by their words. You are aware, aren't you, that if he doesn't listen to them, they punish him with loss of citizen rights, fines and the death penalty?'

'They do indeed,' he said. 'With a vengeance.'

'What other sophist, or what individual arguments, can stand up against them and get the better of them?'

e 'None of them, I imagine.'

'No, they can't. It would be madness even to try. No different type of character ever comes about, nor ever has, nor ever will, trained to virtue in defiance of the education these sophists provide. No human character, that is. The divine or godlike character is what they call the exception which proves the rule. You can be quite sure that if you find a character which survives and turns out in the right way in political systems of this sort, you won't be mistaken in saying it was a divine dispensation

493 which preserved it.'

'I couldn't agree more.'

'In that case,' I said, 'there's a second point I'd like you to agree on as well.'

---

[8] Meetings of the Athenian assembly and most theatrical performances were held in open-air auditoria. Courts of law met in a number of public spaces and buildings, some more enclosed than others.

'What is that?'

'That all the highly paid individuals the public calls sophists, and thinks of as competitors, are teaching exactly the same opinions as those expressed by the general public in its gatherings. Those are what they call wisdom. It's rather like someone keeping a large, powerful animal, getting
b to know its moods and wants, how to approach it, how to handle it, when and why it is most awkward and most amenable, the various sounds it is in the habit of making in different situations, and the sounds which soothe it or infuriate it when someone else makes them. Imagine he'd learnt all this as a result of being with the animal over a long period of time. He might then call what he had learnt wisdom, might organise his findings into an art or science, and take up teaching, though in truth he would have no idea at all which of these opinions and desires was beautiful or ugly, good or bad, just or unjust, and would assign all these names in
c accordance with the opinions of the huge animal. Things which gave the animal pleasure he would call good. Things which annoyed it he would call bad. He would have no other standard by which to judge them, and so he would call things right and good when they were merely necessary. He would never have seen, nor would he be capable of explaining to anyone else, the vast difference which in fact exists between the nature of what is necessary and the nature of what is good. If that were how he behaved, don't you think he would be a pretty odd teacher?'

'Yes, I do,' he said.

'Can you see any difference between him and the person who believes
d that in painting or music, or indeed politics, wisdom consists in having identified the diverse moods and pleasures of the general public in its gatherings? There's no doubt that if someone is presenting the public with a poem or a work of art, or some service done to the city, and gives the public more of a say than he need over what he does, then it's a question of "needs must when the devil drives."[9] He has no option but to do whatever the public approves of. But when they start claiming that what the public likes really is good or really is beautiful, have you ever heard any of them support that claim with an argument which wasn't laughable?'

e   'No, I don't think so,' he said. 'Nor am I ever likely to.'

'Bearing all that in mind, think again about our earlier question. Is it
494 possible for the masses to accept or believe in beauty itself, as opposed to

---

[9] The Greek proverb refers to 'Diomedean necessity'. Its origin is uncertain.

the many beautiful things? Or anything "itself," as opposed to the many examples of it?'

'No.'[10]

'So it's impossible,' I said, 'for the masses to be philosophical.'

'Yes.'

'And the people who *are* philosophers will inevitably be unpopular with them.'

'Inevitably.'

'And also with those private individuals who spend their time among crowds, trying to please them.'

'Obviously.'

'That being so, what hope can you see for the philosophical nature? How can it persevere to the end, and preserve itself, in its chosen way of
b life? Think about our earlier conclusions when you answer. We have agreed that a disposition to learn, a good memory, courage and greatness of spirit were the hallmarks of the philosophical nature.'[11]

'Yes.'

'Well, won't this kind of person stand out above the crowd even in childhood, especially if his appearance and physique match his mind and character?'

'How can he fail to?'

'And when he gets older, I imagine his family and fellow-citizens will want to make use of him in the conduct of their own affairs.'

'Naturally.'

c 'They will lie at his feet, presenting him with their prayers and plaudits, and trying by means of a little flattery in advance to get an option on the power which will one day be his.'

'Yes,' he said, 'that's certainly what is likely to happen.'

'How do you think someone like this will react in these circumstances – particularly if he does in fact come from a large city, and if, in that city, he is rich and well-born, in addition to being tall and good-looking? Won't he be filled with impossible ambitions, and believe himself capable of
d handling the affairs both of Greece and of the barbarians? Won't this give him a very exalted idea of himself, and make him all puffed up – quite irrationally so – with empty pride and vain display?'[12]

---

[10] Previously agreed at 476b.   [11] 490c.

[12] The description in this paragraph and in those that follow fits closely with the person and life of the Athenian statesman Alcibiades, whose ambition was thought partly to blame for the imperialistic disaster of the expedition to Sicily (415–413 BC), who became a traitor to Athens, and who in the Socratic literature is portrayed as intimately involved with Socrates.

'It certainly will,' he said.

'Suppose you quietly take him on one side, when this happens to him, and tell him the truth, which is that he lacks all rationality, desperately though he needs it, and that the only way of acquiring it is to make himself a slave to its acquisition. Do you think it's easy for him to hear, over the noise of all these distractions?'

'No. Far from easy.'

'And suppose again,' I said, 'that as a result of his natural endowments
e and the appeal these arguments have for him he does somehow see the importance of philosophy. Suppose he is attracted and drawn towards it. What do we think will be the reaction of those who think they are losing his help and friendship? Is there any argument they will not use, any action they will not take, in their efforts both to stop him being persuaded and to make things impossible – whether by private intrigue or by taking him to court publicly – for the person persuading him?'

495   'Yes, they're bound to behave like that,' he said.

'Will it be possible for someone like this to pursue philosophy?'

'Certainly not.'

'In which case you can see, can't you, that we weren't so far wrong after all when we said it was the actual elements of the philosophical nature, when subjected to the wrong sort of upbringing, which in some way caused people to give up the philosophical way of life? That, plus such supposed advantages as wealth and all the paraphernalia that goes with it?'

'No, we weren't so far wrong,' he said. 'In fact, we were absolutely right.'

b   'There you are, then. Such is the death and destruction of the finest natures, which are already rare enough, we say, quite apart from this. That is what it is like, and that is how powerful it is. It ruins them for the finest way of life there is. It is from people like this that those who do the greatest harm to cities and individuals come, and also, if that is the way the stream carries them, those who do great good. A nonentity never has any great effect either on an individual or on a city.'

'Very true.'

c   'Well, when those to whom philosophy properly belongs give up in this way, they leave her barren and unfulfilled. Their own life is untrue and unsuited to them, while philosophy, abandoned by her relatives like an orphan, is accosted by a different collection of people, who are unworthy of her and bring shame upon her, together with reproaches of the kind you yourself agree people tend to bring against her – that some of those

who associate with her are worthless, while most of them deserve anything they get.'

'Yes, that's the generally held view.'

'And with good reason,' I said. 'What you get then is inferior people
d instead, who see the field wide open, and the fine titles and prestige
attached to philosophy. It's like escaped prisoners taking refuge in
temples. The ones with the greatest ingenuity in their own trivial occupations are only too glad to break out of these occupations, and into
philosophy. After all, despite the way it is practised, philosophy still has
a very impressive reputation, at least in comparison with other occupations. That's what many people are aiming at, people of no natural excel-
e lence, whose minds are stunted and maimed by menial tasks in the same
way as their bodies are deformed by their occupation or profession. Isn't
that inevitable?'

'It certainly is.'

'And this spectacle,' I asked, 'do you think it differs in any way from
that of some short, balding blacksmith who has come by a bit of money?
No sooner released from chains than he cleans himself up at the baths,
puts on a new cloak and gets himself dressed up as a bridegroom in the
hope of marrying the penniless and neglected daughter of his master.'
496 'No, I can't see any difference at all.'

'What kind of offspring are parents like this probably going to produce?
Won't they be inferior cross-breeds?'

'Yes, they're bound to be.'

'And what happens to these people who are not worth educating, when
they get close to philosophy and form an undeserved association with her?
What kind of thoughts and opinions are we to say they produce? Won't
they produce what can only really be called sophistries – nothing legitimate, nothing belonging to true wisdom?'

'Absolutely.'

'That leaves only a very small fraction, Adeimantus, of those who
b spend their time on philosophy as of right. Some character of noble birth
and good upbringing, perhaps, whose career has been interrupted by
exile, and who for want of corrupting influences has followed his nature
and remained with philosophy. Or a great mind born in a small city, who
thinks the political affairs of his city beneath him, and has no time for
them. And I suppose there may be a small element consisting of those
who reject some other discipline – rightly, since they are too good for it –
and come to philosophy that way. Our friend Theages has a bridle which

c is quite good at keeping people in check. Theages has all the qualifications for dropping out of philosophy, but physical ill-health keeps him in check, and stops him going into politics. Then there's my own case – my divine sign – though that's hardly worth mentioning. Practically nobody in the past, I imagine, has had it happen to him.[13] Those who have become members of this small group have tasted how sweet and blessed a possession is philosophy. They can also, by contrast, see quite clearly the
d madness of the many. They can see that virtually nothing anyone in politics does is in any way healthy, and that they have no ally with whom they could go to the rescue of justice and live to tell the tale. The philosopher would be like a man falling into a den of wild animals, refusing to join in their vicious activities, but too weak to resist their combined ferocity single-handed. He wouldn't get a chance to help his city or his friends. He would be killed before he could be any use either to himself or to anyone else. Taking all this into his calculations, he will keep quiet, and mind his own business, like someone taking shelter behind a wall when he is caught by a storm of driving dust and rain. He sees everyone else
e brimful of lawlessness, and counts himself lucky if he himself can somehow live his life here pure, free from injustice and unholy actions, and depart with high hopes, in a spirit of kindness and goodwill, on his release from it.'

497 'Well,' he said, 'if he could have accomplished that before his departure, it would be no small achievement.'

'And yet not the greatest achievement either – not without finding a political system worthy of him. In one which *is* worthy of him his own growth will be greater, and he will be the salvation of his country as well as of himself. Well, there you are. I think we've dealt satisfactorily with the question why philosophy has got such a bad name, and shown that it is undeserved. Or do you still have something to add?'

'No, I have nothing to add. But when you talk about the political system which is worthy of philosophy, which of the present-day systems do you mean?'

b 'None of them,' I replied. 'That's precisely my complaint. There is no present-day political regime which lives up to the philosopher's nature. That's why his nature is twisted and transformed. It's like the seed of

---

[13] Socrates' divine sign was an inner voice that warned him away from certain courses of action, but never gave positive instruction. Communications from the gods were a part of Greek culture, but typically came in the form of dreams or portents or official proclamations from seers and diviners, not as inner voices.

some exotic plant. When it's sown outside its native land, it tends to lose
its distinguishing properties and vigour, and degenerate into the indig-
enous variety. In the same way, as things stand at present, the philosophic
type tends not to preserve its distinctive power. It degenerates into some
c other sort of character. If it ever does find the best regime – just as it is
itself the best – then it will show that it was a truly divine type, whereas
all other types of nature or life are merely human. And the next question
you're going to ask, obviously, is what this regime is.'

'No, you're wrong,' he said. 'That wasn't what I was going to ask. What
I was going to ask was whether it was the regime we have described in the
course of founding our city, or some other regime.'

'In most respects, the regime we have described. But there was one
proviso we made even then, which was that there would always have to be
d present in the city some element which embodies the principles under-
lying the regime – the same principles on which you, the lawgiver, based
the laws.'

'Yes, there was that proviso.'

'But it wasn't made as clear as it might have been,' I said. 'I was afraid
of the points which you have in fact seized hold of, and whose clarification
has proved so long and difficult. And there's a part we haven't yet dealt
with which is anything but straightforward.'

'What part is that?'

'How a city can handle philosophy without being destroyed. Any great
enterprise involves risk, and in the words of the proverb, what is good
never does come easily.'

e 'All the same, we can't bring our explanation to a close without resolving this question.'

'It will be lack of ability which stops us, if anything does, not lack of
will. You can judge my enthusiasm for yourself at first hand. Here, for
instance. See the reckless enthusiasm in the claim I am now prepared to
make, that the way a city should tackle this pursuit is quite the reverse of
how it is tackled at present.'

'What way do you mean?'

498 'At the moment,' I said, 'those who tackle philosophy at all come to it
as adolescents, straight after childhood, in that period before they start
running households and earning their living. But as soon as they get anywhere near the most difficult part of the subject – the part which is to do
with reasoned argument – they give it up, and are promptly regarded as
experts in philosophy. In later life, they are immensely proud of them-

selves if they are prepared even to accept an invitation to listen to other
people engaged in reasoning. They regard it as a spare-time activity. And
as old age approaches, for all but a handful of them, the fire goes out like
Heraclitus' sun. More so, in fact, since they are never relighted.'

b   'How should they go about it?'

'In exactly the opposite way. When they are adolescents and children,
they should engage in the education and philosophy appropriate to adolescents. While their bodies are growing and reaching manhood, they
should pay a lot of attention to them, and in this way gain philosophy
a useful servant. They should not increase the severity of the soul's
exercises until the time comes in which it begins to reach maturity. And

c when their strength fails, and they are released from politics and military
service, then they can roam the sacred fields at will, and do nothing *but*
philosophy, except in their spare time. That way they will live happy lives,
and on their deaths add a fitting reward in the other world to the life they
have lived here.'

'Well, Socrates, that certainly does strike me as a strongly held view.
But I think it makes most listeners even more strongly opposed to you.
They're not going to believe a word of it. Look at Thrasymachus, for a
start.'

d   'Don't start making trouble between Thrasymachus and me, now that
we've just become friends. Not that we were enemies before, of course.
We're not going to relax our efforts until we either persuade him and the
others, or give them a bit of a helping hand for that moment in some
future life when they find themselves in the same sort of discussion.'

'I see. Not long to wait, then.'

'No time at all,' I said, 'compared with eternity. Mind you, it's no great
surprise if people aren't convinced by what has been said, since they've

e never seen the fulfilment of our prophecy about philosophy – they may
have seen plays on words, the sort of verbal similarities which are created
artificially, but not the ones that occur naturally, as this one did. But men
are different from words. A man who as completely as possible matches
virtue in word and deed, who as it were rhymes with virtue, and who is
the ruler of a city like himself, a man – or men – like that is something
they have never seen. Or do you think they have?'

499   'No, I don't.'

'Nor again, my excellent friend, have they spent enough time listening
to the fine, free talk which in its desire for knowledge looks determinedly
for truth in every way, and which salutes from a safe distance the clever,

combative arguments whose sole aim is prestige and competition, whether in the lawcourts or in private gatherings.'

'No, they haven't had that experience either,' he said.

b   'It was for these reasons, and anticipating these difficulties, that we were apprehensive in the first place.[14] Truth nonetheless compelled us to say that no city or regime, and likewise no man either, can ever be perfect until the few philosophers we mentioned – the ones who are not bad, though at the moment they are labelled useless[15] – are compelled by some chance event, whether they like it or not, to take charge of their city, and until the city is compelled to obey. Either that, or as a result of some divine

c   inspiration the sons of those in positions of authority or sole rule, or the actual holders of those positions, must be seized with a true love of true philosophy. My own personal view is that there is no reason to regard either or both of these events as impossible. If they were impossible, we would quite rightly be a laughing-stock, since our proposals would just be wishful thinking. Isn't that so?'

'It is.'

'Very well. Whether in the boundless past experts in philosophy have ever been compelled to take charge of their city, or whether they are under

d   any compulsion now – in some outlandish country, presumably, far removed from our view – or ever come to be in the future, there is one thing we shall be prepared to take up the cudgels over: it is when the Muse of Philosophy is mistress in the city that the regime we have described either has existed, or does exist, or will exist. It's not impossible for her to be mistress, so we are not talking about impossibilities. That it is difficult, we would none of us deny.'

'I agree,' he said.

'And will you go on to say that most people don't agree?'

'I might well.'

e   'That's all very well for you, but don't be so hard on "most people." If you can avoid being antagonistic towards them, if you encourage them, and remove the prejudice against philosophy, they will think very

500 differently. You have to point out the people you call philosophers, and define the philosophical character and way of life in the way we have just defined it, so that they don't think you are talking about the people *they* regard as philosophers. Or are you going to say that even if they do look at things in this way, they still won't think very differently, or give very

---

[14] 473c–e.   [15] 489b–d, 496b–e.

different answers? Can you imagine anyone showing aggression or malice unprovoked – anyone easy-going and unmalicious, that is? I'll answer for you, and say that while I suppose a nature as unfriendly as this may occur in a few individuals, it does not occur in the majority.'

b   'I agree with you. Of course.'

'In which case, do you also agree that the people responsible for most people's hostility to philosophy are the uninvited outsiders who have gate-crashed the party? Aren't they always at loggerheads with one another, always spoiling for a fight? Aren't their endless *ad hominem* arguments completely alien to philosophy?'

'Yes. Completely.'

'After all, Adeimantus, I don't imagine there's time for the person who
c   truly has his mind fixed on what is to glance down at the affairs of men, or compete with them, and be filled with envy and ill will. No, he fixes his view and his gaze on those things which are properly arranged, which are always the same, which neither wrong one another nor are wronged by one another, and which are all ordered according to a rational plan. These are what he imitates, and tries, as far as possible, to resemble. Do you think it is at all possible to admire something, and spend time with it, without wanting to imitate it?'

'No, that's impossible,' he said.

d   'So the philosopher, spending his time with what is divine and ordered, in fact becomes as ordered and divine as it is possible for a human being to be. Though mind you, there's always plenty of prejudice around, wherever you look.'

'Precisely'

'And if there were some compulsion on him to put what he sees there into effect in human behaviour, both in private and public, instead of simply moulding himself, do you think there will be anything wrong with him as the craftsman of self-discipline, justice and the whole of popular virtue?'

'Certainly not.'

e   'And if the many realise that what we are saying about the philosopher is true, will they be hostile to him? Will they refuse to believe us when we say there is no way the city can ever be happy until it is designed by artists using this divine pattern?'

'No, they won't be hostile to him. Not if they realise we are telling the
501 truth. But this design you are talking about, what form will it take? How will they go about it?'

'They would take as their slate a city, and the character of human beings. They would begin by wiping it clean, which would be far from easy. All the same, you should be in no doubt that they would differ from other draftsmen in refusing, right from the start, to have anything to do with any individual or city, or draft any laws, until they were either given a clean slate or had cleaned it for themselves.'

'Quite right too,' he said.

'After that, would they draw the outline of the constitution, do you think?'

'Of course.'

b   'And then I imagine they would work away, with frequent glances back and forth. First towards what is in its nature just, noble, self-disciplined, and everything of that sort, and then again towards what they are putting into mankind, mingling and blending institutions to produce the true human likeness based on that model which Homer called, when it appeared among mankind, a "godlike form and likeness."'[16]

'How right he was.'

'I suppose they'd rub one bit out, and draw another bit in to replace it,

c doing all they could to make human characters as pleasing to god as human characters can be.'

'It would certainly be a very beautiful picture.'

'Well, then,' I said, 'these people you said were hell-bent on attacking us, are we managing to convince them that the person whose praises we were singing earlier, the one they were hostile to because we were entrusting cities to him, is a constitution-painter of this kind?[17] Are they calming down a bit when they hear what we have to say?'

'Yes,' he said, 'if they're sensible they'll be calming down a lot.'

d   'What possible reason will they have for disagreeing? Are they going to say philosophers are not lovers of truth and reality?'

'No, that would be absurd.'

'Or that the philosopher's nature as we have described it is not akin to what is best?'

'No, they're not going to say that either.'

'How about claiming that this truth-loving nature, when it finds the way of life which is right for it, is not the most completely good and philosophical you can possibly find? Will they prefer the people we ruled out?'

---

[16] 'Godlike' was a standard compliment paid to Homeric heroes.
[17] See 474a, 487c–d, 485a–487a.

e   'I hardly think so.'

'In which case, will they still be angry with us when we say that until the philosophic type takes control in a city, there will be no end to suffering either for the city or for its citizens, and the fairy-tale regime we have been constructing in theory will find no realisation in practice?'

'Less angry, perhaps.'

502   'Never mind "less angry." Can't we say they have become wholly amenable and persuaded? That way they will agree with us out of shame, if for no other reason.'

'By all means let's say that.'

'Let's take it, then,' I said, 'that these people have been convinced on this point. Now, will anyone challenge our contention that it is possible for the sons of kings and rulers actually to be born with philosophical natures?'

'No,' he said. 'No one in the world would challenge that.'

'And if they are born with philosophical natures, can anyone claim they are certain to be corrupted? Even we admit that it is difficult for them to
b survive.[18] But is anyone going to contend that in the whole of time, out of all those who are born, not one is ever going to survive?'

'How could they?'

'But it only needs there to be one, surely, with a city which is obedient to him, to bring about all the things which are now regarded as impossible.'

'Yes, one is enough,' he said.

'After all, if a ruler establishes the laws and way of life we have described, it is presumably not impossible that the citizens will be prepared to follow them.'

'Not in the least impossible.'

'Is it astonishing or impossible that the arrangements which seem a good idea to us should seem a good idea to other people as well?'
c   'Well, *I* don't think so.'

'That they *are* the best arrangements, assuming they are possible, has been satisfactorily shown by our earlier discussion, I think.'[19]

'Yes, it has.'

'So the position we seem to have reached on lawgiving is this. Our arrangements are the best, if only they could be put into effect, and while it is difficult for them to be put into effect, it is not impossible.'

---

[18] 495a.   [19] 427e, 457a, 466c–d, 471c.

'Yes,' he said, 'that is the position we have reached.'

'Well, then, since that topic has struggled to a conclusion, we had better
d go on to deal with the ones which remain. These saviours of our city –
what will prepare them for their task? What course of study and way of
life? And when should each age-group tackle each subject?'

'Yes, we had better deal with that.'

'So much for my cleverness in the earlier part of our discussion,' I said.
'I sidestepped the awkward business of the acquisition of wives, the production of children and the selection of the rulers, when I realised that a
e perfectly true arrangement would be invidious and hard to bring about.[20]
Now the need to deal with these topics has caught up with me just the
same. Our account of women and children has been completed, but the
selection of rulers is something we need to tackle more or less from square
503 one. What we said, if you remember, was that they must prove their patriotism by being tested in the fire of pleasure and pain. It must be clear that
they will not surrender their convictions through hardship, fear or any
other twist of fortune. Those who fail the test must be disqualified, while
those who emerge pure, like gold tested in the fire, should be appointed
rulers, and given rewards and prizes both in their lifetimes and after their
deaths. That was the kind of thing we were saying, while the argument
put on her veil and slipped by us, afraid of stirring up the trouble we now
find ourselves in.'

b   'You're absolutely right,' he said. 'I do remember us saying that.'

'Yes, we were reluctant to say the things we have now been bold enough
to say. Anyway, let's now stand by our new-found boldness, and say that
if we want guardians in the most precise sense of the word, we need
philosophers.'

'Very well. Let's go on record as saying that.'

'You realise there probably won't be very many of them. The elements
of the nature we have described, and which we say they must possess,[21]
are seldom likely to be combined in the same individual. In most people
this kind of nature is fragmented.'

c   'How do you mean?'

'Well, you're aware that those who have a love of learning, a good
memory, intelligence, quickness of wit and everything which follows from
those qualities – and who at the same time are developing energy and

---

[20] Wives and children: 423e–424a; selection of rulers: 412b–414a.
[21] 487a, 490c–d, 494b.

greatness of spirit – are unlikely to become the kind of people who are naturally inclined to lead an orderly, sober and steadfast life. Quickness of wit carries people all over the place, and steadfastness goes out of the window.'

'True,' he said.

'Steadfast characters, by contrast, slow to change, the sort of people you can much more depend on, who in time of war are immovable in the face of danger, are likewise steadfast and slow to change even when it comes to learning. They are immovable and unteachable, as if they had been drugged. They are full of sleep and yawns whenever they have to work hard at something of this sort.'

'Yes, that's true.'

'But we said our guardians must be liberally endowed with both sets of qualities. Otherwise they were not to be given the fullest education, respect or power.'[22]

'Quite right, too.'

'In which case, don't you think the philosophical character will be a rare one?'

'Of course it will.'

'It must be tested in the hardships, fears and pleasures we were talking about earlier. What's more, we can now add something we omitted then, which is that we must exercise it in many branches of study, to see if it will be capable of enduring the most demanding ones, or if it is an intellectual coward, just as some people are cowards in other ways.'

'Yes,' he said. 'It's a good idea to find that out. But what are these most demanding studies of yours?'

'You may remember us distinguishing three elements of the soul, with a view to drawing conclusions about justice, self-discipline, courage and wisdom – about what each of these things was.'

'If I didn't remember *that* I would deserve to miss the rest of this discussion.'

'Can you remember what came just before that?'[23]

'No. What?'

'What we said, I believe, was that we could either get the best possible view of them, but only after a long detour, at the end of which they would be clearly revealed, or we could give an explanation on a level with the discussion so far. You said that was good enough, and as a result what was

---

[22] 484d–485a.   [23] 435c–d.

said then fell short of complete accuracy, in my opinion, though whether it was good enough for your purposes is for you to say.'

c 'As far as I'm concerned,' he said, 'you gave us good measure. And the same goes for the others, I think.'

'In matters like these, my friend, a measure which in any way at all falls short of what really is, is no measure at all. What is incomplete can never be the measure of anything, though for some people there are times when they are satisfied with that, and feel they don't have to look any further.'

'Yes, there are plenty of people who feel like that. It's laziness.'

'Well,' I said, 'it's not a feeling we want a guardian of our city and laws to have.'

'Fair enough.'

d 'In which case, my friend, our guardian must go round by the longer road. He must work as hard at studying as he does at physical training. Otherwise, as we've just been saying, he will never see the most important and appropriate subject of study through to the end.'

'I thought we had dealt with the most important subject. Is there some subject even more important than justice and the things we have been describing?'

'Yes,' I said, 'there is something more important. Also, with these virtues themselves, we shouldn't be looking at a mere outline of them the way we are now. What we want is their realisation in every detail. We must

e not neglect that. Isn't it absurd to make every effort, and do everything we can to reach the greatest possible precision and clarity over things of little significance, and then decide that the most important things deserve less than total precision?'

'Utterly absurd. But this thing you call most important – and its subject-matter, whatever you say that is – do you imagine anyone will let you go without asking you what it is?'

'Of course I don't. Why don't *you* ask me? You've heard the answer

505 often enough before, but now you've either forgotten it, or else this is another plan to make my life difficult by not letting me get away with any-thing. It must be the second reason, I think. You've often heard me say that the most important branch of study is the form or character of the good – that which just things and anything else must make use of if they are to be useful and beneficial. You must know that's what I'm going to say now, and you must also know that it's not something we have adequate knowledge of. But if we don't know it, then however much we know

b about everything else, without that, as you are well aware, our knowledge will be of no more benefit to us than if we possessed something without the good. Do you think it's any use to us to own all there is and yet not own anything good? Or to be wise in everything but the good, and have no wisdom about what is beautiful and good?'

'Good heavens, no. I certainly don't.'

'Another thing you're well aware of is that while most people think the good is pleasure, those with more sophistication think it is knowledge.'

'Of course.'

'And further, my friend, that those who hold this view are unable to show what knowledge it is. They are compelled, in the end, to say that it is knowledge of the good.'

'A pretty absurd definition,' he said.

c   'How can it fail to be absurd? They criticise us for *not* knowing what the good is, and then immediately assume we *do* know what it is. They say the good is knowledge of the good, as if we're bound to understand what they are talking about as soon as they so much as utter the word "good."'

'Absolutely true.'

'What about those who define the good as pleasure? Surely they are just as wide of the mark as the others? Aren't they in their turn compelled to admit that there are bad pleasures?'

'Very much so.'

'Hence, I imagine, they find themselves admitting that the same things
d   are good and bad, don't they?'

'Of course.'

'Is it clear, then, that it is a subject on which there are many serious disagreements?'

'Yes, it is.'

'And isn't something else clear? With justice or beauty, lots of people might settle for the appearance of them. Even if things aren't really just or beautiful, they might choose to do, possess or think them anyway. When it comes to things which are good, on the other hand, no one has ever yet been satisfied with the appearance. They want things that really *are* good; they all treat the appearance of it with contempt.'

'Yes, that's very clear, too,' he said.

e   'This is what every soul follows. All its actions are directed at this. It has a sort of divine intuition that the good is something, but it is in doubt, unable to get a firm grasp on *what* it is, or find any firm belief of the kind it has about other things. As a result it loses whatever benefit it might have got from those other things. Are we to accept that even those best people

506 in the city, to whom we are planning to entrust everything, must remain in the dark about something of this nature and importance?'

'Certainly not.'

'But if it's not known,' I said, 'in what way just and beautiful things are good, and if in particular a guardian does not know this, what kind of guardian will justice and beauty have got for themselves then? One who is not much of an asset to them, in my opinion. And I have an intuition that no one will have a satisfactory knowledge of justice and beauty without knowing this first.'

'A sound enough intuition.'

b   'Well, then, will we get the best arrangements for our society if the guardian supervising it is the kind of person who does know these things?'

'We're bound to. But what about you, Socrates? Do you say the good is knowledge? Or pleasure? Or something else again?'

'Well, you're a fine one,' I said. 'You've been making it quite clear for some time now that you're not prepared to listen to other people's opinions on this subject.'

'I just don't think it's right, Socrates, for someone who spends so much time on the subject to be prepared to come out with other people's opinions, but not his own.'

c   'How about thinking it right for someone to talk as if he knows about things he doesn't know about?' I asked.

'No, of course I don't expect him to speak as if he knows. But I do expect him to have some thoughts, and I do think he should be prepared to say what those thoughts are.'

'Really? Has it never struck you that without knowledge all opinions are hideous? Or at best blind? Can you see any difference between people who have a true opinion without understanding and people who, though blind, are going along the right road?'

'No, I can't,' he said.

d   'In that case, do you prefer to look at what is hideous – what is blind and maimed – when you have the chance of hearing what is illuminating and beautiful from other people?'

'For heaven's sake, Socrates,' said Glaucon, 'don't stop now. Right at the end. We shall be quite happy if you can give us an explanation of the good like the ones you gave us of justice, self-discipline and the other virtues.'

'So shall I, my friend. More than happy. But I'm afraid I shan't be up to it. I shall humiliate myself trying, and make a complete fool of myself.

e For the moment you'll rest content, won't you, if we leave on one side the question of what the good itself is. Getting at my opinions on the subject seems too much for the momentum of our present discussion. No, I want to talk about something which is a child of the good, and very similar to it, if that's all right with you. If it isn't, then let's forget about it.'

'By all means talk about that,' he said. 'You can owe us the description of the father, and pay us some other time.'

507 'I wish I could. And I wish you could receive the father – the full payment – rather than just the child as interest. Anyway, here is the interest payment, the child of the good, for you to take away with you. But you must be careful I don't unintentionally defraud you in some way. You don't want the account of the child I give you to be counterfeit.'[24]

'We'll be as careful as we can,' he said. 'Just give us your account.'

'Not until I have got your agreement – and reminded you – about things which were said earlier in the discussion,[25] and which have been said on many occasions in the past.'

'What things might they be?'

b 'We say there are many beautiful things, and many good things. And the same with everything else. That is how we classify them in speaking of them.'

'Yes, we do say that.'

'We also say there is a beautiful itself and a good itself. And the same with all the things we then said were "many." Applying the procedure in reverse, we relate them to a single form or character of each – since we believe it *is* single – and call it "what each is."'

'That is so.'

'The many things, we say, can be seen but not thought, whereas the forms or characters of things can be thought but not seen.'

c 'Exactly.'

'Very well. Which of our faculties do we use to see the things we see?'

'Our sight,' he said.

'And our hearing for the things we hear, and our other senses for everything we perceive?'

'Of course.'

'Have you ever noticed,' I asked, 'how much more extravagantly the creator of the senses has made the power of seeing and being seen than the other senses?'

---

[24] The Greek word *tokos* means both 'child' and 'interest on a loan'.   [25] 476a.

'No, I haven't.'

'Look at it this way. For hearing to hear, and sound to be heard, do they
d need some other class of thing as well? Without this third thing, will
hearing fail to hear, and sound fail to be heard?'

'No, they don't need any other class of thing,' he said.

'I suspect that many other faculties – I won't say all of them – have no
need for any further thing of this sort. Can you think of any?'

'No, I can't.'

'How about the faculty of sight, and the thing which is seen? Has it ever
struck you that those do need something of this sort?'

'How do you mean?'

'If there is sight in the eyes, and its possessor is trying to make use of
it, you surely realise that even in the presence of colour sight will see
e nothing, and the colours will remain unseen, unless one further thing
joins them, a third sort of thing which exists for precisely this purpose.'

'What thing do you mean?'

'The thing you call light.'

'True,' he said.

'In that case, because it involves a third thing of this important
508 character, the link between the faculty of sight and the ability to be seen
is something more valuable than the links between the other faculties and
their objects. Unless of course light has no value.'

'Well, it certainly *does* have a value.'

'Which of the heavenly gods, then, do you take to be the agent responsible for this? Whose is the light which best enables our faculty of sight to
see, and the things which are seen to be seen?'

'The one you or anyone else would take to be responsible,' he said. 'The
one you're asking about is obviously the sun.'[26]

'Now, do you agree with me about the natural relationship of sight to
this god?'

'What are you saying about it?'

'Sight is not the sun – neither sight itself, nor the place in which it
occurs, and which we call the eye.'

b 'No. It isn't.'

'But of all the organs of perception, I would say, the eye is the most
sun-*like*.'

'Much the most.'

---

[26] It was normal Greek religious practice to treat the heavenly bodies as gods.

'So the power which it has – the ability to see – it receives from the sun, as a kind of grant from an overflowing treasury?'

'Exactly.'

'So too, the sun is not sight, but it is the cause of sight and it can be seen *by* sight?'

'That is so,' he said.

c   'This is what you must take me to mean by the child of the good, which the good produced as its own analogue. In the world of thought the good stands in just the same relation to thinking and the things which can be thought as the sun, in the world of sight, stands to seeing and the things which can be seen.'

'What do you mean?' he said. 'Please explain that a bit further.'

'You know that when the eyes stop being directed at objects whose colours are in daylight, and turn to those whose colours are lit by the lights of the night, they are dimmed, and become virtually blind, as if there were no clear sight in them.'

'They certainly do.'

d   'Whereas when they are directed at things whose colours have the light of the sun shining on them, they see distinctly. The same eyes now manifestly do have sight in them.'

'Of course.'

'You can look at the soul in the same way. When it focuses where truth and that which is shine forth,[27] then it understands and knows what it sees, and does appear to possess intelligence. But when it focuses on what is mingled with darkness, on what comes into being and is destroyed, then it resorts to opinion and is dimmed, as its opinions swing first one way and then another. Now, by contrast, it resembles something with no understanding.'

'None at all.'

e   'You can say that this thing which gives the things which are known their truth, and from which the knower draws his ability to know, is the form or character of the good. Because it is the cause of knowledge and truth, think of it by all means as something known. But you will be right to regard it as different from, and still more beautiful than, knowledge and truth, beautiful though both of these are. Just as in our example it is 509 correct to think of light and vision as sun-*like*, but incorrect to think that they *are* the sun, in the same way here it is correct to think of knowledge

---

[27] Another possible translation would be: 'when it focuses upon what is illuminated by truth and by that which is'.

and truth as good-*like*, but incorrect to think that either of them *is* the good. The good is something to be prized even more highly.'

'It's an incredible beauty you are talking about,' he said, 'if it is the cause of knowledge and truth, but itself surpasses them in beauty. And you of all people, presumably, are not going to say that it is pleasure.'

'Be silent,' I said. 'Don't even mention the word.[28] No, take a closer look at our image of the good.'

b   'How do you want me to look at it?'

'The sun gives to what is seen, I think you would say, not only its ability to be seen, but also birth, growth and sustenance – though it is not itself birth or generation.'

'Of course it isn't.'

'For the things which are known, say not only that their being known comes from the good, but also that they get their existence and their being from it as well – though the good is not being, but something far surpassing being in rank and power.'

c   'Ye gods,'[29] Glaucon exclaimed, making us all laugh. 'What a miraculous transcendence.'

'Don't blame me,' I said. 'You were the one who compelled me to tell you what I thought about the subject.'

'I was. And whatever you do, don't stop now. If nothing else, at least go through your comparison with the sun, to make sure you haven't left anything out.'

'I've left all sorts of things out,' I said.

'Well, don't. Don't omit even the smallest detail.'

'I'm sure I shall omit something. Quite a lot, probably. All the same, as
d   far as is possible on an occasion like this, I won't leave anything out on purpose.'

'No, don't,' he said.

'Very well. You must be aware, as we said, that there are these two things. One of them is ruler of the category and realm of what can be understood. The other is ruler of what can be seen – of the heavenly scene, I could say, only I don't want you to think I'm playing with words. Anyway, be that as it may, you accept that there are these two forms of things, the seen and the understood?'

'Yes, I do.'

---

[28] The phrase refers to the silence of religious rites.
[29] In the Greek Glaucon exclaims 'By Apollo!', a god associated with the sun, although in Plato's day primarily by philosophers rather than in official cult.

'Imagine taking a line which has been divided into two unequal sections, and dividing each section – the one representing the category of the
seen and the one representing the category of the understood – again in
the same proportion. The clearness or obscurity of the sections of the
e line, relative to one another, you will find to be as follows. In the category
510 of the seen the first section is images, by which I mean in the first place
shadows, and in the second place reflections in water, or any dense,
smooth, shiny surface. Everything of that sort, if you see what I mean.'

'Yes, I do.'

'The second section you must regard as what the first section is an
image *of* – the animals we see every day, the entire plant world, and the
whole class of human artefacts.'

'Very well. I so regard it.'

'Now, looking at our division in terms of truth and its opposite, would
you be prepared to say that the relation between the likeness and the thing
it is a likeness *of* is equivalent to the relation between the object of opinion
and the object of knowledge?'

'Yes, I would,' he said. 'Most emphatically.'

b 'Ask yourself next how the section which represents the understood
should be divided.'

'How should it be?'

'Like this. In the first part the soul treats as images the things which in
the other section of the line were originals. It is compelled to work from
assumptions, proceeding to an end-point, rather than back to an origin or
first principle. In the second part, by contrast, it goes from an assumption
to an origin or first principle which is free from assumptions. It does not
use the images which the first part uses, but makes its way in the investigation using forms alone, through themselves alone.'

'I don't entirely follow what you just said.'

c 'Let's try again. You'll find it easier when you've heard what I have to
say by way of introduction. You're aware, I imagine, that when people are
doing things like geometry and arithmetic, there are some things they take
for granted in their respective disciplines. Odd and even, figures and the
three types of angle. That sort of thing. Taking these as known, they make
them into assumptions. They see no need to justify them either to
themselves or to anyone else. They regard them as plain to anyone.
d Starting from these, they then go through the rest of their argument, and
finally reach, by agreed steps, that which they set out to investigate.'

'Yes, I am aware of that,' he said.

'And you will also be aware that they summon up the assistance of visible forms, and refer their discussion to them, although they're not thinking about these, but about the things these are images of. So their reasoning has in view the square itself, and the diagonal itself, not the
e diagonal they have drawn. And the same with other examples. The models they construct, or figures they draw, which have their own shadows, and images in water – these they treat in their turn as images, in their attempt to see the corresponding things themselves which can be seen only through thinking.'

511 'True.'

'That is why I described this category as grasped by the understanding, but as requiring for its investigation that the soul make use of assumptions. The soul cannot make any progress towards a first principle, since it is unable to escape from these assumptions and move in an upwards direction. Instead it treats as images the things which were treated as originals, and copied, by what was in the section below them, and which are thought of as clear by comparison with those images, and valued for their clarity.'

b 'I see,' he said. 'You mean the realm of geometry and its related disciplines.'

'Finally, by the other section of the line representing the objects of understanding you must take me to mean what reason itself grasps by its power to conduct a rational discussion, when it uses assumptions not as first principles, but as true "bases" – points to take off from, entry-points – until it gets to what is free from assumptions, and arrives at the origin or first principle of everything. This it seizes hold of, then turns round and follows the things which follow from this first principle, and so makes
c its way down to an end-point. It makes no use at all of any object of the senses, but only of pure forms – working through them and towards them. And it ends in forms.'

'I sort of see,' he said, 'though not as well as I'd like. I think what you're talking about is an enormous task, but I do at least understand that you want to take that which is, and is understood, and distinguish that part of it which is studied by the knowledge which comes from rational discussion as something clearer than the part which is studied by what are called the sciences. These use assumptions as first principles, and although
d those who study them are compelled to use thinking rather than their senses to do so, still, because their investigation does not make its way upwards to a first principle, but proceeds from assumptions, you do not

regard them as having an intelligent understanding of their subjects, although with a first principle they *could* be understood.[30] I also think that when people are doing subjects like geometry, you call their state of mind thinking rather than understanding,[31] because you regard thinking as a halfway house between opinion and understanding.'

'You've grasped my meaning well enough,' I said. 'And please understand that there are four conditions arising in the soul, corresponding to the four sections of the line. Understanding corresponds to the highest section, thinking to the second, belief to the third, and conjecture to the last.[32] Classify them accordingly, believing that the degree of clarity they possess is proportional to the truth possessed by their objects.'

'I understand. I agree. And I classify them in the way you suggest.'

---

[30] Alternatively, the last clause of this sentence could be translated 'although their subjects belong to the realm of what can be understood, and have first principles'.

[31] As at 510e.

[32] From the description of the line (509d) a mathematician would be able to prove that the two middle sections, corresponding to thought and to belief, are invariably equal in length, regardless of the total length of the line and the location of its first cut. Whether Plato intended this fact to be significant is much disputed. Imagine, for example, that the line is nine units long, and is cut first at the three-unit mark. It must then be cut at the one- and the five-unit marks, in order to comply with the description, making the two central sections both two units long.

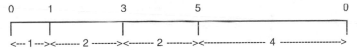

Book 7

514 'If we're thinking about the effect of education – or the lack of it – on our nature, there's another comparison we can make. Picture human beings living in some sort of underground cave dwelling, with an entrance which is long, as wide as the cave, and open to the light. Here they live, from
b earliest childhood, with their legs and necks in chains, so that they have to stay where they are, looking only ahead of them, prevented by the chains from turning their heads. They have light from a distant fire, which is burning behind them and above them. Between the fire and the prisoners, at a higher level than them, is a path along which you must picture a low wall that has been built, like the screen which hides people when they are giving a puppet show, and above which they make the puppets appear.'

'Yes, I can picture all that,' he said.

'Picture also, along the length of the wall, people carrying all sorts of
515 implements which project above it, and statues of people, and animals made of stone and wood and all kinds of materials. As you'd expect, some of the people carrying the objects are speaking, while others are silent.'

'A strange picture. And strange prisoners.'

'No more strange than us,' I said. 'Do you think, for a start, that prisoners of that sort have ever seen anything more of themselves and of one another than the shadows cast by the fire on the wall of the cave in front of them?'

b 'How could they, if they had been prevented from moving their heads all their lives?'

'What about the objects which are being carried? Wouldn't they see only shadows of these also?'

'Yes, of course.'

'So if they were able to talk to one another, don't you think they'd believe that the things they were giving names to were the things they could see passing?'

'Yes, they'd be bound to.'

'What if the prison had an echo from the wall in front of them? Every time one of the people passing by spoke, do you suppose they'd believe the source of the sound to be anything other than the passing shadow?'

'No, that's exactly what they would think.'

c 'All in all, then, what people in this situation would take for truth would be nothing more than the shadows of the manufactured objects.'

'Necessarily.'

'Suppose nature brought this state of affairs to an end,' I said. 'Think what their release from their chains and the cure for their ignorance would be like. When one of them was untied, and compelled suddenly to stand up, turn his head, start walking, and look towards the light, he'd find all these things painful. Because of the glare he'd be unable to see the things whose shadows he used to see before. What do you suppose he'd

d say if he was told that what he used to see before was of no importance, whereas now his eyesight was better, since he was closer to what is, and looking at things which more truly are? Suppose further that each of the passing objects was pointed out to him, and that he was asked what it was, and compelled to answer. Don't you think he'd be confused? Wouldn't he believe the things he saw before to be more true than what was being pointed out to him now?'

'Yes, he would. Much more true.'

e 'If he was forced to look at the light itself, wouldn't it hurt his eyes? Wouldn't he turn away, and run back to the things he *could* see? Wouldn't he think those things really were clearer than what was being pointed out?'

'Yes,' he said.

'And if he was dragged out of there by force, up the steep and difficult path, with no pause until he had been dragged right out into the sunlight,

516 wouldn't he find this dragging painful? Wouldn't he resent it? And when he came into the light, with his eyes filled with the glare, would he be able to see a single one of the things he is now told are true?'

'No, he wouldn't. Not at first.'

'He'd need to acclimatise himself, I imagine, if he were going to see things up there. To start with, he'd find shadows the easiest things to look

at. After that, reflections – of people and other things – in water. The things themselves would come later, and from those he would move on to
b the heavenly bodies and the heavens themselves. He'd find it easier to look at the light of the stars and the moon by night than look at the sun, and the light of the sun, by day.'

'Of course.'

'The last thing he'd be able to look at, presumably, would be the sun. Not its image, in water or some location that is not its own, but the sun itself. He'd be able to look at it by itself, in its own place, and see it as it really was.'

'Yes,' he said, 'unquestionably.'

'At that point he would work out that it was the sun which caused the
c seasons and the years, which governed everything in the visible realm, and which was in one way or another responsible for everything they used to see.'

'That would obviously be the next stage.'

'Now, suppose he were reminded of the place where he lived originally, of what passed for wisdom there, and of his former fellow-prisoners. Don't you think he would congratulate himself on the change? Wouldn't he feel sorry for them?'

'Indeed he would.'

'Back in the cave they might have had rewards and praise and prizes for the person who was quickest at identifying the passing shapes, who had
d the best memory for the ones which came earlier or later or simultaneously, and who as a result was best at predicting what was going to come next. Do you think he would feel any desire for these prizes? Would he envy those who were respected and powerful there? Or would he feel as Achilles does in Homer? Would he much prefer "to labour as a common serf, serving a man with nothing to his name," putting up with anything to avoid holding those opinions and living that life?"[1]

e 'Yes,' he said. 'If you ask me, he'd be prepared to put up with anything to avoid that way of life.'

'There's another question I'd like to ask you,' I said. 'Suppose someone like that came back down into the cave and took up his old seat. Wouldn't he find, coming straight in from the sunlight, that his eyes were swamped by the darkness?'

---

[1] *Odyssey* 11.489–491. The ghost of Achilles is speaking to Odysseus in the underworld. The quotation is among those censored in Book 3 (386c).

'I'm sure he would.'

'And suppose he had to go back to distinguishing the shadows, in
competition with those who had never stopped being prisoners. Before
his eyes had grown accustomed to the dark, while he still couldn't see
properly – and this period of acclimatisation would be anything but short
– wouldn't he be a laughing-stock? Wouldn't it be said of him that he
had come back from his journey to the upper world with his eyesight
destroyed, and that it wasn't worth even trying to go up there? As for
anyone who tried to set them free, and take them up there, if they could
somehow get their hands on him and kill him, wouldn't they do just that?'

'They certainly would,' he said.

'That is the picture, then, my dear Glaucon. And it fits what we were
talking about earlier in its entirety. The region revealed to us by sight is
the prison dwelling, and the light of the fire inside the dwelling is the
power of the sun. If you identify the upward path and the view of things
above with the ascent of the soul to the realm of understanding, then you
will have caught my drift – my surmise – which is what you wanted to
hear. Whether it is really true, perhaps only god knows. My own view, for
what it's worth, is that in the realm of what can be known the thing seen
last, and seen with great difficulty, is the form or character of the good.
But when it is seen, the conclusion must be that it turns out to be the cause
of all that is right and good for everything. In the realm of sight it gives
birth to light and light's sovereign, the sun, while in the realm of thought
it is itself sovereign, producing truth and reason unassisted. I further
believe that anyone who is going to act wisely either in private life or in
public life must have had a sight of this.'

'Well, I for one agree with you,' he said. 'As far as I can follow, at any
rate.'

'Can you agree with me, then, on one further point? It's no wonder if
those who have been to the upper world refuse to take an interest in everyday affairs, if their souls are constantly eager to spend their time in that
upper region. It's what you'd expect, presumably, if things really are like
the picture we have just drawn.'

'Yes, it is what you'd expect.'

'And here's another question. Do you think it's at all surprising if a
person who turns to everyday life after the contemplation of the divine
cuts a sorry figure, and makes a complete fool of himself – if before he can
see properly, or can get acclimatised to the darkness around him, he is
compelled to compete, in the lawcourts or anywhere else, over the

shadows of justice or the statues which cast those shadows, or to argue about the way they are understood by those who have never seen justice itself?'

'No, it's not in the least surprising,' he said.

518   'Anyone with any sense,' I said, 'would remember that people's eyesight can be impaired in two quite different ways, and for two quite different reasons. There's the change from light to darkness, and the change from darkness to light. He might then take it that the same is true of the soul, so that when he saw a soul in difficulties, unable to see, he would not laugh mindlessly, but would ask whether it had come from some brighter life and could not cope with the unfamiliar darkness, or whether it had
b come from greater ignorance into what was brighter, and was now dazzled by the glare. One he would congratulate on what it had seen, and on its way of life. The other he would pity. Or if he chose to laugh at it, his laughter would be less absurd than laughter directed at the soul which had come from the light above.'

'Yes. What you say is entirely reasonable.'

'Well,' I said, 'if it's true, there's one conclusion we can't avoid.
c Education is not what some people proclaim it to be. What they say, roughly speaking, is that they are able to put knowledge into souls where none was before. Like putting sight into eyes which were blind.'

'Yes, that is what they say.'

'Whereas our present account indicates that this capacity in every soul, this instrument by means of which each person learns, is like an eye which can only be turned away from the darkness and towards the light by turning the whole body. The entire soul has to turn with it, away from what is coming to be, until it is able to bear the sight of what is, and in particular the brightest part of it. This is the part we call the good, isn't it?'

d 'Yes.'

'Education, then,' I said, 'would be the art of directing this instrument, of finding the easiest and most effective way of turning it round. Not the art of putting the power of sight into it, but the art which assumes it possesses this power – albeit incorrectly aligned, and looking in the wrong direction – and contrives to make it look in the right direction.'

'Yes,' he said. 'It looks as if that is what education is.'

'So while the other things we call virtues of the soul may perhaps be
e quite close to the virtues of the body, since it's true they are not there to start with, but are implanted by custom and habit, the virtue of rational thought is different. It seems that it really is made of some more divine

material, which never loses its power, but becomes useful and beneficial,
519 or useless and harmful, depending on which way it is facing. Think of
those people who have the reputation of being evil but clever. Have you
never noticed the beady little eyes their souls have, how sharp they are at
picking out the things they are after? This suggests that their soul has
nothing wrong with its eyesight, but that it is coerced into the service of
evil. The more acute its vision is, therefore, the more evil it does.'

'That's certainly true.'

'And yet,' I said, 'if this soul, the soul belonging to a nature of this sort,
had been hammered into shape from earliest childhood, it might have had
b struck from it the leaden weights of birth and of becoming. These cling
to it as a result of eating, gluttony, and pleasures of that sort, and direct
the gaze of the soul downward. If it had rid itself of these weights, and
turned towards the truth, then the same soul, in the same people, would
be able to see things which are true with the same clarity as it sees the
things it is directed towards at the moment.'

'Very likely.'

'And isn't something else very likely?' I said. 'In fact absolutely certain,
on the basis of the discussion so far? Neither those who are uneducated
c and have no experience of the truth, nor those who are allowed to remain
in education until their life's end, could ever manage the city properly.
The uneducated ones lack that single mark in their life at which all their
actions, whether in private life or in public life, must aim. The others, left
to themselves, will never act, because they think they have emigrated
while still alive to the islands of the blest.'[2]

'True,' he said.

'It is up to us, then, as founders of the city, to compel the best natures
d to get as far as that study which we said earlier was the most important[3] –
to make that ascent, and view the good. And when they have made it, and
seen all they need to see, we must not allow them to do what they are
allowed to do at the moment.'

'What is that?'

'Remain there,' I said, 'and refuse to come back down again to the prisoners we were talking about, or share in their hardships and rewards – be
they trivial or substantial.'

---

[2] The islands of the blest were in traditional belief a place reserved for the afterlife of
heroes. Unlike Homeric shades, heroes were permitted to retain the full range of
their faculties, and to engage after death, for eternity, in the activities they enjoyed
in life.   [3] 505a.

'That seems very unfair! Are we going to make them live a worse life when it is in their power to live a better one?'

e   'Now it is your turn to forget, my friend, that the law does not exist for the exclusive benefit of one class in the city.[4] Its aim is to engineer the benefit of the city as a whole, using persuasion and compulsion to bring 520 the citizens into harmony, and making each class share with the other classes the contribution it is able to bring to the community. The law is what puts people like this in the city, and it does so not with the intention of allowing each of them to go his own way, but so that it can make use of them for its own purposes, to bind the city together.'

'True,' he said. 'I had forgotten that.'

'In which case, Glaucon, you should bear in mind that we won't after all be doing an injustice to those who become philosophers in our city. There will be justice in what we say to them when we compel them to look b after and guard what belongs to other people. "It is fair enough," we shall say to them, "for philosophers in other cities not to take a share of the work in those cities. Their philosophy is a spontaneous growth, which arises despite the institutions of the particular city they live in. And what has developed naturally, indebted to nobody for its upbringing, is entitled to be unenthusiastic about paying anyone for its upbringing. But with you it's different. We produced you as guides and rulers both for yourselves and for the rest of the city – like leaders or kings in a hive of bees. You have been better and more fully educated than the rest, and are better able to play your part in both types of life. So you must go down, each of you c in turn, to join the others in their dwelling-place. You must get used to seeing in the dark. When you do get used to it, you will see a thousand times better than the people there do. You will be able to identify all the images there, and know what they are images of, since you have seen the truth of what is beautiful and just and good. In this way the government of the city, for us and for you, will be a waking reality rather than the kind of dream in which most cities exist nowadays, governed by people d fighting one another over shadows and quarrelling with one another about ruling, as if ruling were some great good. The truth is, I imagine, that the city in which those who are to rule are most reluctant to do so will inevitably be the city which has the best and most stable government, whereas the city with rulers of the opposite kind will have a government of the opposite kind."'

[4] Compare 420b, 465e–466a.

'Exactly,' he said.

'Will they disobey us, then, do you think, these people we have brought up? Will they refuse to do their share of work in the city, each group in its turn, even though they can still spend most of their time in each other's company, in the clear air above?'

e   'They can't possibly refuse. It's a just demand, and they are just people. But they will undoubtedly approach ruling, each one of them, as something unavoidable – just the opposite of the people who rule in every city at the moment.'

521   'That's right, my friend. It's like this. If you can find a better life than ruling for the people who are going to be your rulers, then your well-governed city becomes a possibility. It will be the only city ruled by those who are truly rich. Not rich in money, but in a good and wise life, the riches needed for good fortune. If you get beggars – people who are starved of good things in their own lives – going into public life because they believe that the good is something to be taken from there as plunder, then your city is not a possibility. Ruling becomes something to be fought over, and a war of this kind, domestic and internal, destroys both those involved in it and the rest of the city with them.'

'Very true,' he said.

b   'All right, then. Can you think of any life, apart from the life of true philosophy, which has a contempt for public office?'

'Good heavens, no.'

'But ruling must be courted only by those who are not in love with her. Otherwise they will have rival suitors to contend with.'

'Of course.'

'And if you are going to compel people to enter upon the guardianship of the city, who better than those who are wisest in these matters – in what will give the city the best government – and who have their own rewards and their own way of life, better than the political?'

'There is no one better,' he said.

c   'In that case, do you want us now to address the question how people like this are going to come into being, how you can bring them into the light of day, in the way some people are said to have ascended from Hades to the realm of the gods?'

'Of course I do.'

'We are not dealing here, by the looks of it, with something like the spin of a coin, but with the turning of a soul away from that day which is a kind of night, and towards the true day which is the ascent to what is, and which we shall say is true philosophy.'[5]

'Exactly.'

'Does that mean we should ask ourselves which subject of study has the

d   power to do this?'

'Yes, of course.'

'Very well. Which subject, Glaucon, can act as a magnet to the soul, drawing it away from the world of becoming towards the world of what is? But even as I ask the question, I am reminded of something else. Didn't we say it was essential for these young men of ours, as a matter of course, to be warrior-athletes?'[6]

'We did.'

'So the subject we are looking for must possess a second characteristic in addition to the first.'

'What is that?'

'It must be some use to military men.'

e   'Yes,' he said, 'it must have that characteristic, if possible.'

'The education we gave them earlier on had a physical part and a musical part.'[7]

'It did.'

'Physical education busies itself with what comes to be and perishes. It presides over the growth and decay of the body.'

'Apparently.'

522   'So that, at any rate, cannot be the subject we are looking for.'

'No.'

'Could it, in that case, be the musical education we described earlier?'

'No,' he said. 'That, if you remember, was the counterpart to physical education. It trained the guardians by means of good habits, without giving them knowledge. Instead it used its qualities of harmony and rhythm to give harmony and rhythm to the guardians, and in its stories – those of them that were mythical, and those of them that were truer – it offered other qualities akin to these. But there was no subject of study in it which was any good for your present purpose.'

b   'Thank you,' I said, 'for reminding me so exactly. It really didn't

---

[5] In the game that Socrates uses for comparison here a shell or a fragment of pottery was spun in the air. It was painted white on one side (called 'day') and black on the other (called 'night'), and according to the side on which it landed one or other of two teams would chase or be chased.   [6] 403e–404a, 416d–e, 422b.

[7] Announced at 376e.

contain anything of the kind we are looking for. But then, my excellent
Glaucon, what kind of subject would? The practical arts, I think we
decided, are all demeaning.'[8]

'They certainly are. But what other subject *is* there, apart from musical
education, physical education and the practical arts?'

'All right,' I said, 'If we can't find a subject outside this range, let's find
one which applies to all of them.'

c   'Such as?'

'Such as the one which is common to all arts, modes of thought and
sciences, which these all make use of, and which is among the first things
that everybody is obliged to learn.'

'What is that?'

'The small matter of distinguishing one, two and three. Number and
calculation, in fact. Isn't it true of those that every art and science must
necessarily get involved with them?'

'It certainly is,' he said.

'In which case,' I said, 'isn't the art of war necessarily involved with
them?'

'Inevitably.'

d   'There's no doubt that in the tragedies Agamemnon's generalship is
always shown up as utterly laughable by Palamedes. You remember
Palamedes' claim that it was his invention of number which enabled him
to deploy the army at Troy, and count the ships and the rest of the equip-
ment. The suggestion is that these things had never been counted before,
and that apparently Agamemnon, since he didn't know how to count,
hadn't even known how many feet he had. Seriously, what sort of general
do you think that would have made him?'

'A pretty strange one, I'd say – if what Palamedes said was true.'

e   'Shall we just say, then, that calculation and the ability to count are an
essential subject of study for a man interested in warfare?'

'Absolutely essential, if he's to have any understanding of how to
marshal his troops. Or if he's going to be any sort of human being at all,
for that matter.'

'Well, then,' I said, 'do you feel the same way as I do about this subject?'

'What way is that?'

'It may well be that it is one of the subjects we are looking for, and that
523 its natural tendency is to lead us towards understanding, but that no one

---

[8]   475e, 495d–e.

makes the right use of it as the perfect instrument for drawing them towards being.'

'What do you mean?'

'I'll try and explain,' I said, 'how it seems to me. If I distinguish in my own mind between things which lead in the direction we want, and things which don't, then you must keep an eye on them as well. You must say "yes" or "no," so that we can see with greater clarity whether my surmise is correct.'

'Show me the things you mean.'

'Very well. I'll show you – and I hope you can see – that among the
b   things we perceive some do not invite the understanding to examine them, since they are adequately distinguished by perception, whereas others positively demand examination by the understanding, since perception produces no sound result.'

'You obviously mean objects appearing a long way off, and shadow-pictures.'[9]

'No, that's not quite what I mean.'

'What *do* you mean, then?' he asked.

c   'The ones which do not invite examination are the ones which do not at the same time result in an opposite perception. The ones which do result in their opposites I define as those which invite examination, since perception in these cases does not make one thing any more clear than its opposite, regardless of whether it lights upon it at a distance or close by. Let me give you a clearer example of what I mean. Here, we might say, we have three fingers: smallest, second and middle.'

'Yes.'

'Now, take it I'm talking about them as seen close up. Can you answer a question about them?'

'What question?'

d   'Each of them strikes us equally as a finger. It makes no difference whether you see it in the middle or at one end, whether it is dark or pale, thick or thin, or anything of that sort. None of these things would make the soul of an ordinary person feel impelled to ask the understanding what a finger *is*, since sight at no point indicates to it that the finger is also the opposite of a finger.'

---

[9] 'Shadow-painting' was a technique for achieving the illusion of depth in two dimensions. It differed from perspective, but we are unsure how.

'No, of course it doesn't,' he said.

'So you couldn't reasonably expect that sort of thing to appeal to or
e awaken the understanding.'

'No, you couldn't.'

'What about the size of fingers – large or small? Does sight perceive
that in a satisfactory way? Does it make no difference to it whether the
finger is in the middle or at one end? It's the same with touch, when it
perceives thick and thin, or soft and hard. And the other senses as well –
isn't there something defective about the way they show us things like
524 this? Don't we find the same thing with all of them? Isn't the sense with
which we perceive what is hard, for example, bound to be also the sense
with which we perceive what is soft? Doesn't it tell the soul that the same
thing is both hard and soft, when it feels it to be so?'

'Yes, it does,' he said.

'Isn't it bound to be in cases of this sort that the soul is confused? It
wonders what on earth this sense means by hard, if it can also describe
the same thing as soft? And what does the sense of light and heavy mean
by light and heavy, if it indicates that the heavy is light, and the light
heavy?'

b 'Yes, the soul does find messages of this sort puzzling. They do need
examination.'

'It's natural, then, that a situation like this should be the first in which
the soul invites calculation and understanding to examine whether each
of the things it is getting messages about is one or two.'

'Naturally.'

'If it regards them as two, does it regard each of them as separate, and
one?'

'Yes.'

'In which case, if it regards each of them as one, but the two together
as two, it will understand the two as separate. If they weren't separate, it
c would have understood them as one, not two.'

'Correct.'

'But sight also saw large and small – only not as separate, but rather as
some sort of mixture. Isn't this our claim?'

'Yes.'

'Whereas understanding, in the course of trying to make all this clear,
was compelled to see large and small not as a mixture, but as separate. Just
the opposite of sight.'

'True.'

'Is it things like this which first prompt us to ask what large and small can possibly be?'

'It certainly is.'

'Which is why we called one an object of understanding, and the other an object of sight?'

d   'Absolutely right,' he said.

'Well, that's what I meant just now, when I said that some things invite thought to investigate, and others don't. Those which impinge upon the senses in conjunction with their own opposites I classified as inviting the understanding. Those which don't I classified as failing to arouse it.'

'I see what you mean now. And I think you're right.'

'What about number and the one? Which category do you think they come in?'

'I've no idea,' he said.

'You can work it out from what we've said so far. If the one can be seen

e in a satisfactory way – or grasped by some other sense – completely by itself, then it will not draw the understanding towards being in the way we described in our example about the finger. But if some sort of contradiction of it is always seen at the same time, so that it seems to be no more the one than its opposite, then there would be a need for someone to make a decision about it. In a case like this the soul within him would be driven in its confusion to start searching. It would arouse the capacity for

525 reflection within itself, and ask it what the one itself actually was. In this way studying the one would be one of those things which lead and direct us towards the contemplation of what is.'

'Right. And seeing the one does have exactly this effect. After all, we can see the same thing, at one and the same time, both as one and also as an infinite number.'

'Well, if this is true of the one,' I said, 'is it not also true of number in general?'

'Yes, of course.'

'And arithmetic and the theory of number are exclusively concerned with number.'

'Absolutely.'

b 'Clearly, then, the study of number is conducive to truth.'

'To a remarkable degree.'

'In which case it looks like being one of the subjects we are looking for. It is an essential part of a soldier's education, for the deployment of troops, and of a philosopher's education, as he attempts to rise above becoming. He needs to make contact with being if he is ever to become capable of calculation or reasoning.'

'That is so,' he said.

'But our guardian is in fact both a soldier and a philosopher.'

'Of course.'

'So when we are framing our laws, Glaucon, this would be an ideal subject of study for us to demand. We should persuade those in the city
c who are going to have a hand in the most important decisions to take up arithmetical reasoning and practise it – not as a hobby, but until they reach the contemplation of the nature of numbers by means of thought alone. And it shouldn't be for the sake of buying and selling, like tradesmen and dealers. No, it should be for military reasons, and for their very soul's sake, to make it easier to redirect it away from becoming and towards truth and being.'

'I couldn't agree more.'

'What is more,' I said, 'now that we've started talking about the study
d of calculation, I can see how complex it is, and how many uses it has for our present purposes, provided people do it with a view to knowledge, and not with a view to becoming some sort of dealer.'

'What are these uses?'

'The kind we were talking about just now. It gives the soul a strong lead in an upwards direction, compelling it to discuss the numbers themselves, and refusing to allow people to bring numbers with visible or tangible
e bodies into the discussion. You know what these mathematicians are like. If you try and make a division in the one itself, they laugh at you, and tell you you can't. The more you chop it up, the more they multiply it, so making sure that the one is always clearly the one, and never a number of different parts.'

'You are absolutely right,' he said.

526 'Suppose, Glaucon, you asked them the following question: "All right, then, if you're so clever, what *are* these numbers you are discussing – including the one as you assume it to be, with each and every unit being equal to every other unit, and containing no variation at all, and no sub-division into parts?" What do think their answer would be?'

'I think they'd say they are talking about the numbers which can only be thought about, and which it is impossible to approach in any other way.'

'Do you see, then, my friend, how truly essential this subject is likely b to be for us, since it clearly forces the soul to use pure thought as a way of reaching pure truth?'

'Yes, that certainly is what it does,' he said. 'And very effectively.'

'And here's another question for you. Has it ever struck you that people with a natural gift for arithmetical reasoning are naturally quick at virtually all subjects? And those who are slow, if they get some education and training in this subject, do at least all go some way towards becoming quicker than they were before, even if they get nothing else out of it?'

'Yes, that is so,' he said.

c 'What is more, I'm inclined to think you won't easily find any other subjects – you certainly won't find many – which offer greater difficulty to the person learning them or doing them than this one does.'

'No, you won't.'

'So for all these reasons we must include this subject, and our best people must be educated in it.'

'I agree.'

'Very well, then,' I said, 'that's our first subject decided upon. For our second, let's ask ourselves if the one which follows on from it is any use to us.'

'Which do you mean? Geometry?'

'Precisely that.'

d 'Well, the part of it which has a bearing on warfare is obviously some use. In setting up camp, occupying a position, assembling or deploying an army, and all the other manoeuvres involved in the battle itself or on the march, it makes an enormous difference whether someone has a knowledge of geometry or not.'

'Yes,' I said, 'but for that sort of purpose you need only a very small part of geometry and arithmetic. What we must ask ourselves is whether
e the main body of the subject, the part which goes beyond that, is going to contribute to helping us see the form or character of the good. And what *does* contribute, in our view, is anything which forces the soul to turn towards that place where lies the most blessed part of what is, which the soul must do everything it can to see.'

'That is correct,' he said.

'So if geometry forces the soul to contemplate being, it is some use to us. If it forces it to contemplate becoming, then it is no use.'

'That's certainly our claim.'

527 'There's one thing we can say which no one with the slightest acquain-

tance with geometry will challenge. It's a branch of knowledge whose character is the exact opposite of the terminology employed in it by those who practise it.'

'In what way?' he asked.

'Well, they're hard put to it for words to describe what they do – with laughable results, sometimes. All this squaring, extending and adding. They're full of utterances of that kind. Everything they say is in terms of
b doing things, and practical applications, whereas the truth, I take it, is that this is a subject which is pursued entirely for knowledge's sake.'

'Absolutely.'

'And is there something else we have to agree on?'

'What is that?'

'That this knowledge is knowledge of what always is, not knowledge of what at some particular time comes to be, or perishes.'

'That's easily agreed,' he said. 'Geometrical knowledge *is* knowledge of what always is.'

'In that case, my noble friend, it is indeed something that draws the soul towards truth. It is an instrument which produces a philosophical way of thinking by directing upwards that part of us which we now, quite wrongly, direct downwards.'

'Yes, it does do that. More than anything else does.'[10]

c 'More than anything else, then, you must tell the people in your Callipolis, your ideal city,[11] not to neglect geometry in any way. After all, even its secondary benefits are of considerable value.'

'What benefits are those?' he asked.

'The ones you mentioned, to do with war. And in any subject, come to that, if we're looking for an improved ability to learn, I think we can be confident there will be all the difference in the world between those with a grasp of geometry and those without.'

'Heavens, yes. All the difference in the world.'

'In which case, shall we make this the second subject for our young people?'

'Yes, let's,' he said.

d 'And what about astronomy for our third subject? Don't you agree?'

---

[10] The Greek here and in the next sentence could also mean 'To the highest degree possible'.

[11] 'Callipolis' means 'city of beauty', and was the name of some actual Greek cities, none of them grand or influential.

'Yes, I do. An increased awareness of the moon's cycle, or the season of the year, is useful not only in farming or sailing, but also, just as much, in commanding an army.'

'I can't help being amused,' I said, 'by your apparent fear that people will see no practical value in the subjects you are putting in your curriculum. The truth is that it is not at all easy – in fact, it is extremely hard –
e   to accept that it is these subjects which purify and rekindle that instrument in each person's soul which is destroyed and blinded by his other pursuits, and whose preservation is more important than the sight of a thousand eyes, since truth cannot be seen without it. Those who agree with you will find your ideas extraordinarily convincing. Those who've never become aware of the existence of this instrument in the soul will probably think you're talking nonsense, since they can see no benefit worth
528   speaking of in these subjects. So make up your mind, here and now, which group you are talking to. Or are you talking to neither group, and constructing your arguments chiefly for your own benefit – though you would have no objection to others deriving what benefit they can from them?'

'Yes, that's what I would choose: to speak and ask and answer mainly for my own benefit.'

'In that case,' I said, 'it's time to retreat a little. We were wrong just now in what we took to be the next thing in order after geometry.'

'What did we take to be next?'

b   'After plane surfaces, we went on to rotating solids, before taking solids in isolation. But the thing which comes next, after the increase from one dimension to two, is the increase from two to three. I take it this concerns itself with cubic increase, and anything that has volume.'

'Yes. But solutions to these problems don't seem to have been found yet, Socrates.'

'There are two kinds of reason for that. In the first place, the solutions are difficult, and not pursued with any determination, since no city puts a high value on them. And in the second place, those looking for the solutions need a director or supervisor. They won't find the answers without one. Finding such a director is a problem, to start with. And even if you did find one, as things stand now, the people interested in this kind of enquiry would be too conceited to do what he tells them.

c   'But if a whole city were to become joint-director, and put a high value on these studies, then the people trying to find the solutions would do what they were told. Systematic, energetic investigation would lead to

clear answers being found. Even now, when the subject is undervalued
and belittled by most people – including those who pursue it, since they
can give no reason why it is of value – it still has enough natural appeal to
force its way forward in the face of all these handicaps. So it will be no
d surprise if solutions are found.'

'Yes,' he said, 'the subject does have a remarkable natural appeal. But
please explain something you said just now. You were taking geometry,
presumably, to be the study of plane surfaces.'

'Yes.'

'And you began by putting astronomy after it, though you subse-
quently retreated from that position.'

'It was a question of more haste, less speed, I'm afraid. I was trying to
get through things in a hurry. The next in order was the study of the
e dimension of depth, but the study of that is in such a laughable state that
I left it out, and put astronomy, which is solid bodies in motion, after
geometry.'

'Correct,' he said.

'Let's make astronomy our fourth subject, then, not our third. Let's
assume that the subject we are leaving out at the moment is only waiting
for a city to get interested in it.'

'Fair enough. And since you accused me just now, Socrates, of praising
astronomy for mundane reasons, let me praise it now for the reasons
529 which attract you to it. I think it's clear to everyone that astronomy
compels the soul to look upwards, directing it away from things here and
towards things up there.'

'Well, it may be clear to everyone,' I said, 'but it isn't clear to me. *I* don't
think that's what it does at all.'

'What *do* you think it does, then?'

'As currently tackled by those leading us on the upward path to
philosophy, I think its effect is entirely to direct the gaze downwards.'

'What do you mean?'

'I admire the freedom,' I said, 'with which you put forward your
b personal view of the nature of the higher learning! Imagine someone lying
on his back, looking at a decoration or pattern on a ceiling, and observing
something about it. It sounds as if you would say he was studying the
ceiling with his intellect, not his eyes. Well, you may be right, and I may
be being naive, but as far as I'm concerned the only subject *I* can regard
as making the soul look upwards is the one which concerns what is, what
can *not* be seen. Anyone trying to learn about objects of perception by

gaping up at the sky or frowning down at his feet can never learn anything, I would say – since no object of perception admits of knowledge.
c His soul is looking down, not up, even if he makes his observations lying
on his back – whether on land or floating in the sea.'

'I plead guilty as charged,' he said. 'Your criticisms are quite justified.
But if people are going to study astronomy in a way which will be useful
for the purposes we have in mind, in contrast with the way it is studied
nowadays, how *did* you mean them to study it?'

'Like this. The decorations or patterns in the vault of heaven, since
d their workmanship appears in the realm of sight, can by all means be
regarded as the most beautiful and perfect of visible objects. But they
should also be regarded as falling far short of the true motions, those
with which genuine velocity and genuine slowness, using true number
and following in every case a true orbit, move relative to one another and
cause the objects which they contain to move. These true motions are
to be grasped by reason and thought, not by sight. Or would you disagree?'

'Certainly not,' he said.

'Well, then, this heavenly pattern is to be used as a set of examples or
models, as a way of learning about the true patterns. It's exactly like
e finding diagrams drawn and executed with great skill, by Daedalus or
some other artist or draftsman. If you were an expert in geometry, you
would no doubt think they were technically excellent when you saw them,
but you would regard it as absurd to study them seriously in the expectation of finding in them the truth about things which are equal, or double,
or in any other ratio.'

530   'Of course it would be absurd.'

'Don't you think that's just how the true astronomer will feel when he
looks at the motions of the stars? He will regard heaven and everything in
it as having been put together by its maker as beautifully as such things
can be put together. But as for the ratio of night to day, of these to the
b month, of the month to the year, or of the other stars to the sun, moon
and one another, don't you think he'll regard as extremely odd anyone
who believes that these things are always the same – never varying in any
way, though they are corporeal and visible – and who makes a determined
effort to learn the truth from them?'

'Yes, I do think he will, now that I hear you putting it like that.'

'In which case,' I said, 'our approach to astronomy will be like our
c approach to geometry. It will be based on problems. If we want to take

part in true astronomy, and make the naturally rational part of the soul useful instead of useless, we shall forget about the heavenly bodies.'

'That's a much, much larger task you are requiring of us, compared with the way astronomy is done at the moment.'

'Yes, and if we are going to be any use as lawgivers, I think we shall have to impose the same requirements in other subjects as well. Can you suggest any other subjects that might be useful?'

'No, I can't,' he said. 'Not on the spur of the moment.'

'Well, I'm sure motion doesn't take just a single form. It takes several.
d No doubt an expert could give you a comprehensive list. But there are two which are obvious even to us.'

'What are they?'

'The one we've just been talking about, and its counterpart.'

'What is its counterpart?'

'The chances are,' I said, 'that our ears can be fixed on harmonic motion in the same way as our eyes on astronomical motion. These may well be in some sense sister sciences. That's what the Pythagoreans say, and you and I agree with them, Glaucon. Or do we not?'

'We do.'

e 'Very well. It's a massive task, so let's ask them what they have to say on the subject – and possibly other subjects as well. Meanwhile we will stick to our maxim throughout.'

'What maxim is that?'

'We should not allow the people for whose upbringing we are responsible ever to try and learn any pointless part of the subject, any part that is not constantly leading them to the goal that all things must reach – as
531 we were proposing in the case of astronomy just now. You must be aware that students of harmonics behave in more or less the same way. In trying to make comparative measurements of the harmonies and sounds which can be heard, they set themselves an endless task, just as the astronomers do.'

'Good god, yes,' he said. 'They certainly do. They make complete fools of themselves with their "close" intervals, applying their ears to the instrument as if they were eavesdropping on their neighbours. One group claims it can still distinguish an intermediate sound, and says this is the smallest interval which should be used as a unit of measurement. Others
b disagree. They say the two sounds are the same. Both groups trust their ears in preference to their reason.'

'You mean the worthy individuals who make life a misery for their strings by torturing them and using pegs to stretch them on the rack. I don't want to labour the metaphor – the plectrum striking and accusing, the strings refusing to speak or noisily defiant[12] – so I'll abandon it, and simply say that those aren't the people I mean. The people I'm talking about are the ones we said just now we would ask about harmonics. What

c they do is the same as what the astronomers do. They look for the numerical ratios in these harmonies which can be heard, without ever rising above those to an approach based on problems. They don't investigate which ratios are harmonious, which are not, and why.'

'That would be a superhuman task,' he said.

'Well, it would certainly be a useful one, in the pursuit of the beautiful and the good. Pursued for any other reason it is useless.'

'Very likely.'

d 'It's my opinion,' I said, 'that if the investigation of all these subjects we've outlined arrives at what they have in common with one another, their kinship with one another, and if it can work out how they are related to one another, then it's not a pointless task. It's an activity which contributes to what we are trying to achieve. Otherwise it is pointless.'

'I agree. I have the same presentiment myself. But it's an enormous task you're proposing, Socrates.'

'And that's merely the prelude. Or don't you agree? Are we in any doubt that all these subjects are merely preludes to the main theme we have to learn?[13] After all, you presumably don't regard people as dialecticians just because they are good at these subjects.'

e 'Good heavens, no,' he said. 'A very few perhaps of those I've ever come across.'

'And did you think that people who were incapable of explaining or understanding the basis of their subject were ever going to know any of the things we say they need to know?'

532 'Again, the answer is no.'

'Well, Glaucon, isn't this finally the true tune or theme which the study of dialectic plays? It is in the realm of thought, though the power of sight can imitate it, as when we said that sight attempts to look at animals themselves, and stars themselves, and even finally at the sun itself.[14] In the same way, when someone tries to use dialectic to arrive at what each thing itself is, by means of reason, without using any of the senses, and does not give

---

[12] The metaphor is drawn from the lawcourts, where the evidence of slaves was taken under torture.

[13] Socrates follows his discussion of harmonics with a musical metaphor, but the word *nomos*, 'theme' or 'tune', also means 'law'.   [14] 516a–b.

b up the attempt until he grasps what good itself is, by means of thought itself, then he has come to the true end or goal of the intelligible, just as the man in the cave, in our earlier example, came to the true end or goal of the visible.'

'Exactly,' he said.

'Very well. Isn't "dialectic" the name you give to this journey?'

'Of course.'

'And the release from chains?' I asked. 'The turning away from the shadows towards the images and the firelight? The upward path from the
c underground cave to the daylight, and the ability there to look, not in the first instance at animals and plants and the light of the sun, but at their divine reflections in water and the shadows of real things, rather than the shadows of models cast by a light which is itself a shadow in comparison with the sun? All this practice of the sciences we have just outlined has precisely this power to direct the best element in the soul upwards, towards the contemplation of what is best among the things that are – just as earlier on the clearest element in the body was directed to the contemplation of what was brightest in the corporeal and visible region.'

d 'Personally speaking, I accept that,' he said, 'though I find it extremely hard. But then again, in another way it is very hard *not* to accept. Still, this won't be our only opportunity to hear what you have to say on the subject. We shall often have to return to it in the future. So let's take it these things are as we have just said they are, and go on to the main theme
e itself, and describe that in the same way we described the prelude. Tell us, how does it operate, this power of dialectic? Into what forms is it divided? And by what routes, again, does it progress? After all, it is these routes which can apparently take a man to the destination which is his place of rest after the road, and the end of his journey.'

533 'My dear Glaucon, you will not be able to follow me that far – though not for any want of enthusiasm on my part. From now on what you would be seeing would not be an image or model of what we are talking about, but the truth itself – at least as it seems to me. Whether it's precisely like this doesn't seem worth insisting on. But that there is something *like* this to see – that we must insist on, mustn't we?'

'Of course.'

'Do we insist also that the power of dialectic is the only power which can reveal this? That it reveals it to the person who is expert in the subjects we have just been talking about? And that it is impossible in any other way?'

'Yes, these are things we should insist on,' he said.

b   'At the very least, then, no one will quarrel with us if we claim it is a distinct and separate inquiry which systematically and universally attempts, for each thing just by itself, to grasp what that thing is. All other arts and sciences, without exception, are directed either towards human opinions and desires, or towards creation or manufacture, or towards the care of things which are growing or being manufactured. As for the subjects which we said *did* grasp some part of what really is – studies in
c   geometry and the disciplines which go with geometry – we can now see that as long as they leave the assumptions they use untouched, without being able to give any justification for them, they are only dreaming about what is. They cannot possibly have any waking awareness of it. After all, if the first principles of a subject are something you don't know, and the endpoint and intermediate steps are interwoven out of what you don't know, what possible mechanism can there ever be for turning a coherence between elements of this kind into knowledge?'[15]

'None,' he said.

'Very well,' I said. 'The dialectical method is the only one which in its determination to make itself secure proceeds by this route – doing away
d   with its assumptions until it reaches the first principle itself. Dialectic finds the eye of the soul firmly buried in a kind of morass of philistinism. Gently it pulls it free and leads it upwards, using the disciplines we have described as its allies and assistants in the process of conversion. We have generally followed convention in calling these disciplines branches of knowledge, but they really need some other name. Something clearer than opinion, but more obscure than knowledge. We may have used the term
e   "thinking" at some point earlier on.[16] But I don't think people need argue about names when they have as many important matters still to investigate as we have.'

'No, they needn't,' he said.

'We'll be happy enough, then, to do what we did before. We'll call the
534 first section or category knowledge, the second thinking, the third belief, and the fourth conjecture. Three and four taken together we can call opinion, and one and two taken together, understanding. We'll say that opinion has to do with becoming, whereas understanding has to do with being; that as being is to becoming, so understanding is to opinion; and as understanding is to opinion, so knowledge is to belief, and thinking is to

---

[15] Socrates is recalling the description of geometry at 510c–511a.   [16] 511d–e.

conjecture. As for the proportions holding between the objects in these categories, and the division of the objects of opinion or the objects of understanding into two parts, let's leave all that on one side, Glaucon. Otherwise it will overwhelm us with a discussion many times as long as the one we've had so far.'

b   'Very well. But as far as the rest of it goes, I for one agree with what you say. As far as I can follow it, that is.'

'In which case, is "dialectician" the name you give to the person who grasps the explanation of the being of each thing? As for the person who has no explanation, will you say that to the extent that he is unable to give an account of it, to himself or to anyone else, he has no intelligent understanding of it?'

'Of course I will,' he said.

'The same goes for the good. Anyone who cannot use reason to c distinguish the form of the good from everything else, who cannot fight his way through all attempts to disprove his theory in his eagerness to test it by the standard of being rather than the standard of opinion, who cannot make his way through all these dangers with his explanation unscathed – won't you say that a person who is in this state knows neither the good itself nor any other good? That if at any point he does lay hold of some image of it, he does so using opinion, not knowledge? That he is dreaming and dozing away his life on earth, and that one day d he will come to Hades and go to sleep for good, without ever waking up here at all?'

'Yes, all that is exactly what I shall say. And with some emphasis.'

'These children of yours, then, for whom you are providing this theoretical upbringing and education   suppose one day you found yourself bringing them up in real life. If they had as little reason to them as incommensurable lines in mathematics,[17] I don't imagine you would still allow them to be rulers in your city and exercise control over matters of the greatest importance.'

'No, I wouldn't,' he said.

'Will you enact a law, then, requiring them to have a particularly good grasp of that branch of education which will give them the ability to ask and answer questions in the most expert way?'

e   'Yes. I will enact such a law – with your help.'

'Would you say, in that case, that dialectic sits as a kind of coping-stone

---

[17] 'Incommensurable' lines are, in Greek, 'irrational' (*alogos*) lines.

on the top of our educational edifice, and that there is no other subject left which we'd be justified in putting on top of it? Do you think our list of subjects for study is now complete?'

535   'I do,' he said.

'That just leaves you with the question of allocation, then. Who are we going to give these subjects to? And how are we going to give them?'

'Yes, that obviously needs to be decided.'

'Do you remember our selection of rulers earlier on? Do you remember the kind of people we selected?'[18]

'Of course I do.'

'Well, you can take it that in general those must be the natures we should select. We must choose the most steadfast, the bravest and as far

b   as possible the best-looking. In addition, not only must we look for noble and virile character; we also need people with a natural talent for this kind of education.'

'What talent is that?'

'I tell you, they must be like razors when it comes to studying,' I said, 'and they must find learning easy. The soul gives up much more easily during hard study than it does during physical exercise, since when it is studying the pain is more its own – specific to it, not shared with the body.'

'True.'

'The person we are looking for must also have a good memory, great

c   resilience and tremendous energy. How else, do you suppose, will anyone be prepared both to endure the physical hardships and to complete such an extensive course of study and training?'

'I don't suppose anyone will be prepared to. Not unless he is altogether exceptional.'

'The trouble at the moment,' I said, 'the reason why philosophy has fallen into disrepute, as I was saying a little while ago, is that the wrong kind of people are taking it up.[19] We didn't want bastard, or illegitimate, philosophers taking it up. We wanted legitimate philosophers.'

'What do you mean by "legitimate"?'

d   'Well, take love of hard work, for a start. It's no good having a gammy leg if you're going to take up philosophy. No good working really hard in one half of the subject, and doing no work in the other half. That's what

---

[18] 374e–376c (character of guardians); 412b–414a (testing and selection of rulers from among the guardians); 485a–487a (character of philosophers, with retrospective summaries at 490c–d and 494b); 503a–504a (testing and selection of philosopher-rulers).   [19] 495c–496a.

happens when you get someone who is athletic, fond of hunting, and ready to work hard in all branches of physical exercise, but with no love of learning, no love of listening, no love of enquiry – in fact, bone idle in all these subjects. And anyone whose love of hard work is one-sided in the opposite direction is just as lame.'

'Very true,' he said.

e   'Then there's the question of truth. Won't we in the same way define a soul as crippled if it hates a deliberate lie, cannot bear to tell one itself, and gets furious when other people tell them, but is quite content to put up with falsehoods which are not deliberate, doesn't mind some deficiency in its knowledge being revealed, and wallows happily in ignorance like a wild pig?'

536   'We certainly will.'

'And when it comes to self-discipline, courage, greatness of spirit, and all the other parts of virtue, we should be particularly careful to distinguish the illegitimate from the legitimate. Individuals and cities who don't know how to look for these characteristics can't help using those who are lame and, for their need of the moment, illegitimate. As a result individuals choose the wrong friends, and cities the wrong rulers.'

'Yes, that's exactly how it is,' he said.

'This is an area where we have to proceed with extreme caution,' I said.
b   'If the people we introduce to an education in such an important branch of knowledge and such an important discipline are sound of limb and sound of mind, then justice herself will have no fault to find with us, and we shall be the saviours of our city and its regime. But if we introduce people of a quite different character, we shall achieve entirely the opposite result, and expose philosophy to a further flood of ridicule.'

'That would certainly be something to be ashamed of,' he said.

'It would indeed. Meanwhile *I* seem to be making a bit of a fool of myself, here and now.'

'In what way?'

c   'I forgot this is just a game we are playing, and I got rather carried away. My eye fell on philosophy as I was speaking, and I think I got annoyed when I saw her undeservedly covered in filth. I spoke with too much heat, as if I were angry with those responsible.'

'You didn't speak with too much heat. Not for this hearer's taste, anyhow.'

'Well, it was too much for the *speaker's* taste,' I said. 'And there's another point we don't want to lose sight of. In our original selection of d　rulers we were choosing old men,[20] but this time that won't do. We must not believe Solon when he tells us how good the old are at learning things. They are worse at learning than they are at running. Great and repeated effort is always the province of the young.'

'Inevitably.'

'So arithmetic, geometry, and all the education our future rulers need as a preliminary to dialectic – these are things we should offer them while they are still children. But we shouldn't present these subjects as a compulsory syllabus they have got to learn.'

'Why is that?'

e　'Because for a free man learning should never be associated with slavery. Physical exertion, imposed by force, does the body no harm, but for the soul no forced learning can be lasting.'

'True,' he said.

537　'In which case, my friend, when you're bringing children up, don't use compulsion in teaching them. Use children's games instead. That will give you a better idea what each of them has a natural aptitude for.'

'There is some sense in what you say.'

'Do you remember us saying that children should be taken to war, mounted on horseback, as spectators? And that if the situation allowed it they should be taken in close and given a taste of blood, like young hounds?'[21]

'Yes, I do,' he said.

'Well, in all these situations – exertion, or study, or when exposed to
b　danger – we should select those who seem quickest, and put them on a shortlist.'

'At what age?'

'When they are finished with their compulsory physical education, that being a period of two or three years when it is impossible for them to do anything else.[22] Exhaustion and sleep are the enemies of study. Besides, the performance of each individual in physical training is one of the yardsticks – and an important one at that.'

'Of course.'

'At the end of this period,' I said, 'the chosen few among the
c　twenty-year-olds will win greater recognition than the others. They must now take a unified view of subjects that were all mixed up in the course

---

[20]　412c.　　[21]　466e–467e.

[22]　Eighteen-year-old males at Athens in Plato's time entered a two-year period of compulsory military training and guard duty at frontier posts.

of their education as children, so that they can get an overall picture of these subjects' kinship with one another and to the nature of what is.'

'Yes,' he said, 'there's no doubt that learning of that kind – for those who possess it – is the only sort of learning which can be relied on.'

'It's also the most important test of the dialectical and non-dialectical nature. Anyone who has this overall picture is dialectical. Anyone who doesn't have it is not.'

'I agree.'

d   'In that case, this is something you will have to keep an eye open for. You will have to see which among them must possess this quality, and which are resolute in their studies as well as being resolute in war and the other activities expected of them. These are the ones, when they reach the age of thirty, whom you must choose from among the chosen, and promote to greater distinctions. You must use the power of dialectic as your yardstick to decide who is capable of giving up eyesight – and sense-perception in general – and progressing, with the help of truth, to that which by itself is. This is an area, my friend, where we must be very much on our guard.'

'Over what, in particular?'

e   'Aren't you aware of the damage done at the moment in the name of dialectic?'

'What damage?' he asked.

'Its students are filled with what I suppose we'd call contempt for the law.'

'Yes, utter contempt.'

'Do you find it at all surprising that they should be like that?' I asked. 'Can't you find excuses for them?'

'What excuses?'

538   'It's like the supposed child of a large and influential family, brought up in the midst of great wealth and among numerous flatterers, who realises, when he grows up to be a man, that he is not the son of these people claiming to be his parents, but can't find the people who really were his parents. Can you hazard a guess at his attitude both to the flatterers and to those who made the substitution – first during the time when he didn't know about the substitution, and then during the time when he did know? Or would you like to hear my guess?'

'Yes, I would,' he said.

'Very well. My guess is that during the time when he didn't know the
b   truth he would have more respect for his father, mother and other

members of his supposed family than he would for those who flattered him. He would be unlikely to ignore their needs, unlikely to break the law at all in the way he treated them or spoke to them, and unlikely to disobey them in anything important. But he would disobey the flatterers.'

'Very likely,' he said.

'But then when he realised the truth, my guess is that it would all change. His respect and enthusiasm for his relatives would dwindle, and
c he'd turn to the flatterers instead. He'd take their advice more than he did before, start living by their values, and spend his time quite openly in their company. Unless he was an exceptionally well-balanced character, he would completely lose interest in his former father and the rest of those who made themselves out to be his family.'

'Yes, that's exactly the kind of thing that would happen. But what's your comparison got to do with people who take up argument?'

'This. We all have strongly held beliefs, I take it, going back to our childhood, about things which are just and things which are fine and beautiful. They're like our parents. We've grown up with them, we accept their authority, and we treat them with respect.'
d 'That is so.'

'But then we have other habits which are opposed to these opinions. They bring us pleasure, flattering our soul and trying to seduce it. People with any sense pay no attention to them. They value the opinions they got from their parents, and those are the ones they obey.'

'True.'

'When someone like this encounters the question "What is the beautiful?", and gives the answer he used to hear from the lawgiver, and argument shows it to be incorrect, what happens to him? He may have many of his answers refuted, in many different ways, and be reduced to
e thinking that the beautiful is no more beautiful or fine than it is ugly or shameful. The same with "just", "good", and the things he used to have most respect for. At the end of this, what do you think his attitude to these strongly held beliefs will be, when it comes to respect for them and obedience to their authority?'

'It's impossible for him to go on feeling the same respect for them, or obeying them.'

'In which case,' I said, 'if he no longer regards these opinions as his own, or worthy of respect, in the way he once did, and if he cannot find
539 the true opinions, where else can he possibly turn, except to the life that flatters him?'

'Nowhere else,' he said.

'I imagine he'll be thought to have changed from a law-abiding citizen into a criminal.'

'Bound to be.'

'Isn't that just what you'd expect to happen to people who take up argument in this sort of way? As I said a few moments ago, it entitles them to a large measure of forgiveness.'

'Yes, and pity,' he said.

'Very well, then. If you don't want your thirty-year-olds to qualify for this kind of pity, you will have to take the greatest possible care how you allow them to take up argument.'

'I certainly will.'

b   'Isn't one very effective safeguard not to let them get a taste for argument while they are young? You can't have forgotten what adolescents are like, the first time they get a taste of it. They regard it as a kind of game to be constantly turning arguments into their opposites. They imitate those they hear proving other people wrong by going out and doing the same thing themselves. They're like puppies in the delight they take in tugging at anyone within reach, and tearing them to pieces with their arguments.'

'Yes, they really do overdo it, don't they?'

'And when they have themselves often proved other people wrong, and
c   often been proved wrong, they suffer a sudden and disastrous lapse into the state of not believing any of the things they believed before. The result is that they themselves come in for a lot of criticism in the eyes of the world – and so does everything to do with philosophy.'

'That's absolutely true,' he said.

'An older man would refuse to take part in that kind of madness. He will imitate the person who chooses to employ dialectic in the search for truth, rather than the person who engages in a game of contradiction for
d   entertainment's sake. He will be a more balanced person himself, and will make philosophy more respected, not less respected.'

'Rightly so.'

'Hasn't everything that has been said so far been said precisely with a view to making sure that only people with orderly and reliable natures are to be introduced to argument? Not like now, when anybody at all, however unsuitable, can go in for it.'

'Exactly,' he said.

'Is it enough if they devote themselves to argument, and nothing else, continuously and energetically, in a training equivalent to their physical training in the gymnasiums, only twice as long?'

e   'Does that mean six years, or four?' he asked.

'It doesn't really matter. Call it five. After that you will have to make them go back down into the cave we were talking about. You will have to compel them to hold military command, and any other position which is suitable for the young, so that others will not have an advantage over them

540   in practical experience. And even in these positions they must be on trial, to see if they will stand firm when they are pulled in different directions, or if they will to some extent give way.'

'And how long do you think this stage should be?'

'Fifteen years,' I said. 'Then, when they are fifty years old, those who have survived and been completely successful in every sphere, both in practical affairs and in their studies, should now be conducted to the final goal, and required to direct the radiant light of the soul towards the contemplation of that which itself gives light to everything. And when they

b   have seen the good itself, they must make that their model, and spend the rest of their lives, each group in turn, in governing the city, the individuals in it, and themselves. They can spend most of their time in philosophy, but when their turn comes, then for the benefit of the city each group must endure the trials of politics, and be rulers. They will regard it as a necessity rather than a privilege. In this way, after educating a continuous succession of others like themselves, and leaving them behind to take their place as guardians of the city, they will finally depart,

c   and live in the islands of the blest. The city will put up memorials to them, and institute sacrifices, at the public expense, honouring them as divine spirits, if the Pythian priestess permits – or if not, as divinely inspired and fortunate.'

'What wonderful men you have fashioned as your rulers, Socrates. Just like a sculptor.'

'Men *and women*, Glaucon. You mustn't think that in what I have been saying I have had men in mind any more than women – those of them who are born with the right natural abilities.'

'Quite right,' he said. 'Assuming, that is, that they are going to be equal partners with men in the way we described.'[23]

d   'Very well. Do you agree that our ideas about the city and its regime have not just been wishful thinking? What we want is difficult, but not

---

[23]   451c–466d.

impossible. However, it is possible only in the way we have described, when true philosophers – it might be a number of them, or it might be just one – become rulers in our city. They will show their contempt for what are now regarded as honours, believing them to be worthless and

e   demeaning. They will set the highest possible value on what is right, and the honours resulting from it. Their most important and demanding guide will be justice. They will serve justice, watch over its growth, and in this way keep their city on the right lines.'

'How will they do that?' he asked.

541   'Let them send everyone in the city over the age of ten into the country-side. Then they can isolate these people's children from the values they hold at the moment – their parents' values – and bring the children up according to their own customs and laws, which are of the kind we described earlier. Don't you agree that this will be the quickest and sim-plest way for the city and regime we were talking about to come into being, making itself happy and bringing a large number of benefits to the nation in which it originates?'

b   'Yes. Much the quickest and simplest. I think you have given us a good idea, Socrates, of the way it would come about, if it ever did come about.'[24]

'In that case,' I said, 'isn't our discussion of this city, and the corre-sponding individual, now complete? After all, I imagine it's pretty clear what we are going to say that individual should be like.'

'Yes, it is clear,' he said. 'And in reply to your question, I do think this subject of discussion is complete.'

---

[24] Banishing elements of a population from a city to the surrounding countryside was not without historic parallel (see pp xv–xvii of the introduction), and in the Greek world in general populations were relocated with what to us would seem alarming frequency. But there was no historic parallel for removing a whole class of parents to the countryside without their children.

Book 8

543 'Very well, Glaucon. The agreed characteristics of the city which is to reach the peak of political organisation are community of women, community of children and the whole system of education, community likewise of everyday life, both in wartime and peacetime, and the kingship of those among them who have developed into the best philosophers, and the best when it comes to war.'

'Yes,' he said, 'those are the agreed characteristics.'

b 'What is more, we also agreed that when the rulers assume power, they will take the soldiers and move them to housing of the kind we described earlier – common to all of them, and offering no private property to anyone.[1] And in addition to the nature of their housing, we even reached agreement, if you recall, on the kind of possessions they will have.'[2]

'I do recall. We thought that none of them should have any of the
c possessions which most people nowadays have. They should be guardians and warrior-athletes of some sort, receiving from the rest of the citizens, as annual pay for their guardianship, just as much maintenance as they need for this purpose. Their duty would be to protect themselves and the rest of the city.'

'You are right,' I said. 'But after we'd finished dealing with all that, can we remember the point where we began this digression, so that we can carry on from the same place?'

'That's easy enough,' he said. 'You were talking, in pretty much the way you are talking now, as if you had completed your account of the city.
d You were saying you regarded the kind of city you had just described –

---

[1] 415d–416a.   [2] 416d–417b.

252

544 and the individual who resembled it – as a good one, despite the fact that
you apparently had an even finer city and individual to tell us about. You
certainly said that if this was the right sort of city, then the others must
have something wrong with them. And you said, if I remember rightly,
that there were four other kinds of regime – or four others worthy of discussion, at any rate. You said we should look at their faults, and at the individuals who resemble them, so that when we had examined all the
individuals, and reached agreement on which was the best and which was
the worst, we could ask whether the best individual is the happiest and

b   the worst the most wretched, or whether that's all a mistake, I asked you
which four regimes you meant, but then Polemarchus and Adeimantus
interrupted, and that started you on the discussion which has brought
you here.'[3]

'What an excellent memory!'

'In which case, could you do what a wrestler does when he offers his
opponent the same hold again? If I ask the same question again, try and
give me the answer you were going to give me then.'

'Certainly,' I said. 'Assuming I can, that is.'

'Apart from anything else, I have reasons of my own for wanting to
know which four regimes you meant.'

c   'There will be no difficulty in telling you that. They even have names,
the ones I'm talking about. There's the one which is pretty generally
approved, the Cretan or Spartan.[4] Next – and next in the scale of general
approval – is the one called oligarchy, a form of government filled with all
sorts of evils. In contrast to oligarchy, and the form of government which
arises next, is democracy. And then there is the wonderful institution of
tyranny, standing   head   and   shoulders   above   all   the   others,

d   the fourth and last diseased state of the city. Can you think of any other
kind of regime which forms a distinct category of its own? I take it that
hereditary rule by families, kingships which go to the highest bidder, and
other similar regimes, which you will find are no less common among the
barbarians than among the Greeks, are all intermediate between the
forms I have mentioned.'

'Yes,' he said, 'we certainly do hear about plenty of extraordinary
regimes.'

'Well, then, are you aware that for individuals also there must

---

[3] See the transition between Books 4 and 5 (445a–449b).

[4] At 545b these relatively parochial terms will be replaced by the coinages 'timocracy'
or 'timarchy'. For historical information see 'Crete' and 'Sparta' in the glossary.

necessarily be as many kinds of character as there are kinds of regime? Or
e do you think that regimes somehow come into being "from oak or
stone"?[5] Isn't it rather from the characters of people in the city, which tip
the scale, as it were, taking the rest with them?'

'No, I think it's entirely the character of the inhabitants.'

'In which case, if there are five types of city, then for individuals there
will likewise be five dispositions of the soul.'

'Of course.'

'Well, we have finished describing the person who resembles aristocracy. And we say, quite rightly, that he is good and just.'

545   'Yes. We have described him.'

'Is the next thing, then, to describe the ones who are less good – the
lover of victory and honour, who corresponds to the Spartan regime, and
then in turn the oligarchic character, the democratic, and the tyrannical?
That way we can contrast the most unjust, when we find him, with the
most just. Our investigation into how pure justice fares, relative to pure
injustice, in terms of the happiness or wretchedness of the person who
possesses it, will be complete. And we can either follow Thrasymachus'
b advice and pursue injustice, or follow the argument which is unfolding
before us now, and pursue justice.'

'Yes,' he said, 'that's exactly what we have to do.'

'All right, then. In our earlier enquiry we started with the character of
regimes rather than that of individuals, because we thought that would be
clearer.[6] In the same way now, shall we start by taking a look at the honour-
loving regime? I can't think of another term in general use that would
c apply to it. Its name ought to be "timocracy" or "timarchy."[7] Then we can
look at the timocratic individual in relation to that regime – followed by
oligarchy and the oligarchic individual. After that we can turn to democracy and study the democratic individual, and fourthly we can turn to the
city which is ruled by a tyrant, and look at that, before studying the tyrannical soul. Will that be a way of trying to become competent judges of the
question we have asked ourselves?'

'It would certainly be a logical way of going about our observations and
judgments.'

'Very well. Let's try and describe the way in which timocracy might

---

[5] The phrase is proverbial of the fact that we all have ancestors, and is so used in
Homer's *Odyssey* (19.163) and Plato's *Apology* (34d).   [6] 368d–369a.
[7] The etymological components of these coinages are 'honour' ('timo-'), 'power'
('-cracy'), and 'rule' ('-archy').

d arise out of aristocracy. Is it a general rule that the cause of change in any
regime is to be found in the sovereign body itself – when civil war arises
within this group? That as long as this group, however small it may be,
remains united, it is impossible for the regime to be altered?'
    'Yes, that's true.'
    'In that case, Glaucon, how *will* the regime of our city be altered? How
will civil war break out either between our auxiliaries and our rulers, or
e among them? Do you want us, like Homer, to invoke the Muses to tell us
"how first dissension fell upon them"?[8] Shall we imagine that they speak
to us in high-flown, tragic tones, as if they were playing with little children and teasing them by pretending to be speaking seriously?'
546   'What would they say?'
    'Something like this. "It is no easy matter for a city founded in this way
to be altered. But since destruction awaits everything that has come to be,
even a foundation of this kind will not survive for the whole of time. It
will fall apart, and this will be the manner of its falling. Both for plants in
the ground and for animals above the ground it is a fact that souls and
bodies are produced or not produced when the cycles of begetting for
each species complete their revolutions – short revolutions for short-lived
species, and the opposite for long-lived species. In the case of your
species, wise though the people you have educated as leaders of the city
b are, still they will not quite hit the mark when they apply calculation –
together with observation – to their programme of breeding and birth-
control. Success will elude them, and they will sometimes produce children they should not produce. For the birth of a divine being there is a
period embraced by a perfect number,[9] while for a human being it is the
first number in which increase to the power of roots combined with
squares – taking on three dimensions and four defining limits – of the
c numbers which create likeness and unlikeness, and which wax and wane,
makes all things conversable and rational with one another. Of these
numbers the ones that form the basis of the musical fourth, when coupled
with five and three times increased, produce two harmonies. The first

---

[8] An adaptation of *Iliad* 16.112–113.
[9] The divine being is presumably the cosmos. It is described in the *Timaeus* as a living
creature, the most perfect of those made by the creator-god. It is unclear whether
the period in question is a gestation-period (the time it took for the creator-god to
bring the cosmos into being) or some cosmic period such as the Great Year (the time
it takes for the various orbiting bodies in the cosmos to come back to the same positions relative to one another). For an explanation of the remainder of this paragraph,
see the glossary under 'Number'.

harmony is a square, the product of equals, so many times 100. The second harmony is of equal length one way, but a rectangle. One side is the square of the rational diagonal of a five-by-five square, minus one, times 100, or the square of the irrational diagonal of a five-by-five square, minus two, times 100. The other side is three cubed times 100. Taken as a whole, this geometrical number is master of this domain – of better and

d   worse births. When your guardians fail to understand these births, and make injudicious unions of brides and grooms, the children will not have the right nature, and they will not be fortunate. The previous generation will select the best of them for office, but they will not deserve selection, and when they in their turn inherit the powers of their fathers, the first thing they will neglect as guardians will be us, the Muses, since they will put too low a value on musical and literary education. And the second thing they will neglect will be physical education. The result will be a younger generation which has even less regard for us. And from their number rulers will be appointed who completely lack a guardian's ability

e   to discriminate between Hesiod's classes, or the classes in your city – gold,

547   silver, bronze and iron.[10] When iron is compounded with silver, and bronze with gold, then you will get unlikeness and discordant inequality. And when you get those, wherever they occur, they always breed war and hostility. This is sedition's noble line,[11] we have to say – always, and wherever it arises.'''

'Yes, that is the answer the Muses will give. And we cannot deny that they are right.'

'They must be right,' I said, 'if they are Muses.'

'In which case,' he asked, 'what else do the Muses have to say?'

b   'When civil war breaks out, the classes or natures are divided into two. The iron and bronze draw the state towards commerce, and the possession of land and housing, of gold and silver. The other pair, by contrast, the gold and silver, since in their souls they are not poor, but naturally wealthy, lead the state towards virtue and the traditional order. In fighting

c   and struggling against one another they arrive at a compromise. The land and housing is to be divided up and owned privately, and they agree to enslave those who were previously watched over by them as free men,

---

[10] Originally described at 415a–c.

[11] Socrates quotes the first part of a line that appears twice in Homer, to cap a hero's description of his ancestry: 'This is my line, my blood – and this my boast' (*Iliad* 6.211, 20.241).

friends and providers. They now hold them as serfs and slaves, while their role is to watch them, and conduct warfare.'

'Yes,' he said, 'I think that is the origin of this sort of change.'

'In which case,' I said, 'would this regime be a kind of halfway-house between aristocracy and oligarchy?'

'It certainly would.'

'That is how the change will take place, then. But how will the state d be organised *after* the change? It's obvious, isn't it, since it is midway between the two, that it will in some ways be modelled on the original regime, and in other ways on oligarchy, but that it will also have an element which is peculiar to itself?'

'Yes,' he said.

'Very well. Will the points it has in common with the original regime be these: respect for the rulers; the disqualification of the warrior element in the state from agriculture, manual employment or any other kind of business; the establishment of communal living quarters; and the concentration on physical education and training for war?'

e   'Yes.'

'Whereas fear of putting the wise into positions of power – since the wise men it has are now complex, not simple and direct any more – a leaning towards people who are spirited, more straightforward and 548 naturally cut out for war rather than peace, the value it places on military deceptions and stratagems, and the way it spends its entire time at war – will most of these characteristics be peculiar to itself?'

'Yes.'

'Now that they possess their own treasuries and strongrooms where they can put their gold and silver, and keep it hidden, people like this will be avaricious, like the members of an oligarchy, with a fierce and secret passion for gold and silver. And to protect it all they will have walls around b their houses – real private nests where they can spend a fortune on women or anyone else they fancy.'

'Very true,' he said.

'The value they put on money, and their inability to acquire it openly, will make them mean with their own money, while their desires and the secret pleasures they enjoy will make them extravagant with other people's. They will run away from the law like children running away from their father, since their education will not have been a matter of conviction, but something imposed on them by force. This in turn is the c result of neglecting the true Muse, the Muse of argument and philosophy, and setting a higher value on physical education than on education in the arts.'

'It's certainly a mixed regime you are describing – partly bad and partly good.'

'Yes, it is a mixture,' I said. 'But it has one striking characteristic, which comes from the dominance of the spirited element. Love of victory and honour.'

'Absolutely.'

'So much for this regime, then. That's how it would have come into
d existence, and that's what it would be like. It's just an outline sketch of the regime, without filling in the details, but even a sketch will give us a good enough picture of the completely just man and the completely unjust man. It's an impossibly long task to describe every regime and every character without leaving anything out.'

'Quite right,' he said.

'Well, then, who is the man corresponding to this regime? How did he come into existence, and what is he like?'

And Adeimantus replied, 'When it comes to love of victory, I think he's pretty close to Glaucon here.'

e 'Maybe he is,' I said, 'as far as that goes. But there are some ways in which I think his nature is different.'

'What ways are those?'

'He'd have to be more self-willed, and with less education in the arts,
549 though still a lover of them. Interested in listening to speeches, but no speaker. He'll be one of those people who are hard on his slaves, a man like this, since he doesn't feel the superiority the truly educated man feels towards his slaves. He'll be courteous towards free men, and his love of power and success will make him extremely deferential to those in authority. He is an avid hunter and loves physical exercise, and he feels entitled to rule not because of what he says, or anything like that, but because of his warlike deeds and achievements in war.'

'Yes, because this is the character of that regime.'

b 'As for money,' I said, 'someone like this would despise it in his youth, but the older he got, the more fond of it he would become. This is because he shares in the money-loving temperament, and is not purely directed towards virtue, since he has missed out on the finest of all guardians.'

'What guardian is that?' Adeimantus asked.

'Reason, blended with musical and artistic education. Reason is the only thing which once it is born in a man, remains with him throughout his life as the protector of virtue.'

'You are right.'

'Well,' I said, 'that is undoubtedly what the timocratic man is like in his youth. He is very similar to the timocratic city.'

'Absolutely'

c   'The way he comes into existence is something like this. You sometimes get the young son of a good man who lives in a badly governed state. The father avoids success, public office, the lawcourts, and all that kind of minding other people's business. He's prepared to settle for less than his due, in the interests of a quiet life.'

'How does the son become timocratic, then?'

d   'It happens when he starts listening to his mother complaining about her husband not being one of the ruling group, and her own failure, in consequence, to receive the respect she is entitled to from the other women. She can see that her husband is not particularly keen on money, that he does not fight, he is not argumentative – either as a private citizen in the lawcourts, or in public life – that he is indifferent to all this kind of thing. She notices that his attention is constantly directed towards himself, whereas for her he feels neither marked respect nor marked disrespect. The boy hears her complaining on all these counts, and saying

e   that his father is a coward, far too easy-going, and all the rest of it. You know the kind of litany women tend to recite on these occasions.'

'I do indeed,' Adeimantus said. 'It's a long litany, and all too typical.'

'And you're aware too,' I said, 'that even the servants of men like this, the supposedly loyal servants, will sometimes say this kind of thing to the son behind the father's back. If they see someone owing the father money, or doing him some other wrong, and the father not prosecuting him, they

550   tell the son he must get his own back on all these kinds of people when he grows up, and be more of a man than his father. When he goes out, he hears and sees more of the same kind of thing. People who mind their own business in the city are called simpletons, and regarded as of little account, while those who don't mind their own business are respected and admired. The young man is constantly hearing and seeing this kind of thing, but at the same time he listens to what his father says. He can observe his way of life close to, and compare it with other people's way of

b   life. At that point he is torn between the two, his father feeding the rational element in his soul, and making it grow, while the others feed the desiring and spirited elements. Since he is not a naturally bad man, but is influenced by the bad company he keeps, he is torn between these two extremes, and finishes up somewhere in the middle. He hands over power to the compromise candidate, the competitive and spirited element, and in this way becomes arrogant and ambitious.'

'Yes, I'm happy with that as an explanation of the way this man comes into being.'

c   'In that case,' I said, 'we have both our second regime and our second individual.'

'Yes, we have.'

'Should we move on, then, with apologies to Aeschylus, to "another man before another state"?[12] Or would we rather, sticking to our original plan, deal with the state first?'

'By all means,' he said.

'I imagine the next regime after the one we've just described would be oligarchy.'

'And what form of political organisation do you mean by oligarchy?'

d   'The regime based on property qualifications,' I said. 'The one where the rich rule, and a poor man is excluded from power.'

'I see.'

'Do we have to explain how the change from timarchy to oligarchy first takes place?'

'Yes.'

'Mind you,' I said, 'even a blind man could see how it happens.'

'How does it happen?'

'The regime we described is destroyed by the strongroom full of gold which each man possesses. They start by inventing extravagances for

e   themselves, and then they bend the laws in that direction, since neither they nor their wives are prepared to obey them.'

'That's likely enough.'

'The next step, I suppose, will have been for them to start eyeing one another and competing with one another, and in this way they would reduce the whole population to their own level.'

'Very likely.'

'After that, presumably, they would become still further involved in making money. And the higher the value they put on that, the lower the value they would put on virtue. Isn't virtue always at odds with wealth in

---

[12] The phrase puns on 'another man before another gate' (the jingle is preserved in translation), itself an amalgam of two lines from Aeschylus' *Seven against Thebes* (451, 570).

this way? As if they were in the two scales of a balance, always trying to move in opposite directions?'

'Exactly,' he said.

551 'And as wealth and the wealthy are valued more in a city, so goodness and the good are valued less.'

'Obviously.'

'What is valued at any particular time becomes the common practice. What is not valued is neglected.'

'Yes.'

'Eventually, then, they stop being competitive and ambitious, and become mercenary and money-loving. They praise and admire the rich man, and admit him to positions of power. The poor man they treat with contempt.'

'Absolutely.'

b 'At that point they pass a law defining the oligarchic regime. They establish a wealth qualification – larger in an extreme oligarchy, smaller in a more moderate oligarchy – and declare that anyone whose property does not reach the prescribed value is debarred from the government. Either they put this into effect by force of arms, or else they've already established this kind of regime earlier by intimidation. Isn't that how it's done?'

'It is.'

'So that, more or less, is how it becomes established.'

'Yes,' he said. 'But what are the characteristics of this regime? And c what are the kind of faults we said it possessed?'

'Well,' I said, 'the first fault is this very thing which defines its nature. Think what it would be like if you appointed ships' captains in this way, on the basis of a property qualification, and refused a command to a poor man even if he was better qualified.'

'I think it'd be a sorry voyage they'd find themselves making,' he said.

'And the same with any position of command over anything?'

'That's certainly my opinion.'

'With the exception of a city? Or including a city?'

'It is especially true of a city,' he said, 'since the responsibility a city brings is the greatest and the most demanding.'

d 'This would be one great failing, then, possessed by oligarchy.'

'It looks like it.'

'What about its second failing? Is that any less serious?'

'What would it be, this second failing?'

'That a city of this kind is bound to be two cities, not one: a city of the poor and a city of the rich, living in the same place, but constantly scheming against one another.'

'That is, god knows, as big a failing as the first.'

'Nor is it much of a recommendation that they are unlikely to be able to fight any kind of war. They must necessarily either arm their own e own common people and use them, in which case they will fear them more than the enemy, or else not use them, and show themselves, when it comes to the actual fighting, to be true oligarchs, with few under their command.[13] What is more, their love of money makes them reluctant to contribute to the cost of a war.'

'No, that's not much of a recommendation.'

'What about the criticism we made some time ago,[14] that in a regime of 552 this kind the same people are farmers, businessmen and soldiers all at the same time – that they are jacks of all trades and masters of none? Do you think it is right for things to be like that?'

'Not in the least.'

'You must ask yourself, however, if this city isn't also the first to introduce an evil which is greater than any of these.'

'What evil is that?'

'There is nothing to stop one person selling all his property, and a second person acquiring it.[15] Nothing to stop the first person still living in the city after selling his property, without being one of the elements which make up the city. He is neither businessman nor skilled worker, b neither cavalryman nor infantryman[16] – just a poor man, what they call a man without means.'

'Yes,' he said, 'this city is the first to introduce this evil.'

'Certainly in cities with oligarchical regimes this kind of thing is not prohibited in any way. If it were, you wouldn't get one group of people who are very rich, and the rest living in complete poverty.'

'That's right.'

'And here's another question you might ask yourself. At the point where someone like this was rich, and spending all his money, was he even at that time any use to the city for the purposes we've been talking about?

[13] Socrates is punning on the etymology of olig-archy, 'rule of the few', as if it meant 'rule over the few'.   [14] 434a–b.

[15] In Sparta – the model for timocracy – such transactions were at least frowned upon and may have been forbidden. At Athens they were permitted.

[16] Since citizens equipped themselves for military service out of their own pockets, 'cavalryman' and 'infantryman' were designations of wealth and status.

Or was it an illusion, his being one of the rulers? Was he in truth neither a ruler nor a servant of the city, but merely a spendthrift?'

c   'Yes,' he said, 'it was an illusion. He was nothing more than a spendthrift.'

'Do you want us to say, then, that just as a drone born in a cell is a blight on the hive, so a man like this is born as a drone in a household, and is a blight on the city?'

'By all means, Socrates.'

'Well, then, Adeimantus, is it the case that god has made the winged variety of drone all stingless, whereas of these two-legged drones some

d   are stingless, but others have very nasty stings? Do those who finish up as beggars in their old age come from the stingless class, and all those who are labelled criminals from the class with stings?'

'Yes, that's true,' he said.

'It's obvious, then, that anywhere in a city you see beggars, there you can expect to find a secret nest of thieves, pickpockets, robbers of temples, and all these sorts of malefactors.'

'Yes, that's obvious.'

'And don't you find beggars in cities with oligarchic regimes?'

'Yes. Practically the whole population apart from the rulers.'

e   'Can we avoid the conclusion, then, that in these cities there is a large number of criminals with stings, and that the authorities systematically and forcibly keep them under control?'

'No, we can't,' he said.

'And can we not say that the cause of people like this coming into existence there is lack of education, together with poor upbringing and constitutional arrangements?'

'Yes, we can.'

'Well, that's roughly what the oligarchic city would be like. And those are the evils it would contain – plus some others besides, perhaps.'

553   'Yes, that's about it.'

'Then that's another regime we can regard as dealt with – the one known as oligarchic, whose rulers are chosen on the basis of a property qualification. Let's look next at the man who resembles it – how he comes into existence, and what he's like when he does.'

'By all means,' he said.

'Doesn't the change from the timocratic character to the oligarchic take place more or less like this?'

'Like what?'

'He has a son, who starts by emulating his father's achievements and
b following in his footsteps. But then one day he sees him suddenly fall foul
of the city, like a ship striking a reef. He sees all his father's possessions,
and even his life, spilled out over the waves. He may have been general, or
held some other high office, but then been dragged into the lawcourts, and
injured by the evidence of informers. He may have been put to death,
exiled or disfranchised, and lost everything he possessed . . .'[17]

'More than likely,' he said.

'When the son sees this, my friend, when he lives through it, and loses
everything he possesses, he is gripped by fear, I imagine. He promptly
c tumbles the love of honour and that spirited element we were talking
about headlong from their throne in his soul. Demeaned by poverty, he
turns to making money. Greedily and gradually he saves and works, and
so amasses wealth. The next step, don't you think, for someone like this,
is to enthrone the desiring and avaricious element, and crown that as the
great king within his soul, girding it with chains and ceremonial swords
and tiaras?'[18]

'Yes,' he said.

d 'As for the rational and spirited parts of the soul, he makes them sit on
the ground, one on each side, below the desiring element, reducing them
to slavery. The rational part he bans from all subjects of calculation or
inquiry other than ways of turning a little money into a lot, while the only
things he allows the spirited part to admire and respect are wealth and
wealthy people. The only thing it may pride itself on is the acquisition of
money, or anything which contributes to this end.'

'There is no swifter or surer way to turn an ambitious young man into
an avaricious one.'

e 'And is this the oligarchic type?' I asked.

'Well, he certainly develops from the kind of man who is very like the
regime from which oligarchy developed.'

554 'Let's see, then, if he will be like the oligarchic regime.'

'Yes, let's.'

'And won't the first point of similarity be his regarding money as of
supreme importance?'

'Yes, naturally.'

---

[17] Athenian generals were chosen by popular election, and were held to account in the
lawcourts, before a popular jury.
[18] Greeks referred to the Persian monarch as the 'great king'. He was emblematic for
them of vast empire and wealth, and of absolute sovereignty over a servile populace.

'And of course in his being a toiler, counting every penny, who satisfies only the most pressing and necessary of the desires he has, refuses to spend money on anything else, and keeps all his other desires in subjection, since he regards them as idle.'

'Absolutely.'

b 'A sordid little fellow,' I said, 'looking to turn everything to his advantage. A miser. And this is what most people admire. Won't this be the man who is like this regime?'

'Yes,' he said, 'if you ask me he certainly will. And certainly money is the ultimate value both for this city and for the person who is like it.'

'And the reason, I take it, is that this kind of person never applied himself to his education.'

'I don't think he can have done. Otherwise he wouldn't have chosen himself a blind chorus-leader, and treated him with such respect.'[19]

c 'Good,' I said. 'Now, the next question. Can we say of him that his lack of education gives him drone-like desires – some beggarly, some vicious – but that they are forcibly suppressed by his habitual cautiousness?'

'Certainly we can.'

'So do you want to know the best place to look for these people's crimes?' I asked.

'Where?'

'When they are guardians of orphans, or in any situation of that kind where they find they have a free hand to behave unjustly.'

'True.'

'Isn't this a clear indication that when this kind of person has a good reputation in most of his business dealings, and is generally regarded as a d just man, he is using something decent in himself to suppress by force other, evil desires that he possesses? He does not persuade them that what they want is wrong, or use reason as a civilising influence. He uses compulsion and fear, because he is afraid of losing the rest of his fortune.'

'Exactly,' he said.

'Though god knows, my friend, when it's a question of spending other people's money, you will find then that most of them possess drone-like desires.'

'And strong desires at that.'

'In which case, someone of this sort will not be free from conflict within

---

[19] The god of wealth, Plutus, was represented as blind.

e himself. He is two individuals, not one, though for the most part his better desires have the upper hand over his worse desires.'

'That's right.'

'That, I think, is the reason why someone of this sort makes a comparatively good impression. But he's a far cry from the true excellence of the harmonious and well-tuned soul.'

'I agree.'

555 'And of course, for any prize in public life, or any other highly regarded distinction, the penny-pincher, as an individual, is a poor competitor. He refuses to spend money in the cause of reputation or this kind of success, because he is frightened of awakening his extravagant desires and entering into alliance with them in order to compete. He brings only a small part of himself to the fray, fighting with slender resources, oligarchically.[20] So he generally loses – and remains rich.'

'Exactly.'

'Does that leave us in any doubt, then,' I asked, 'that if we are asking about similarity, the penny-pinching and money-loving man is in the same class as the oligarchic city?'

b 'No, it doesn't.'

'Democracy, then, would seem to be our next object of enquiry – how it arises, and what it is like when it does arise. Then we can recognise the character of the democratic man in his turn, and bring him forward for appraisal.'

'Yes, if we want to be consistent, that would be the right approach.'

'Very well,' I said. 'Isn't the way a city changes from oligarchy to democracy something like this? Isn't it the result of their greed in pursuing the ideal they have set themselves – the requirement to become as rich as possible?'

'How do you mean?'

c 'Well, the reason the rulers in it *are* rulers, I take it, is because of their great wealth. So if any of the young turn out to have no self-restraint, the rulers, predictably, are not prepared to restrain them by a law prohibiting them from spending what they own, and losing it all. Their aim is to buy up the property of people like this, or lend them money with the property as security, and in this way become even richer and more highly respected.'

'Yes, that is their overriding aim.'

---

[20] The pun on olig-archy is the same as at 551e (note 13 above).

'And isn't it obvious by now that a high regard for wealth in a city is
d incompatible with the possession of self-discipline on the part of the citizens? They will inevitably lose interest in one or the other.'

'Yes, that's reasonably clear,' he said.

'So through negligence, and the consistent licence they give well-born
individuals to behave without restraint, the rulers in oligarchies can
sometimes drive them into poverty.'

'They certainly can.'

'And these people, I take it, sit around armed in the city – in debt, or
disfranchised,[21] or both. They are drones with stings. Eager for revolution, they hate and plot against those who now possess their property,
and the others like them.'

e   'True.'

'The money-makers, eyes fixed on the ground, pretend not to see
them. And they inject the poison of their money into any of the other
556 citizens who offer no resistance, gaining for themselves in interest many
times the original sum lent. In this way they create a large class of drones
and beggars in the city.'

'Yes, it's bound to be large,' he said.

'As the flames of discontent begin to take hold, they refuse to put them
out either in the first way, by forbidding people to dispose of their possessions as they wish, or again in a different way, using a second law which
can stop this kind of thing happening.'

'What law is that?'

'Well, it's the next best after the first one I mentioned. And it does
compel the citizens to pay some regard to virtue. If you have a law that
b voluntary agreements should in general be entered into at each party's
own risk, there would be less shameless money-making in the city, and
fewer dangers of the kind we've just been talking about would arise there.'

'Far fewer,' he said.

'As it is, for all the reasons we have given, the rulers treat the subjects
in the city in the way I have described. As for themselves and their families, don't they bring their children up to be luxurious, incapable alike of
c physical and mental exertion, weak when it comes to resisting pleasure or
pain, and lazy?'

'Of course they do.'

---

[21] A disfranchised person lost more than just the right to vote, he was also forbidden
to hold any public office, to be a litigant in court, and even to show his face in certain
important public places.

'Haven't they themselves lost interest in everything other than making money? Have they paid any more attention to virtue and excellence than the poor have?'

'No, they haven't.'

'With this background, what do you think happens when rulers and ruled come into close contact, on a journey, perhaps, or in some other
d joint activity – an embassy or military expedition, or sailing in the same ship, or as fellow-soldiers? Or when they watch each other in the actual moment of danger, and the poor find that here at least they are not looked down on by the rich? In fact it often happens that a poor man, lean and sunburnt, is stationed in battle alongside a rich man who has had a comfortable upbringing in the shade, and who is carrying a good deal of superfluous flesh. When he sees him wheezing and struggling, don't you suppose he blames his own cowardice for the fact that people like this
e are rich? Don't they egg one another on when they are alone together? "They're ours for the plucking," they say. "There's nothing to them."'

'Yes,' he said. 'Speaking for myself, I'm quite sure that's their reaction.'

'It's like an unhealthy body. It only takes a trivial external cause to tip the balance towards actual illness. Or the body can sometimes come to be at war with itself without any outside intervention at all. It's just the same with a city. An unhealthy city needs only the slightest pretext – one side appealing for outside help to an oligarchy, or the other to a democracy – to become ill, and start fighting against itself. Can't it even sometimes be at war with itself without any outside intervention at all?'

557   'It can. Ferociously.'

'And presumably it turns into a democracy when the poor are victorious, when they kill some of their opponents and send others into exile, give an equal share in the constitution and public office to those who remain, and when public office in the city is allocated for the most part by lot.'

'Yes,' he said, 'that is the way democracy becomes established, whether it happens by force of arms or because their opponents lose their nerve and go into exile.'

'Very well, then. How will these people live? What will this regime, in
b its turn, be like, since it's obvious that the man who resembles it will prove to be a democratic man of some sort?'[22]

---

[22] The picture of the democratic regime that follows owes many of its touches to the social life of Plato's Athens. But there was something of Athens in the description of the oligarchic regime also.

'Yes, that's obvious.'

'Well, aren't they free men, for a start? Isn't it a city full of freedom, and freedom of speech? Isn't there liberty in it for anyone to do anything he wants?'

'Yes, that's the reputation it has,' he said.

'And where there is liberty, then obviously each person can arrange his own life within the city in whatever way pleases him.'

'Obviously.'

c   'The most varied of regimes, I would think, as far as human character goes.'

'Of course.'

'It's probably the most attractive of the regimes,' I said. 'Like a coat of many colours, with an infinite variety of floral decoration, this regime will catch the eye with its infinite variety of moral decoration. Lots of people are likely to judge this regime to be the most attractive – like women or children looking at prettily painted objects.'

'Indeed they will.'

d   'And I tell you, it's a good place to look if you want a particular kind of constitution.'

'Why?'

'Because the liberty it allows its citizens means it has every type of constitution within it. So anyone wanting to found a city, as we have just been doing, will probably find he has to go to a city with a democratic regime, and there choose whatever political arrangements he fancies. Like shopping for constitutions in a bazaar. Then, when he has made his choice, he can found a city along those lines.'

e   'Yes,' he said, 'he's not likely to find any shortage of models to choose from.'

'There's no compulsion to hold office in this city,' I said, 'even if you're well qualified to hold office, nor to obey those who do hold office, if you don't feel like it, nor to go to war when the city is at war, nor to be at peace when everyone else is, unless peace is what you want. Then again, even if there's a law stopping you holding office or being a member of a jury, there's nothing to stop you holding office and being a member of a jury

558 anyway, if that's how the mood takes you. Isn't this, in the short term, a delightful and heaven-sent way of life?'

'It probably is, in the short term.'

'And what about the relaxed attitude of those sentenced by the courts? Isn't it civilised? Or have you never seen people who have been condemned to death or exile in a regime of this kind, who nonetheless remain in person, hanging about at the centre of things, and haunting the place like the spirit of a departed hero,[23] without anyone caring or noticing?'

'I've seen plenty,' he said.

b   'Then there's the tolerance of this city. No pedantic insistence on detail, but an utter contempt for the things we showed such respect for when we were founding our city – our claim that only someone with an outstanding nature could ever turn out to be a good man, and only if from earliest childhood he played in the best company and the right surroundings, and did all the right kinds of things. How magnificently the city tramples all this underfoot, paying no attention to what kind of life someone led before he entered political life! All anyone has to do to win

c   favour is say he is a friend of the people.'

'Ah, yes, that's true nobility!'

'These and related qualities will be the ones possessed by democracy. You'd expect it to be an enjoyable kind of regime – anarchic, colourful, and granting equality of a sort to equals and unequals alike.'

'Yes, that's a pretty familiar story,' he said.

'Look and see, then,' I said, 'what the individual resembling this regime is like. Or rather, should we ask first, as we did with the regime, how he comes into being?'

'Yes.'

'Doesn't it happen like this? He might come into being, I imagine, as a

d   son of the thrifty oligarchic character we were talking about, brought up under his father's direction and with his father's habits.'

'He might well.'

'So he too will use force to master those desires within him which are extravagant and not money-making – the ones called unnecessary desires.'

'Obviously,' he said.

'Would you like us to start by defining necessary and unnecessary desires? We don't want to be completely in the dark about what we're discussing.'

'Yes, I would.'

'Very well. Is it the ones we can't deny which can properly be called

---

[23] In Greek religion, heroes became minor deities after death and were worshipped in their place of origin.

e necessary – plus the ones whose satisfaction does us some good? Our
nature demands that we try to satisfy both these classes, doesn't it?'

'Very much so.'

559 'So we shall be justified in using the name "necessary" for these desires.'

'We shall.'

'What about the desires you *can* get rid of, if you work at it from childhood, the ones moreover whose presence does you no good – may even
perhaps do you some harm? Wouldn't we be right in saying that all these
are unnecessary?'

'We would.'

'Let's take an example of each class. It's easier to grasp them if we have
a pattern, or model.'

'That's a good idea.'

b 'Won't the desire to eat for one's health and well-being, the desire just
for bread and cooked food, be a necessary desire?'

'Yes, I think it will.'

'The desire for bread is necessary on both counts. It is not only
beneficial, but also the difference between life and death.'

'Yes.'

'Whereas the desire for cooked food is necessary if it can contribute in
some way to our well-being.'

'Precisely.'

'What about the desire, over and above this, for other sorts of foods?
This desire can be eliminated, in most people, by discipline and education
from early childhood. And since it is harmful to the body, and harmful to

c the soul's capacity for thought and self-control, would it be correct to call
it unnecessary?'

'Absolutely correct.'

'In which case, shall we say that these desires are extravagant, whereas
the others are productive, because they contribute to some function?'

'By all means.'

'And we'll say the same about sex, and the rest of our desires.'

'Yes, we shall.'

'Well, then. Did we say that this person we were calling a drone a few
moments ago was the one who was stuffed with pleasures and desires of this
sort, and that he was ruled by unnecessary pleasures and desires? Whereas

d the person ruled by necessary desires was thrifty and oligarchical?'[24]

---

[24] 555c–556a vs. 554a.

'We did indeed.'

'Let's return, then,' I said, 'to our account of the way the democratic man comes into being from the oligarchic. I think it generally happens like this.'

'Like what?'

'Imagine a young man who has been brought up in the uneducated and stingy way we described just now, but who gets to taste the honey the drones enjoy, and spend his time with wild, fiery creatures who can offer e him pleasures of every kind, hue and variety. That's probably the point you must regard as the beginning of the change from the oligarchy within him to democracy.'

'No question about it,' he said.

'Just as the city changed when one party received support from an external ally of a similar persuasion,[25] doesn't the young man now change in the same way when one group of his desires in its turn receives support from a class of external desires which are related and similar to it?'

'He certainly does.'

'And if some countervailing help comes to the oligarchic element within him – from his father, perhaps, or from the lectures and reproaches 560 of the rest of his family – I imagine that's when faction and counterfaction arise, and internal warfare against himself.'

'Of course.'

'Sometimes, I imagine, the democratic element loses ground to the oligarchic element, and some of his desires are either destroyed or banished, as some sense of shame is born in the young man's soul, and order is restored.'

'Yes, it sometimes happens like that,' he said.

'But as one set of desires is banished, I imagine another related set has grown up in succession. The father, who has no idea how to bring up his b son, cannot prevent these desires becoming numerous and powerful.'

'Yes, that's certainly what tends to happen.'

'These desires, then, draw the young man to the same company as before, and secret intercourse breeds a mob of further desires.'

'And then?'

'Finally, I imagine, they seize the citadel of the young man's soul, realising that it is empty of learning, good habits and true arguments, which are of course the best defenders and guardians in the minds of men loved by the gods.'

[25] 556e.

272

c   'Much the best,' he said.

'False, seductive arguments and opinions run up and seize this stronghold in the young man's mind, I expect, replacing the true defenders.'

'They do indeed.'

'Doesn't he then return to that land of the Lotus-eaters, and take up residence there quite openly? If any help from his family reaches the thrifty part of his soul, those seductive arguments bar the gates of the
d   royal walls within him.[26] They will neither allow entry to the actual allied force, nor even admit an embassy of wise words, in a private capacity, from the young man's elders. They join battle, and the seductive arguments win. A sense of shame is classed as simple-mindedness, deprived of rights, and driven into exile. Self-discipline is called cowardice, heaped with insults, and sent packing. As for moderation and economy, don't the seductive arguments persuade the young man that these are mean and parochial? Don't they join forces with his many useless desires, and despatch these qualities beyond the borders?'

'Absolutely.'

'And when they have somehow emptied and purged the soul of the
e   young man they are taking possession of and initiating with solemn rites, they then promptly bring insolence, anarchy, extravagance and shamelessness back from exile, in a blaze of glory, with a great retinue, and crowned with garlands.[27] They sing their praises, and find flattering names for them. Insolence becomes sophistication, anarchy freedom,
561   extravagance generosity, and shamelessness courage. Isn't this likely to be the way a young man exchanges an upbringing among necessary desires for the liberation and release of unnecessary and useless desires?'

'Yes, it is,' he said. 'Quite clearly.'

'From then on, I imagine, a young man of this sort lives his life spending at least as much money, effort and time on unnecessary as on necessary desires. If he is lucky, he may not get too carried away by his
b   orgy. As he grows older and the first flush of excitement fades, he may accept back some elements of the party he exiled, and avoid complete surrender to the usurpers. Putting all his pleasures on an equal footing, he grants power over himself to the pleasure of the moment, as if it were a magistrate chosen by lot. And when he has had his fill of it, he surrenders

---

[26] The citadel or acropolis of a Greek city was typically the seat of its ancestral kings.
[27] The imagery parodies the ritual of the Eleusinian Mysteries. (For mystic cults in general, see note 9 to 363c above.)

himself in turn to another pleasure. He rejects none of them, but gives sustenance to all alike.'

'He does indeed.'

c 'If someone tells him that some pleasures are the result of fine and good desires, others of evil desires, and that he should follow and value the first, and punish and hold in subjection the second, he does not admit this truth, or allow it into the fortress. He shakes his head at any claims of this sort, saying that all desires are equal, and must be valued equally.'

'Yes,' he said, 'that's exactly how he feels, and exactly how he behaves.'

'And so he lives out his life from day to day, gratifying the desire of the moment. One day he drinks himself under the table to the sound of the
d pipes, the next day he is on a diet of plain water. Now he is taking exercise, but at other times he is lazing around and taking no interest in anything. And sometimes he passes the time in what he calls philosophy. Much of his time is spent in politics, where he leaps to his feet and says and does whatever comes into his head. Or if he comes to admire the military, then that is the way he goes. Or if it's businessmen, then that way. There is no controlling order or necessity in his life. As far as he is concerned, it is pleasant, free and blessed, and he sticks to it his whole life through.'

e 'You've given us an excellent account of the life of the man who puts equality before everything.'

'Yes. I take it to be a variegated life, full of all sorts of characteristics. This democratic man is elegant and colourful, just like the democratic city. Many men and women might envy him his life, with all the examples of regimes and characters it contains within it.'

'Yes, that is what it is like,' he said.

562 'Very well, then. Can a man like this be ranked on a par with democracy? Can he properly be called democratic?'

'Yes, he can.'

'In that case,' I said, 'that leaves us with the task of describing the most delightful of regimes, and the most delightful of individuals. Tyranny and the tyrant.'

'It certainly does,' he said.

'Very well, my good friend, how does tyranny manifest itself? That it is a change from democracy is pretty obvious.'

'Yes, it is.'

'In which case, does tyranny in its turn arise out of democracy in rather the same way as democracy arises out of oligarchy?'

b   'How do you mean?'

'The thing they held up as an ideal,' I said, 'the thing which formed the basis of oligarchy, was wealth, wasn't it?'

'Yes.'

'It was the insatiable longing for wealth, and the neglect of everything else in the pursuit of profit, which destroyed oligarchy.'

'True,' he said.

'And is it the insatiable longing for what it defines as good which destroys democracy too, in its turn?'

'What is it you say it defines as good?'

c   'Freedom,' I said. 'This is the thing, I imagine, which in a democratic state you will hear described as its finest attribute, and what makes it, for any man of free spirit, the only place worth living in.'

'Yes, that is certainly something you often hear said.'

'Well, then, as I was saying just now, is it the insatiable longing for this good, and the neglect of everything else, which brings about a change in this regime too, and creates the need for tyranny?'

'How does that happen?' he asked.

'I imagine it's when a democracy, in its thirst for the wine of freedom,

d   finds the wine being poured by unscrupulous cupbearers, and when it drinks more deeply than it should of pure, unmixed freedom.[28] Then if its magistrates are not totally easy-going and do not offer it that freedom in large quantities, it accuses them of being filthy oligarchs, and punishes them.'

'Yes,' he said. 'That is what they do.'

'Those who obey the rulers are heaped with insults. They are regarded as servile nonentities. Praise and respect, whether in private or public life, go to rulers for behaving like those they rule, and to those they rule for behaving like rulers. Isn't the desire for freedom in a city of this type

e   bound to run to extremes?'

'Of course it is.'

'And isn't the anarchy bound to make its way, my friend, into private households? Until finally it starts appearing among dumb animals.'

'And how do we reckon this happens?'

'A father, for example, gets used to being like a child, and being afraid of his sons. A son gets used to being like his father. He feels no respect or

563   fear for his parents. All he wants is to be free. Immigrants are put on a par

---

[28] The Greeks drank their wine diluted with water.

275

with citizens, and citizens with immigrants. And the same with visiting foreigners.'

'Yes, that's what happens.'

'That, plus a few more trivial examples of the same kind,' I said. 'In a society of this sort teachers are afraid of their pupils and curry favour with them. Pupils have an equal contempt for their teachers and their attendants. In general, the young are the image of their elders, and challenge them in everything they say and do. The old descend to the level
b of the young. They pepper everything with wit and humour, trying to be like the young, because they don't want to be thought harsh or dictatorial.'

'Precisely,' he said.

'But the high-water mark of mass-freedom in a city of this kind comes when those who have been bought as slaves – whether male or female – are every bit as free as those who bought them. As for the relationship of women to men and men to women, I all but forgot to mention the extent of the legal equality and liberty between them.'
c 'Shall we then, borrowing a phrase from Aeschylus, say whatever it was that "came to our lips" just now?'[29]

'By all means,' I said. 'It's certainly what *I'm* going to do. You wouldn't believe, without seeing it for yourself, how much more free domestic animals are here than in other cities. Dogs really *are* like the women who own them, as the proverb says. And horses and donkeys are in the habit of wandering the streets with total freedom, noses in the air, barging into
d any passer-by who fails to get out of their way. It's all like that – all full of freedom.'

'Talk about telling people their own dreams,' he said. 'I've often had that experience myself on my way out of the city.'

'To generalise, then, from all these collected observations, have you noticed how sensitive it makes the souls of the citizens, so that if anyone seeks to impose the slightest degree of slavery, they grow angry and cannot tolerate it? In the end, as I imagine you are aware, they take no
e notice even of the laws – written or unwritten[30] – in their determination that no one shall be master over them in any way at all.'

'Yes, I am well aware of that,' he said.

---

[29] The Aeschylean play from which this phrase derives is unknown.
[30] 'Unwritten law' was a common phrase for the customary beliefs and social strictures respected in any particular community.

'This is the form of government, my friend, so attractive and so head-strong, from which I believe tyranny is born.'

'Certainly headstrong,' he said. 'But what is the next step?'

'The same ailment which arose in oligarchy, and destroyed that, arises in this regime also – only more widespread and virulent because of the licence it is given. Here it enslaves democracy. Indeed, excess in one 564 direction generally tends to produce a violent reaction in the opposite direction. This is true of the seasons of the year, of plants and animals, and particularly true of political regimes.'

'Probably so,' he said

'Yes, since the only likely reaction to excessive freedom, whether for an individual or for a city, is excessive slavery.'

'Very likely.'

'In which case,' I said, 'the chances are that democracy is the ideal place to find the origin of tyranny – the harshest and most complete slavery arising, I guess, from the most extreme freedom.'

'That makes sense,' he said.

'However, that doesn't by itself answer your question, presumably. b What you wanted to know was the nature of this ailment which arises not only in oligarchy but also in democracy, enslaving it.'

'True.'

'Very well,' I said. 'What I had in mind was that class of idle and ex-travagant men, the most courageous element leading, the less courageous element following. We compared them to drones – the leaders to drones with stings, the followers to drones without stings.'[31]

'Rightly so.'

'Both these classes,' I said, 'disturb the balance of any regime in which c they arise. Like phlegm and bile in the body.[32] The good doctor and law-giver for a city must be far-sighted in his precautions against both of them – just like a good beekeeper. His intention, ideally, should be to prevent their occurrence at all. If they do occur, he should make sure they are cut out, cells and all, as swiftly as possible.'

'Heavens, yes. And as completely as possible.'

'All right, then,' I said. 'To help us see what we are after in a more clear-cut way, let's tackle the question like this.'

---

[31] 552c–e.
[32] These were two of the so-called 'humours' – the Greek term simply means 'juices' – upon whose balance in the body much of Greek medicine made physical health depend.

'Like what?'

'Let's make a theoretical division of the democratic city into three
d parts. After all, this is how it is in fact composed. This class of drones, I
imagine, is one part, and because of the absence of restrictions it grows at
least as freely in a democracy as in an oligarchy.'

'That is so.'

'But it is much fiercer in a democracy than in an oligarchy.'

'In what way?'

'In an oligarchy it is treated as of no value, and excluded from power.
So it gets no exercise, and does not develop its strength. In a democracy,
by contrast, barring a few individuals, it is the dominant influence in the
state. The fiercest element in this class does the talking and acting; the
remainder sit around the rostrum buzzing, and refusing to allow the
e expression of any other view. The result is that in a regime of this kind
everything, with very few exceptions, is run by the class of drones.'

'Exactly,' he said.

'Then there's a second class which always separates itself off from the
majority.'

'What class is that?'

'When everyone is engaged in making money, presumably it is those
with the most disciplined temperament who generally become the
richest.'

'Very likely.'

'They provide a plentiful supply of honey for the drones, I imagine,
and an easy source from which to extract it.'

'Yes,' he said. 'After all, they can't extract much from those who haven't
got much.'

'They're called the rich, these people we are talking about, the drones'
feeding-ground.'

'That's about it,' he said.

565   'The general populace would be the third class – manual labourers with
little interest in politics, and very little property of their own. This is the
most numerous and powerful class in a democracy, but only when it is
assembled together.'

'It is indeed,' he said. 'But if it isn't getting some share of the honey, it
is reluctant to assemble very often.'

'That's why it always does get a share of it, if its leaders have anything
to do with it. They take it away from those who possess property and distribute it among the people, keeping only the lion's share for themselves.'

b   'Yes, the people do get a limited share of that sort,' he said.

'Those whose property is taken away are presumably compelled to defend themselves by speaking in the assembly and taking whatever other action they can.'

'Of course.'

'Even if they have no desire at all for revolution, they are accused by the others of plotting against the people and being oligarchs.'

'Naturally.'

'In the end, when they see the people attempting to injure them – not
c   maliciously, but out of ignorance, misled by their opponents – at that point, whether they like it or not, the rich really do become oligarchs, though not from choice. This too is an evil implanted in them by the stings of the drone we were talking about.'

'It is indeed.'

'Then you get impeachments, litigation and lawsuits between the two classes.'

'You certainly do.'

'And isn't there a universal tendency for the people to set up one single individual who is their own particular champion? Don't they feed him up and make him mighty?'[33]

'They do.'

d   'So when we look at the growth of a tyrant,' I said, 'one thing at least is clear. This position of champion is the sole root from which the tyrant springs.'

'Yes, that's absolutely clear.'

'In that case, what prompts the change from champion to tyrant? Isn't it pretty obvious that it happens when the champion of the people starts acting like the character in the story about the temple of Zeus the wolf-god in Arcadia?'

'What story?' he asked.

'That there is one piece of human innards chopped up among all the pieces of the other sacrificial offerings, and that anyone who tastes it will inevitably turn into a wolf. Or haven't you heard that story?'

[33] This narrative, although a generalised composite, alludes most particularly to two instances of struggle between democratic and oligarchic factions: the turmoil in late fifth-century Athens, and the rise of Dionysius I as popular champion in Sicily (see pp. xi–xiii and xxii of the introduction). There was no people's champion who became tyrant at Athens in Plato's time. What this fits is rather the rise of Dionysius, as well as that of Pisistratus, ruler of Athens in the mid-sixth century, when the city was first becoming prominent.

e   'Yes, I have heard it.'

'Isn't it the same with a champion of the people? Once he really wins the mob over, the blood of his kinsmen is no bar to him. He accuses someone falsely, as such people do. He brings him to trial and murders

566   him, and as he rubs out a man's life his unholy mouth and lips taste the blood of a butchered kinsman. He drives people into exile or kills them, hinting at a cancellation of debts and the redistribution of land. What is the inevitable and predestined next step for someone like this? Doesn't he either have to be destroyed by his enemies, or else become tyrant, turning from man into wolf?'

'Yes. That is absolutely inevitable,' he said.

'He becomes the architect of civil war against those who own property.'

'He does.'

'Well, then. If he is sent into exile, but returns despite his enemies, doesn't he return as an out-and-out tyrant?'

'Yes. Obviously.'

b   'And if his enemies are unable to drive him into exile or kill him by attacking him publicly, then they start plotting to kill him secretly by assassination.'

'Yes, that's certainly what tends to happen,' he said.

'The tyrant's response to this is the famous request which everyone who has reached this stage discovers. He asks the people for a personal bodyguard, to guarantee the safety of their people's champion.'

'Indeed he does.'

'And they give him one. More worried about his safety than their own, presumably.'

c   'Much more.'

'When a man with money sees this, one who in addition to his money has reason to be an enemy of the people, then this man, my friend, in the words of Croesus' oracle,

> Without delay to Hermus' pebbled shore
> Flees straight, nor thinks it shame to play the coward.'[34]

'That's right,' he said. 'He certainly wouldn't get a second chance to think it shame.'

'No. I imagine anyone they can get their hands on is done to death.'

---

[34] The Hermus is a large river in Lydia that would have provided an escape-route for its king, Croesus, in the event of his overthrow. The oracle was the reply given to Croesus when he asked how long he would reign. See Herodotus 1.55.

'Bound to be.'

d   'And this champion of ours is obviously not going to be the one lying there, "measuring his full length"[35] in the dust. After destroying all these other people, he'll stand tall in the chariot of the city, having graduated from champion to tyrant.'

'Of course,' he said. 'What's to stop him?'

'Shall we then describe the happiness of this man and of the city where such a creature comes into being?'

'By all means let's describe it,' he said.

'Very well. To start with, in the early days, doesn't he have a smile and
e   a friendly word for everyone he meets? He says he's no tyrant, and is full of promises both to individuals and to the state. Won't he have freed them from their debts, and divided up the land among the people and among his supporters? Doesn't he pretend to be universally kind and gentle?'

'He's bound to.'

'But I imagine that once he feels safe from his enemies in exile, being reconciled with some and destroying others, his first concern is to be constantly starting wars, so that the people will stand in need of a leader.'

'Very likely.'

567   'And perhaps with the further intention that their contributions to the war will impoverish them, compel them to concentrate on their daily occupations, and make them less likely to plot against him?'

'Undoubtedly.'

'And if there are some independent-minded people whom he suspects of challenging his rule, doesn't he try to find a good excuse for handing them over to the enemy and destroying them? For all these reasons, isn't a tyrant always bound to be stirring up war?'

'Yes, he is.'

b   'Doesn't this tend to make him increasingly unpopular with the citizens?'

'Of course it does.'

'Then the boldest of those who helped to make him tyrant, and who are now in positions of power, start to speak their minds freely, don't they, both to him and to one another, criticising what is going on?'

'Probably.'

'So the tyrant, if he wants to go on ruling, must be prepared to remove all these people, until he is left with no one who is any use – whether friend or enemy.'

[35] Homer, *Iliad* 16.776.

'Obviously he must.'

c   'He will need a sharp pair of eyes, then. He needs to pick out the brave, the noble, the wise and the rich, since it is his unavoidable good fortune, whether he likes it or not, to be the enemy of all of them. He must plot their downfall, until he has got the city clean.'

'A fine way to clean a city,' he said.

'Yes. The exact opposite of what doctors do to the body. They remove what is worst, and leave what is best. With the tyrant it is the other way round.'

'That's what he *has* to do, apparently, if he is to go on ruling.'

d   'In which case,' I said, 'he is firmly and inevitably impaled on the horns of a delightful dilemma, which requires him either to spend his life with the worthless mob – and be hated by them into the bargain – or not to live at all.'

'That's about the size of it,' he said.

'And the more hated by the citizens his behaviour makes him, the larger and more reliable a bodyguard he will need, won't he?'

'Of course.'

'Who are these reliable people, then? Where can he send to for them?'

'They'll come winging their way of their own accord,' he said. 'Any number of them, as long as he pays the going rate.'

e   'Ye dogs!³⁶ Drones again! Foreign ones, all kinds of them, I think you're talking about.'³⁷

'Good. I haven't given you the wrong impression, then.'

'And from the city itself? Might he not bring himself . . .'

'To do what?'

'To deprive the citizens of their slaves, set the slaves free, and make them part of his bodyguard?'

'Indeed he might. They are, after all, the most reliable people he can find.'

568   'What a wonderful thing you make a tyrant out to be,' I said, 'if these are the people he has as his friends, the people he can trust, once he has destroyed the friends he started with.'

'Well, these certainly *are* the kind of friends he has.'

'So while he enjoys the admiration of these friends, and the company of these new citizens, do decent people hate him and avoid him?'

---

³⁶ See note 50 to 399e above on Socrates' habit of using this oath.

³⁷ Mercenaries were increasingly used in warfare throughout the Greek world in the fourth century, but it was characteristic only of tyrants to use them for a personal bodyguard.

'How can they help doing so?'

'It's no wonder,' I said, 'that tragedy in general, and Euripides in particular, has such a reputation for wisdom.'

'Why?'

b   'Because among other insight-filled utterances he produced this one:
"A tyrant's wisdom comes from wise companions."[38] Clearly it was these
associates of the tyrant that he was referring to as the wise.'

'Yes,' he said. 'And Euripides also praises tyranny as "godlike"[39] – and
a whole lot else besides. And not just Euripides – other poets as well.'

'That's why writers of tragedies, being so wise, will forgive us and those
with regimes like ours, if we refuse to accept them into our state on the
grounds that they are apologists for tyranny.'

'Well, if you want my opinion,' he said, 'they will forgive us. Or the
more civilised of them will, at any rate.'

c   'They can tour the other cities, presumably, drawing great crowds and
hiring actors with fine, loud, persuasive voices, and so seduce those states
into tyranny and democracy.'

'They certainly can.'

'What is more, they get paid for this, and are treated with respect. First
and foremost by tyrants, as you might expect, but also by a democracy.[40] But
d   the higher they climb in the ascending scale of political regimes, the
fainter respect for them becomes, as if it were short of breath, and unable
to progress further.'

'Exactly.'

'We have strayed from the point, however,' I said. 'Let us return to that
army the tyrant has – that fine, large, varied and ever-changing army –
and ask how it is going to be maintained.'

'Well, obviously, if there is money in the city's temples, then as long as
it lasts he will spend that. Plus the money of his victims, allowing him to
exact smaller contributions from the people.'

e   'But what happens when these run out?'

'He will use his father's money, obviously – to support himself, his
drinking-companions, and his male and female friends.'

---

[38] The play from which this statement comes is lost, and some sources attribute it to
Sophocles rather than Euripides. Poets and intellectuals were frequently to be found
at the courts of powerful patrons.

[39] *Trojan Women* 1169.

[40] Pindar, Simonides and Aeschylus are said to have attended the court of the Sicilian
tyrant Hiero, while Euripides and Agathon – the tragedian featured in Plato's
Symposium – attended the court of the Macedonian tyrant Archelaus. We also know
of non-Athenians who came to Athens to have their dramas performed.

'I see. The people, who spawned the tyrant, will support him and his friends.'

'It will have no choice,' he said.

'What if the people resent this?' I asked. '"It is not right," they might say for a start, "for a grown-up son to be supported by his father. Quite the reverse, in fact. A father should be supported by his son. What is more, the reason we fathered you and put you in power was not so that we could ourselves become slaves to our own slaves, as soon as you became powerful, and support you and them and the rest of your collection of human flotsam. No, with you as our champion we wanted our political freedom from the rich and the so-called aristocracy. We order you to leave the city now, you and your friends." Suppose the people spoke to him in this way, like a father driving his son and his unruly drinking-companions from the house? What do you think would happen then?'

'My god!' he said. 'Then the people really will find out what they are, and what kind of offspring they have fathered, taken to their hearts, and allowed to grow. They'll realise it's a case of the weaker trying to drive out the stronger.'

'What do you mean?' I asked. 'Will the tyrant have the effrontery to use force against his parent? Will he beat him if he disobeys?'

'Yes – once he has taken away his weapons.'

'A parricide, then, this tyrant you are describing. A cruel guardian for man's old age. At this point, it seems, the thing is an acknowledged tyranny. The people have jumped out of the proverbial frying pan into the fire, from their enslavement to free men to a despotism of slaves. They have exchanged the ample – too ample – freedom they had before for the hair shirt of the most harsh and galling form of slavery, the slavery imposed by slaves.'

'Yes, that is precisely how it happens.'

'Will there be any objection, then,' I asked, 'to our saying that we have given an adequate description of the way tyranny evolves out of democracy, and of what it is like when it has done so?'

'No,' he said, 'our description is perfectly adequate.'

Book 9

571 'That still leaves the tyrannical man himself,' I said. 'We must ask how he develops out of the democratic man, what sort of person he is, and what manner of life he leads. Is he wretched or blissful?'

'Yes, we are still left with him.'

'And there's something else I need before I can deal with him. Shall I tell you what it is?'

'What?'

'I'm not very satisfied with our analysis of the nature and extent of our
b desires.[1] Until we remedy that, we shall be pretty much in the dark in our present enquiry.'

'And is it too late now?' he asked.

'Not at all. I want to make the following distinction between desires. Think about it. Among the unnecessary pleasures and desires there are some which seem to me to be violent or lawless. Everyone is born with them, in all probability, but in some people, under the control of the laws and the better desires, allied with reason, they are either eliminated completely, or remain few and weak. In other people, however, they become stronger and more numerous.'

c 'Which desires do you mean?'

'Those which are aroused in sleep,' I said, 'when the rest of the soul – the rational, gentle and ruling element in it – slumbers, and the bestial, savage part, filled with food or drink, suddenly comes alive, casts off sleep, and tries to go out and satisfy its own nature. In this state, as you know, since it is released and set free from all shame or rational judgment, it can

---

[1] 558d–559d.

285

bring itself to do absolutely anything. In its imaginings it has no hesitation

d in attempting sexual intercourse with a mother – nor with anyone or anything else, man or god or animal. There is no murder it will not commit, no meat it will not eat. In short, it will go to any length of folly and shamelessness.'

'How right you are,' he said.

'I imagine someone with a healthy and self-disciplined disposition will awaken the rational part of himself before going to sleep, feast it on fine

e arguments and enquiries, and so bring himself into a state of harmony

572 with himself. As for his desiring part, he will expose it neither to want nor to excess. He wants it to go to sleep, and not disturb what is best in the soul with its pleasure or pain, but allow it all by itself, solitary and pure, to follow its enquiries and reach out for a vision of something – be it past, present or future – that it does not know. The same goes for the spirited part of the soul. He will calm it down, and avoid getting into a rage with anyone and going to sleep with his spirit in a state of turmoil. Before retiring to rest he needs to pacify two elements in the soul and awaken the third, which is the birthplace of reason. Under these conditions, as you

b know, he can most easily grasp truth, and the visions which appear in his dreams are least lawless.'

'I entirely agree.'

'Well, we've been carried along slightly further than we needed. What we need to know is that there is in everyone a terrible, untamed and lawless class of desires – even in those of us who appear to be completely normal. This becomes quite clear in our sleep. Am I talking sense? Do you agree?'

'Yes, I do.'

'Take the democratic man, then, the man of the people. Remember

c what we said he was like.[2] He was the result, I think I'm right in saying, of an upbringing from earliest childhood under a thrifty father, who valued only the money-making desires, and felt contempt for the unnecessary desires whose aim is entertainment or display. Is that right?'

'Yes.'

'When he met more sophisticated men, who were full of the desires we have just described, hatred of his father's stinginess made him plunge into excess of every kind, and into these people's kind of behaviour. However,

[2] 558d.

d because he had a better nature than those who were corrupting him, he was drawn in both directions, and finished up midway between the two positions. He enjoyed the benefits of each in moderation – or so he thought – and led a life that was neither mean nor lawless. In this way he developed from the oligarchic type into the democratic.'

'Yes,' he said. 'That was – and still is – our opinion about this kind of person.'

'Imagine, in that case, that someone like this has now grown old in his turn, and that again a young son has been brought up in his father's way of life.'

'All right, I'm imagining that.'

c 'Now imagine further that the same happens to him as happened to his father before him. He is led into all kinds of lawlessness – or "liberty," as those who are leading him call it. His father and the rest of his household come to the support of the intermediate desires, while his seducers support his other desires. When these cunning magicians and tyrant-makers despair of keeping control of him any other way, they contrive to
573 implant in him a kind of lust or passion,[3] a champion of those idle desires which want to consume whatever is available, a kind of giant winged drone. Isn't that the only description for the lust found in people of this kind?'

'The only possible description, if you ask me.'

'Very well. When the other desires come buzzing round, full of incense, perfumes, garlands, wine and the dissolute pleasures typical of such gatherings, they feed this drone, help it grow to an enormous size, and so
b plant the sting of yearning in it. Then this champion of the soul takes madness for its bodyguard, and goes berserk. If it detects in the man any desires or opinions which can be regarded as decent and which still feel some sense of shame, it kills them off or banishes them from its presence, until it has purged the soul of restraint and filled it with foreign madness.'

'Yes, that's a perfect description of the way a tyrannical man comes into being.'

---

[3] 'Lust or passion' translates *erōs*, which in Greek normally means the kind of love we fall in rather than the love we bear to family or friends; hence it also refers to sexual passion, and, by extension, any vehement desire. It is in addition the name for Love personified, who was depicted on vase-paintings of the time as a winged boy-god. Plato exploits this semantic range, particularly its darker reaches, in describing the tyrannical character. The word is variously translated 'passion', 'lust' (or 'Lust') or 'Eros', according to context.

'Is that the kind of reason, then,' I asked, 'why Eros has traditionally been called a tyrant?'[4]

'Probably,' he said.

c   'And does a man who is drunk also have something of the tyrant in him, my friend?'

'He does.'

'And of course someone who is mad or deranged attempts to rule over gods as well as men, and imagines himself capable of doing so.'

'Absolutely.'

'Strictly speaking, then, a man becomes tyrannical when either his nature or his habits, or both, lead him to drink, lust and madness.'

'Precisely.'

'That is the origin of the tyrannical man in his turn, apparently. But what is his life like?'

d   'This is like one of those question-and-answer jokes. All right, then, I don't know. What *is* the tyrannical man's life like?'

'I'll tell you. The next step, I think, for those in whom Lust dwells as an internal tyrant, directing the entire course of their soul, is for there to be feasting and parties, celebrations and call-girls, and everything of that sort.'

'Yes, there's bound to be.'

'And each day and night countless unspeakable desires, with countless needs, spring up in addition, don't they?'

'Yes, countless.'

'Any source of income there may be is speedily exhausted.'

'Of course.'

e   'After that comes borrowing, and drawing on his capital.'

'Naturally.'

'And when it's all gone, isn't there bound to be an outcry from the dense mass of fledgling desires? When people are driven both by the stings of the other desires and in particular by Lust itself, which stands at the head of them all like a tyrant at the head of his bodyguard, aren't they bound to run amok, and start looking for anyone with anything which can be taken from them by deception or force?'

574   'They certainly are,' he said.

'They have no choice, then, but to help themselves to anything they can

---

[4] In myth and in poetry the irresistible power of love over men and gods is frequently acknowledged. Love also figures as a primeval and mighty power in some traditions and speculations concerning the origins of the cosmos.

lay their hands on, or else find themselves labouring in the grip of pain and agony.'

'No, they have no choice at all.'

'The behaviour of the tyrannical man himself is just like that of the pleasures within him, isn't it? They came along after the older pleasures, took over from them and usurped their enjoyment. Won't he, young as he is, make up his mind in the same way to take over from his father and mother and usurp what is theirs, awarding himself a share in his father's property now that he has spent what is his own?'

b   'Of course he will,' he said.

'If they refuse, won't his first resort be theft and fraud against his parents?'

'Absolutely.'

'And whenever he can't get away with that, won't his next step be to seize what he wants by force?'

'I imagine so.'

'Really? And if the old man and the old woman resist him, and put up a fight, how careful will he be to steer clear of anything tyrannical?'

'I wouldn't give much for his parents' chances,' he said, 'if they do resist him.'

'For god's sake, Adeimantus, are you saying that for something
c   inessential, like his latest mistress, someone like this would come to blows with his mother, dear to him all his life, his essential kin? And for an inessential such as his latest pretty boy, would he come to blows with his father, who is aged, past his prime, essential to him, and the oldest of those dear to him? And if he brought these people under the same roof, would he enslave his parents to them?'

'Heavens, yes.'

'Blessed are those, apparently, who produce a tyrannical son.'

'Blessed indeed,' he said.

d   'How about when his father's and mother's possessions start to run out, and the swarm of pleasures now accumulated within him has grown large? Won't someone like this turn his hand, initially, to a little gentle house-breaking, or to the cloak of some late traveller – and follow that up with a clean sweep of some temple? In all these exploits, his original childhood opinions about good and bad, opinions which are generally regarded as right, will be overwhelmed by those new opinions just released from slavery, which are the bodyguard of Lust, and act in company with it.
e   Previously, while he was still under the control of the laws and of his

father, and his mind was a democracy, they were set free only in sleep, as
dreams, but now that he is tyrannised by Lust, and has become per-
manently, in his waking life, that which he used to be only occasionally, in
his dreams, there will be no foul murder, no food, no deed, from which he
575 will abstain. Lust will dwell within him as a tyrant, in total anarchy and
lawlessness. As you'd expect of a sole ruler, it will lead its possessor, like
a tyrant leading a city, into every kind of outrage, as it attempts to provide
upkeep for itself and the mob surrounding it – some of them brought in
from outside, the result of the bad company the man keeps, others native
to him, released and liberated by the same bad habits in himself. Isn't that
an accurate picture of the life of the tyrannical man?'

'It is,' he said.

b   'If there are not many of them in a city, if most of the population is sensible, people like this emigrate. They become bodyguards to some foreign
tyrant, or serve as mercenaries, if they can find a war somewhere. But if
they arise at a time of peace and quiet, then they stay where they are, and
commit all sorts of minor crimes in the city.'

'What sort of crimes?'

'Theft, housebreaking, picking pockets, stealing clothes, robbing
temples, kidnapping. Malicious prosecution, perhaps, if they are persuasive speakers, perjury, accepting bribes.'

c   'Minor crimes? Only if the people committing them are few in
number.'

'No, they *are* minor,' I said. 'Minor crimes are defined with reference
to major crimes. And when it comes to the wretchedness and misery of
the city, none of these can hold a candle, as the saying goes, to the tyrant.[5]
When you get a large number of these people in a city, and others
following them, when they become aware of their own numbers, then it
is they, aided and abetted by the folly of the common people, who give
d   birth to the tyrant – that one who stands out among them as possessing
the greatest and most bloated tyrant in the soul within him.'

'Very probably,' he said. 'After all, he would be the most tyrannical.'

'That's assuming they submit to him willingly. If the city does not
prove compliant, then he will punish his country in its turn, if he can, in
the same way as he punished his mother and father earlier. He will bring
in new, foreign friends, and he will keep in slavery to them the fatherland

---

[5] That is, to the misery that a tyrant can inflict on his city. The saying in Greek is
archaic language for 'does not even hit close'.

– or motherland, as the Cretans call it – he once loved. That is how he will cherish it. And this would be the ultimate goal at which the tyrannical man's desire is directed.'

e 'It certainly is.'

'And what are they like as private individuals before they come to power? Shall I tell you? The company they keep, for a start. They either associate with people who flatter them, who are prepared to do anything
576 for them. Or if they want something from someone, they get down on their knees themselves, and have no hesitation in putting on a full show of being close friends. Once they've got what they want, then they are strangers.'

'Complete strangers.'

'Throughout their life, then, they are never friends with anybody. They are always one man's master and another man's slave. The tyrannical nature never gets a taste of freedom or true friendship.'

'Exactly.'

'Wouldn't we be right in calling people like this distrustful?'

'Of course we would.'

'Not to mention unjust – outstandingly unjust, if we were correct in
b our earlier conclusions about the kind of thing justice is.'

'Which we undoubtedly were,' he said.

'Let us sum up this worst of all men. He is, I take it, the waking embodiment of the kind of man we described as existing in dreams.'

'Precisely.'

'Anyone with a highly tyrannical nature who becomes sole ruler ends up like this. And the longer he spends in his tyranny, the more like this he becomes.'

'Inevitably,' said Glaucon, taking up the argument.

'Well, then, will whoever proves to be the most wicked prove also to be
c the most unhappy? And will be the one who is tyrant for the longest time, who is tyrant to the fullest extent, prove, if truth be told, the most unhappy, and for the longest time? Though mind you, for the general run of people, it's a question of everyone having their own opinion.'

'That *has* to be true, of course.'

'Isn't it the case that the tyrannical man corresponds to and resembles the city ruled by a tyrant?' I asked. 'And that the democratic man corresponds to the city ruled democratically? And the others likewise?'

'Yes, of course.'

'And is the comparison between man and man, when it comes to goodness and happiness, the same as the comparison between city and city?'

'Naturally.'

d   'In terms of goodness, then, what is the relation between a city ruled by a tyrant and a monarchy of the kind we described as the first of our regimes?'

'They are exact opposites,' he said. 'One is the best, the other is the worst.'

'I won't ask which is which, because it's obvious. But when it comes to happiness and unhappiness, is your verdict still the same, or different? And let's not dazzle ourselves by looking at one individual – the tyrant – or at some few who surround him. No, since the entire city is the proper

e   object of our journey and enquiry, let us not present our opinion to the world until we have burrowed our way right into the heart of the city, and viewed the whole thing.'

'That's a fair requirement,' he said. 'Anyone can see that there is no unhappier city than the one ruled by a tyrant, and no happier city than the one ruled by a king.'

577   'And would it be fair to impose the same requirement when it comes to the men as well, if I think that the best judge of these matters is the person who can mentally worm his way into a man's character, and take a long, hard look at it? He must not see it from the outside, like a child, and be dazzled by the display of grandeur which tyrants put on for outward show, but must look at it fairly and squarely. And if I were to think that we should all listen to the man who is qualified to form a judgment, who has lived under the same roof as a tyrant, who has been in a tyrant's company and seen his behaviour – both in his private life, the way he deals

b   with each member of his household, where he can best be seen stripped of his theatrical costume and props, and then again in public, when he is in danger – should we tell the person who has seen all this to give us his report on how the tyrant compares, in terms of happiness and unhappiness, with other people?'

'Yes, it would be absolutely correct to impose this requirement as well.'

'In which case,' I said, 'do you want us to pretend that *we* are among those who would be qualified to form a judgment, and who have met tyrants in the past? That would at least give us someone to answer our questions.'[6]

---

[6] It is usually assumed that Plato the dramatist and stage-director here pops his head from the wings to remind the audience that he was himself guest at a tyrant's palace in Sicily and eyewitness to his behaviour (see p. xxii of the introduction).

'Yes, please.'

c   'Can I ask you to go about it like this, then? Remembering the similarity between the city and the man, examine each of them in turn, point by point, and tell us how things are for each of them.'

'What sort of things?' he asked.

'Start with the city. Are you going to describe a city ruled by a tyrant as free or enslaved?'

'Enslaved. As enslaved as it is possible to be.'

'Though of course you can see masters and free men in it.'

'I can see a small element of that,' he said. 'Not much. But more or less the whole thing – and certainly the most decent element in it – is shamefully and miserably enslaved.'

d   'In which case,' I said, 'if the man is like the city, won't we inevitably find the same arrangement of elements in him as well? Won't we find his soul crammed with all sorts of slavery and servility, with those parts of his soul enslaved which used to be the most decent, and a small element, the most evil and insane, possessing the mastery?'

'Yes. Inevitably.'

'All right, then. What are you going to call a soul of this kind? Slave or free?'

'Slave, I guess. Well, that's my opinion, anyway.'

'And the slave city, the city ruled by a tyrant, is the one least able to do what it wants.'

'By far the least.'

e   'In which case, the soul which is ruled by a tyrant will also be least able to do what it wants – at any rate if we are talking about the entire soul. Despite itself, it will be forever driven onward by the gadfly of desire, and filled with confusion and dissatisfaction.'

'Of course it will.'

'And is it certain to be rich or certain to be poor, this city ruled by a tyrant?'

'Certain to be poor.'

578   'So the tyrannical soul too is certain always to be impoverished and insatiable.'

'True,' he said.

'What about fear? Aren't the tyrannical city and the tyrannical man bound to be full of it?'

'Yes. Bound to be. Inevitably.'

'Do you think there is any other city in which you will find more wailing, groaning, lamentation and grief?'

'No.'

'And in a man – do you think anyone possesses these qualities more abundantly than this tyrannical individual, maddened as he is by desires and lusts?'

'No, that's impossible,' he said.

b   'I'd imagine that one look at all these drawbacks, and others like them, would be enough to make you pronounce this city the unhappiest of cities.'

'And that's a correct verdict, isn't it?'

'Absolutely correct. But what about the tyrannical man, in his turn? Taking a look at these same drawbacks, what have you got to say about him?'

'I'd say he is by a long way the unhappiest of all.'

'Now, there,' I said, 'you are no longer correct.'

'How so?' he asked.

'The tyrannical man, I believe, is not yet the unhappiest.'

'Who is, then?'

'There is someone else you may think unhappier still.'

'Who?'

c   'The tyrannical man who does not live the life of a private individual, but is unfortunate enough to be given the opportunity, by some mischance, of actually *becoming* a tyrant.'

'From what we have said already, I take it you must be right.'

'Yes. All the same, claims like this should not be a matter of belief. We should use careful argument in examining an individual of this sort. After all, the object of our enquiry – the good life and the bad life – is of the highest importance.'

'Precisely,' he said.

d   'Ask yourself, in that case, whether I am right in my belief that when we are examining the tyrant, there is one particular example we should concentrate on.'

'What example is that?'

'The example presented in our cities by each and every one of those wealthy individuals who own a lot of slaves. What they have in common with tyrants is that they exercise control over a large number of people. Though there's a difference in the number the tyrant controls.'

'Yes, there is that difference.'

'You are aware, aren't you, that these rich people feel quite secure. They are not afraid of their slaves, are they?'

'No, of course not. What is there for them to be afraid of?'

'Nothing,' I said. 'And do you know why?'

'Yes. Because each one of these individuals has the support of the whole city.'

e   'Exactly. But suppose some god or other were to whisk one of these owners of fifty or more slaves away from the city, and put him down – the man himself, with his wife and children, together with all his property and slaves – in a deserted place where none of the free population could give him any help? Can you imagine the terrible fear he would feel for himself, his children and his wife – fear that they would all be killed by his slaves?'

'Every kind of fear, if you ask me.'

579 'Would he have any choice but to start flattering some of these same slaves, and making them all sorts of promises, and setting them free – quite gratuitously?[7] Wouldn't he reveal himself to be an appeaser of slaves?'

'He would have no choice at all,' he said. 'It would be that, or perish.'

'And suppose the god moves other people as well, and surrounds him with a whole lot of neighbours who cannot bear to see one man laying claim to mastery over another, and who will probably inflict the severest punishments on anyone they catch behaving in this way?'

b   'He would be in all kinds of trouble, I imagine – even more so than before – surrounded and besieged entirely by enemies.'

'So, then, isn't this the kind of prison in which the tyrant is chained? He has the nature we have described, full of many and varied fears and lusts. And greedy though his soul is, he is the only one living in the city who cannot go abroad anywhere, or go and see any of the things other free

c   men are so keen to see. He spends most of his life buried in his house, like a woman. He even envies the other citizens if one of them does go abroad and sees some fine sight.'

'Exactly,' he said.

'This, then, is the additional crop of evils reaped by that man whom you just now judged to be the unhappiest[8] – the one with a bad political regime established in him, the man with a tyrannical nature – if he stops living as a private citizen, is compelled by some misfortune to become tyrant, and tries, lacking any mastery over himself, to be ruler over others. It's like someone having some physical ailment which stops his body

---

[7] That is, not as a reward for faithful service.   [8] 578b.

d   being in control of itself, and yet not being allowed to live quietly at home,
but being required to spend his whole life in competition and conflict with
other bodies.'

'Yes, it's exactly like that,' he said. 'You are absolutely right, Socrates.'

'Isn't his situation utterly wretched, my dear Glaucon? And isn't there
an even harsher life than that of the person whose life you judged to be
the harshest, namely the life of such a person when he actually is a tyrant?'

'That's absolutely right.'

'The truth is, whatever some people may think, that the true tyrant is
e   a true slave – abjectly ingratiating and servile, and flatterer of the worst
people. If you know how to look at the entire soul, it is clear that he does
not satisfy his desires in the slightest, that he lives in the greatest need and
in true poverty. His whole life through, laden with fear, he is a mass of
uncontrollable pains and convulsions, if his condition is like the condition
of the city over which he rules. Which it is, isn't it?'

'Yes. Exactly like.'

580   'Shall we, on top of all this, award the man the qualities we mentioned
earlier?[9] We said he would inevitably – and increasingly, because of his
position – be envious, distrustful, unjust, friendless, impious, host and
nurse to all manner of evil. We said the effect of all these qualities was first
and foremost to make the man unhappy himself, and secondly to cause
unhappiness in those closest to him.'

'No one with any sense will argue with that,' he said.

b   'This is your moment, then,' I said. 'Your time has finally come. Like
the judge of the contest making the final decision. There are five con-
tenders: the kingly, the timocratic, the oligarchic, the democratic and the
tyrannical. In terms of happiness, which of them in your opinion comes
first? Which comes second, and so on with the other places?'[10]

'That's not a difficult decision. In terms of goodness and badness, and
happiness and its opposite, I will rank them like choruses; and my ranking
follows the order of their appearance.'

'Shall we hire a herald, then?' I asked. 'Or shall I announce the result

---

[9]   The qualities Socrates is about to list fit the earlier descriptions both of the tyrant in
Book 8 (565e, 567a–568a) and of the tyrannical character in Book 9 (573d–575a,
575e–576b).

[10] The metaphor is drawn from the ranking of plays in the dramatic competitions at
Athens – hence Glaucon's reference to choruses in his reply – but we do not know
enough about the method of judgment to understand what corresponded to the
'final' decision, or, in another meaning of the phrase, the 'overall' decision. The
results were announced by a public herald.

c   myself? "The verdict of the son of Ariston is this. The best and most just
character is the happiest. This is the one who is the most kingly, the one
who is king over himself. The worst and most unjust is the unhappiest,
and he is in fact the one with the most tyrannical nature, the one who is
the greatest tyrant over himself and his city."'

'Thank you,' he said. 'Let's take it that the announcement has been
made.'

'And shall I add a clause saying "whether or not they escape detection,
in the sight of all men and gods"?'

'Yes, do add that clause.'

d   'Very well,' I said, 'let that stand as one proof for us. Now, have a look
at this second proof, and see if you think it has any force.'

'What is the second proof?'

'Since the soul of each person was divided into three in exactly the
same way as the city was divided into three classes, I think it will provide
us with a second proof as well.'

'How does the proof go?'

'Like this. The three parts of the soul seem to me to have three forms
of pleasure, one for each individual part. Likewise three forms of desire,
and three forms of rule.'

'Can you explain that?'

'The first element, we say, is the one which allows a man to learn, the
second the part which allows him to act in a spirited way. To the third, on
e   account of its diversity, we found it impossible to give its own unique
name, so we gave it the name of its largest and strongest element. We
called it desiring – because of the strength of its desires for food, drink,
581 sex and everything that goes with these – and money-loving, because
money is the principal means of satisfying these desires.'[11]

'And we were right,' he said.

'So if we were to say that the thing it took pleasure and delight in was
profit, would that be our best way of concentrating our argument under
one general heading? Would that make it clear to ourselves what we mean
when we talk about this part of the soul? And if we were to call it money-
loving and profit-loving, would we be justified?'

'Well, *I* certainly think we would.'

'What about the spirited part? Can we say, by contrast, that *its* sole and
b   constant aim is power, victory and reputation?'

[11]   For the various roles and names assigned to the different elements of the soul see
Book 4, 435e–436a, 439d–e, and Book 8, 550a–b, 553c–d.

'Yes, we can.'

'So if we called it a lover of victory and a lover of honour, would that be appropriate?'

'Absolutely appropriate.'

'And of course it's obvious to anyone that the part we learn with is entirely and constantly intent upon knowing where the truth lies, and that of the three it is the least concerned with money and reputation.'

'Easily the least.'

'Would it be in order, then, for us to call it a lover of learning and a lover of wisdom?'[12]

'It would.'

c   'Very well,' I said. 'Is this the ruling element in some people's souls? And is one of the other two elements – it could be either – dominant in others?'

'Yes,' he said.

'Does this explain why we say that there are three fundamental human types: the lover of wisdom, the lover of victory and the lover of profit?'

'Of course.'

'And three classes of pleasures, one corresponding to each type?'

'Exactly.'

'You realise,' I said, 'that if you took the trouble to ask three people of this sort, one after another, which of these lives is the most pleasant, each

d   would sing the loudest praises of his own? Certainly the money-maker will say that, in comparison with profit, the pleasures of honour and learning are worthless, unless there is something in them which can make money.'

'True.'

'What about the lover of honour?' I asked. 'Doesn't he regard the pleasure which depends on money as sordid, and the pleasure which depends on learning – except to the extent that learning brings reputation – as a load of hot air?'

'He does.'

'As for the lover of wisdom, or philosopher,' I said, 'what view do we

e   imagine he takes of the other pleasures, compared with the pleasure of knowing where the truth lies and always enjoying some similar sort of pleasure while he is learning it? Won't he regard them as far inferior? And won't he call them truly necessary, or compulsory, since but for necessity he could get on perfectly well without them?'

---

[12] The word translated 'lover of wisdom' can also mean 'philosopher'.

'Yes,' he said, 'we can be confident this is his view.'

'When the pleasures, indeed the very life, of each human type are in dispute – a dispute not just about which is more beautiful or ugly, or
582 better or worse, but actually about which is more pleasant or painful – how can we tell which type is speaking most truly?'

'I can't begin to answer that question,' he said.

'Look at it like this. If things are going to be judged correctly, by what should they be judged? Isn't it by experience, reflection and reasoning? Or could someone come up with a better standard of judgment than these?'

'Of course not.'

'Now, think about it. Here are three men. Which of them has most experience of all the pleasures we have mentioned? Does the lover of profit learn about the nature of truth itself? Do you think he has more
b experience of the pleasure of knowledge than the lover of wisdom has of the pleasure of gain?'

'There's no comparison,' he said. 'The lover of wisdom is compelled to taste both pleasures right from his earliest years. The lover of profit, on the other hand, is not compelled to learn about the nature of things, or taste and experience the sweetness of this pleasure. Even if he really wanted to, he would find it difficult.'

'In which case,' I said, 'when it comes to experience of both sets of pleasures, the lover of wisdom has a great advantage over the lover of profit.'

'Yes, a great advantage.'

c 'And does he have an advantage over the lover of honour? Or does he have less experience of the pleasures of being respected than the lover of honour has of the pleasure of knowledge?'

'No,' he said. 'If they accomplish what each individually sets out to achieve, they all find that recognition follows. The rich man is widely respected. So is the courageous man, and so is the wise man. So they all experience the pleasure of being respected. They all know what it is like. But only the lover of wisdom, the philosopher, is in the position of having tasted the contemplation of what is, and the pleasure it brings.'

d 'On grounds of experience, then,' I said, 'he is the best judge out of these men.'

'Much the best.'

'What is more, won't he be the only one whose experience has been accompanied by reflection?'

'Of course.'

'And the instrument with which judgment should be made does not belong to the lover of profit or the lover of honour, but to the lover of wisdom.'

'What instrument is that?'

'We said judgment should be made using reasoned arguments, didn't we?'

'Yes.'

'And reasoning is essentially the instrument of the philosopher, the lover of wisdom.'

'Of course.'

e   'If wealth and profit were the best means of deciding questions, the truest recommendations or criticisms would necessarily be those of the lover of profit.'

'Necessarily.'

'And if honour and victory and courage were the best means, wouldn't the truest recommendations be those of the lover of honour or lover of victory?'

'Obviously.'

'But since experience, reflection and reasoning are the best means . . .'

'The truest recommendations will necessarily be those of the lover of wisdom and lover of reasoning.'

583   'Of these three pleasures, then, will the one belonging to the part of the soul with which we learn be the most enjoyable? And does the person in whom this part rules have the most enjoyable life?'

'How can he fail to?' he said. 'At the very least, he's certainly giving an expert opinion, the reflective man, when he recommends his own life.'

'Which life does our judge put in second place? And which pleasure?'

'The pleasure of the warlike lover of honour, obviously. It is closer to him than the pleasure of the money-maker.'

'So he puts the lover of profit's pleasure third, apparently.'

'Yes, of course,' he said.

b   'That's two wins out of two, then, for the just over the unjust. Now we come to the third round – the Olympic round, which is for Olympian Zeus the saviour.[13] If you think about pleasure, you can see that for anyone other than the wise, it is not true and pure, but a kind of shadow-picture.

---

[13] Drinking-parties maintained an established sequence of libations or toasts in honour of the gods, the third of which was to Olympian Zeus the saviour or preserver. Socrates is also alluding to the wrestling contest at the Olympic games – in wrestling, the third throw decided victory.

Or so I think I've been told by some expert.[14] Now if *that* were true, it would be the biggest and most important throw of the contest.'

'Easily the most important. But please explain why pleasure is a shadow-picture.'

c 'I can find the answer to that,' I said, 'if I ask the questions, and you answer them.'

'Start asking, then,' he said.

'And you start answering. Don't we say that pain is the opposite of pleasure?'

'We certainly do.'

'And that there is such a thing as feeling neither pleasure nor pain?'

'Yes.'

'Intermediate between those two, a kind of rest or respite for the soul from pain and pleasure? Or isn't that how you would describe it?'

'That *is* how I would describe it,' he said.

'Think of the things people who are ill say at times when they are ill.'

'What sort of things?'

'That there is no greater pleasure than good health, but that they
d hadn't realised it was the greatest pleasure until they were ill.'

'Yes, I do remember hearing people say that,' he said.

'And have you heard people in the grip of some agonising pain saying that there is no pleasure to compare with relief from agony?'

'Yes, I've heard that.'

'I expect you can think of plenty of similar painful situations people find themselves in, where the pleasure they praise most highly is the absence of pain – a rest from pain – rather than any enjoyment.'

'Yes. At times like that maybe rest becomes something pleasant and delightful.'

e 'So too, when someone stops feeling enjoyment, the rest from pleasure will be painful.'

'Possibly,' he said.

'In which case, this thing we described just now as intermediate between the two, this rest or respite, will at one time or another be both those things – both pain and pleasure.'

'Apparently.'

'Is it really possible for something which is neither of those things to come to be both of them?'

[14] Which expert, if indeed any, we cannot tell. 'Shadow-painting' was a technique for achieving the illusion of depth in two dimensions.

'I don't think so.'

'Besides, when pleasure and pain arise in the soul, they are both a kind of motion or agitation, aren't they?'

'Yes.'

584   'But hasn't what is neither painful nor pleasurable just been shown to be a rest or respite, occupying a position midway between the two?'

'It has.'

'How can it be right, then, to regard the absence of pain as something pleasant, or the absence of pleasure as something painful?'

'It can't.'

'So it's not that this rest or respite *is* pleasant. It *seems* pleasant beside what is painful, and painful beside what is pleasant. As far as the truth about pleasure goes, there is nothing sound or reliable in these illusions. It's all sorcery.'

'That's what the argument suggests, at any rate,' he said.

b   'Well, take a look at pleasures which are not preceded by pain,' I said. 'I wouldn't want you to think, in this context, that it is the nature of pleasure simply to be the cessation of pain, and of pain simply to be the cessation of pleasure.'

'What sort of pleasures do you mean? Where are they?'

'There are any number of them,' I said, 'but you might like to think particularly about the pleasures of smell. You don't have to have felt pain beforehand. They come out of the blue. They are incredibly powerful. And when they are over, they leave no pain behind.'

c   'Absolutely true.'

'We shouldn't accept, then, that pure pleasure is a release from pain, or pain a release from pleasure.'

'No, we shouldn't.'

'However, of the so-called pleasures which reach the soul through the body, surely the most numerous and powerful are of this type – some sort of relief from pain.'

'Yes, they are.'

'Very well. And are anticipated pleasures and pains caused by the expectation of some future relief from pain or pleasure, of the same nature?'

'They are.'

d   'Do you know what sort of thing these pleasures and pains are, then,' I asked, 'and what they most resemble?'

'What?'

'Do you believe that there is in nature a top, a bottom and something in between?'

'Yes, I do.'

'Don't you think if someone were taken from the bottom to the middle, he'd be bound to think he was travelling to the top? And standing in the middle, looking back at where he'd come from, wouldn't he be bound to think he was at the top, if he hadn't seen the real top?'

'If you ask me,' he said 'that's exactly what someone would think in that situation.'

e   'And if he were taken back again,' I asked, 'would he think – and think rightly – that he was travelling to the bottom?'

'Of course he would.'

'Would the cause of all this be his not having experienced the true range of top, middle and bottom?'

'Obviously.'

'In which case, would it surprise you to find that people with no knowledge of truth are the same? They have unsound opinions on all sorts of subjects, and their condition, when it comes to pleasure, pain, and what
585 is in between, is such that when they move in the direction of what is painful their supposition is true – they really *are* in pain – but when they move from pain to what is in between, they are firmly convinced they have reached fulfilment and pleasure. It's like comparing black and grey when you have no knowledge of white. Lacking any knowledge of pleasure, they compare the absence of pain with pain, and come to the wrong conclusion.'

'Would it surprise me?' he said. 'Good heavens, no. It would surprise me much more if it *weren't* like that.'

b   'Think of it like this,' I said. 'Aren't hunger and thirst, and things like that, a kind of emptiness – an empty condition of the body?'

'Yes, of course they are.'

'Aren't ignorance and stupidity likewise an empty condition of the soul?'

'They certainly are.'

'And how are people filled? By taking in food? By gaining understanding?'

'Of course.'

'Which gives the truer fulfilment, that which is more something or that which is less something?'[15]

---

[15] The ambiguity of the phrase 'to be something' is explained in the note 39 to 476e above.

'Obviously that which is more something.'

'Which kinds of thing, then, do you think have a greater share in pure being? Things like bread, drink, cooked food, and nourishment in general? Or the kind made up of opinion, knowledge, understanding and in fact the whole of human excellence? The choice you have to make is this. Which do you think is more something? That which is connected with what is always the same, immortal and true – itself possessing these qualities, and being found in the context of things with these qualities? Or that which is connected with what is never the same, and mortal – itself possessing those qualities, and being found in the context of things with those qualities?'

'That which is connected with what is always the same is far superior,' he said.

'Well, does anything have a greater share in the being of what is always the same than knowledge does?'[16]

'No.'

'Does anything have a greater share in truth than knowledge does?'

'Again, no.'

'And if anything has a smaller share in truth, doesn't it also have a smaller share in being?'

'Necessarily.'

'As a general rule, then, will the kinds of things involved in care of the body have a smaller share both of truth and of being than the kinds involved in care of the soul?'

'Much smaller.'

'And don't you think the body itself has a smaller share than the soul has?'

'Yes, I do.'

'Very well. Is what is filled with things which have more being, and itself has more being, more genuinely filled than what is filled with things which have less being, and itself has less being?'

'Of course.'

---

[16] The Greek text of the sentence transmitted in the manuscripts at this point has long been acknowledged to make little sense as it stands. In its place we are using a text emended by the editor of this translation. The transmitted text of this and the following sentences would be translated: 'Does the being of what is always the same have any greater share in being than it does in knowledge?' 'No.' 'Or any greater share in being than it does in truth?' 'Again, no.' 'And if it had a smaller share in truth, wouldn't it also have a smaller share in being?' The emended text that we are using at 585c7–8 is: ἢ οὖν ἀεὶ ὁμοίου οὐσίας τι μᾶλλον ἐπιστήμης (or ἢ ἐπιστήμη) μετέχει;

'So if being filled with things appropriate to our nature is pleasurable, then that which is more genuinely filled, and filled with things which have
e more being, would make people more truly and genuinely happy, giving them true pleasure, whereas that which takes in things which have less being would be less truly and lastingly filled, and get hold of a pleasure which was less trustworthy and less true.'

'That inescapably follows,' he said.

586   'In which case, those who know nothing of wisdom and human excellence, who are always engaged in things like feasting, apparently go down to the region at the bottom and back again to the middle. They spend their whole lives wandering in this way. Higher than this they never go. They never look up at the true top, nor go there. They are not truly filled with true being, nor do they taste any lasting or pure pleasure. They are like cattle, their gaze constantly directed downwards. Eyes on the
b ground – or on the table – they fatten themselves at pasture, and rut. The struggle for these things makes them kick and butt – with horn and hoof of iron – until they kill one another. But they cannot be filled, since they do not fill the part of them which truly is, the retentive part, nor do they fill themselves *with* what truly is.'

'Hear the words of the oracle,' said Glaucon. 'You have given us a full and complete description, Socrates, of the life most people lead.'

'Aren't they bound to live among pleasures mingled with pains, images of the true pleasure and shadow paintings, in which both the pleasure and
c the pain take their colour from their proximity to one another? This is why they appear so strong, why they breed insane passions in the foolish, for the pleasure they offer, and why they are fought over as Stesichorus says the image of Helen was fought over by those at Troy, in their ignorance of the truth.'

'Yes,' he said, 'they are bound to be pretty much like that.'

'What about the spirited part of the soul? Aren't the same sorts of things bound to happen to anyone who concentrates on that? Love of
d honour leads to envy, love of victory to violence, and bad temper to anger. Without reason or understanding, he sets out in pursuit of his full measure of success, or victory, or anger.'

'Yes,' he said, 'the spirited part too is bound to be as you describe.'

'What is the conclusion, then?' I asked. 'Can we say one thing with confidence? That when it comes to those parts of the soul which love profit or victory, if the desires associated with them follow knowledge and rational thought, and with these as their guides pursue and capture the

pleasures wisdom prescribes, then, since they are following the truth, they
e will gain pleasures which are both the truest – or the truest possible for
them – and also their own, if what is best for each thing is also what is
most its own.'

'Which it unquestionably is.'

'If the entire soul, then, follows without rebellion the part which loves
wisdom, the result is that each part can in general carry out its own
587 functions – can be just, in other words – and in particular each is able to
enjoy pleasures which are its own, the best, and as far as possible the
truest.'

'Absolutely.'

'When one of the other parts takes control, there are two results: it fails
to discover its own proper pleasure, and it compels the other parts to
pursue a pleasure which is not their own, and not true.'

'That's right,' he said.

'Would this result be most noticeable with those elements which are
furthest removed from philosophy and reason?'

'Yes. Easily the most.'

'And isn't the element furthest removed from reason the one which is
furthest removed from law and order?'

b 'Obviously.'

'Wasn't it the lustful and tyrannical desires which were clearly revealed
to be the furthest removed?'

'Much the furthest.'

'And the kingly and orderly desires which were the least far removed?'
'Yes.'

'In which case, I imagine, the tyrant will be furthest removed from true
pleasure – his own proper pleasure – while the king will be least far
removed.'

'Bound to be.'

'So the most unpleasant life,' I said, 'will be the tyrant's, and the most
pleasant will be the king's.'

'Absolutely bound to be.'

'Do you know *how much* more unpleasant the tyrant's life is than the
king's?'

'Not unless you tell me,' he said.

'It seems there are three pleasures – one legitimate and two illegitimate.
c In his flight from law and reason, the tyrant has gone to the farthest limits
of the illegitimate, and now dwells with a bodyguard of slavish pleasures.

It is hard to say precisely how much worse off he is, but perhaps there is a way we can get at it.'

'What way is that?' he asked.

'The tyrant was in one sense at the third remove from the oligarchic man, since the man of the people came in between them.'

'Yes.'

'In terms of truth, then, assuming our earlier conclusions are sound, will he live with an image of pleasure at the third remove from the oligarchic man's image?'

'He will.'

d   'But the oligarchic man in his turn is at the third remove from the kingly man, if we put the aristocratic and kingly into the same category.'

'Yes, the third remove.'

'Numerically, then, the tyrant is three times three removes from true pleasure.'[17]

'So it seems.'

'And as for the total length of this distance,' I said, 'it looks as if the image of the tyrant's pleasure is a plane number.'

'Just so.'

'And by squaring and cubing it becomes clear how far removed the tyrant is.'

'Clear enough,' he said, 'to anyone who can do the arithmetic.'

e   'Conversely, if you are talking about how far removed the king is from the tyrant, in terms of true pleasure, you will find, when you complete the multiplication, that his life is nine- and twenty- and seven hundred-fold more pleasurable, and that a tyrant is more wretched by the same amount.'[18]

'What a horrendous piece of arithmetic,' he said. 'A real deluge. And is

588   that the difference between the two men – the just and the unjust – when it comes to pleasure and pain?'

'Yes, and not only is this the true answer, but it is also appropriate to human life – if days and nights and months and years are appropriate.'[19]

'Which they certainly are,' he said.

'And if the good and just man is so far ahead of the bad and unjust in

---

[17] Socrates is counting the oligarchic man twice, as the last in the series aristocrat, timo-crat, oligarch, and the first in the series oligarch, democrat, tyrant.

[18] 729 is 9×9×9. But it is unclear why Socrates does not rest content with 9 as the multiple of the tyrant's distance from true pleasure.

[19] Presumably because the year was thought to contain 364.5 days and the same number of nights, which together add up to 729.

terms of pleasure, won't he be an unbelievable distance ahead of him in the grace, beauty and excellence of his life?'

'Heavens, yes. An unbelievable distance.'

b   'Very well,' I said. 'Having got this far in the argument, let's go back to the original claim which brought us to this point. The claim was, I think, that for anyone who was completely unjust, but had a reputation for justice, injustice was profitable. Wasn't that the claim?'[20]

'It was.'

'Well, this seems a good moment to talk it over with the person who made the claim, now that we have reached agreement on unjust and just behaviour, and the value of each.'

'How shall we do that?' he asked.

'Let's imagine we are sculpting a model of the soul, to show the person who made the claim what it was he was claiming.'

c   'What sort of model?'

'One of those creatures the ancient stories tell us used to exist. The Chimaera, or Scylla, or Cerberus, or any of the other creatures which are said to be formed by a number of species growing into one.'

'Yes, I know the stories,' he said.

'Start with a single species, then. A complex, many-headed beast, with a ring of animal heads – some gentle, some fierce – which it can vary and produce out of itself.'

d   'It sounds like a job for a skilled sculptor,' he said. 'Still, words are easier to shape than wax and things like that, so consider the model made.'

'For your second single species, make a lion. And for your third, a man. And let the first creature be much the biggest, followed by the second.'

'That's easier,' he said. 'Look, they are made.'

'Now join the three of them into one, so that they've grown into one another in some way.'

'There they are,' he said. 'Joined.'

'Enclose them in the external appearance of one of the creatures – that
e of the human being – so that to those who see only the outer shell, and can't see the inside, it looks like a single living creature. Like a human being, in fact.'

'They are enclosed,' he said.

'Good. When someone claims it pays this human being to be unjust, and that it is not good for him to behave justly, let's tell him it amounts to

---

[20] 360c–d, 361a–362c.

saying that it pays him to fatten up the many-headed creature, and let it
589 grow in strength – along with the lion and everything to do with the lion.
That it pays him to starve and weaken the human being, so that it can be
dragged wherever either of the others chooses to take it. And that it pays
him to leave the two of them to themselves, allowing them to fight among
themselves, biting one another and eating one another, rather than getting
them used to one another or making them friends with one another.'

'Yes,' he said, 'that's exactly what the person who recommends injustice is saying.'

'If someone says justice pays, on the other hand, wouldn't he be saying
that the aim of speech and action should be to give the inner human
b complete control over a person, and get him to be like a farmer in the way
he tends the many-headed creature, feeding and domesticating the gentle
animals, and not allowing the fierce ones to grow? He should make the
lion's nature his ally, have a common care for all and tend all, making them
friends with one another and with himself.'

'Yes, that's certainly what the person who recommends justice, in his
turn, is saying.'

'However we look at it, then, what the person who praises justice says
would be true, and what the person who praises injustice says would be
c false. By the standard of pleasure, or of reputation, or benefit, the sup-
porter of justice is right, and the criticism of the critic is unsound and
based on ignorance.'

'Complete ignorance, if you ask me.'

'Should we reason gently with him, then? After all, he's not getting it
wrong on purpose. We could ask him: "Look at it this way, if you'd be so
good. Couldn't we say also that conventional views of what is shameful
d and what is praiseworthy have this as their basis? Praiseworthy actions are
what bring the savage elements of our nature under the control of the
human – or rather, perhaps, of the divine – while shameful actions are
what makes the gentle element a slave to the fierce." Will he agree with
that? Or what?'

'He will if he takes my advice,' he said.

'Is there anyone, then, on this argument, who profits by taking money
unjustly, if all that happens is that by taking the money he makes the best
e part of him a slave to the worst part? If taking it would make one of his
sons or daughters a slave – and a slave to dangerous and evil men, at that
– even an enormous sum of money would not, on these terms, profit him
in the slightest. So if he shows no mercy to the most divine part of

himself, and makes it the slave of the part which is most ungodly and
590 polluted, is he not an object of pity? Isn't his reward for taking bribes a
far worse fate than that of Eriphyle, when she accepted the necklace at the
price of her husband's soul?'

'Yes, far worse,' Glaucon replied. 'I'll answer for him, if you like.'

'And do you think the reason why lack of discipline has always been
regarded as a fault is that it gives that terrible creature, the great beast
with many heads, too much freedom?'

'Obviously,' he said.

b   'And the vices we call obstinacy and bad temper – aren't they caused
by the lion-like or snake-like[21] part straining or waxing beyond measure?'

'Absolutely.'

'And luxury and timidity? Aren't they the vices arising out of atrophy
and slackness of this same element, introducing cowardice into it?'

'Of course.'

'Aren't flattery and meanness of spirit the result of subjecting this same
spirited element to the mob-like beast? In their desire for money and the
constant satisfaction of the beast's needs, don't people allow the spirited
element to get used to being trampled on, right from their childhood, so
that it turns into a monkey instead of a lion?'[22]

'Absolutely,' he said.

c   'Why do you think someone is looked down on for engaging in menial
tasks, or working with his hands? Isn't the reason just this? The best
element in him is naturally weak, and so he is unable to control the creatures within him, but instead becomes their servant. All he can do is learn
how to appease them.'

'Apparently.'

'So if we want someone like this to be under the same kind of rule as
d the best person, we say he must be the slave of that best person, don't we,
since the best person has the divine ruler within him? And when we say
he needs to be ruled, it's not that we mean any harm to the slave, which
was Thrasymachus' view of being ruled.[23] It's just that it's better for
everyone to be ruled by what is divine and wise. Ideally he will have his
own divine and wise element within himself, but failing that it will be

---

[21] Snakes in Greek religion were fierce guardians of sacred places. This in combination
with their deviousness and associations with secret zones below the earth makes
them a darker counterpart of the lion.

[22] Small monkeys were kept as pets. They were regarded as comically ugly, and also as
devious.   [23] 343b–c.

imposed on him from outside, so that as far as possible we may all be
equal, and all friends, since we are all under the guidance of the same commander.'

'Yes, that is what we say. And rightly.'

e   'It is clearly the aim,' I said, 'both of the law, which is the ally of all the
inhabitants of the city, and of our own governance of our children. We
591 don't allow them to be free until we have established a regime in them, as
in a city. We use what is best in us to care for what is best in the child, and
we give him a guardian and ruler similar to our own, to take our place.
Only then do we give him his freedom.'

'Yes,' he said, 'that clearly *is* the aim.'

'How, in that case, Glaucon – by what standard of judgment – can we
claim that it pays to be unjust or undisciplined, or to behave badly? To do
things that degrade a person, even though they may give him more money
or power of some other sort?'

'There is no way we can make that claim.'

'How can we say, either, that it pays to get away with injustice and go
b unpunished? Doesn't the person who gets away with it become even more
depraved, whereas in the person who *doesn't* get away with it, and who *is*
punished, the savage element is tamed and put to sleep, the gentle part is
set free, and the entire soul turns in the direction of its best nature? In
acquiring self-discipline and justice together with wisdom, it attains a
more precious state – in exact proportion as the soul is more precious than
the body – than the body does when it gains strength and beauty together
with good health.'

'Absolutely,' he said.

c   'Isn't this, then, what anyone with any sense will concentrate all his
lifetime's efforts on? In the first place, won't he value the learning which
will bring his soul into this condition, and reject other kinds of learning?'

'Obviously.'

'Secondly, as regards the condition and care of his body, it will be out
of the question for him to entrust it to savage and unreasoning pleasure,
and spend his life in that state. He won't even make health his aim, or take
d any thought for being strong, healthy or good-looking, unless these things
will give him self-discipline. As he tunes the harmony in his body, it is
clear that what he has in mind will always be the concord in his soul.'

'It certainly will,' he said. 'If he wants to be truly musical, that is.'

'And will he observe the same order and concord in the acquisition
of money? He won't be dazzled, will he, by what the many regard as

happiness, and gain himself evils without number by amassing a huge quantity of money?'

'No, I don't think he will do that,' he said.

e   'He will concentrate instead on the regime within him, and keep watch over that, being careful not to disturb any of the elements in it either by too much wealth or by too little. This is the star he will follow, to the best of his ability, in adding to his store of wealth or spending from it.'

'Naturally.'

592   'Similarly when it comes to honours, he will keep the same end in view. Some he will share in and taste of willingly – the ones he thinks will make him a better person. But he will avoid, both in his private life and in public life, the ones he thinks will upset the established condition of his soul.'

'He certainly won't be prepared to go into politics, then, if those are his priorities.'

'Ye dogs!' I said.[24] 'He'll be quite prepared to go into politics – in the city which is his own. But in his native country, barring some heaven-sent piece of good fortune, perhaps not.'

'I see,' he said. 'You mean in the city we have just been founding and
b   describing, our hypothetical city, since I don't think it exists anywhere on earth.'

'No, though there may perhaps be a pattern or model laid up in heaven somewhere, for anyone who chooses to see it – and seeing it, chooses to found a city within himself. It makes no difference whether it exists anywhere, or ever will. It, and no other, is the only city whose politics he would engage in.'

'Very likely,' he said.

[24] For this characteristically Socratic oath see note 50 to 399e above.

Book 10

595 'There are many reasons,' I said, 'why I feel sure we have gone about founding our city in the right way, but I am thinking particularly of poetry.'

'What in particular about poetry?'

'Our refusal to accept any of the imitative part of it. Now that we have
b distinguished the elements of the soul from one another, it is clearer than ever, in my view, that imitative poetry is the last thing we should allow.'

'Why do you say that?'

'Between ourselves – I'm sure you won't denounce me to the writers of tragedy and all the other imitative poets – everything of that sort seems to me to be a destructive influence on the minds of those who hear it. Unless of course they have the antidote, the knowledge of what it really is.'

'What do you have in mind when you say that?'

'I'd better explain,' I said, 'though the affection and respect I have had
c for Homer since I was a child makes me very reluctant to say it. He seems to me to have been the original teacher and guide of all these wonderful tragedians of ours. All the same, no man is worth more than the truth. So as I say, I had better explain myself.'

'You certainly had.'

'Listen, then. Or rather, answer.'

'Ask away.'

'Can you give me any idea what exactly this thing "imitation" is? Speaking for myself, I don't really understand what it aims to be.'

'In which case, of course I'm *bound* to understand it.'

596   'That wouldn't be so very unusual,' I said. 'People who don't see well are often quicker to see things than people whose eyesight is better.'

'That's true,' he said. 'But even if something does occur to me, I'm not going to summon up much enthusiasm for saying so with you here. You'd better rely on your own eyes.'

'Very well. Would you like us to follow our usual procedure in starting the enquiry? We generally postulate a certain form or character – a single form or character, always – for each plurality of things to which we give the same name.[1] Do you follow that?'

'Yes, I do follow it.'

'In which case, let's take any plurality you care to name. For example,
b I take it there are many couches, if you like, and many tables.'

'Of course.'

'But when it comes to forms for these pieces of furniture, there are presumably two. A single form of a couch, and a single form of a table.'

'Yes.'

'Don't we usually say also that for each type of furniture the person who makes it looks at the appropriate form? Then one will make the couches we use, another will make the tables, and so on with other kinds
c of furniture. But the form itself is presumably not the work of any of the craftsmen. How could it be?'

'It couldn't.'

'Now, turn your attention to a maker of a different kind. What name are you going to give him?'

'What kind of maker is that?'

'The kind who can create all the objects which the individual craftsmen can create.'

'It's a clever man you're talking about. Remarkably clever.'

'Wait till you hear the rest of it. This same craftsman is not only capable of making any sort of furniture. He can also create all the things that grow out of the earth. He produces all living creatures – including himself – and on top of that produces heaven and earth, the gods, everything in heaven, and everything under the earth in Hades.'

d   'A complete and astonishing genius, you mean.'

'Don't you believe me?' I said. 'Tell me this. Do you think it's altogether impossible for there to be a craftsman of this kind? Or do you think

---

[1] Compare 476a–c, 507b. The sentence could also be translated: 'We typically postulate a certain form or character – a single form or character, always – whenever we find ourselves applying the same name to a plurality of things.'

that in one way there *could* be a creator of all these things, though in another way there couldn't? Can't you see that there is a way in which you would be capable of creating all these things for yourself?'

'What way is that?'

'There's nothing very difficult about it,' I said. 'This kind of work-manship is often – and easily – practised. I suppose the quickest way is if you care to take a mirror and carry it around with you wherever you go.
e That way you'll soon create the sun and the heavenly bodies, soon create the earth, soon create yourself, other living creatures, furniture, plants, and all the things we've just been talking about.'

'Yes,' he said. 'I could create them as they appear to be. But not, I take it, as they truly are.'

'Good. That's exactly the point. Isn't that just the kind of craftsman a painter is?'

'Indeed it is.'

'Of course you can say the things he creates are not real. Yet there *is* a sense in which the painter does create a couch, isn't there?'

'Yes. The painter too creates a couch as it appears to be.'

597   'What about the carpenter who makes a couch? Didn't you just say he creates a particular couch, but not the form or character which we say is what a couch is?'

'Yes, I did.'

'Then if he does not create what a couch is, he can't be creating the real thing. Something *like* the real thing, but not itself the real thing. So if you were to say that it fully is – this thing made by a carpenter who makes couches, or by any other craftsman – you probably wouldn't be telling the truth.'

'No. Or not in the opinion of those who occupy themselves with argu-ments of this sort, at any rate.'

'In which case, let's not find it at all surprising if the carpenter's couch,
b too, is in fact rather shadowy by comparison with truth.'

'No, we shouldn't find that surprising.'

'Now,' I said, 'this imitator of ours. When we ask our question "Who exactly is he," would you like us to use the same examples?'

'Yes, if you like.'

'Very well. We have these three sorts of couch. There's the one which exists in the natural order of things. This one, I imagine we'd say, was the work of a god. Or would we say someone else?'

'No, I don't think we would.'

'Then there's the one made by the carpenter.'

'Yes,' he said.

'And then the one made by the painter, isn't there?'

'Let's take it there is.'

'Painter, carpenter, god, then. Three agents responsible for three kinds of couch.'

c   'Yes, three.'

'Now, either from choice or because there was some necessity for him not to produce more than one couch in the natural order of things, god has made only this one couch – what a couch is, just that. Two, or more than two, of these were never brought forth by god, nor could they be.'

'Why not?'

'Because if he made even two, then another would make an appearance in its turn – the one whose form both the others possessed. And this one would be what a couch is, rather than the two.'

'Correct,' he said.

d   'God was aware of this, I imagine, and wanted to be the true creator of the true couch. Not just any old maker of any old couch. That's why he gave it an essentially unique nature.'

'Probably.'

'So do you want us to call him its natural creator, or something of that sort?'

'We'd certainly be justified in calling him that, given that he has created both this and everything else in its essential nature.'[2]

'What about the carpenter? Shouldn't we call him a craftsman who makes couches?'

'Yes, we should.'

'And the painter? Is he too a craftsman and creator of such things?'

'Certainly not.'

'What are you going to say he does to a couch, then?'

e   'I think the most reasonable description would be to say that he is an imitator of what those craftsmen make.'

'Very well,' I said. 'So you call "imitator" the maker of the product which is two removes from nature, do you?'

'I do indeed,' he said.

'In that case, this is what the writer of tragedies, if he is an imitator, will

---

2 The phrase could also mean 'given that it is by means of nature that he has created both this and everything else [i.e. everything else that he has made]'.

be. Someone whose nature it is to be two removes from the king and the truth.[3] And the same with all other imitators.'

'It looks like it.'

'So, we are in agreement about the imitator. Now, tell me something
598 about the painter. Do you think, in each case, he is trying to imitate the thing itself, the one which exists in the natural order of things? Or is he trying to imitate the work of craftsmen?'

'He is trying to imitate the work of craftsmen,' he said.

'As it is? Or as it appears to be? Can you make your definition a little more precise?'

'What do you mean?'

'I mean this. When you look at a couch from the side or from the front, or from anywhere else, does the couch itself change? Or does it stay the same, and merely look different? And the same with other things.'

b   'Yes, that's how it is,' he said. 'It looks different, but it's really the same.'

'Well, that's the point of my question. In each individual case, what is the object of painting? Does it aim to imitate what is, as it is? Or imitate what appears, as it appears? Is it imitation of appearance, or of truth?'

'Of appearance,' he said.

'In that case, I would imagine, the art of imitation is a far cry from truth. The reason it can make everything, apparently, is that it grasps just a little of each thing – and only an image at that. We say the painter can
c   paint us a shoemaker, for example, or a carpenter, or any of the other craftsmen. He may know nothing of any of these skills, and yet, if he is a good painter, from a distance his picture of a carpenter can fool children and people with no judgment, because it looks like a real carpenter.'

'Of course it can.'

'I suppose the thing we have to remember in all these cases is this. When someone tells us, in any particular context, that he has met a man
d   who has knowledge of all these crafts, and of all the things each individual practitioner of them can know, and that this man's knowledge is in every respect more accurate than anyone else's, the answer we should give someone like this is that he is some sort of simpleton, who has apparently come across a magician and imitator, and been taken in by him. He has decided this man is an expert, because he himself is incapable of distinguishing knowledge from ignorance or imitation.'

---

[3] An obscure phrase. The 'king' is presumably the god who created what a couch is – the true couch, the real thing.

'Absolutely true.'

'Very well,' I said. 'Now, our next question concerns both tragedy and
e its mentor Homer. It arises out of the claim that the tragedians know
about all the arts, that they know about everything human – as it relates
to virtue and vice – and everything divine as well.[4] The good poet, they
say, if he is to do a good job of creating the things he does create, must
necessarily create them with knowledge. He could not create it otherwise.
So the questions we have to ask are these. Are the people they have come
599 across imitators? Have they been deceived by them? Don't they realise,
when they look at their works, that these are two removes from the real
thing, and easy for someone who does not know the truth to create? After
all, it is appearances, not realities, they are creating. Or is there some truth
in what these people say? Do good poets really have knowledge of the
things the general public thinks they write so well about?'

'Yes,' he said. 'Those *are* the questions we have to ask.'

'Do you think, then, assuming someone had the ability to create both
things – the object of the imitation *and* its image – that he would allow
b himself to show any enthusiasm for the production of images? Would he
make this his chief aim in life, his proudest possession?'

'No, I'm sure he wouldn't.'

'If he really knew about the things he imitates, I imagine, he'd be much
keener on action than on imitation of it. He'd try to leave many fine
actions as memorials to himself, and be much more interested in having
poetry written in honour of him than in writing poetry in honour of
others.'

'I'm sure he would. In terms of prestige and benefit, there's no comparison.'

'Very well, then. For most subjects, we needn't ask Homer or any of the
c other poets to justify himself. We needn't ask if any of them has any
medical knowledge, rather than just being an imitator of medical language. Or which patient any poet, old or new, is ever said to have made
healthy, in the way Asclepius did. Or what students of medicine he left
behind him, as Asclepius left his descendants. Nor need we ask the poets
about most of the arts. We can forget about them. But when it comes to
d the greatest and finest of the things Homer tries to tell us about – war,
military command, the founding of cities, a man's education – then I

---

[4] Greek culture lacked a canonical religious text, and literature performed some of the
functions – inspirational, edifying, instructive, exemplary – for which Christians
would look to the Bible.

think we *are* entitled to be curious. "My dear Homer," we can say to him, "if you are not two removes from truth in this matter of goodness – not a maker of images, what we defined as an imitator – if you are even at one remove from truth, and if you were capable of distinguishing the behaviour which makes men better or worse in private life or in public life, then tell us which city has ever been better governed because of you.

e Sparta is better governed because of Lycurgus, and so are many other cities, great and small, because of many other individuals. What about you? Which city says that *you* are its great lawgiver, or attributes its success to you? Italy and Sicily say it is Charondas. We say it is Solon. Which city says it is you?" Will he be able to name a city?'

'No, I don't think so,' said Glaucon. 'Even Homer's most devoted supporters don't make that claim.'[5]

600 'Is any war in Homer's day recorded as having been won by his leadership or strategy?'

'No.'

'Do we find a number of ingenious contributions to the arts, or other human activities, attributed to him? That's what you'd expect to find in the life of a wise man. The kind of thing we are told about Thales of Miletus, for example. Or Anacharsis the Scythian.'

'No, absolutely nothing of that sort.'

'Well then, in his private life, if not in public life? Does Homer have the reputation of being a formative influence on people during his lifetime?

b Did they love him for his company, and hand down some "Homeric" way of life to their successors? Take Pythagoras. Not only was Pythagoras himself very much loved for this reason, but even to this day his successors call their way of life "Pythagorean," and can be easily identified as Pythagoreans.'

'No,' he said, 'there's nothing of that kind told about him either. As far as education and culture go, Socrates, Homer's disciple Creophylus might well strike us as even more absurd than his name, if the stories about Homer are true. It is said that Creophylus showed not the slightest

c interest in the man himself when he was alive.'

'Yes, I've heard that story,' I said. 'But if Homer really had been able to educate men and make them better, Glaucon – because he had knowledge of these things, and not just the ability to imitate them – do you think he could have failed to gain himself a lot of disciples, and be respected and

---

[5] 'Homer's supporters' (the 'Homerids') seem to have been a guild dedicated to preserving the tradition of Homeric poetry and promoting its performance.

loved by them? Think of Protagoras of Abdera, Prodicus of Ceos, and any
number of others. They have this ability to persuade any of their con-
d temporaries who takes private lessons from them that he will not be
capable of managing either his own household or his own city unless they
themselves take charge of his education. So greatly are they loved for this
wisdom that their disciples all but carry them around on their shoulders.
If Homer had been capable of helping men on the path towards goodness,
would his contemporaries have allowed him and Hesiod to roam the
world giving recitations?[6] Wouldn't they have grabbed hold of them
e as something more valuable than gold, and compelled them to come home
and live with them? And if they couldn't persuade them, wouldn't they
themselves have acted as their attendants wherever they went, until they
had completed their education?'

'I think you're absolutely right, Socrates,' he said.

'In that case, shall we say that all artists, starting with Homer, are imitators of images of goodness and the other things they create, without
having any grasp of the truth?[7] As we've just been saying, the painter will
601 create what *looks* like a shoemaker, though he himself knows nothing
about shoemaking and the kind of people who look at his painting know
nothing about it either. They judge things by their colours and shapes.'

'Exactly.'

'The same goes for the poet, too, I take it. We can say that he colours
his pictures of all these skills with his words and phrases, and that the only
thing he knows anything about is imitation. The result is that people like
himself, people who judge things on the basis of language, think that what
he has to say seems excellently said – whether he is using his metre,
b rhythm and harmony to describe shoemaking, or generalship, or anything
else. Such is the power of bewitchment naturally possessed by the tools
he uses. And yet a poet's words, when stripped of the colours provided by
his art, and taken by themselves – well, I think you know what they're like.
You've seen them, after all.'

'Indeed I have.'

'It's like the faces of people who have youth without beauty,' I said.
'Like looking at them when they lose their bloom of youth.'

---

[6] Reciters (or 'rhapsodes') were in Plato's day not themselves epic poets but professional performers of epic poetry, who would appear at festivals across the Greek
world.

[7] In Greek, 'to imitate x' is ambiguous between 'to take x as a model for imitation'
and 'to produce an image of x', 'to represent x'. Accordingly, the phrase translated
'imitators of images' could also mean 'producers of images'.

'Exactly,' he said.

'Very well. Now, here's another thing for you to think about. The
c creator of images, the imitator, has no knowledge of what is, but only of
what appears to be. Isn't that our claim?'

'Yes.'

'But that's only half the story. Let's not leave it there. Let's look at the
whole story.'

'Explain.'

'A painter, we say, can paint reins and a bridle?'

'Yes.'

'But when it comes to making them, that's done by a leather-worker
and a blacksmith?'

'Of course.'

'Well, then, does the painter know what reins and bridle should be like?
Even the people who make them – the blacksmith and leather-worker –
do they know? Isn't it only the person who knows how to use them, the
horseman?'

'That's exactly how it is.'

'And won't we say that this is universally true?'

'That what is universally true?'

d 'That in every sphere there are these three skills using, making and
imitating?'

'Yes.'

'So the goodness, beauty and correctness of any manufactured object,
living thing or action are entirely a question of the use for which each of
them was made, or for which it developed naturally?'

'Yes.'

'In which case, it's the person who uses a particular object who must
necessarily have the most experience of it. He must act as a messenger to
the person who makes it, telling him the good and bad points, in use, of
e the instrument he is using. A player of the pipes, for example, gives his
views on pipes to the maker of them, telling him which ones are any use
for playing. He will instruct the maker what sort of pipes to make, and
then the maker will be of use to him.'

'Of course he will.'

'Is it the person who knows, in other words, who tells the maker which
instruments are good and which are no good? And will the maker take this
information on trust when he makes the instrument?'

'Yes.'

'So for a given object the maker will have correct opinion about what is good and what is bad, from being with the person who knows, and being compelled to listen to the person who knows, whereas the person who uses it will have knowledge.'

'Exactly.'

'What about the imitator? Will he have used the things he paints, and so have knowledge of whether they are good and right, or not? Will he have correct opinion about them through being compelled to associate with the person who does know, and receive instructions on what sorts of things to paint?'

'No, neither of those things.'

'So the imitator will have neither knowledge nor correct opinion about the goodness or badness of the things he imitates.'

'Apparently not.'

'What a wonderful guide the poetic imitator must be, then, if we want wisdom on the subjects he writes about.'

b   'He's no guide at all.'

'And yet he'll still carry on imitating, even though he doesn't know what makes any particular thing good or no good. And it looks as if what he imitates will be the kind of thing that appears good to the ignorant majority.'

'What else?'

'In which case, or so it appears, we have pretty well reached agreement on two points. First, the imitator has no knowledge worth mentioning of the things he imitates. His imitation isn't serious. It's a kind of play. And second, all those who turn their hand to tragic poetry, in iambic or epic,[8] are out-and-out imitators.'

'Absolutely.'

c   'And this sort of imitation,' I said, 'really and truly is connected with something twice removed from the truth, isn't it?'

'Yes.'

'Then here is another question. What part of a person does it have its effect on?'

'What kind of thing do you mean?'

'I'll tell you. If we rely on our eyesight, presumably, the same thing does not look the same size close to and far off.'

'No, it doesn't.'

---

[8] Socrates treats Homeric epic as a kind of tragedy, although typically the two genres would be kept distinct. Compare 595b.

'And the same things can look crooked and straight to people looking at them first in water and then out of water. Or concave and convex,
d because of our eyes' variable perception of colours or shades. Our souls are clearly full of this kind of confusion. Things like shadow-painting,[9] conjuring, and all the other arts of the same kind rely on this weakness in our nature to produce effects that fall nothing short of witchcraft '

'True.'

'Isn't that why measuring, counting and weighing proved to be a wonderful help to us? They meant we were not ruled by what *looked* bigger or smaller, or more, or heavier, but by the thing which did the calculating or the measuring – or the weighing, for that matter.'

'Naturally.'

e 'And these operations, of course, are the function of the rational element in the soul.'

'Yes, the rational element.'

'Quite often this element makes its measurements, indicates that one group of things is bigger or smaller than another – or the same size – but simultaneously finds that the same group of objects presents exactly the opposite appearance.'[10]

'Yes.'

'But didn't we say it was impossible for one thing to have opposite opinions about the same things at the same time?'[11]

'We did. And rightly.'

603 'In which case, the part of the soul whose opinions conflict with the measurements cannot be the same as the part whose opinions agree with the measurements.'

'No, it cannot.'

'Well, the part which puts its trust in measurement and calculation will be the best part of the soul.'

'Of course.'

'And the part which disagrees with this part will be one of the weaker elements in us.'

'Bound to be.'

---

[9] A technique for achieving the illusion of depth in two dimensions. Compare 523b, 583b, 586b.

[10] The sentence could also be translated: 'Quite often, when this element has made its measurements and is indicating that one group of things is bigger or smaller than another – or the same size – the same group of objects simultaneously presents exactly the opposite appearance.' That is, the indications would conflict in the person rather than in a single element.   [11] 436b.

'This was the point of agreement I wanted to reach when I said that painting – and imitation in general – operates in an area of its own, far
b removed from the truth, and that it associates with the element in us which is far removed from intelligence – a liaison and friendship from which nothing healthy or true can result.'

'Precisely,' he said.

'An inferior art, then, imitation. And its union with what is inferior produces inferior offspring.'

'That's the way it looks.'

'And is that only imitation in things we see?' I asked. 'Or is it also imitation in things we hear – what we call poetry?'

'Poetry as well, I would guess.'

'Well,' I said, 'let's not trust to guesswork alone, and the analogy with
c painting. Let's turn directly to the actual part of our thought which poetic imitation has to do with, and see whether that is something trivial or something important.'

'Yes, that is what we should do.'

'We can put it to ourselves like this. Imitation, we say, imitates men performing actions freely or under compulsion. As a result of their actions, they believe they have done well or badly, and in all these situations they feel pain or pleasure. There wasn't any more to it than that, was there?'

'No.'

d 'Now, is a man's attitude consistent in all these activities? Or is it the same with actions as it was with vision? Then he was in a state of civil war, and held opposite opinions about the same things within himself. Is he at odds with himself in the same way when it comes to his actions? Is he at war with himself? Come to think of it, though, that isn't a question which is still waiting to be answered. We answered all those questions quite satisfactorily in the earlier part of our discussion, when we agreed that there were countless contradictions of this kind, that the soul was full of them.'[12]

'Correct,' he said.

e 'Yes, it was correct,' I said. 'But there was something we left out then which I think we now have to explain.'

'What is that?'

'What we said then, I think, was that if something happens to a good

---

[12] 439c–441c.

man – losing a son, perhaps, or something else of great value – he will more easily endure it than anyone else would.'[13]

'He certainly will.'

'The question we now have to ask ourselves is whether he will feel no pain at all. Or if that is impossible, will he nonetheless observe some moderation in his grief?'

'Yes,' he said, 'that seems closer to the truth.'

604   'Right. In that case, tell me something else about him. Do you think he will put up a better fight and resistance against his grief when he is being observed by his equals, or when he is on his own, in a deserted place, all by himself?'

'I should think there'll be a big difference when he is being observed,' he said.

'Yes. When he is on his own, I imagine, he will not be ashamed to say all sorts of things which he would be embarrassed if anyone else heard him saying. And he'll do all sorts of things which he wouldn't be prepared to have anyone see him doing.'

'That is so,' he said.

'Are reason and established custom the things which encourage him to
b   resist, while what drags him back to his grief is his misfortune itself?'

'Yes.'

'And when a human being has opposing impulses, relating to the same thing, at the same time, we say these must necessarily be two different elements.'

'Yes, of course.'

'Is one element prepared to follow custom wherever custom leads?'

'And where would that be?'

'Custom says, presumably, that in misfortune the best thing is not to be upset, but to be as calm as possible – for a number of reasons. In the first place, it is not clear how much is good and how much bad in situations of
c   this sort. Second, if we look to the future, it does no good to take things hard. Third, nothing in human affairs is worth taking that seriously. And fourth, grieving gets in the way of the thing which ought, in these situations, to come to our assistance as swiftly as possible.'

'What thing do you mean?' he asked.

'Reflection on what has happened,' I replied. 'People should accept the way things have fallen out the way they accept the fall of the dice, and then

---

[13] 387d–e.

325

make their plans in the way reason prescribes as best for them. They
shouldn't spend their time howling, clutching hold of the part which is
d   hurt, like children who have fallen over. They should always accustom
their souls to concentrate straight away on curing and repairing the
damaged and injured part. They should use healing to do away with
lamentation.'[14]

'Yes,' he said, 'that would certainly be the right attitude to take towards
misfortune.'

'So it's the best element, we say, which is prepared to use this kind of
rational calculation as a guide.'

'Clearly.'

'Whereas the element which draws us towards mourning and the re-
collection of our sufferings, which can never get its fill of these things –
won't we describe this as irrational, lazy and a friend to cowardice?'

'Yes, we will.'

e   'This element, the fretful element, is highly susceptible to all sorts of
varied imitation. The calm, thoughtful character, on the other hand,
unchanging and true to itself, is hard to imitate, and not a simple matter
to understand if it is imitated – particularly in public, when you get a
diverse collection of people in the theatre.[15] What is being imitated is
quite unfamiliar to them.'

605   'Absolutely.'

'The imitative poet's nature is obviously not adapted to this element in
the soul, nor is his wisdom framed to appeal to it. Not if he's going to be
popular with the general public. His concern is with the fretful, variegated character, because that is the one which is easy to imitate.'

'Obviously.'

'So we'd be justified now in taking him and putting him on a par with
the painter. His products, like the painter's, are inferior by comparison
b   with the truth, and he resembles him also in associating with an inferior
part of the soul, not with the best part. By rights, therefore, we ought not
to admit him into a city which is going to be well governed, since it is an
inferior part of the soul that he arouses and feeds, and by making this
strong destroys the rational part. It's the same with a city. If you give

---

[14]   The evidence for conventional Greek attitudes towards grieving speaks more ambig-
uously than the voice of custom here. Greek males were less inhibited from weeping
than those in some modern cultures. On the other hand, appeals for restraint in
mourning were not uncommon. See *GPM* 167–169.

[15]   Greek drama was mass entertainment, peformed at festivals on public holidays.

power to those who are bad, and hand the city over to them, you destroy
those who are better. In exactly the same way, we shall say, the imitative
c poet sets up a bad regime in the soul of each individual, gratifying the
senseless part of it, the part which cannot distinguish larger from smaller,
and which regards the same things at one time as large and at another time
as small. He is nothing but an image-maker, and he stands far removed
from the truth.'

'He does indeed.'

'However, we haven't yet brought our most serious accusation against
imitative poetry. Its ability to corrupt even good people – with a very few
exceptions – is surely a disgrace.'

'Of course it is, if that really is what it does.'

'Listen, and see what you think. The best of us, I imagine, when we
d hear Homer or one of the tragic poets imitating some hero in a state of
grief, as he drags out a long speech of lamentation, or even breaks into
song, or starts beating his breast . . . well, you know how it is. We enjoy it,
and surrender ourselves to it. We follow and share the hero's sufferings,
treat them as real, and praise as an excellent poet the person who most
affects us in this way.'

'Yes, I know how it is. How could I fail to?'

'And yet when some misfortune affects one of us personally, you're
aware how we pride ourselves on doing the exact opposite – if we can have
e the strength to remain silent, and endure. We seem to regard this as men's
behaviour, and what we praised in the poetic context as women's behaviour.'

'Yes, I'm aware of that,' he said.

'Is praise of that sort justified, then – if you see a man behaving in a
way you wouldn't dream of behaving yourself, a way you'd be ashamed to
behave, and are not repelled by it, but take pleasure in it and praise it?'

606 'Heavens, no,' he said. 'That kind of praise sounds quite unreasonable.'

'Yes, it does,' I said. 'At least, it does if you look at it like this.'

'Like what?'

'Think about it. Here we have this element which in one situation – in
our private misfortunes – is forcibly held in check, though it has this
hunger which can only be satisfied by weeping and wholesale lamentation, since these are the satisfactions this kind of thing by its nature
desires. Then in another situation this same part is fulfilled and gratified
by the poets, and what is by nature the best part of us, inadequately
b educated by reason or habit, abandons its watch over grieving of that

kind. It says the sorrows it is watching are another's, and if someone else, who claims to be a good man, is grieving inappropriately, there is nothing for us to be ashamed of in applauding him and pitying him. We believe there is a positive benefit, which is pleasure, and would not be prepared to lose that by rejecting the whole poem. It is given to few people, I suspect, to work out that the pleasure they take in what happens to others necessarily carries over into what happens to them. If they allow the faculty of pity to grow strong, by feeding it on the sorrows of others, it is hard to restrain it when it comes to their own sorrows.'

'Very true,' he said.

c   'The same argument applies to laughter, doesn't it? If there are jokes you wouldn't dream of making yourself, but which you very much enjoy when you hear them in the comic theatre, or even in private company – if you don't regard them as the wrong sort of jokes, or hate them, isn't what you are doing the same as with the things you pity? That element in yourself which wanted to make jokes, but which you kept in check by means of reason because you were frightened of being thought a buffoon, you now release. You don't realise that giving it its head in this way results in your playing the comedian, over and over again, in your own life.'

d   'Exactly.'

'Doesn't it apply also to sex, anger, and all the desires, pains and pleasures in the soul which we say accompany any of our actions? Isn't the effect of poetic imitation on us the same? It feeds and waters these things, when they ought by rights to wither away. And it makes them our rulers, though if we want to be better and happier rather than worse and more wretched, they ought to be ruled by us.'

'I have to agree with you,' he said.

e   'In that case, Glaucon, when you come across Homer's admirers saying that this is the poet who has educated Greece, that he is worth studying both for our general education and for the management of human affairs,

607   that we should learn from him and follow this poet in the arrangement and conduct of the whole of our own lives, then by all means show them the warmth of friendship and affection. They are, after all, excellent people within their limitations. By all means agree that Homer is highly poetic, and first among tragic writers, but be aware that the only poetry we can accept into our city are hymns to the gods and verses in praise of good men. If you accept the honeyed Muse, in song or poetry, pleasure and pain will be twin kings in your city in place of established custom and the thing which has always been generally accepted as best – reason.'

'Very true,' he said.

b   'Well, since we've brought up the subject of poetry again, let our defence be this. Since that is what she is like, it was not unreasonable of us to banish her from our city. Reason demanded it. And let us say to her, if she looks like accusing us of being harsh or uncultured, that there is a long-standing antagonism between poetry and philosophy. The "howling dog" which "yelps against its master," "great in the empty eloquence of fools," "the mob of wise men who have mastered Zeus," "how

c   subtle thinkers are but beggars yet," and countless other passages, are evidence of their long-standing opposition.[16] And if, despite this, imitation, the poetry which is for pleasure, has any argument to show that she should be included in a well-governed city, let our reply be that left to ourselves we would gladly allow her back. We know how beguiling we ourselves find her. But it is wrong to abandon what we believe

d   to be true. Don't you find that as well, my friend? Don't you find her beguiling, especially when it is through Homer that you behold her?'

'Yes, very.'

'So is she entitled to make her return – but only after having defended herself, in lyric or some other metre?'

'Absolutely.'

'And I suppose we might allow those of her defenders who have no gift for poetry, but are lovers of poetry, to speak in prose on her behalf, and tell us she is not only pleasurable but also a good thing – for political regimes and individual human lives. We'll be good listeners, since I

e   imagine it will clearly be to our advantage if she is shown to be a good thing as well as pleasurable.'

'How can it not be to our advantage?' he said.

'And if they can't tell us that, my dear friend, then we must do what lovers do when they have fallen in love with someone and decided their love is not a good thing. They stay away. It may be a struggle, but they stay away nonetheless. It's the same with us. The love of imitative poetry has

608   grown in us as a result of our being brought up in these wonderful regimes of ours, and this will predispose us to believe that she is as good and as true as possible. But while she remains incapable of making this

---

[16] The quotations are all taken from poetic attacks on philosophers, for their useless chatter, their unjustified arrogance, their irregularity in religion, their inability to achieve worldly success. We do not know the sources of the citations here, but at least some of them probably come from comic drama, which loved to take pot-shots at philosophers.

defence, we shall recite to ourselves, as we listen to her, this argument we have put forward, as a kind of charm to prevent any relapse into our childish but popular passion. And this will be the spell we shall recite, that this kind of poetry is not something to be taken seriously, as something

b important, with some bearing on the truth. The listener should be on his guard against it if he is concerned about the regime within him, and his views on poetry should be the ones we have put forward today.'

'I couldn't agree more,' he said.

'It's a great test, Glaucon, greater than people realise – this question of turning out good or bad. We shouldn't be led by success, money, power – or even poetry – into neglecting justice, or virtue in general.'

'After what we have said today, I agree. So would anyone else, I imagine.'

c 'And that's without even mentioning the greatest of the rewards and prizes which are on offer for virtue.'

'Greater than we can imagine, you must mean, if there are other rewards greater than the ones we have described.'

'Nothing great can happen in a short space of time,' I said. 'And presumably, compared with eternity, our whole span of time from childhood to old age *is* a short space of time.'

'A mere nothing,' he said.

'Well, then. Do you think something which is immortal should be

d seriously interested in this short period of time, and not in the whole of time?'

'No, I think it should be interested in the whole of time. What are you getting at?'

'Don't you know for a fact,' I said, 'that our soul is immortal, that it never dies?'

He looked at me in astonishment. 'Good heavens, no,' he said. 'I don't know that for a fact. What about you? Are you in a position to say so for certain?'

'Yes, I am – unless I'm greatly at fault. So are you, I imagine. There's no difficulty about it.'

'There is for me,' he said. 'So I'd very much like you to tell me about this thing which presents no difficulty.'

'Listen, then,' I said.

'Tell me.'

e 'Do you say there is a good and a bad?'

'Yes, I do.'

'And is your opinion about them the same as mine?'

'What is your opinion?'

'That what corrupts and destroys is always the bad, whereas what saves and preserves is the good?'

'Yes, I do believe that,' he said.

'What about a bad and a good for each thing? Do you accept those? 609 Ophthalmia for the eyes, for example. Or if it's the whole body, disease. For corn it's blight, for wood it's rot, and for bronze and iron it's rust. Doesn't practically everything, as I say, have its own characteristic evil and disease?'

'Yes, I accept that.'

'When one of these agents attacks something, does it weaken the thing it attacks? Does it in the end break it down and destroy it completely?'

'It's bound to.'

'So it's this characteristic evil each thing has, and the weakness it b causes, which destroys each thing. And if this doesn't destroy it, then nothing else can destroy it either. The good is certainly never going to destroy anything. Nor will what is neither good nor bad.'

'No, of course not,' he said.

'So if we find among existing things something which has an evil which makes it bad, and yet this evil is incapable of destroying it and breaking it down, won't we then know that in that case it was never in its nature to be destroyed?'

'That would be reasonable,' he said.

'Very well. What about the soul? Doesn't that have something that makes it bad?'

c 'It certainly does,' he said. 'All the things we've just been describing. Injustice, lack of discipline, cowardice, ignorance.'

'Well, then, does any of these break it down and destroy it? Be careful, now. We don't want to make the mistake of thinking, when someone unjust and foolish is detected being unjust, that he has been destroyed by injustice, which is the defect of the soul. Look at it like this instead. In the case of the body, the defect of the body – which is disease – wastes it away, corrupts it, and brings it to the point of not even being a body at all. In the same way all the things we've just been talking about reach the point d of not being, when their own specific evil attaches itself to them, occupies them, and destroys them. Isn't that right?'

'Yes.'

'Good. Now, look at the soul in the same way. When injustice and the

other forms of vice are present in it, does their presence, and their attachment to it, corrupt and decompose the soul until they bring it to the point
of death, and separate it from the body?'

'No, that they certainly can't do,' he said.

'But it's illogical,' I said, 'to imagine that something can be destroyed
by the defect of something else, if it can't be destroyed by its own defect.'

'Yes, that is illogical.'

e   'Don't forget, Glaucon, we don't regard the defect of food, whatever
the specific defect of food is – age, or being rotten, or whatever – as
responsible for the destruction of the body. If the specific defect of food
imparts bodily decay to the body, we shall say the body has been destroyed
by its own evil, which is disease, arising out of those things. But we shall
610 never accept that the body, which is one thing, can be destroyed by the
defect of food, which is a quite different thing. It cannot be destroyed by
an external evil, unless that in turn implants the body's own characteristic evil.'

'Absolutely right,' he said.

'By the same argument, therefore, if the defect of the body does not
implant in the soul the soul's own defect, we shall never accept that the
soul is destroyed by an external evil, in the absence of its own defect. We
can't have one thing destroyed by the evil of another.'

'That makes sense.'

b   'In which case, either let's prove this claim of ours to be false or, until
it is proved false, let us never admit that fever, or any other illness, or
murder – even if someone cuts the entire body up into the smallest
pieces you can imagine – can bring about the soul's destruction. At least,
not until someone demonstrates to us that these things happening to the
body make the soul itself more unjust or more unholy. We shall not
allow anyone to say that the soul, or anything else, is destroyed by an
c   external evil happening to something else, if its own evil does not
happen to it.'

'And that's something,' he said, 'which no one will ever be able to show
– that the souls of the dying are made more unjust by death.'

'If anyone has the nerve to challenge our argument, because he doesn't
want to be compelled to admit that souls are immortal – if he says that the
dying person becomes worse and more unjust, I imagine our view will be
d   that if what he says is true, then injustice must be fatal to its possessor,
like a disease. Those who catch it must die because the disease itself kills
them by its own nature – the most unjust more quickly, the less unjust

more slowly – and not, as now, because the unjust are put to death for their injustice by other people who inflict this penalty on them.'

'Good heavens,' he said. 'Injustice will turn out to be not such an alarming thing after all, if it really is fatal to anyone who catches it. It

e would be an escape from his troubles. But I'm much more inclined to think it will turn out to be just the opposite – that it kills others, if it can, but gives added vitality to the person who possesses it. And not just vitality, but alertness as well. That shows, I think, how far it is from being fatal. Misses it by miles.'

'You're right,' I said. 'After all, if the soul's own particular defect and own particular evil are not enough to kill or destroy it, the evil allocated to the destruction of something else is hardly going to destroy it – or anything else apart from the thing it is allocated to.'

'No, it is hardly likely to.'

'In which case, if it is not destroyed by any evil – neither its own nor

611 anything else's – it's obvious that it must necessarily be something which always is. And if it always is, then it must be immortal.'

'Necessarily,' he said.

'Very well. Let's take it that's how things are. And if that *is* how they are, you realise it must always be the same souls which are in existence. There can never be any fewer of them, I take it, if none can be destroyed. Nor can there be any more of them, since if it were ever possible for any more of the class of immortal things to come into being, you can see they would have to come into being from what is mortal, and you would end up with everything being immortal.'

'True.'

b   'That's not something we want to contemplate,' I said. 'Reason will not allow it. And let's not think, either, that the soul is in its truest nature the kind of thing which is highly variegated, or full of difference and inconsistency.'

'What do you mean?'

'If something is composed of many constituents, and its composition is less than perfect – as we have found with the soul – then it's not easy for it to be immortal.'

'No, it probably isn't.'

'Very well. That the soul is something immortal is a conclusion we might be driven to both by this recent argument and by other arguments.

c   But if we want to know what it's really like, we shouldn't look at it in the form we currently see it in, crippled by its partnership with the body and

other evils, but in its pure state. And that's something which can only be
seen adequately by means of reason. We'll find it far more beautiful, and
get a much clearer view of justices and injustices, and all the things we
have so far described. All we've said so far is the truth about the way it
d appears at present. And all we've seen of it is something like Glaucus who
lives in the ocean, if people were to see him. They would no longer find
it easy to make out the shape he started with, because some of the original parts of his body have been broken off, others have been worn away
and completely eroded by the waves, while things like shells, seaweed and
stones have grown on to him. As a result, he no longer resembles his original nature. He looks like some kind of wild beast. It's the same with us,
looking at the soul when it is afflicted with all these evils. No, Glaucon,
we should be looking in a different direction.'

'Which direction?' he said.

e 'We should look to the soul's love of wisdom. We should bear in mind
what it clings to, the kind of company it yearns for, since it is kin to that
which is divine, immortal and always existing, and what it could become
if it devoted itself entirely to this, and if this enthusiasm brought it up out
612 of the sea in which it now is, striking from it the stones and shells, all those
coarse accretions of earth and stone which have now grown round it as a
result of its supposedly " happy" feasting upon earth.[17] Then you would
see the soul's true nature, whether it is complex or simple – or however
exactly it is. For the moment, however, I think we have given an adequate
description of the things that can happen to it, the shapes it can assume,
in human life.'

'We certainly have,' he said.

'There you are, then,' I said. 'In the course of our discussion we have
b removed the various objections to our claim. We haven't had to resort to
the rewards and reputation of justice, as you two were saying Homer and
Hesiod did.[18] Haven't we found that the thing itself, justice, is best for the
soul itself, and that the soul should do what is just, whether or not it
possesses the ring of Gyges – or even the ring of Gyges *and* the cap of
Hades?'[19]

'Very true. We have.'

---

[17] When the soul associates with the body it is as if it eats dirt. Compare how in the
Phaedo (81c–d) some souls are said to become weighed down by the admixture of
earth and incapable of escaping to the divine realm.   [18] 363a–b.

[19] The ring of Gyges was introduced by Glaucon in Book 2, 359d–360b. Its power to
confer invisibility was also attributed to the cap or helmet of Hades, god of the
underworld.

'In which case, Glaucon, can there still be any objection to our going
c further, and restoring to justice and the rest of virtue the great rewards
which they characteristically bring to the soul, from men and gods alike,
both during a man's lifetime and after his death?'

'No. No objection,' he said.

'Then will you now repay the loan I made you in the course of our discussion?'

'What loan?'

'I granted you that the just man should appear to be unjust, and the
unjust man just. You both thought that however things might appear in
the eyes of gods and men, we should still make that allowance for
d argument's sake, so that pure justice could be judged in comparison with
pure injustice. Or don't you remember saying that?'[20]

'I would be guilty of injustice if I forgot it,' he said.

'In that case, since they now have been judged, in the name of justice I
hereby ask for the return of the reputation she in fact has among gods and
men. I request that we too should agree that this is the reputation she has.
Let her bear off the prizes of victory which she gets from *appearing* to be
just, and which she gives to those who possess her, now that we've seen
how she does indeed provide the good things that come from *being* just,
and that she does not deceive those who truly take hold of her.'

e   'There's justice in that request.'

'Will you start,' I said, 'by granting that the gods at least are not fooled
about what either of them, the just or the unjust, is like?'

'We will.'

'And if the gods are not fooled, then one is loved by the gods, and the
other hated, in the way we agreed originally.'[21]

'That is so.'

613   'Can we agree that for the one the gods love, everything that comes
from the gods is the best that possibly can come, unless he started with
some unavoidable evil as a result of a fault already committed?'

'Indeed we can.'

'In the same way, then, we must take it that if the just man falls into
poverty or sickness, or any of the other things which are generally
regarded as evils, it will all turn out well for him either in his lifetime or
after his death. He will never be neglected by the gods if he is willing to

---

[20] Glaucon imposed this condition at 360e–361d, and Adeimantus seconded him at
367b–c.
[21] This was agreed, or rather, not opposed, by Thrasymachus in Book 1 (352b).

be serious about becoming just, practise virtue, and become as much like a god as it is possible for a man to be.'

b   'That's fair enough. A person like that ought not to be neglected by one who is like him.'

'And our opinion of the unjust man? Should that be the exact opposite?'

'Absolutely.'

'So those are the kind of prizes the just man will receive from the gods.'

'That's certainly my view,' he said.

'What about the prizes he will receive from men? Isn't this the position, if we're really going to say how things are? Aren't clever, unjust people

c   just like runners who are good at running the outward leg, but not the inward leg?[22] They leap off eagerly at the start, but end up making fools of themselves. Ears laid back, they come away uncrowned. True runners make it to the end, carry off the prizes, and wear the crown. Isn't that generally what happens with people who are just? At the end of any of their actions or dealings with other people, and at the end of their life, don't they have a good reputation, and walk off with the prizes in the human realm?'

'Indeed they do.'

'In which case, can you put up with it if I say about them what *you* said

d   about the unjust?[23] I shall say that as they get older, the just can, if they wish, hold political office in their own city. They can marry where they choose, and give their children in marriage to anyone they like. Everything *you* said about the unjust, I am now going to say about the just. When it comes to the unjust, by contrast, I shall say that even if they get away with it when they are young, by the end of the race most of them have made fools of themselves, and been overtaken. By the time they are

e   old they are in a wretched state – insulted by foreigners and citizens, whipped, and all the things you described as crude and uncivilised. Rightly so, what with them being put on the rack, and having their eyes burnt out. Imagine you've heard me saying that all these things happen to the unjust. What do you think? Are you going to accept what I say?'

'I certainly am,' he said. 'What you say has justice on its side.'

614   'Well,' I said, 'those would be the prizes, rewards and gifts the just man gets during his lifetime, both from gods and men, on top of the good things we were talking about, which justice herself has to offer.'

---

[22] Socrates is referring to a particular type of race, the 'double-pipe': a sprint up the straight track and back again.   [23] 361d–362c.

'Very fine and reliable, too.'

'But these are nothing,' I said, 'in number or magnitude, when compared with the rewards and punishments which await each of them after death. You ought to hear those too, if each is to receive in full the payment the argument owes him.'

'Please tell us,' he said. 'I can think of few things I'd rather hear about.'

b   'Well, it's not the tale of an ancient mariner I am going to tell you. More the tale of an ancient foreigner [24] – a hero from Pamphylia, Er the son of Armenius. He was killed in battle, and on the tenth day, when the dead, by now decomposed, were taken up for burial, his body was found to be perfectly sound. He was taken home, and on the twelfth day, as he was lying on the funeral pyre, ready for burial, he came to life again. And having come to life, he told people what he had seen in the place where he had been.

'He said that when his soul left his body, it went on a journey, with
c   many others like it, until they came to a wonderful place where there were two openings side by side in the ground, and two others, up above in the heavens, corresponding to these. In between were seated judges, who when they gave their judgments ordered the just to take the way which led to the right and upwards, through the heavens, and to wear on their front the marks of the judgments made about them. The unjust they
d   ordered to take the left-hand, downward way. And they too wore, on their backs, the marks of everything they had done. When he himself stepped forward, they said they wanted him to act as a messenger to mankind, to tell them what was going on there. They urged him to hear and observe everything which happened in that place. There he saw souls departing, as judgment was passed on them, through the two exits, the opening in the heavens and the opening in the ground. Meanwhile through the other two openings souls were either rising up, parched and dusty in
e   appearance, from the one in the ground, or coming down all clean from the one in the heavens. The ones who were just arriving looked as if they had got there after a long journey. They were very glad to come out into the meadow, and camp there, as if they were at a festival. They greeted

---

[24] In the Greek, Socrates announces, 'It's not an Alcinous-story I am going to tell you, more a brave man's story.' The phrase 'Alcinous story' became proverbial for a tale both long-drawn-out and tall, after the narration of his travels that Odysseus tells to King Alcinous in Books 9–12 of Homer's *Odyssey* – travels which included a journey to the underworld. 'Alcinous-story' and 'brave man's story' make a pun in Greek: *Alkinou* ('of Alcinous') and *alkimou* ('of a brave man'). The name Alcinous means 'strong of mind'.

one another – those who were acquainted – and exchanged news. Those coming out of the ground asked the others about things up there, while those coming from the heavens asked them in return how things were 615 where they had been. As they exchanged accounts, the first group were wailing and weeping as they recalled all the terrible things they had seen and experienced in their journey – their thousand-year journey – beneath the earth. Those who had come from the heavens, by contrast, were recounting the wonderful things that had happened to them and the indescribably beautiful sights they had seen.

'To give a full account, Glaucon, would take a very long time. But the main point, he said, was this. Whatever wrongs they had done anyone, and whatever people they had all wronged, for all these in turn they had

b to pay a penalty – ten times over for each offence. Ten periods of a hundred years each, in other words, this being the measure of a human life. This made sure they would pay a tenfold payment for the offence. For example, if any of them had been guilty of the deaths of many people – betraying cities or armies and casting people into slavery, perhaps, or playing a part in any other cruelty – on all these counts they earned

c tenfold pain for each offence. Equally, due rewards were earned for any good deeds, and for showing themselves just and holy. And he said something, though nothing of note, about those who died at birth or lived only a short time. He also described the still greater rewards and penalties for piety or impiety towards gods and parents, and for murder.

'He said he came across one person who was being asked by another where Ardiaeus the Great was. This Ardiaeus had been tyrant in some

d city in Pamphylia a thousand years before. He had killed his aged father and his older brother, and done many other wicked deeds, so it was said. "He has not come to this place," replied the one being asked. "Nor will he ever come. That was one of the appalling sights we saw. When we had been through everything we had to go through, and were close to the opening, just about to come up, we suddenly caught sight of Ardiaeus and

e some others. They were tyrants, most of them, though there were some private citizens who had committed heinous crimes. When these people thought it was their turn to go up, the opening refused to allow them through. Its mouth gave a loud roar whenever one of these irredeemably wicked people, or one of those who had not been sufficiently punished, attempted to pass through. And there were savage men standing there, of fiery aspect, who recognised the sound. Some of the people they seized,

616   and took them away, but as for Ardiaeus and others like him, they
      bound their hands, feet and heads, threw them on the ground, and
      flayed them. Then they dragged them over the thorn bushes beside the
      road, tearing and rasping them. They explained to those passing by at
      any particular moment why the people were being dragged away, and
      said they were going to be thrown into Tartarus." He said that for each
      of them, out of the whole range of fears they were exposed to in that
      place, this was the greatest – that when they came up to the opening the
      voice might be heard. And each of them was only too glad to pass
      through in silence.

b   'So much, then, for the kinds of penalties and punishments – and the
      corresponding rewards. For each group, the stay in the meadow lasted
      seven days. At the end of it, on the eighth day, they had to get up and go
      on a journey, arriving after four days at a place from which they could see
      a shaft of light, like a pillar, extending from above through the whole
      heaven and earth. The light was more like a rainbow than anything else,

c   only brighter and more pure. A day's journey brought them to where the
      light was, and there in the middle of the light they could see, extended
      from heaven, the extremities of its chains. This light binds the heavens.
      It is like the cables of a trireme in the way it holds the whole revolving
      firmament together. And from the extremities they saw extended the
      spindle of Necessity, by which all the separate rotations are set in motion.
      The shaft and hook of the spindle are of adamant, the whorl is partly of
      adamant and partly of other materials.[25]

d   'The nature of the whorl is as follows. In appearance it is like the whorls
      we have here, but from what he said we have to think of it like this.
      Imagine a single large whorl which has been completely hollowed out
      with a chisel, and a second, smaller whorl inside it, fitting exactly into it,

[25] On the question of what the souls get to see, interpreters agree only that it is a vision
     of the central axis of the cosmos and of the revolutions of the heavenly bodies around
     this axis. The motif of a column or shaft stretching between heaven and earth would
     be familiar from mythology – for example, in connection with the mountain-god
     Atlas who supports the heavens. It is disputed whether trireme cables passed under
     the hull and bound the ship across its width, or were stretched lengthwise to bind
     stern to bow. Nor is it clear whether the light is being described as *shaped* like trireme
     cables or simply as *functioning* like them. A Greek spindle was a rod with a weight at
     one end, the whorl, to stabilise its rotation. The image of the Fates as goddesses who
     spun the thread of each human life was a traditional way to express the power of
     destiny over human beings, and it appears explicitly at 620e. It was not traditional,
     however, to personify 'Necessity', as is done here and again at 617d.

like those pots that fit inside one another. Similarly a third, fourth, and then four more, making a total of eight whorls in all, one inside another.[26]

e Their rims show as so many circles from above, and form a single whorl round the shaft, with a continuous surface. The shaft is driven right through the middle of the eighth whorl. The first and outermost whorl is the broadest, in terms of the breadth of the circular rim. The rim of the sixth comes second, the fourth rim comes third, the eighth rim comes fourth, the seventh rim comes fifth, the fifth rim comes sixth, the third

617 rim comes seventh, and the second comes eighth. The rim of the largest whorl is spangled, that of the seventh is the brightest, that of the eighth derives its colour from the seventh shining on it. The second and fifth are very similar to one another, and yellower than the others. The third has the whitest light, the fourth is reddish, and the sixth is the next whitest after the third.

'The spindle is rotating. Seen as a whole, it all goes round at the same speed, but within the whole, as it revolves, the seven inner circles are

b gently revolving in the opposite direction to the whole. Of these inner circles number eight turns fastest, followed by numbers seven, six and five, which all travel at the same speed. Third in the speed of its counter-rotation, as it appeared to them, was the fourth whorl. Fourth was number three, and fifth number two. The spindle itself turns in the lap of Necessity. On the rim of each of its circles is perched a Siren, who is carried round with it, uttering a single sound, a single musical note. All

c eight together combine to produce one single harmony.[27] There are three others seated in a circle, at equal distances, each on a throne. These are the Fates, the daughters of Necessity: Lachesis, Clotho and Atropos. They are clothed in white, with garlands on their heads, and they sing to the accompaniment of the Sirens. Lachesis sings of the past, Clotho of the present, and Atropos of the future. Clotho has her right hand on the

d outer circumference of the spindle, turning it at intervals. Atropos, with

[26] In Plato's cosmology the planets, sun, and moon orbit the central earth in a series of concentric bands, with the fixed stars contained together in the outermost band. What the variation in the width of the bands represents is uncertain. The counter-revolution of the seven inner bands represents the various independent movements of sun, moon and planets in relation to the overall movement of the heavens. The order of the whorls, from first and outermost to eighth and innermost, is: (1) fixed stars, (2) Saturn, (3) Jupiter, (4) Mars, (5) Mercury, (6) Venus, (7) Sun, (8) Moon.

[27] The Sirens in Homer were poetic goddesses who knew all that happened and whose singing lured sailors to their deaths (*Odyssey* 12.165–200), but in Pythagorean imagery were responsible, as here, for the 'music of the spheres', a musical concord of sounds caused by the motions of the heavenly bodies.

her left hand, does the same for the inner rims. Lachesis touches both
inner and outer in turn, one with each hand.

'They themselves, when they arrived, had immediately to go before
Lachesis. A kind of prophet, or speaker, started off by lining them up.
Then from the lap of Lachesis he took numbers for drawing lots and patterns of lives. Ascending a high platform, he began to speak. "The word
of the maiden Lachesis, daughter of Necessity. Souls, creatures of a day,
here begins another cycle of mortal life and the death it brings. Your
e guardian spirit[28] will not be given to you by lot. You will choose a guardian
spirit for yourselves. Let the one who draws the first lot be the first to
choose a life. He will then be joined to it by Necessity. Virtue knows no
master. Your respect or contempt for it will give each of you a greater or
smaller share. The choice makes you responsible. God is not responsible."
With these words he threw the lots among them all, and each picked up
the lot which fell closest to him. All except Er. He was not allowed to pick
618 one up. But anyone who did pick one up could see clearly what number
lot he had drawn. Next he spread the patterns of lives before them on the
ground. There were many more of them than there were people present,
and they were of every possible kind – lives of all the animals in addition
to all the human lives. There were lives of tyrants among them – some
lasting, others destroyed in mid-career, and ending in poverty and exile,
b or beggary. There were lives of men distinguished, some for their looks,
beauty and in general for their strength and prowess, others for their families and the virtues of their ancestors, lives of men who by the same criteria were not distinguished, and a similar range of women's lives as well.
The overall arrangement of the soul was not included, because the soul is
inevitably altered by the kind of life it chooses. But the other characteristics were mingled with one another, with wealth and poverty, disease and
health – or with some balance between these extremes.

'It looks, my dear Glaucon, as if that is where the whole danger lies for
c a man. It is why the greatest care must be directed towards having each
and every one of us disregard all other branches of study, and be a follower
and student of this branch of ours, in the hope that he can learn and
discover who it is who will give him the ability and knowledge to
distinguish the good life from the bad, and choose always and everywhere,

---

[28] A *daimōn* in Greek religion is generally a lesser god, often a deified human hero, and
always closely attached to localised doings in the human world. Sometimes, as here,
it is a spirit attached to the interests of a single person, in which case it can be syn-
onymous with a person's fortune or luck in life.

out of all those possible, the life which is better. He must take into consideration all the things we have talked about here today, comparing them with one another and choosing between them in terms of excellence

d of life. He needs to know what the effect is, for good or bad, of beauty when mingled with poverty or riches – and what the effect is of noble or ignoble birth, of private life or public office, of strength or weakness, of ease or difficulty of learning, and all such matters as are connected with the soul either by nature or acquisition, when they are all mingled with one another. Taking all these things into consideration, he must be able to choose, defining the worse and better life with reference to the nature

e of the *soul*, calling that worse which leads the soul along the road to greater injustice, and that better which leads along the road to greater justice. He will pay no attention to anything else. After all, this is the crucial choice, as we have seen, both during his lifetime and after his death. Fast as adamant must he hold to this opinion as he goes to Hades,

619 so that even there he can avoid being distracted by evils like wealth, and so plunging into the life of a tyrant, into the sort of behaviour in which he will commit countless crimes for which there is no remedy, and suffer an even worse fate himself. No, he will know how to choose the middle way in such matters, avoiding the two extremes both in this life, as far as he can, and in the whole of the life hereafter. This is the way to the greatest happiness for a man.

b   'The next thing the Speaker had to say, according to this messenger from the afterworld, was this. "Even the last to come forward, provided he chooses sensibly and lives with integrity, has a worthwhile life before him, not a bad life. There is no cause for carelessness if you choose first, no cause for despair if you choose last." When he finished speaking, the person who had drawn the first lot came straight up and chose the greatest tyranny. In his folly and greed he did not look hard enough at what he was choosing. He had not seen that within its fate was included, among

c other evils, the devouring of his own children. When he did have time to look at it, he beat his breast and lamented his choice. Paying no attention to the instructions the Speaker had issued earlier, he refused to blame himself for his misfortunes, blaming fate, the gods, anything rather than himself. He was one of those who had come from the heavens, and in his previous life he had lived in a well-ordered society. He had had his share

d of virtue, but it had been a matter of habit rather than philosophy. Generally speaking, the bulk of those caught in this kind of predicament

342

were those who had come from heaven, since they were without the experience of hardship. Most of those who came from the earth, having both suffered themselves and seen others suffer, were in no hurry to make their choice. For this reason, and because of the way the lot fell out, for the majority of the souls there was an alternation between good and evil. However, if there is anyone who every time he enters this life here, consistently pursues philosophy in the right way, then provided the way

e   the lot falls out does not put him among the last to choose, the chances are, if Er's report is correct, not only that he will be happy here, but also that his journey from here to there and back again will be along the smooth, heavenly road, not the rough, terrestrial one.

'This choice of lives among the various souls, Er said, was a sight well
620 worth seeing – and one which commanded pity, laughter and amazement. For the most part their choice matched the character and habits of their previous life. He saw the soul of what had once been Orpheus choose the life of a swan. His death at the hands of women had given him a hatred of the female sex, and he refused to be conceived and born of a woman again. He saw the soul of Thamyras choose the life of a nightingale. He saw a swan choose a human life, by way of a change, and the same with other

b   musical creatures. The soul which drew number twenty in the lottery chose the life of a lion. This was the soul of Ajax the son of Telamon, shunning the life of a man as he remembered the decision over the weapons. The one after him was the soul of Agamemnon. Because of what had happened to it, this soul too had a hatred of the human race. It chose the life of an eagle instead. The soul of Atalanta had drawn a number somewhere in the middle. When she saw the wonderful prizes of

c   a man who was an athlete, she couldn't resist them, and chose those. And after her he saw the soul of Epeius the son of Panopeus, taking on the nature of a woman skilled in the arts. Among the very last to choose he saw the soul of that clown Thersites taking the form of a monkey. He also saw the soul of Odysseus, which as it turned out had drawn the last lot of all, coming up to make its choice. Remembering the hardships of its previous life, it rejected ambition, and spent a long time wandering round looking for the life of a private citizen who minded his own business. After

d   a long search he found one lying somewhere. It had been rejected by everyone else. When he saw it, he chose it gladly, saying he would have done the same even if he had drawn the first lot. Similarly among the wild animals there were moves into human beings, and into one another – the unjust changing into savage creatures, the just into gentle ones. Every kind of intermingling was taking place.[29]

e 'When all the souls had chosen their lives, they approached Lachesis in the same order they had made their choices. She gave each the guardian spirit it had chosen, to go with it, watch over its life and fulfil its choices. This spirit first brought the soul before Clotho, passing beneath her hand and the whirl of the revolving spindle, to confirm the fate which the lot had allowed it to choose. When the soul had touched her, the spirit took it to where Atropos was spinning, so making the spun thread impossible

621 to unwind. And from there, without turning back, it went beneath the throne of Necessity. When it had been under that, and when the other souls had passed through as well, they all travelled to the plain of Forgetting, through terrible, stifling heat, since the plain is devoid of trees or anything else the earth brings forth. By now it was getting to be evening, so they camped by the river of Lost Cares, whose water no vessel can hold.[30] Drinking a limited amount of the water was compulsory for

b all of them, but those who were not saved by reason drank more than a limited amount. And as each drank, he forgot everything he had seen. They went to sleep, and around the middle of the night there was a thunderstorm and an earthquake, and they were suddenly carried away from there, upwards to their births, all in different directions, like shooting stars.[31] Er himself was not allowed to drink any of the water. As for where and how he returned to his body, he didn't know. All of a sudden he woke up, and found himself, early in the morning, lying on his funeral pyre.

'In this way, Glaucon, his story was saved and not lost.[32] And so it can

c be our salvation, since if we believe it we shall pass the river of Forgetting in the right way, without polluting our souls. And if we take my advice, we shall believe that the soul is immortal and capable of coping with all evils and all goods, and we shall keep always to the upper way, doing what-

---

[29] Belief in the transmigration of souls between humans and animals is attributed to Pythagoras and claimed in the fragments of the fifth-century Sicilian sage Empedocles. It seems connected to a larger context of shamanistic and magical practice in Anatolian and Asiatic cultures.

[30] These topographic features of Socrates' underworld probably derive from Orphic and Pythagorean belief.

[31] That our souls become stars after death, and conversely that stars are living intelligences, are ideas to be found in a variety of contexts in antiquity.

[32] The expression was proverbial, and plays on two senses of the Greek: 'the story was preserved', and 'the story came home safe'. The second of these phrases means that a story has reached its appropriate conclusion.

ever we can to practise justice with wisdom. That way we shall be friends
to ourselves and to the gods, both while we remain here and when we
d carry off our prizes afterwards, like winning athletes on their victory tour.
And so, here and on the thousand-year journey we have described, let us
fare well.'

Glossary

All dates in the glossary entries are BC. *Among alphabetically arranged works of reference that can usefully supplement this glossary are: S. Hornblower and A. Spawforth, eds.,* The Oxford Classical Dictionary *(3rd edn, Oxford: Oxford University Press, 1996), and P. Grimal,* The Dictionary of Classical Mythology *(Oxford: Blackwell, 1985).*

ACHILLES. Legendary champion of the Greeks in the Trojan War, and hero of Homer's *Iliad.* He was the son of a mortal, Peleus, and a goddess, Thetis. In response to his mother's prophecy that if he joined the expedition to Troy he would die young, though gloriously, whereas if he remained in his homeland he would live a long but uneventful life, he famously chose glory. Socrates in Plato's *Apology* (28b–d), on trial for his life, cites Achilles' contempt for death as a model.

ADEIMANTUS, son of Ariston and Perictione, brother of Glaucon and of Plato. The order of age, from oldest to youngest brother, is usually taken to be: Adeimantus, Glaucon, Plato. Adeimantus is mentioned as one of the companions present with Plato at Socrates' trial in the *Apology* (34a). (Glaucon is not.) We would not know of Plato's brothers were it not for their relationship to Plato. Adeimantus in the *Republic*, unlike Glaucon, is not given explicit characterising labels, beyond the credit that he shares with his brother for heroism in war (368a), but is rather characterised by his behaviour. He seems as capable as his brother of firm interventions (e.g. 419a, 487b), and is not lacking in the spirit of competition (362d, 548d). He is if anything better acquainted than Glaucon with Socrates' philosophic practice (487b–d). He is passionate about the importance of education and the cultural environment, which is the focus of his long speech in Book 2 (362e, and compare 376d, 424d–e).

ADRASTEIA. As the personification of necessity or fate, she imposed on mortals the inevitable consequences of their actions, and was therefore the divinity to appease in advance (as at 451a) when undertaking something rash.

AESCHYLUS (525–456). The earliest of the great writers of tragic drama at Athens.

AGAMEMNON. Legendary king and supreme commander of the Greek forces in the Trojan War. On his return from Troy he was murdered by his wife and her lover. His choice of an eagle's life in the myth of Er (620b) matches his status; the eagle was regarded as a kingly bird, and was sacred to Zeus, king of the gods.

AJAX. The archetype of the mighty warrior and man of honour. The Greek kings in the army at Troy (including Agamemnon) awarded the armour of the dead Achilles to Odysseus rather than to him, either succumbing to Odysseus' rhetorical skill or else because of some outright collusion instigated by Odysseus. Ajax reacted with a bout of madness, then committed suicide out of shame at what he had done while mad.

ANACHARSIS (sixth century). Sage and traveller from Scythia – an extensive non-Greek area north of the Black Sea. The Scythians were known among the Greeks for their nomadism and general wildness; Anacharsis was therefore an exceptional figure, an intellectual and an admirer of Greek ways despite being raised among barbarians. He was credited with inventing the anchor, and the potter's wheel. Some, although not Plato, list him among the Seven Sages.

ARCADIA. Backward region in the central Peloponnese. At 565d Socrates alludes to its cult of Zeus on 'Wolf-mountain' (Mt Lycaeum). The legendary King Lycaon was said to have sacrificed a child at Zeus' altar, for which he was turned into a wolf. It was thought that on each occasion of sacrifice in the cult that derived from this incident someone else became a werewolf.

ARCHILOCHUS of Paros (an island in the Cyclades chain), fl. 680–640, was one of the earliest iambic and elegiac poets, and one of the most renowned.

ARDIAEUS. Described as tyrant of Pamphylia at 615c, he is not a character known to history, and may be Plato's invention.

ARGOS. Greek city, home to King Agamemnon.

ARISTOPHANES (*c.* 455–386). The greatest writer of the kind of comic drama ('Old Comedy') that prevailed at Athens in the late fifth and early fourth century – although his final plays participate in the new style known as 'Middle Comedy'. Several of his plays have utopian themes, and one, *Women at the Assembly* (or *Ecclesiazusae*), produced in the late 390s, has many elements in common with the *Republic* (see pp. xvii–xviii of the introduction). Socrates is the comic butt of the *Clouds*, produced in 423. Plato has Socrates make much of this in the *Apology*; nevertheless, he gives Aristophanes one of the most memorable speeches in the *Symposium*.

ARISTOTLE (384–322). One of the greatest philosophers of antiquity, and the most famous of those who studied with Plato in the Academy. He came from Stagira in north Greece, near Macedon, and his Macedonian ties were in part the cause of his leaving Athens after Plato's death. He was for a time the tutor to Alexander the Great, son of Philip II of Macedon. He returned to Athens in 335 and founded his own school. He produced important work in almost all aspects of philosophy, but most directly relevant to the *Republic* are his *Politics* and *Nicomachean Ethics*; also the *Topics*, which codifies dialectical argument. Book 2 of the *Politics* begins with a critique of the *Republic* and *Laws*, as well as of the utopian schemes of Hippodamus and Phaleas (see pp. xvii–xviii of the introduction).

ASCLEPIUS, mythical patron of medicine. Asclepius was a mortal, or according to some a demi-god, who was raised to full divine status after his death. Zeus struck him dead with a thunderbolt as punishment for having taken the healing art so far as to restore a dead (or in some versions a near-dead) man to life. At 408c Socrates mentions the claim that Asclepius' motive for this act was mercenary: see Pindar, *Pythian* 3.47–58. His sons, Machaon and Podalirius, were the medical experts in the Greek army at Troy (Homer, *Iliad* 11.833). The phrase 'descendants of Asclepius', however, which is used at 599c, can also embrace the members of the Asclepiad school, since 'Asclepiad' can mean both 'of Asclepius' family' and 'intellectually affiliated with Asclepius'. By the late fifth century the cult of Asclepius was firmly established and his temples had become popular centres of healing, with his priests the presiding physicians. The preferred method of therapy was by 'incubation': the patient slept in the temple and hoped for a dream that the priests could interpret in such a way as to reveal the cause of his malady and indicate the path of cure.

ASIA MINOR. A region of the ancient world roughly coterminous with modern Turkey.

ATALANTA. A legendary tomboy, who loved hunting and other masculine pursuits, and evaded marriage by challenging her suitors to a running-race, which she consistently won. It took a stratagem to defeat her: a suitor dropped apples of gold in her path, unique treasures which she could not resist pausing to pick up.

BENDIS. Thracian divinity, one of several known to have acquired devotees at Athens from the fifth century onwards. Unusually for a Thracian cult, that of Bendis acquired official status within the Athenian religious calendar. The evidence of inscriptions places the date of the first celebration of the type described in Book 1 no earlier than 431 and no later than 411. By our calendar, the festival took place in June. The sanctuary of Bendis was located in the Piraeus. She was compared to the native goddesses Artemis, Hecate and Persephone – all three connected with death and the underworld. The way of referring to her at 327a, simply as 'the goddess', was widely used of Persephone. The double parade mentioned there, co-ordinated between Athenian citizens and Thracians in separate groups, was a distinctive feature of her festival. Also unusual was the torch race, because it took place on horseback. By comparison with the rites of native gods, those honouring Thracian divinities were wilder, louder, riskier.

BIAS of Priene (a Greek city on the coast of Asia Minor). Active in the early sixth century, he was considered among the wisest of the Seven Sages. He is named with Pittacus in Socrates' listing of the seven in Plato's *Protagoras* (343a) – further details under 'Pittacus'. His best-known saying was 'most men are bad'.

CEPHALUS. A wealthy immigrant who came to Athens from Syracuse in Sicily at the invitation of Pericles. As metics (resident aliens), he and his sons Polemarchus and Lysias could not become landowners in Attica, and were excluded from formal participation in the political institutions of

Athens, although they could certainly foster political sympathies and connections, as we know Lysias did. Economic activity, however, was fully open to them, and metics were liable for a full range of taxes, including a special levy on their right of residence, as well as for civic services, among them service in the military. It may have been Cephalus who set up the workshop manufacturing weapons that we know his sons directed. The Piraeus, the port-district of Athens, was in any case a businessman's natural home, and it was here that Cephalus lived for thirty years, undisturbed. A similarly peaceful life was not the lot of his sons (see 'Lysias', and pp. xi–xiii of the introduction).

CERBERUS. The dog who stood guard at the gates of the underworld. He had three heads, and his body ended in a snake's tail. He is sometimes pictured with snake-heads growing from his spine.

CHARMANTIDES. On the assumption that he and Cleitophon are present with Thrasymachus at Cephalus' house in the role of associates and supporters of Thrasymachus, it would make sense that he should be the same Charmantides mentioned by the rhetorician Isocrates as one of his students (*Antidosis* 93–94). The anachronism would be gross, however, since Isocrates was either a child or no more than a youth at the time of the *Republic*'s action; in which case the Charmantides of the dialogue would be the grandfather of Isocrates' student, whom we know to have served as one of the many public treasurers in the year 427/6. It is possible, nevertheless, that Plato is using the grandfather's name as a mischievous allusion to the pupil of his rival Isocrates. The family must have been a wealthy one. Paeania is one of the demes or districts of Attica. That Charmantides is designated by his deme would be sufficient to show that he was an Athenian citizen.

CHARONDAS (sixth century). Wrote the lawcodes for a number of Greek colonies, including his native Catana in Sicily, and others in Sicily and south Italy. He is credited with the law that contracts should be entered into at each party's own risk, mentioned at 556b. It was not part of the Athenian lawcode.

CHEIRON. A centaur, skilled in many arts, to whom the boy Achilles was entrusted for his education.

CHIMAERA. A mythical monster, part lion, part snake, part goat.

CLEITOPHON, son of Aristonymus. Plutarch (*On the Fortune of Alexander* 328c) mentions him in a list of associates of Socrates who eventually rejected Socrates' influence, although it is unclear whether this judgment is more than an inference from Cleitophon's intervention in support of Thrasymachus at 340a together with his challenge to Socrates on themes from the *Republic* in the eponymous dialogue *Cleitophon* (whose Platonic authorship is a matter of dispute). He may well be the Cleitophon who was an ally of Theramenes, the leader of a moderate oligarchic coup at Athens in 411, and an opponent of the extreme oligarchy of the Thirty – an opposition for which Theramenes receives little credit from the democrat Lysias (*Against Eratosthenes* 62–78). This Cleitophon is also described along with Theramenes in Aristophanes' *Frogs* (967) as an enthusiast of Euripidean sophistry, and is associated by implication in the charge of political trimming that the playwright lays there against Theramenes.

CREOPHYLUS. We know little about him. Late sources make him a relative of Homer's as well as an epic poet. The name is built from the words for 'meat' and 'tribe'. When Socrates mocks it at 600c, this is probably for its suggestion of uncultured excess. The Greeks reserved meat for ritual occasions. The sophisticated delicacy, by contrast, was fish. There may also be an implicit contrast, in context, with the vegetarianism of the Pythagoreans.

CRETE. Major island in the south Aegean, whose inhabitants were of the same Dorian tribe as the Spartans, and whose culture, like that of Sparta, stood out in the Greek world for its militarism and for the practice of dining in common mess halls. Plato's *Laws* is set in Crete. Aristotle, *Politics* 1271b20–1272b23 is an important source of information on the Cretan way of life.

DAEDALUS. Legendary master-craftsman and inventor, designer of the Cretan Labyrinth and patron of all sculptors. He is mentioned twice in the Platonic dialogues for having made statues so life-like they were able to move and had to be chained down (*Euthyphro* 11b–e, *Meno* 97d), and is twice claimed as an ancestor by Socrates, whose father was a sculptor (*Euthyphro* 11b, *Alcibiades* 121a).

DAMON. An Athenian intellectual who flourished in the second half of the fifth century, and was influential with the leading statesman Pericles

– a political involvement which eventually caused him to be exiled. Inspired by Pythagorean ideas, he developed a theory of the influence of the different modes and rhythms of music on the emotions, hence of its importance in the education of character. He seems also to have been a creative musician, and is credited with the invention of the 'relaxed Lydian' mode (one of those that Socrates declares unsuitable for his warlike guardians, 398e). He receives further respectful mention elsewhere in the Platonic dialogues: *Laches* 180d, 197d; *Alcibiades* 118c. Plutarch (*Life of Pericles* 4) describes his specialisation in music as a cover for his political ideas and for his desire to influence the powerful – but the claim is perhaps not independent of the generalisation Plato puts in the mouth of Protagoras, *Protagoras* 316e.

DORIAN. Name of a Greek tribe whose principal members were found in the Peloponnese and in Crete and included the Spartans. Also the name of a musical mode traditionally associated with this tribe.

EGYPT. In Plato's day, an important trading partner for the Greek states, noted for its *entrepôts* as much as for its long and distinguished history.

EPEIUS. The master-craftsman who designed the Trojan horse – the tool of deception by which Troy was finally captured. The stratagem was devised by Odysseus.

ER, son of Armenius. The names 'Er' and 'Armenius' are not Greek. We do not know whether Plato made them up or took them over from foreign sources. A Christian writer later identified Plato's Er with the Iranian Zoroaster, founder of a religious system in which light and dark are equal and opposing powers, who was known to the Greeks by the fifth century. But the myth in which Er figures in Book 10 seems to borrow from a variety of religious and mystic traditions.

ERIPHYLE. Wife of Amphiaraus, the wise seer who took part in the legendary expedition featured in Aeschylus' *Seven against Thebes*, quotations from which, referring to Amphiaraus, occur at 361b, 362a, 550c. He refused at first to join the expedition, having foretold his own death if he did, but Eriphyle, to whom the decision was referred for arbitration, took the bribe of a gold necklace and sent him off to his doom. She was eventually murdered by her own son.

EURIPIDES (*c.* 480–406). The most overtly intellectual and innovative of the great writers of tragic drama at Athens, and satirised for it by

Aristophanes in his comedy *Frogs*. He spent the last two years of his life as a guest of King Archelaus of Macedon – one of several artists who came to that court – and wrote a play about one of the king's ancestors. Archelaus is portrayed as a typical tyrant in Plato's *Gorgias*.

EURYPYLUS. Greek soldier whose wounds are treated by Patroclus in Homer's *Iliad*. Socrates' account of this incident at 405e, however, is garbled. The mulled wine is in fact given to the wounded physician Machaon, son of Asclepius, and for refreshment and sustenance rather than as a treatment for his wound (*Iliad* 11.618–664). Patroclus is present only to ask after Machaon's condition; he does not treat Eurypylus until later, and then with an herbal poultice rather than a wine posset (11.822–848). Plato gives an accurate version of the incident in the *Ion* (538b–c). One effect of substituting Eurypylus for Machaon is to pass over in notable silence a classic example of a physician in need of healing himself.

EUTHYDEMUS, son of Cephalus and brother to Polemarchus and Lysias. Nothing further is known of him. He is not the Euthydemus who appears in Plato's dialogue of that name.

GLAUCON, son of Ariston and Perictione, brother of Adeimantus and of Plato. The order of age, from oldest to youngest brother, is usually taken to be: Adeimantus, Glaucon, Plato. Xenophon (*Memorabilia* 3.6.1) portrays Glaucon as politically ambitious and says that he attempted to speak in public assembly before he was even twenty, allowing himself to be dissuaded only by Socrates. In the *Republic* he (like Adeimantus) is a war-hero (368a), and is described as competitive (548d), a bold and determined character (357a), a passionate lover (474d), and musically sophisticated (398e). He makes a well-disposed audience for Socrates (474a), and is reasonably familiar with Socratic practice (475e), but his interventions often border on the impatient and dismissive. For a list of them, consult the index under 'Glaucon'.

GLAUCUS. Legendary character who began life as an ordinary mortal and became a god of the sea by accident, as a result of eating a magical herb. The story was told that he fell in love with Scylla, one of the monsters to which the wax model of the soul is compared at 588c.

GYGES. One historical character who bore this name was the founder of the third dynasty of kings of Lydia (a wealthy territory in what is now western Turkey). The dynasty ended with the reign of Croesus in the mid-sixth century, after which Lydia became a dependency of Persia. Herodotus 1.8–13 tells a story somewhat resembling Glaucon's in Book 2 (359c ff.), at least insofar as the throne is usurped through adultery with the queen, but he makes no mention of the ring of invisibility, and attributes the actions to Gyges himself rather than, as Glaucon does, to Gyges' ancestor. It was common for ancestors and descendants to share the same name, but Glaucon's manner of identifying the hero of his story ('the ancestor of the Lydian Gyges') would then be peculiar, since it was the usurper who was the famous Gyges – indeed, Herodotus records no other of that name in the line. Moreover, in Book 10 Socrates speaks directly of the 'ring of Gyges' (612b), rather than of the ring of Gyges' ancestor. Possibly Glaucon's allusion to the ancestor is an attempt to isolate the fabulous details of his story in a suitably unhistorical past, even at the cost of solecism, and this in turn is intended by Plato to reveal something about Glaucon. Some emend the text at 359d to read 'Gyges the ancestor of the Lydian [i.e. Croesus]'.

HADES. The god of the underworld and ruler of the dead. His cap, mentioned at 612b, conferred invisibility on its wearer.

HERACLITUS (fl. 500). Philosopher from Ephesus (a Greek city on the coast of Asia Minor), notorious for his obscure and riddling style. He constructed paradoxes involving the unity of opposites and the idea that, despite appearances, everything is in continuous flux. Aristotle describes his work as an important influence on Plato. The reference to 'Heraclitus' sun' at 498a is to his statement that the sun's fire is extinguished each night and rekindled each morning: 'the sun is new each day' (DK 22 B 6).

HERODICUS. A figure satirised in Plato's dialogues as a hypochondriac and a quack physical trainer. In addition to his appearance at 406a he is mentioned at *Phaedrus* 227d for his regimen of long walks, and at *Protagoras* 316e figures in Protagoras' list of intellectuals whose specialisation masked wider intellectual pretensions.

HESIOD (fl. 700). Along with Homer, treated by the Greeks as their second great epic poet. His most important works are the *Theogony* and the *Works and Days* – the first a genealogy of the gods, the second a work of instruction and exhortation comparable to examples of 'wisdom literature' from other ancient cultures. Aristotle vacillates between treating him as an embryonic philosopher and dismissing him as a mythologer (*Metaphysics* 984b23, 989a10 vs. 1000a9).

HOMER. Acknowledged by the Greeks as their greatest epic poet, and – given the high status of the epic genre, and given Homer's antiquity by Plato's time – their most venerable poet *tout court*. His work is to be dated at least as early as the eighth century. He was thought in antiquity to have composed not only the *Iliad* and *Odyssey* but also the comic poem *Margites*.

HYDRA. Mythical monster whose many venomous heads had the property of re-sprouting when cut off – two heads for each one that was severed – rendering it almost impossible to kill.

INACHUS. A river-god. His daughter Io, originally a priestess of Hera, was persecuted by Hera for being the object of Zeus' passion, and transformed into a cow. The 'life-giving sons' of Inachus mentioned at 381d are presumably his tributaries.

IONIAN. Tribal name for the Greeks of Attica, the region around Athens, and also the name of a musical mode traditionally associated with this region.

ISMENIAS. Theban politician and general, leader of an anti-Spartan faction, who helped restore democracy at Athens in 403. He went on to foment the Corinthian War, in which an alliance of major Greek cities attempted to subdue Sparta. He was said to have taken Persian money to do it, and to have represented Persian interests to the detriment of Greek. In the *Meno* (90a) he is mentioned as a bribe-taker. He is the odd man out in the list at 336a, both because the others named there are famous autocrats and because his most notable political achievements post-date the dramatic action of the *Republic*.

ISOCRATES (436–338). An Athenian rhetorician, writer and educator of major importance. His early associations were with a wide variety of intellectual figures, including Socrates, Prodicus and Theramenes, the last of whom came to represent the moderate oligarchic opposition to the tyrant Critias (see pp. xi–xiii of the introduction). Around 390 he opened a school of what he called 'philosophy', although its technical training was confined to the art of words, and he explicitly avoided the more abstruse metaphysical, epistemological and scientific investigations pursued in

Plato's Academy, interesting himself rather in practical ethics and political matters. He is regarded as a founding theorist of what has come to be called 'liberal' education. He attracted students from abroad as well as from Athens, and many became important statesmen, while others were historians and poets. He made a name for himself with a series of political writings cast mainly in the form of speeches. A favourite theme was to urge the Greek states to find their common good in united resistance against Persia ('panhellenism'). Another was kingship – its duties, goals, and capacity to inspire. Isocrates also made requests to monarchs to resolve political crises, notably to Dionysius I and, later, Philip of Macedon. For more on his relation to Plato, see pp. xviii–xxii of the introduction.

ITHACA. Island-kingdom of Odysseus, and scene of much of Homer's *Odyssey*.

LACHESIS. One of the three traditional 'Fates', who control the destiny of mortals and immortals. Her name means 'the Allotter'. The names of the other two Fates, Clotho and Atropos, mean respectively 'the Spinner' and 'the Unswayable'. The image of their spinning the thread of each human life was conventional. Their wearing of white robes at 617c, however, may allude to Orphic tradition in particular.

LOTUS-EATERS. A people visited by Odysseus on his return voyage (Homer, *Odyssey* 9.82–104). When Odysseus' scouts share the food of the Lotus-eaters they lose all sense of responsibility and no longer wish to make the journey home.

LYCURGUS. Of uncertain historicity. Tradition credited him with establishing the legal constitution of Sparta and, more generally, its militarism and devotion to discipline, which he modelled on the institutions of Crete. See Herodotus 1.65–66, Xenophon's *Spartan Constitution*, and Plutarch's *Life of Lycurgus*.

LYSANIAS. Father of Cephalus, not otherwise known.

LYSIAS, son of Cephalus, brother of Polemarchus and Euthydemus, and an important orator and writer. While still young he emigrated with his brothers to the new colony of Thurii (in the arch of Italy's boot). The place had about it a utopian flair: its townplan was ultra-modern, and its settlers, unusually, came from all parts of Greece, responding to the panhellenic initiative of Pericles. Eventual factionalism between oligarchic and democratic interests drove the brothers, who grouped themselves with the democrats, back to Athens in 412, where they directed a large workshop in the Piraeus that manufactured weapons. In 404 their wealth, democratic sympathies and vulnerability as resident aliens attracted the hostility of the oligarchic junta ('the Thirty') that a victorious Sparta had newly established at Athens. (The leader of the Thirty, Critias, was a relative of Plato's.) Polemarchus was executed, while Lysias escaped into exile, from which he returned when democracy was restored in the following year, and worked for the remainder of his life as a writer of speeches for legal clients. The speech *Against Eratosthenes* is his own prosecution of his brother's murderer. In the *Olympic Speech* he represents the tyrant Dionysius I of Syracuse – Plato's first Sicilian host – as a danger to all Greece. In Plato's *Phaedrus* a speech on love purporting to be by Lysias is read out and subjected to criticism. On the question why the action of the *Republic* is set in his family home, see pp. xi–xiii of the introduction.

MARSYAS. One of the satyrs – bawdy creatures, part man, part animal. As an enthusiast of the reed-pipe he challenged the lyre- and cithara-playing god Apollo to a musical contest, and lost. The penalty inflicted by the god of music was to flay Marsyas alive. Despite Socrates' claim at 399e to be doing nothing radical in banning the reed-pipe, its absence would in fact have made a difference to Athenian musical life comparable to that of banning amplified instruments from modern music. Alcibiades in the *Symposium* (215b–c) compares Socrates himself to Marsyas, claiming he can excite and inspire with his words as Marsyas did with his reed-pipe.

MIDAS. A proverbially wealthy – and foolish – king of Phrygia (in the area of what is now central Turkey)

MIXOLYDIAN. Name of a musical mode traditionally associated with Lydia, a region of Asia Minor. It means 'mixed Lydian'.

MUSAEUS. Legendary poet, prominent in the genealogy of the clan in charge of the Eleusinian mysteries. Cosmogonies, hymns, oracles and healing pronouncements were attributed to him in antiquity. Like Orpheus, his association with mystic rites and regimen renders him half-poet, half-shaman.

MUSE. The Muses were patron goddesses of artistic expression in all its forms. Poets conventionally appealed to them, as Socrates does at 545e, for direct knowledge of truths that come to human beings only at second hand, and are subject to distortion over time (as in Homer, *Iliad* 2.484–486). But equally familiar to Plato's audience would be the lines that Hesiod attributes to the Muses as a way of authorising his poetic vocation: 'Lies that seem genuine – there's our repertoire; yet now and then we'll choose to sing a truth' (*Theogony* 27–28). To speak of the 'Muse' of philosophy, as Socrates does at 499d, is to lay emphasis on the philosopher as performer or communicator. Strict assignment of particular Muses to particular arts was the pleasure of a later age, but in the *Phaedrus* (259d) Socrates names Calliope ('Beautiful-Voice') and Ourania ('Heavenly') as the philosophic Muses. Calliope was said by Hesiod to be the Muse who aids kings in their political rhetoric (*Theogony* 79–93).

NICERATUS. His father Nicias was an Athenian general important to the conduct of the Peloponnesian War, who orchestrated a temporary peace between Athens and Sparta in 421, and perished leading the disastrous Athenian expedition against Syracuse in 413. In the *Laches* Nicias displays great concern for the education of his son, and an eagerness to entrust him to Socrates. Niceratus, like Polemarchus, was executed by order of the Thirty during their reign in 404–403. In Xenophon's *Hellenica* (2.3.39) his fate is described as particularly outrageous given his refusal to curry favour with the common people.

NUMBER. The number that governs the reproduction of human beings, described at 546c–d, has become so renowned for its obscurity as to merit a title: the 'nuptial number', or simply 'Plato's number'. Interpreters even disagree as to how obscure the description was originally intended to be. The numbers that form the basis of the musical fourth are 3 and 4, because this interval is expressible as the proportion 4:3. Couple them with 5 and we have $3 \times 4 \times 5 = 60$. To increase this number three times is to raise it to the power of 4, which gives 12,960,000. This in turn can be geometrically represented in two ways: as a square of side 3,600 ('so many times 100'); or as a rectangle of sides $4,800 \times 2,700$. (Greek mathematicians built a series of squares out of odd numbers and rectangles out of even numbers, the squares being similar and the rectangles dissimilar; so odd numbers cause similarity and even numbers dissimilarity.) Take the long side of the rectangle first. The length of the diagonal of a 5×5 square is the square root of 50 – an irrational number. The *rational* diagonal is the rational number nearest to this, i.e. 7. Square this, subtract one, and multiply by 100, and you have 4,800. You can reach the same figure by the alternative route of squaring the square root of 50, subtracting 2, and multiplying by 100. Now take the short side of the rectangle. 2,700 is $(3\times3\times3)\times100$. The sentence preceding this whole calculation is taken by some to be a further analysis of it, by others – as in this translation – to refer to a different number, 216. This is the sum of the cubes of 3, 4 and 5, and it is their cubing that is described as the taking on of three dimensions and four limits. The symbolism of these numbers is variously explained. For example, 216 is the number of days in a seven-month pregnancy (regarded as a standard gestation period – see 461d). 12,960,000 is assumed to be the number of days Plato reckoned in the Great Year – one complete cycle of the cosmos. The relation between these numbers would then suggest a correspondence between microcosm and macrocosm. Quite different is the approach and translation of Edit Ehrhardt, 'The word of the Muses', *Classical Quarterly* 36 (1986) 407–420, for whom the passage does not reveal a mystic number but describes a series of right-angled triangles with rational sides. One of the sides is always odd, the other even, representing male and female bound together by the hypotenuse. The rulers must marry odd and even, as it were, to build the series, and the problem that arises with such a series – the problem Socrates describes, on this interpretation – is that it becomes impossible to decide which numbers should be paired with which. This approach has the advantage that Socrates would be alluding, poetically but not impenetrably, to a mathematical series well known in the ancient world and of mathematical interest in its own right, rather than constructing a riddle around a quite straightforward arithmetical calculation that would not otherwise pose a problem. On the other hand, the disjunction between elaborate riddle and simple answer may be Plato's point. On either approach, the importance of the numbers 3, 4 and 5 is that they define the first right-angled triangle with rational sides. Pythagorean sources praise its beauty and endeavour to find it at work in the cosmos.

ODYSSEUS. Legendary king of Ithaca. His ten-year return journey from the Trojan War is the theme of Homer's *Odyssey*. As a heroic type he is noted not only for his prowess in battle but especially for his craftiness and sagacity.

ORPHEUS (ORPHICS). Not only was Orpheus the supreme poet and musician of legend but in classical times his name was associated with purificatory and healing rites and with a special regimen of life (Plato at *Laws* 782c calls vegetarianism 'Orphic'). His origins were Thracian. He died at the hands of Thracian women who tore him apart in the course of a frenzied occult ritual. His choice of a swan's life in the myth of Er (620a) matches his previous life in so far as the swan was a creature sacred to Apollo, god of music, and famous for singing when on the point of death.

PALAMEDES. Greek hero of the Trojan War. It was characteristic of Greek myth to regard the attributes of civilisation as the creation of individual inventors, divine or heroic. Palamedes was one such, credited with inventing not only number (as at 522d) but writing and the concept of the code of law. If Agamemnon, supreme commander of the Greek army, is the type of the king, Palamedes is the type of the philosopher – indeed of the persecuted philosopher, since he was unjustly tried and executed. Socrates in Plato's *Apology* takes him as a model in that respect (41b). Aeschylus, Sophocles and Euripides all wrote plays, now lost, that centred on the story of Palamedes.

PAMPHYLIA. A region in south-western Asia Minor. In Plato's day it was under Persian control. Its etymology in Greek suggests the meaning 'region of every sort of tribe'.

PERDICCAS II usurped the kingship of Macedon and ruled *c.* 450–413. During the Peloponnesian War he showed notable *realpolitik* in shifting his allegiance many times between Athens and Sparta. In Plato's *Gorgias* (471a–d) it is his son Archelaus who is the type of the unscrupulous tyrant.

PERIANDER, renowned tyrant of Corinth from *c.* 625 to 585. He is again listed with Perdiccas as a classic tyrant in the *Theages* (124c–e). (The Platonic authorship of this dialogue is insecure.) He also figures among the Seven Sages, but notably not in Plato's enumeration of them at *Protagoras* 343a, in which he is replaced by Myson, an obscure Spartan philosopher.

PHOCYLIDES. Aphoristic poet of sixth-century Miletus (a Greek city on the coast of Asia Minor), of whose work only a few fragments survive. The saying of his mentioned at 407a may have meant simply that it is difficult to concentrate on virtue if you are dirt poor – compare Cephalus' description of the advantages of wealth at 331b.

PHOENICIA. Coastal region of the eastern Mediterranean roughly co-terminous with modern Lebanon, inhabited by Semites who were noted sea-traders. The story that Socrates tells at 414c is 'of Phoenician origin' because it features citizens springing full-grown from the earth, as hap-

pened when Cadmus, originally from Phoenicia, populated his new city –
the Greek city of Thebes – by sowing a dragon's teeth, each of which
became an armed man. Cadmus' citizens, unlike those in Socrates' myth,
immediately set about fighting each other. The politically useful claim
that one's ancestors sprang from the very land still occupied by one's
people was made by other Greek communities also, notably Athens. Plato
puts it to different work in the myth of the *Statesman* (269b).

PHRYGIAN. Name of a musical mode traditionally associated with
Phrygia, central Asia Minor.

PINDAR (518–438). Important lyric poet, whose victory odes, performed
in celebration of athletic success in contests such as the Olympic games,
survive almost entire. His style is solemn and sententious. His mode of
poetry was old-fashioned, although classic, by the time in which the
Republic is set.

PIRAEUS. The port district of Athens, located approximately five miles
south-west of the city. At the interface with foreign trade and foreign cultures, it was a natural home for resident aliens (such as Cephalus and
family), many of whom were merchants, as well as for the cults of foreign
gods (such as Bendis). Partly for this reason, and partly because it served
as base for the naval fleet, whose sailors were drawn from the lower eche-
lons of Athenian society, it was also the natural home for radical democrats (such as Cephalus' son Lysias), who were known as 'the party of the
Piraeus'. The Athenian Stranger in the *Laws* (704d–705b) decries the
unsettling effect on public morality of having a port nearby.

PITTACUS of Mytilene (the main city of Lesbos, an island off the coast of
Asia Minor), lived between the late seventh and early sixth centuries. He
is named with Bias among the Seven Sages in the *Protagoras* (343a), where
Socrates is analysing a poem by Simonides that criticises Pittacus' apoph-
thegm 'it is hard to be good'. Socrates makes a point of the laconic,
proverbial manner in which the Seven Sages philosophised. Having
joined with the poet Alcaeus in the overthrow of the tyrant of Lesbos, he
became in turn a famous target of Alcaeus' invective in a contest for political influence.

POLEMARCHUS, son of Cephalus, brother of Lysias and Euthydemus.
For details of Polemarchus' life see under 'Lysias', who achieved greater
renown and is our principal source of information for the family's story.

In the *Phaedrus* (257b) Polemarchus is described as having turned himself to philosophic activity. His name means 'War Leader'.

POLYDAMAS. Famous athlete from Thessaly (north Greece) who won the pancratiasts' event – a combination of wrestling and boxing – in the Olympic games of 408.

PRODICUS of Ceos (an island in the Cyclades chain). A sophist, contemporary with Socrates, who is portrayed by Plato as a specialist in the study of language, particularly in the drawing of fine distinctions among words. The portrayal is often comic: see *Protagoras* 337a–c. He also wrote on other matters: Xenophon (*Memorabilia* 2.1.21–34) paraphrases his 'Choice of Heracles', in which the hero chooses between virtue and vice; and he is reported to have given a naturalistic account of the origin of man's worship of gods. Socrates in Plato's dialogues likes to call himself a disciple of Prodicus (*Protagoras* 341a, *Meno* 96d).

PROTAGORAS of Abdera (a Greek city on the coast of Thrace), *c.* 490–420. The most famous of the sophists, he was welcomed by the Athenian elite and invited by the Athenian leader Pericles to write the constitution for Thurii (see under 'Lysias'). Few fragments of his voluminous writings survive, but the titles cover a wide variety of topics. He proposed agnosticism with regard to the gods, and that 'man is the measure of all things'. The latter doctrine is attacked in the *Theaetetus*. The *Protagoras* shows him discoursing on political and ethical matters, and makes him a sympathetic theorist of democracy.

PYTHAGORAS (PYTHAGOREANS). Pythagoras was a late sixth-century sage who emigrated from Samos (an island off the coast of Asia Minor) to Croton in south Italy, where he founded a community of initiates into his system of beliefs. Features of this system were its mathematical and musical bent, by which harmonic ratios were associated with the structure of the entire cosmos, and its treatment of the soul as a prisoner in the body – a prison from which it escapes at death, but only to be reincarnated in successive bodies until a life sufficiently pure can release it from the cycle for good (the idea is adapted by Plato in the *Phaedo*). Details of the way of life of the Pythagorean community are known only from late and not especially reliable sources, but there are elements in it akin to the life of Plato's guardians: women were said to have been equal members, strict purity and discipline were enjoined on all, and eugenic practices governed marriage and procreation. There were also strict dietary regulations: vegetarianism (as among the Orphics) and abstention from eating beans. The community rose to political power in Croton and made the city influential. Eventually it aroused hostility and was disbanded by the end of the fifth century. Archytas of Tarentum, with whom Plato associated, revived the way of life in Italy in the fourth century. He is the Pythagorean, mentioned at 530d, who called astronomy and music sister sciences, although he added geometry, arithmetic and 'spherics' to the list (DK 47 B 1).

PYTHIAN. Title of Apollo. The 'Pythian priestess' was the channel for the oracle of Apollo at Delphi.

SCYLLA. A mythical monster in the shape of a woman with six dog-heads growing from her waist.

SCYTHIA. A region that is now the Crimea and part of the Ukraine, inhabited by non-Greeks who were reputed to be fierce warriors and skilled horsemen.

SELENE. The moon – which, like all heavenly bodies, was traditionally thought of as divine.

SEVEN SAGES. A traditional roll call of wise men from the archaic age of Greece.

SERIPHUS. A small, barren, insignificant island of the Cyclades chain in the Aegean sea.

SIMONIDES (556–468). Famous poet of whose work little survives. Plato devotes a long scene in the *Protagoras* (339a–348a) to the satirical analysis of a poem addressed by Simonides to his patron, the Thessalian tyrant Scopas, in which Socrates makes a point of Simonides' having put his poetry at the service of tyrants (346b). Again, it is in the entourage of the Athenian tyrant Hipparchus that Simonides appears in the *Hipparchus* (228c), enticed there by the large fees (his avarice was notorious). (The Platonic authorship of the *Hipparchus* is disputed.) He also spent many years at the court of the Sicilian tyrant of his day, Hiero, and is represented in dialogue with him on the subject of tyranny in Xenophon's *Hiero*. As a fee-charging poet of untypically speculative range on moral and theological topics he may have been regarded by Plato as a proto-sophist – a precursor of the professional intellectuals against whom Socrates is often pitted in the dialogues. The phrase 'appearance overpowers truth', quoted without attribution by Adeimantus in Book 2 (365c), is his.

SOCRATES (470/69–399). Plato's philosophic mentor and protagonist of the majority of his dialogues. Plato is not our sole contemporary source of information about him: Xenophon's Socratic writings survive entire, as do fragments of works by other members of Socrates' circle. He was a favourite butt of comic drama, most famously in Aristophanes' *Clouds*. An Athenian citizen who served in its wars and took his turn in the political committee-work shared by all citizens of its democracy, he became notorious for neglecting his material affairs in favour of philosophic discussion. This he conducted by asking questions rather than offering answers. Those giving the answers typically discovered that they did not understand the topic half as well as they had imagined before Socrates began his work. Socrates would nevertheless insist that he did not himself possess the knowledge that they had been shown to lack (see 354c, 368b, 450e–451a, 506c, and compare *Apology* 23a–b). His insistence could seem ironic (as at 337a), and his technique then came across as a kind of entrapment (see 350e, 487b–c, and compare *Meno* 80a–b). He was reputed to seek out the young for his partners in philosophic conversation (328a; compare *Apology* 24b, 33c–d). In the *Republic* he is at least forty. Among his associates were leaders of the oligarchic junta, the Thirty, that took power in 404. After the restoration of democracy, Socrates was brought to trial as a subversive, on charges of impiety and of corrupting the young people with whom he so often associated (at 538a–539b Socrates admits that philosophic doubts can lead to cynicism). This was in 399, when he was seventy years old. He was found guilty by a narrow margin, and executed.

SOLON. Sixth-century Athenian statesman, sage and poet. Of aristocratic lineage, and an ancestor of Plato, he introduced reforms and drafted laws that struck a balance between the interests of higher and lower social classes at Athens, including the cancellation of enslavement for debt, the rearrangement of classes on the basis of property, and the proportional reassignment of political privileges to these classes. He was seen as a founding father of the Athens of the fifth and fourth centuries. He is portrayed as travelling to distant lands in the manner of an enquiring intellectual in Herodotus 1.29–33 and in Plato's *Timaeus* (21–25), and is listed among the Seven Sages. His political poetry survives in fragments: for a translation see *EGPT* 25–30. The line of his verse referred to at 536d runs: 'As age takes hold, it finds me learning much.'

SOPHISTS. Professional, itinerant teachers and intellectuals. Plato casts them as the opposite of the unprofessional Socrates, rooted in Athens, and often subjects them to satire, most tellingly in the *Protagoras*.

SOPHOCLES (*c.* 496–406). One of the greatest and most successful writers of tragic drama at Athens.

SPARTA. The major city of the Peloponnese, and Athens' great rival in the late fifth and early fourth century. Its way of life was distinctive, and Socrates' proposals for social reform in Book 5 reflect its influence: see pp. xiv–xvi of the introduction. Important ancient sources of information on the Spartan way of life are Xenophon, *Spartan Constitution*, Aristotle, *Politics* 1269a29–1271b19 and Plutarch, *Life of Lycurgus*.

STESICHORUS. Lyric poet, active in the first half of the sixth century. The story was told that he was struck blind for having written a poem criticising Helen of Troy for her infidelity, but recovered his sight by writing a retraction, according to which not Helen but her phantom eloped with Paris to Troy. The retraction is quoted in the *Phaedrus* (243a). Euripides used the story of the phantom in his play *Helen*.

SYNTONOLYDIAN. Name of a musical mode traditionally associated with Lydia, a region of Asia Minor. It means 'tense Lydian' – perhaps with reference to high tessitura.

TARTARUS. A traditional place of punishment, usually conceived as a chasm far beneath the underworld. In the eschatological myths of Plato's dialogues it serves as the repository for the worst criminals, as in the myth of Er (616a): see *Gorgias* 523b, 525c and *Phaedo* 114b.

THALES of Miletus (a Greek city on the coast of Asia Minor). Sixth-century sage and cosmologist, credited with various discoveries and inventions in astronomy, geometry and engineering – among them, predicting an eclipse, and measuring the height of the Egyptian pyramids by their shadow. Aristotle treats him as the first natural philosopher. Plato includes in the *Theaetetus* (174a) the story of his falling down a well because he was sky-gazing as he walked, a story which made him emblematic of the philosopher with his head in the clouds. He is a fixture in lists of the Seven Sages.

THAMYRAS (or Thamyris). Like Orpheus, a legendary musician and singer of Thracian origin, and often paired with him. He was said to have challenged the Muses themselves to a singing contest and been punished for his arrogance.

THEAGES. A member of Socrates' circle. In Plato's *Apology* (33e) he is mentioned at Socrates' trial as someone already deceased, although he was a generation younger than Socrates. In the *Theages*, commonly thought not to be by Plato, Socrates is shown taking him on as a student.

THEMISTOCLES (*c.* 524–459). One of the most prominent Athenian statesmen of his time, he served as a general in the Greek forces that combined to repulse the invading Persians. His career ended, however, in disgrace and exile.

THERSITES. Comic character in Homer's *Iliad* (2.211–277) – a common soldier, an ugly fellow, who likes to try raising a laugh from the troops by insolent banter at the expense of his superiors. But he ends up being made a laughing-stock himself, at the hands of Odysseus.

THRACE. Inhabited by non-Greeks and stretching across the north Aegean mainland in a region including modern Bulgaria, Thrace was an important trading partner for Athens. Thracians had a reputation as fierce warriors and expert horsemen, and were much used as mercenaries in the Greek world. Their organisation, both military and political, was looser than the Greek: their light-armed troops fought without strict formation; they lived in scattered villages and were never united under a single king. At Athens they could be objects both of fear and of derision (Aristophanes, *Acharnians* 135–173). A military alliance with their most powerful chieftain, Sitalces, was important to Athens in the early stages of the Peloponnesian War. In the *Charmides* (156d–157c) Socrates speaks respectfully of the skills of the Thracian healer Zalmoxis.

THRASYMACHUS of Chalcedon (a Greek-speaking city on the Asiatic side of the Bosporus opposite Byzantium). A professional practitioner and teacher of rhetoric, he was an important figure in the development of the discipline, known to us from many sources other than Plato. In Plato's *Phaedrus* (267c) he is credited with particular expertise in the manipulation of strong emotions and in mounting and dispelling accusations. A fragment of a political speech attributed to him expresses conservative views (DK 85 B 1, translated in *EGPT* 254–255). His name means 'Bold-in-Battle'.

XENOPHON (*c.* 427–354). Athenian writer and military man. In his youth he was a companion of Socrates, and later wrote Socratic dialogues and a Socratic notebook or series of recollections (the *Memorabilia*). He left Athens in 401 to serve as officer in a mercenary army called to assist in a conflict within the Persian royal family (the story is told in his *Anabasis*). Always a Spartan sympathiser, he was exiled in the 390s, probably for his fighting on the Spartan side against Athens at the battle of Coronea. He lived most of his life in territory controlled by Sparta, but seems to have returned to Athens, or to have been reconciled with Athens, towards the end. In addition to the Socratic works, his widely varied writings include history, historical romance, political theory and technical treatises (e.g. on horsemanship and hunting).

XERXES. King of Persia from 486 to 465, he led the great expedition against Greece which ended in defeat at Salamis and made way for the ascendancy of the Athenian empire in the mid fifth century.

Index

Reference to Plato's text is made by Stephanus page (i.e. by the numbers and letters that appear in the margin of the text). Roman numerals refer to the introduction. When a term or an identification appears in an editorial note rather than in Plato's text, reference is made to the Stephanus page together with the note (e.g. 'Aeschylus ... 381d with note 42'). Information on people and places mentioned in the text and in the introduction can be found in the glossary.

Cambridge Texts in the History of Political Thought

Titles published in the series thus far

Aristotle *The Politics* and *The Constitution of Athens* (edited by Stephen Everson)
  0 521 48400 6 paperback
Arnold *Culture and Anarchy and Other Writings* (edited by Stefan Collini)
  0 521 37796 x paperback
Astell *Political Writings* (edited by Patricia Springborg)
  0 521 42845 9 paperback
Augustine *The City of God against the Pagans* (edited by R. W. Dyson)
  0 521 46843 4 paperback
Austin *The Province of Jurisprudence Determined* (edited by Wilfrid E. Rumble)
  0 521 44756 9 paperback
Bacon *The History of the Reign of King Henry VII* (edited by Brian Vickers)
  0 521 58663 1 paperback
Bakunin *Statism and Anarchy* (edited by Marshall Shatz)
  0 521 36973 8 paperback
Baxter *Holy Commonwealth* (edited by William Lamont)
  0 521 40580 7 paperback
Bayle *Political Writings* (edited by Sally L. Jenkinson)
  0 521 47677 1 paperback
Beccaria *On Crimes and Punishments and Other Writings* (edited by Richard Bellamy)
  0 521 47982 7 paperback
Bentham *A Fragment on Government* (introduction by Ross Harrison)
  0 521 35929 5 paperback
Bernstein *The Preconditions of Socialism* (edited by Henry Tudor)
  0 521 39808 8 paperback
Bodin *On Sovereignty* (edited by Julian H. Franklin)
  0 521 34992 3 paperback
Bolingbroke *Political Writings* (edited by David Armitage)
  0 521 58697 6 paperback
Bossuet *Politics Drawn from the Very Words of Holy Scripture* (edited by Patrick Riley)
  0 521 36807 3 paperback
The British Idealists (edited by David Boucher)
  0 521 45951 6 paperback
Burke *Pre-Revolutionary Writings* (edited by Ian Harris)
  0 521 36800 6 paperback
Christine De Pizan *The Book of the Body Politic* (edited by Kate Langdon Forhan)
  0 521 42259 0 paperback

Cicero *On Duties* (edited by M. T. Griffin and E. M. Atkins)
    0 521 34835 8 paperback
Cicero *On the Commonwealth* and *On the Laws* (edited by James E. G. Zetzel)
    0 521 45959 1 paperback
Comte *Early Political Writings* (edited by H. S. Jones)
    0 521 46923 6 paperback
Conciliarism and Papalism (edited by J. H. Burns and Thomas M. Izbicki)
    0 521 47674 7 paperback
Constant *Political Writings* (edited by Biancamaria Fontana)
    0 521 31632 4 paperback
Dante *Monarchy* (edited by Prue Shaw)
    0 521 56781 5 paperback
Diderot *Political Writings* (edited by John Hope Mason and Robert Wokler)
    0 521 36911 8 paperback
The Dutch Revolt (edited by Martin van Gelderen)
    0 521 39809 6 paperback
Early Greek Political Thought from Homer to the Sophists (edited by Michael
    Gagarin and Paul Woodruff)
    0 521 43768 7 paperback
The Early Political Writings of the German Romantics (edited by Frederick C.
    Beiser)
    0 521 44951 0 paperback
The English Levellers (edited by Andrew Sharp)
    0 521 62511 4 paperback
Erasmus *The Education of a Christian Prince* (edited by Lisa Jardine)
    0 521 58811 1 paperback
Fenelon *Telemachus* (edited by Patrick Riley)
    0 521 45662 2 paperback
Ferguson *An Essay on the History of Civil Society* (edited by Fania Oz-
    Salzberger)
    0 521 44736 4 paperback
Filmer *Patriarcha and Other Writings* (edited by Johann P. Sommerville)
    0 521 39903 3 paperback
Fletcher *Political Works* (edited by John Robertson)
    0 521 43994 9 paperback
Sir John Fortescue *On the Laws and Governance of England* (edited by Shelley
    Lockwood)
    0 521 58996 7 paperback
Fourier *The Theory of the Four Movements* (edited by Gareth Stedman Jones
    and Ian Patterson)
    0 521 35693 8 paperback
Gramsci *Pre-Prison Writings* (edited by Richard Bellamy)
    0 521 42307 4 paperback

William of Ockham *A Letter to the Friars Minor and Other Writings* (edited by
A. S. McGrade and John Kilcullen)
0 521 35804 3 paperback
Wollstonecraft *A Vindication of the Rights of Men* and *A Vindication of the
Rights of Woman* (edited by Sylvana Tomaselli)
0 521 43633 8 paperback